SEVEN SEAS ENTERTAINMENT PRESENTS

CW00544110

story and art

TRANSLATION
M. Fulcrum

ADAPTATION
Jeffrey Thomas

LETTERING
Arbash Mughal

COVER DESIGN
Nicky Lim

LOGO DESIGN
George Panella

COPY EDITOR
Dawn Davis

EDITOR
Nick Mamatas

PREPRESS TECHNICIAN
iannon Rasmussen-Silverstein

PRODUCTION ASSOCIATE
Christa Miesner

PRODUCTION MANAGER
Lissa Pattillo

MANAGING EDITOR
Julie Davis

ASSOCIATE PUBLISHER
Adam Arnold

PUBLISHER
Jason DeAngelis

LEVEL ONE DEMON LORD & ONE ROOM HERO Volume 2
© toufu 2020
Originally published in Japan in 2020 by HOUBUNSHA CO., LTD., Tokyo.
English translation rights arranged with HOUBUNSHA CO., LTD., Tokyo,
through TOHAN CORPORATION, Tokyo.

Seven Seas press and purchase enquiries can be sent to Marketing Manager Lianne Sentar at press@gomanga.com. Information regarding the distribution and purchase of digital editions is available from Digital Manager CK Russell at digital@gomanga.com.

Seven Seas and the Seven Seas logo are trademarks of Seven Seas Entertainment. All rights reserved.

ISBN: 978-1-64827-615-6
Printed in Canada
First Printing: October 2021
10 9 8 7 6 5 4 3 2 1

//// READING DIRECTIONS ////

This book reads from *right to left*, Japanese style. If this is your first time reading manga, you start reading from the top right panel on each page and take it from there. If you get lost, just follow the numbered diagram here. It may seem backwards at first, but you'll get the hang of it! Have fun!!

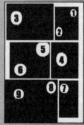

Follow us online: www.SevenSeasEntertainment.com

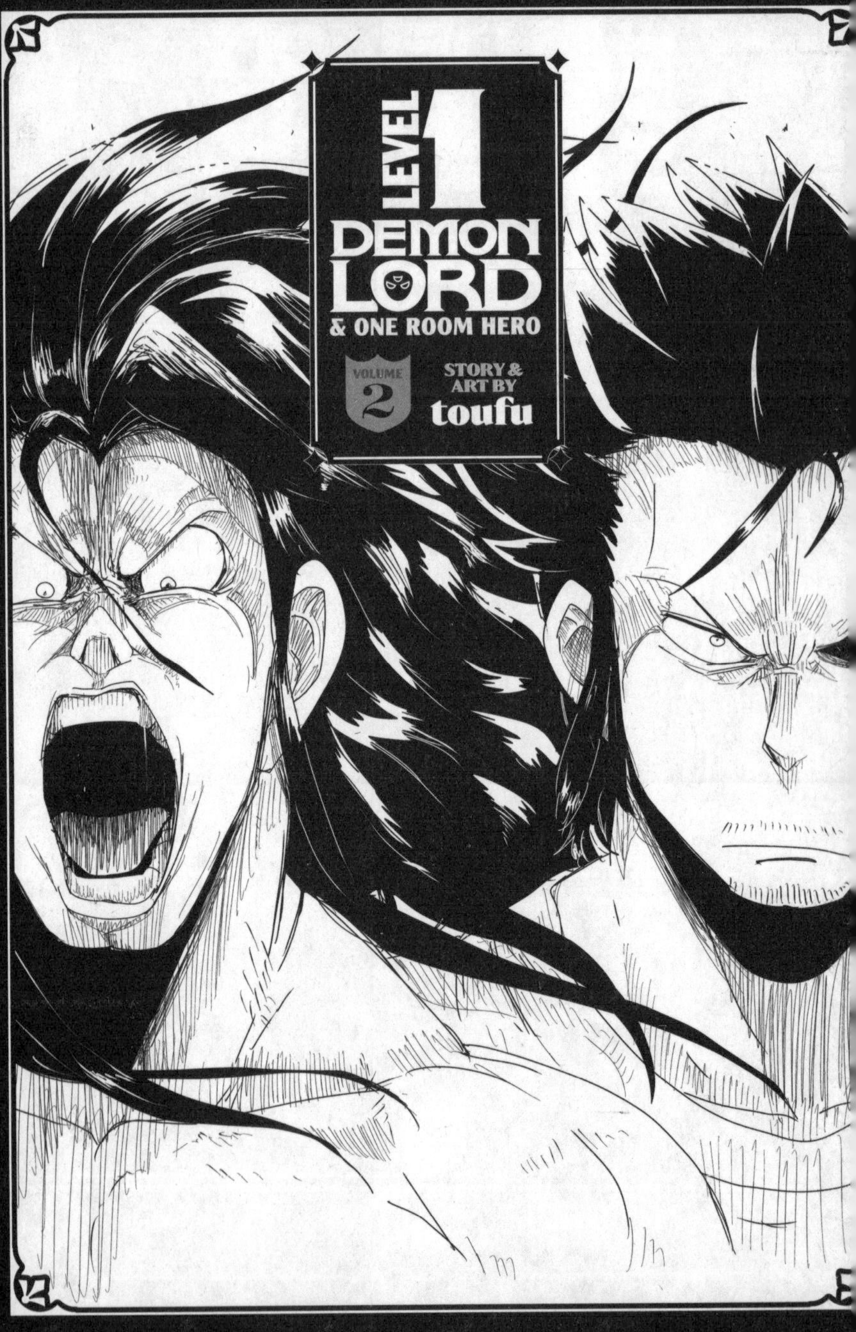
LEVEL 1
DEMON LORD
& ONE ROOM HERO
VOLUME 2
STORY & ART BY
toufu

LEVEL 1 DEMON LORD & ONE ROOM HERO

✦ CONTENTS ✦

2

STORY &
ART BY
toufu

Episode 8: Perks of Transmutation

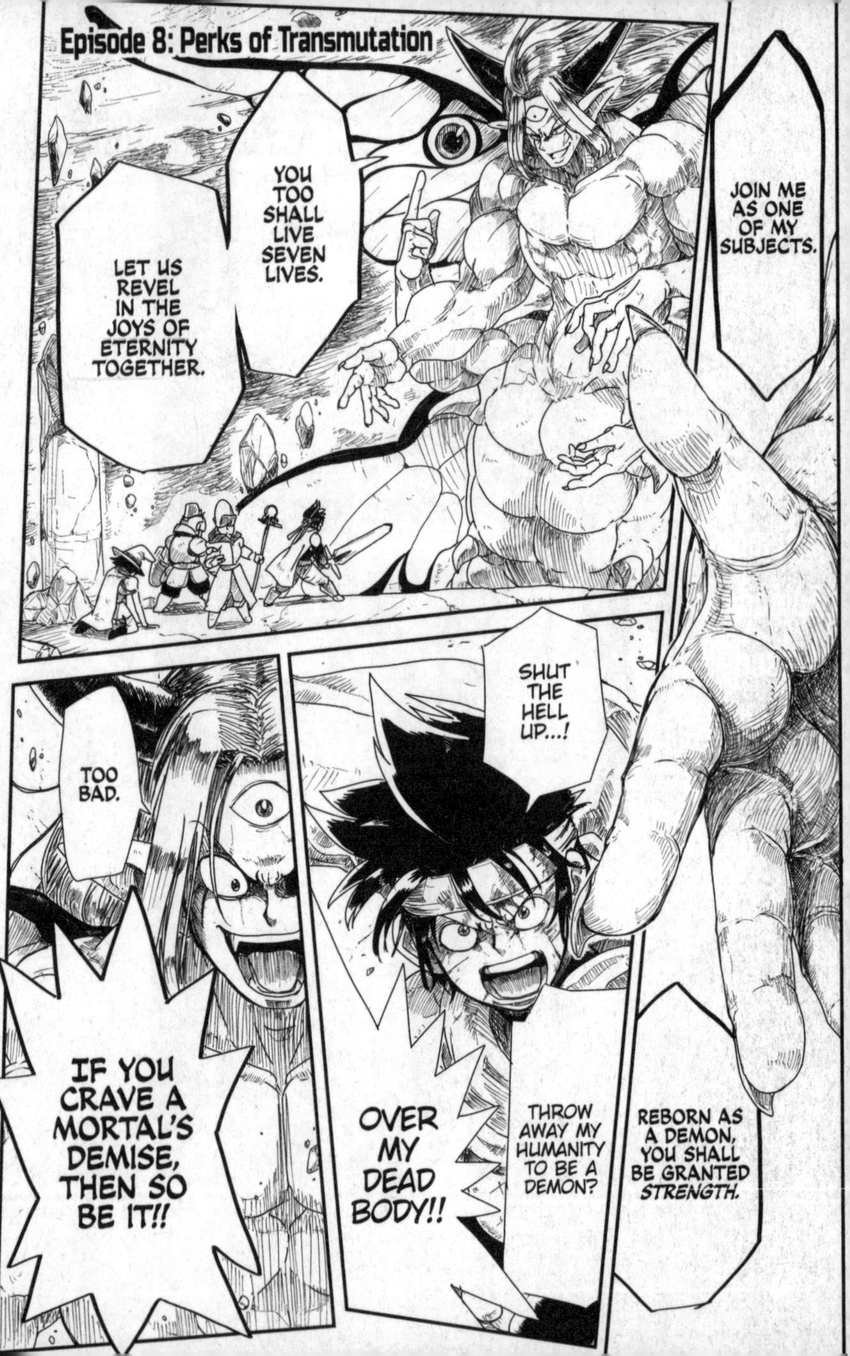
JOIN ME AS ONE OF MY SUBJECTS.
YOU TOO SHALL LIVE SEVEN LIVES.
LET US REVEL IN THE JOYS OF ETERNITY TOGETHER.
REBORN AS A DEMON, YOU SHALL BE GRANTED *STRENGTH.*
SHUT THE HELL UP...!
THROW AWAY MY HUMANITY TO BE A DEMON?
OVER MY DEAD BODY!!
TOO BAD.
IF YOU CRAVE A MORTAL'S DEMISE, THEN SO BE IT!!

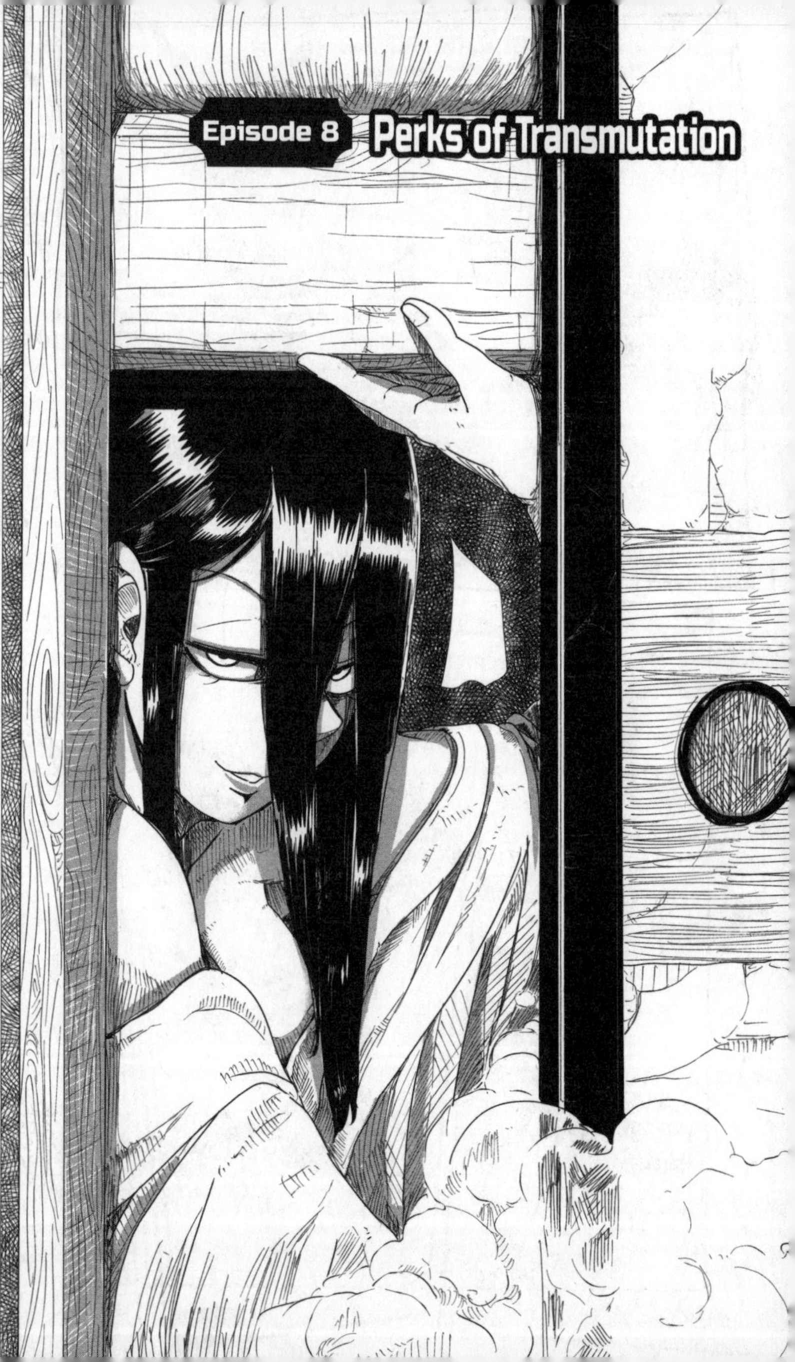
Episode 8
Perks of Transmutation

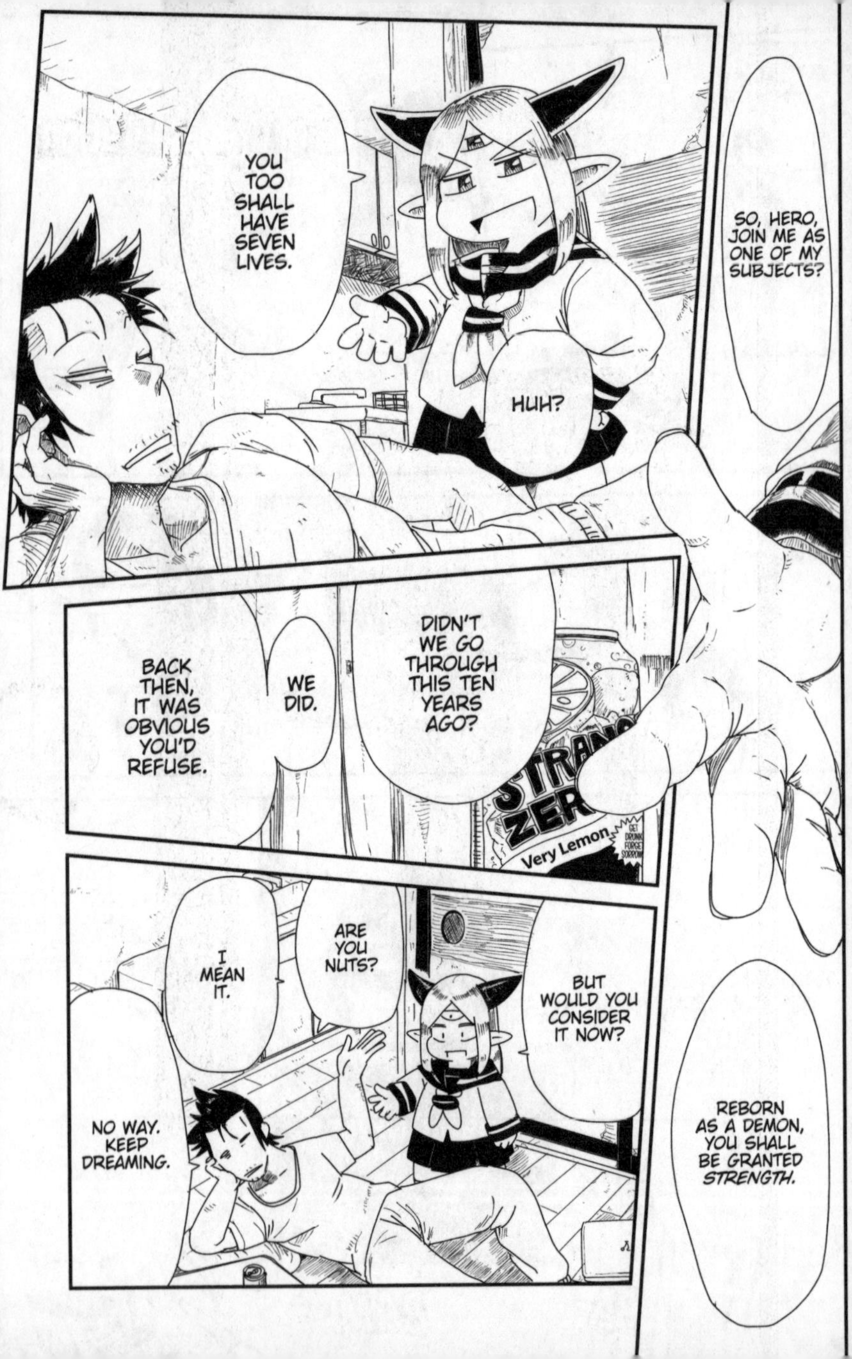
SO, HERO, JOIN ME AS ONE OF MY SUBJECTS?
REBORN AS A DEMON, YOU SHALL BE GRANTED *STRENGTH.*
YOU TOO SHALL HAVE SEVEN LIVES.
HUH?
DIDN'T WE GO THROUGH THIS TEN YEARS AGO?
WE DID.
BACK THEN, IT WAS OBVIOUS YOU'D REFUSE.
Very Lemon
GET DRUNK FORGET SORROW
BUT WOULD YOU CONSIDER IT NOW?
ARE YOU NUTS?
I MEAN IT.
NO WAY. KEEP DREAMING.

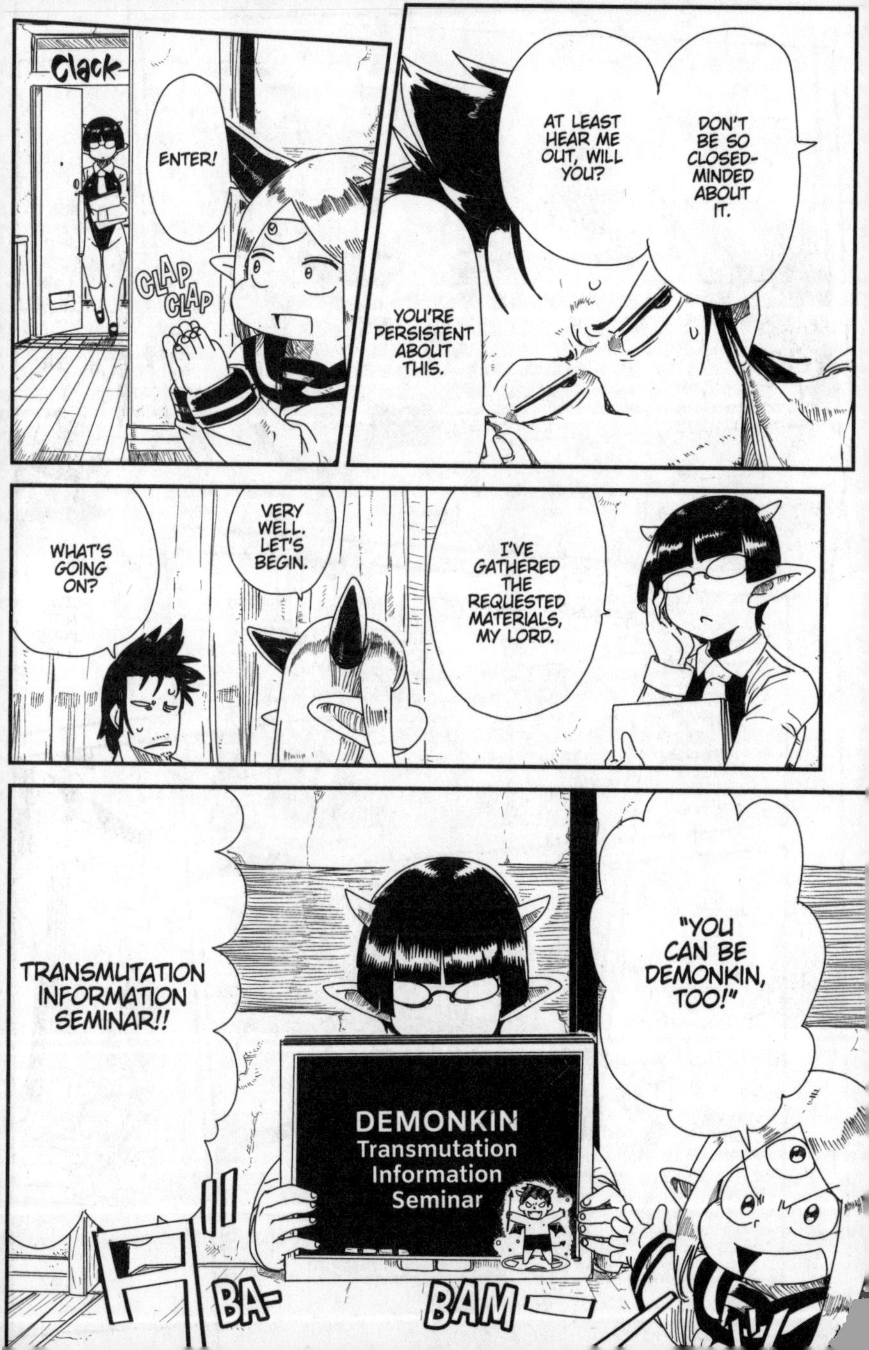
DON'T BE SO CLOSED-MINDED ABOUT IT.
AT LEAST HEAR ME OUT, WILL YOU?
YOU'RE PERSISTENT ABOUT THIS.
ENTER!
Clack
CLAP CLAP
I'VE GATHERED THE REQUESTED MATERIALS, MY LORD.
VERY WELL. LET'S BEGIN.
WHAT'S GOING ON?
"YOU CAN BE DEMONKIN, TOO!"
TRANSMUTATION INFORMATION SEMINAR!!
DEMONKIN
Transmutation
Information
Seminar
BA-
BAM

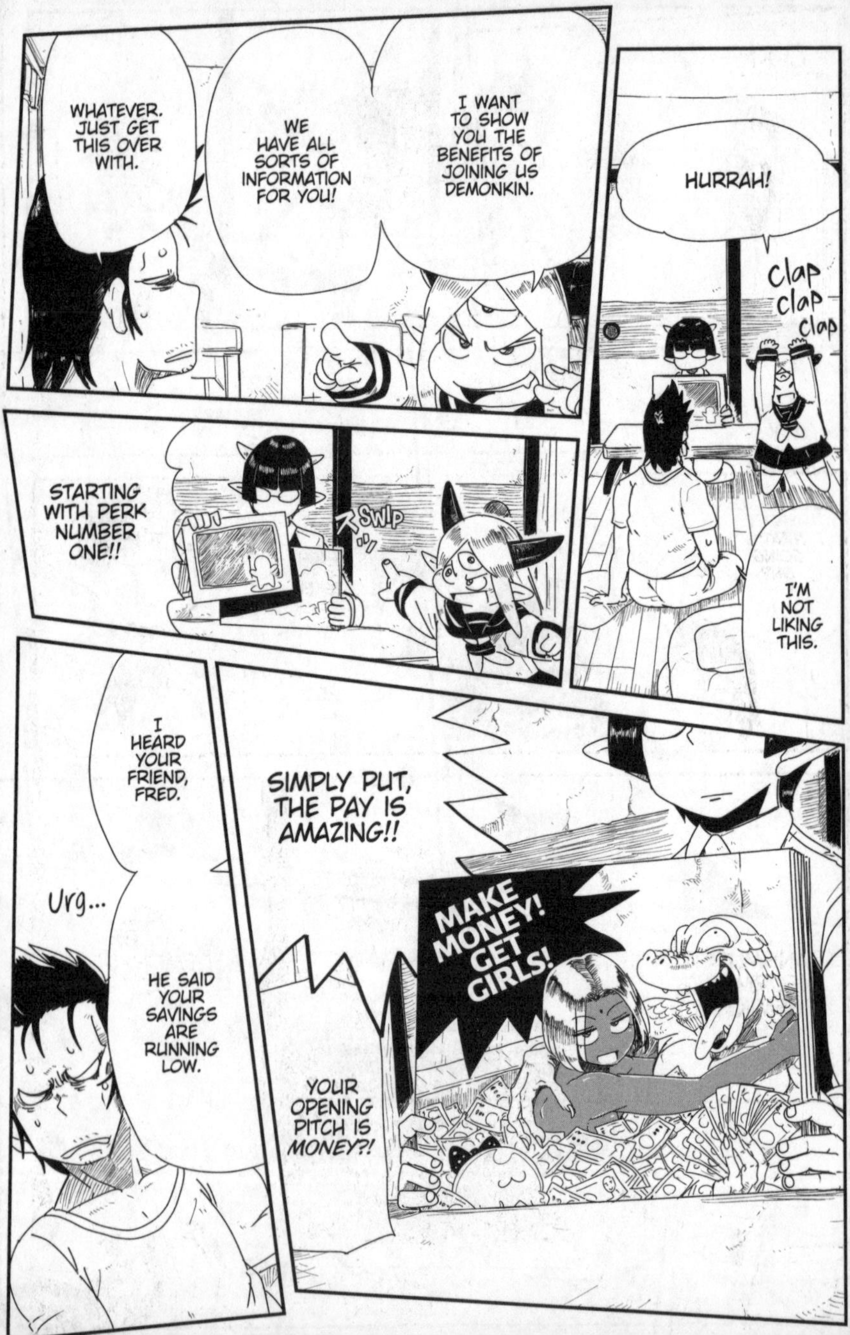
HURRAH!
Clap
Clap
Clap
I'M NOT LIKING THIS.
I WANT TO SHOW YOU THE BENEFITS OF JOINING US DEMONKIN.
WE HAVE ALL SORTS OF INFORMATION FOR YOU!
WHATEVER. JUST GET THIS OVER WITH.
SWIP
STARTING WITH PERK NUMBER ONE!!
SIMPLY PUT, THE PAY IS AMAZING!!
MAKE MONEY! GET GIRLS!
YOUR OPENING PITCH IS *MONEY?!*
I HEARD YOUR FRIEND, FRED.
Urg...
HE SAID YOUR SAVINGS ARE RUNNING LOW.

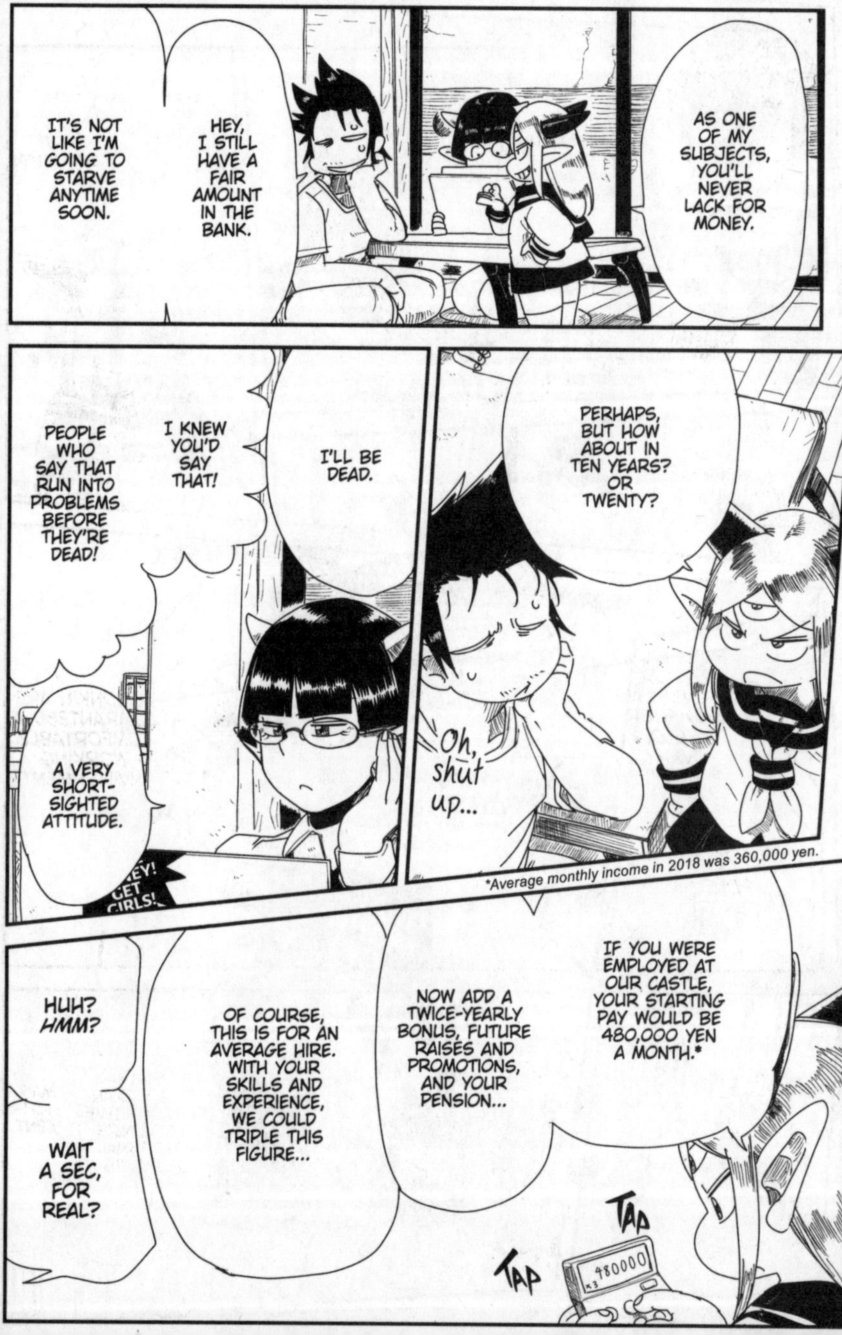
AS ONE OF MY SUBJECTS, YOU'LL NEVER LACK FOR MONEY.
HEY, I STILL HAVE A FAIR AMOUNT IN THE BANK.
IT'S NOT LIKE I'M GOING TO STARVE ANYTIME SOON.
PERHAPS, BUT HOW ABOUT IN TEN YEARS? OR TWENTY?
Oh, shut up...
I'LL BE DEAD.
I KNEW YOU'D SAY THAT!
PEOPLE WHO SAY THAT RUN INTO PROBLEMS BEFORE THEY'RE DEAD!
A VERY SHORT-SIGHTED ATTITUDE.
IF YOU WERE EMPLOYED AT OUR CASTLE, YOUR STARTING PAY WOULD BE 480,000 YEN A MONTH.*
TAP
TAP
480000
×3
NOW ADD A TWICE-YEARLY BONUS, FUTURE RAISES AND PROMOTIONS, AND YOUR PENSION...
OF COURSE, THIS IS FOR AN AVERAGE HIRE. WITH YOUR SKILLS AND EXPERIENCE, WE COULD TRIPLE THIS FIGURE...
HUH? HMM?
WAIT A SEC, FOR REAL?
*Average monthly income in 2018 was 360,000 yen.

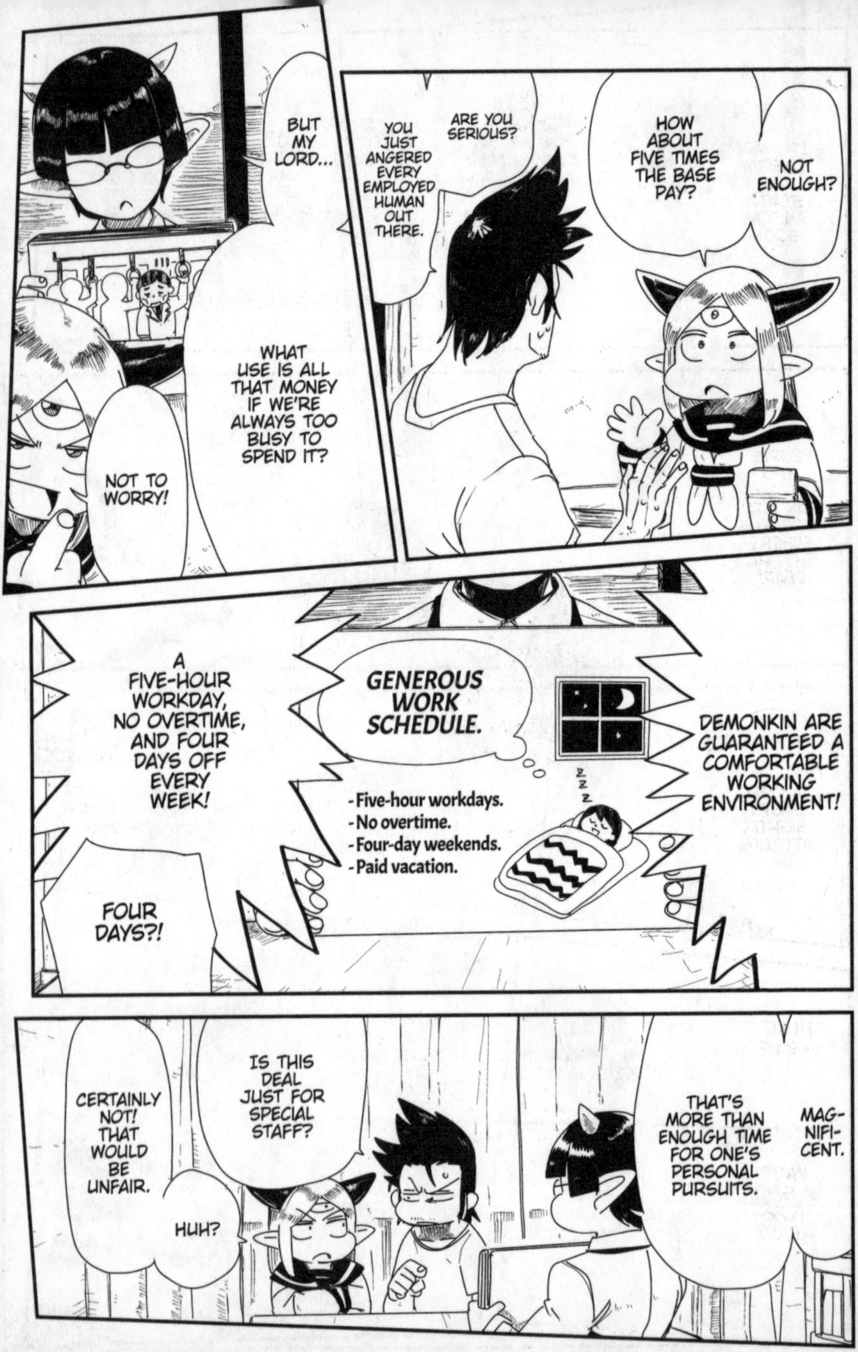
NOT ENOUGH?
HOW ABOUT FIVE TIMES THE BASE PAY?
ARE YOU SERIOUS?
YOU JUST ANGERED EVERY EMPLOYED HUMAN OUT THERE.
BUT MY LORD...
WHAT USE IS ALL THAT MONEY IF WE'RE ALWAYS TOO BUSY TO SPEND IT?
NOT TO WORRY!
DEMONKIN ARE GUARANTEED A COMFORTABLE WORKING ENVIRONMENT!
GENEROUS WORK SCHEDULE.
- Five-hour workdays.
- No overtime.
- Four-day weekends.
- Paid vacation.
A FIVE-HOUR WORKDAY, NO OVERTIME, AND FOUR DAYS OFF EVERY WEEK!
FOUR DAYS?!
MAG-NIFI-CENT.
THAT'S MORE THAN ENOUGH TIME FOR ONE'S PERSONAL PURSUITS.
IS THIS DEAL JUST FOR SPECIAL STAFF?
CERTAINLY NOT! THAT WOULD BE UNFAIR.
HUH?

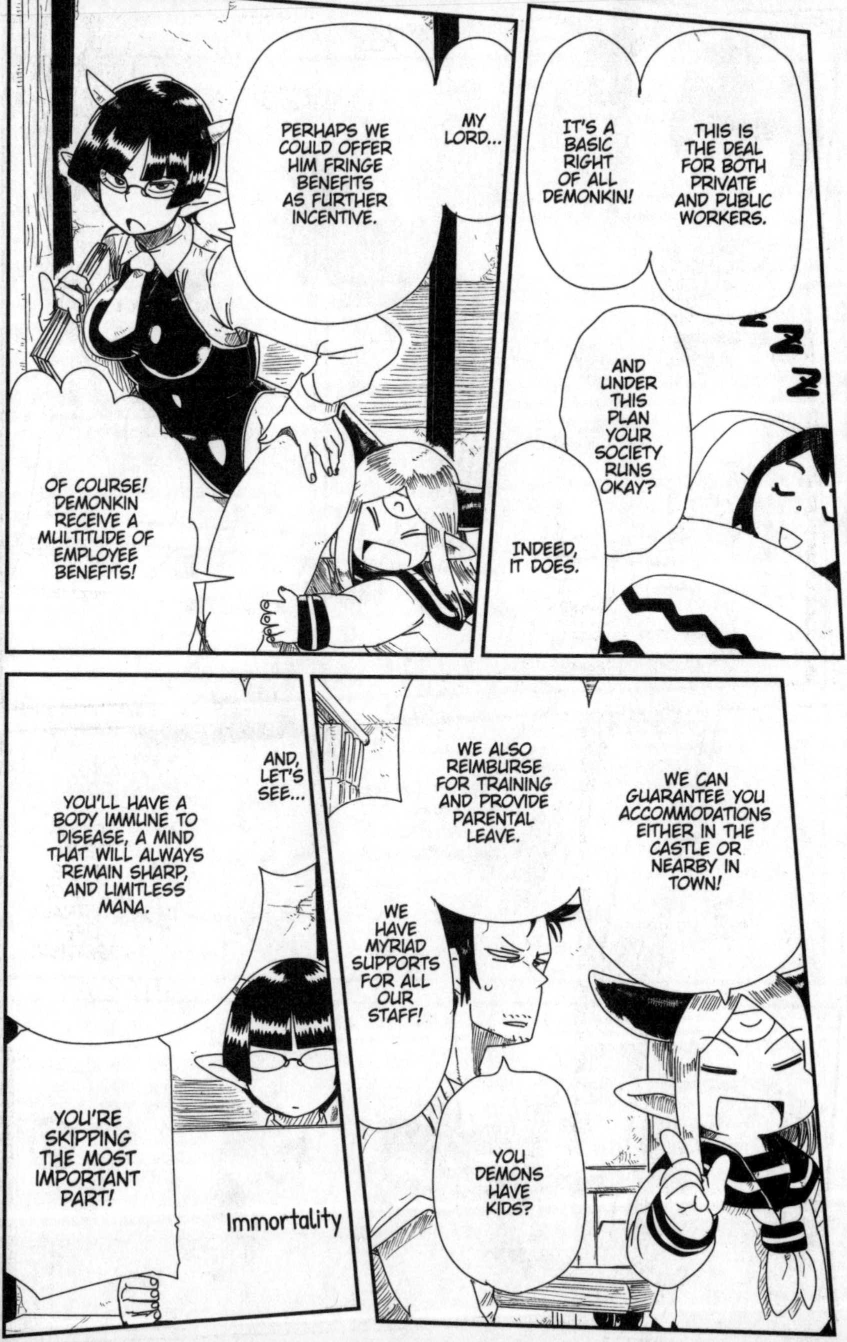
THIS IS THE DEAL FOR BOTH PRIVATE AND PUBLIC WORKERS.
IT'S A BASIC RIGHT OF ALL DEMONKIN!
ZZZ
AND UNDER THIS PLAN YOUR SOCIETY RUNS OKAY?
INDEED, IT DOES.
MY LORD...
PERHAPS WE COULD OFFER HIM FRINGE BENEFITS AS FURTHER INCENTIVE.
OF COURSE! DEMONKIN RECEIVE A MULTITUDE OF EMPLOYEE BENEFITS!
WE CAN GUARANTEE YOU ACCOMMODATIONS EITHER IN THE CASTLE OR NEARBY IN TOWN!
WE ALSO REIMBURSE FOR TRAINING AND PROVIDE PARENTAL LEAVE.
WE HAVE MYRIAD SUPPORTS FOR ALL OUR STAFF!
YOU DEMONS HAVE KIDS?
AND, LET'S SEE...
YOU'LL HAVE A BODY IMMUNE TO DISEASE, A MIND THAT WILL ALWAYS REMAIN SHARP, AND LIMITLESS MANA.
YOU'RE SKIPPING THE MOST IMPORTANT PART!
Immortality

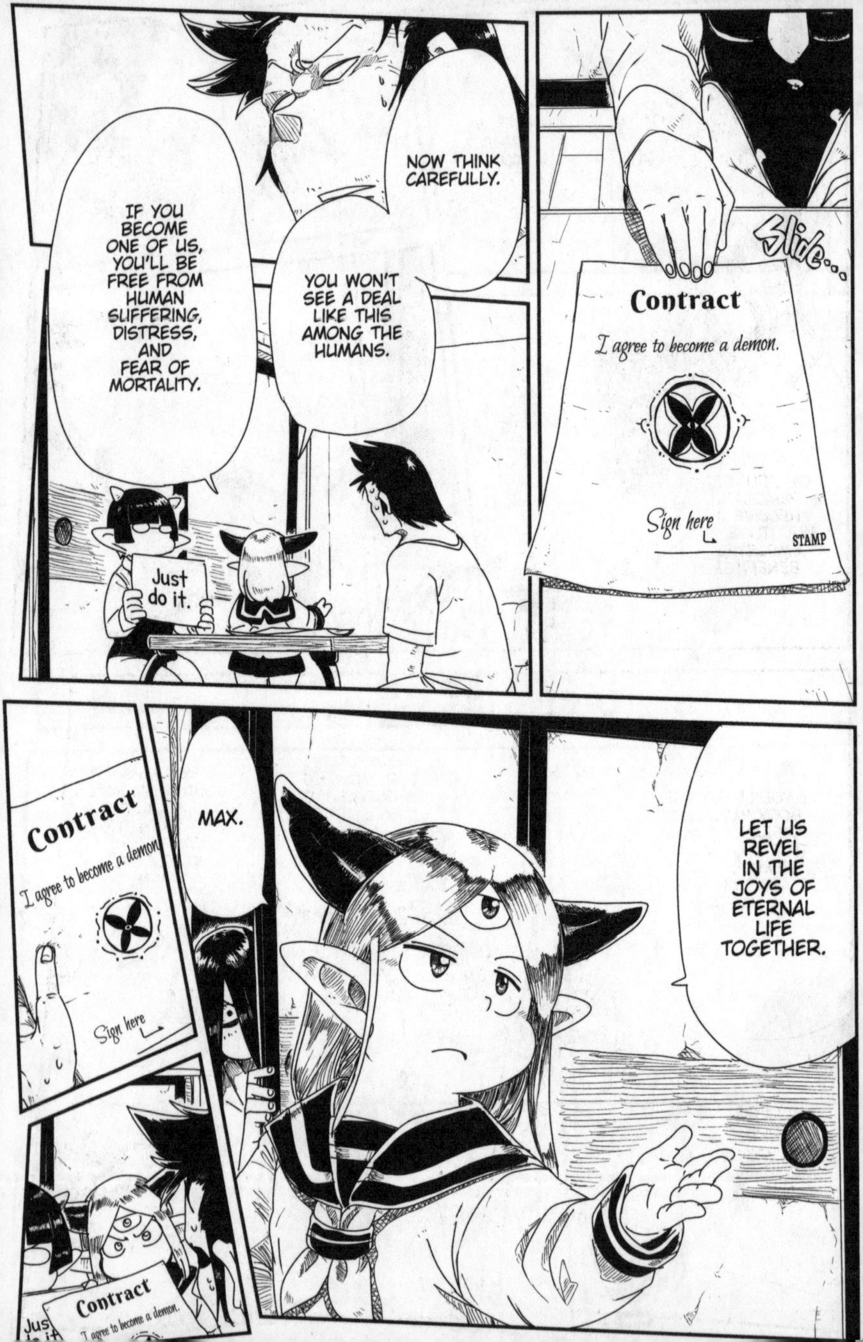
Slide...
Contract
I agree to become a demon.
Sign here
STAMP
NOW THINK CAREFULLY.
YOU WON'T SEE A DEAL LIKE THIS AMONG THE HUMANS.
IF YOU BECOME ONE OF US, YOU'LL BE FREE FROM HUMAN SUFFERING, DISTRESS, AND FEAR OF MORTALITY.
Just do it.
LET US REVEL IN THE JOYS OF ETERNAL LIFE TOGETHER.
MAX.
Contract
I agree to become a demon
Sign here
Contract
I agree to become a demon.

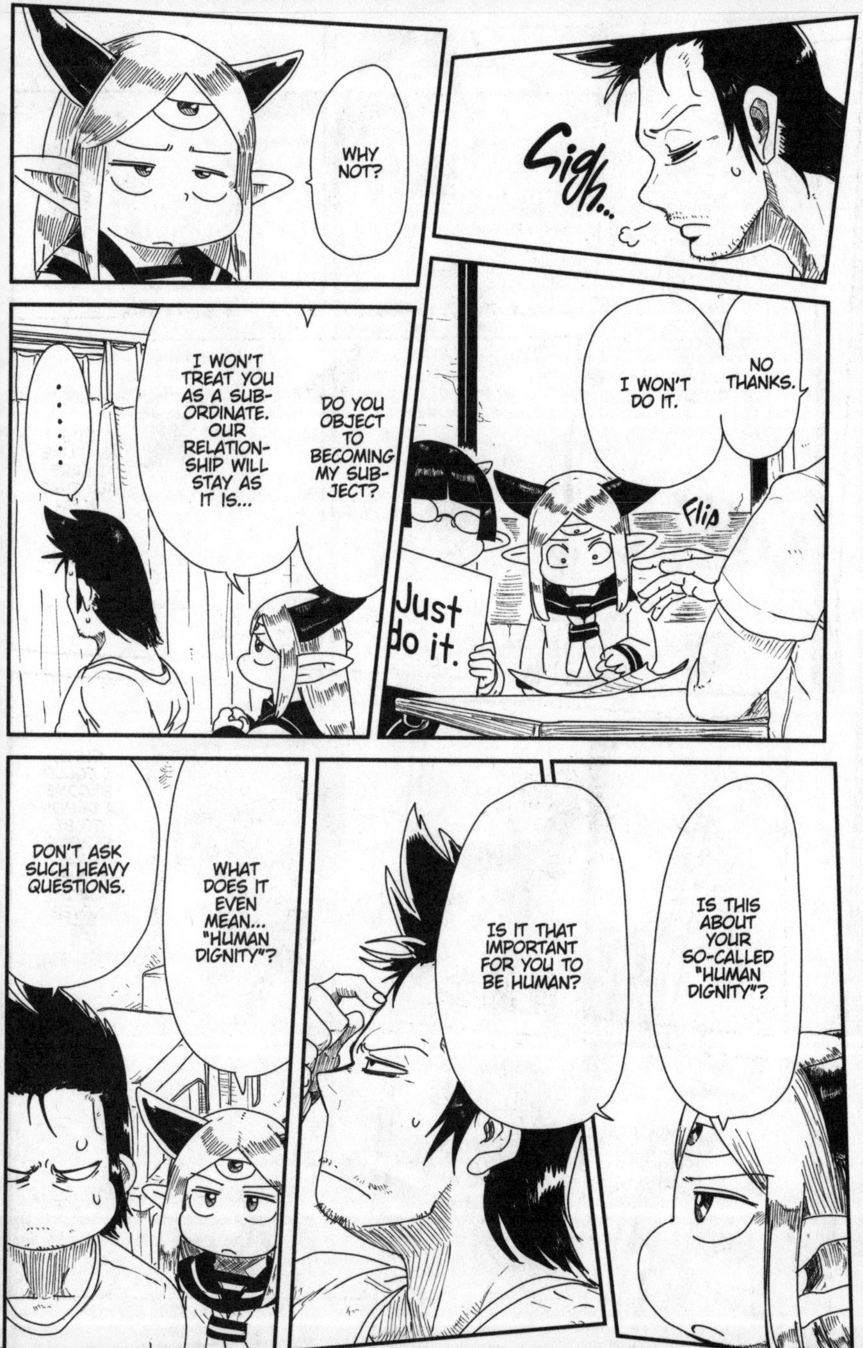
Sigh...
WHY NOT?
NO THANKS.
I WON'T DO IT.
Flip
Just do it.
DO YOU OBJECT TO BECOMING MY SUBJECT?
I WON'T TREAT YOU AS A SUBORDINATE. OUR RELATIONSHIP WILL STAY AS IT IS...
......
IS THIS ABOUT YOUR SO-CALLED "HUMAN DIGNITY"?
IS IT THAT IMPORTANT FOR YOU TO BE HUMAN?
WHAT DOES IT EVEN MEAN... "HUMAN DIGNITY"?
DON'T ASK SUCH HEAVY QUESTIONS.

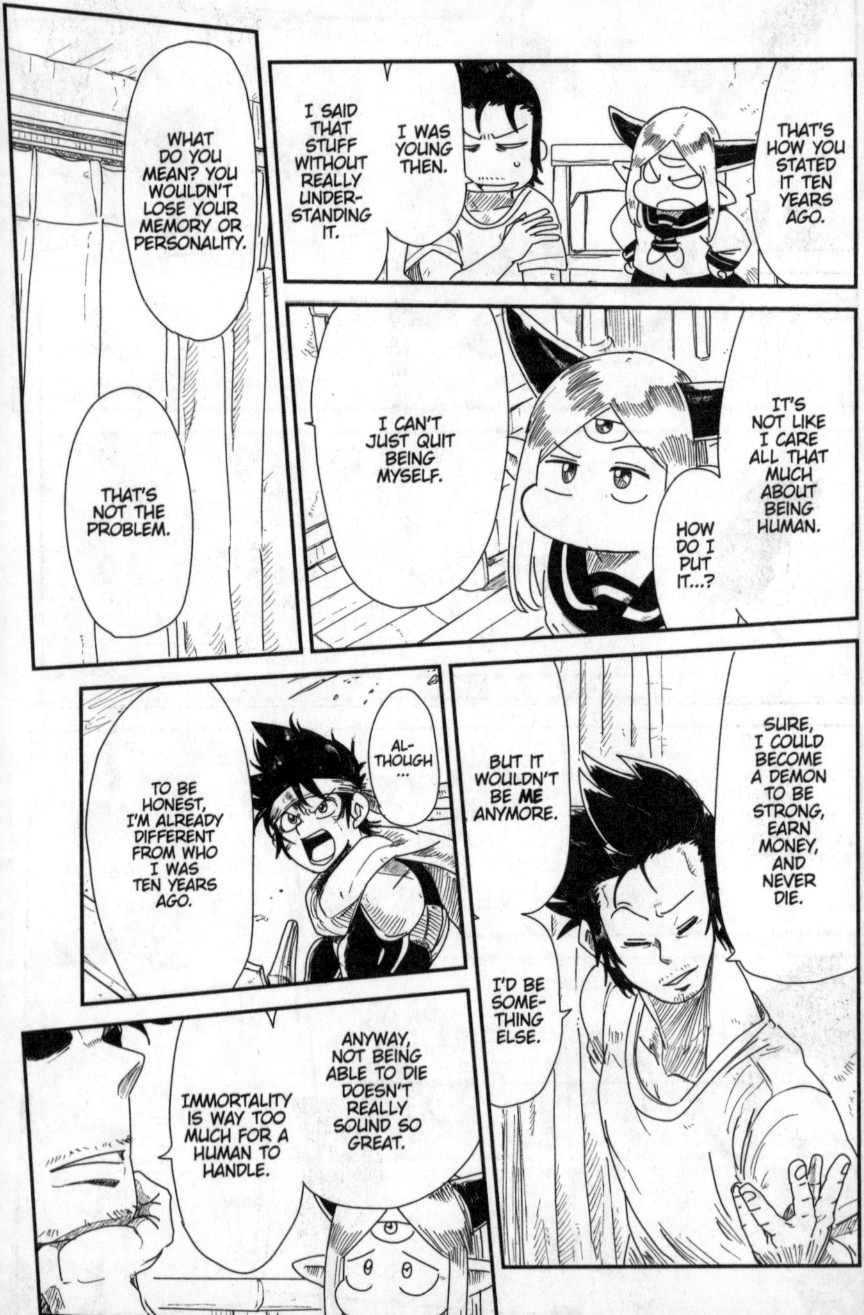
THAT'S HOW YOU STATED IT TEN YEARS AGO.
I WAS YOUNG THEN.
I SAID THAT STUFF WITHOUT REALLY UNDER-STANDING IT.
IT'S NOT LIKE I CARE ALL THAT MUCH ABOUT BEING HUMAN.
HOW DO I PUT IT...?
I CAN'T JUST QUIT BEING MYSELF.
WHAT DO YOU MEAN? YOU WOULDN'T LOSE YOUR MEMORY OR PERSONALITY.
THAT'S NOT THE PROBLEM.
SURE, I COULD BECOME A DEMON TO BE STRONG, EARN MONEY, AND NEVER DIE.
BUT IT WOULDN'T BE ME ANYMORE.
I'D BE SOME-THING ELSE.
AL-THOUGH ...
TO BE HONEST, I'M ALREADY DIFFERENT FROM WHO I WAS TEN YEARS AGO.
ANYWAY, NOT BEING ABLE TO DIE DOESN'T REALLY SOUND SO GREAT.
IMMORTALITY IS WAY TOO MUCH FOR A HUMAN TO HANDLE.

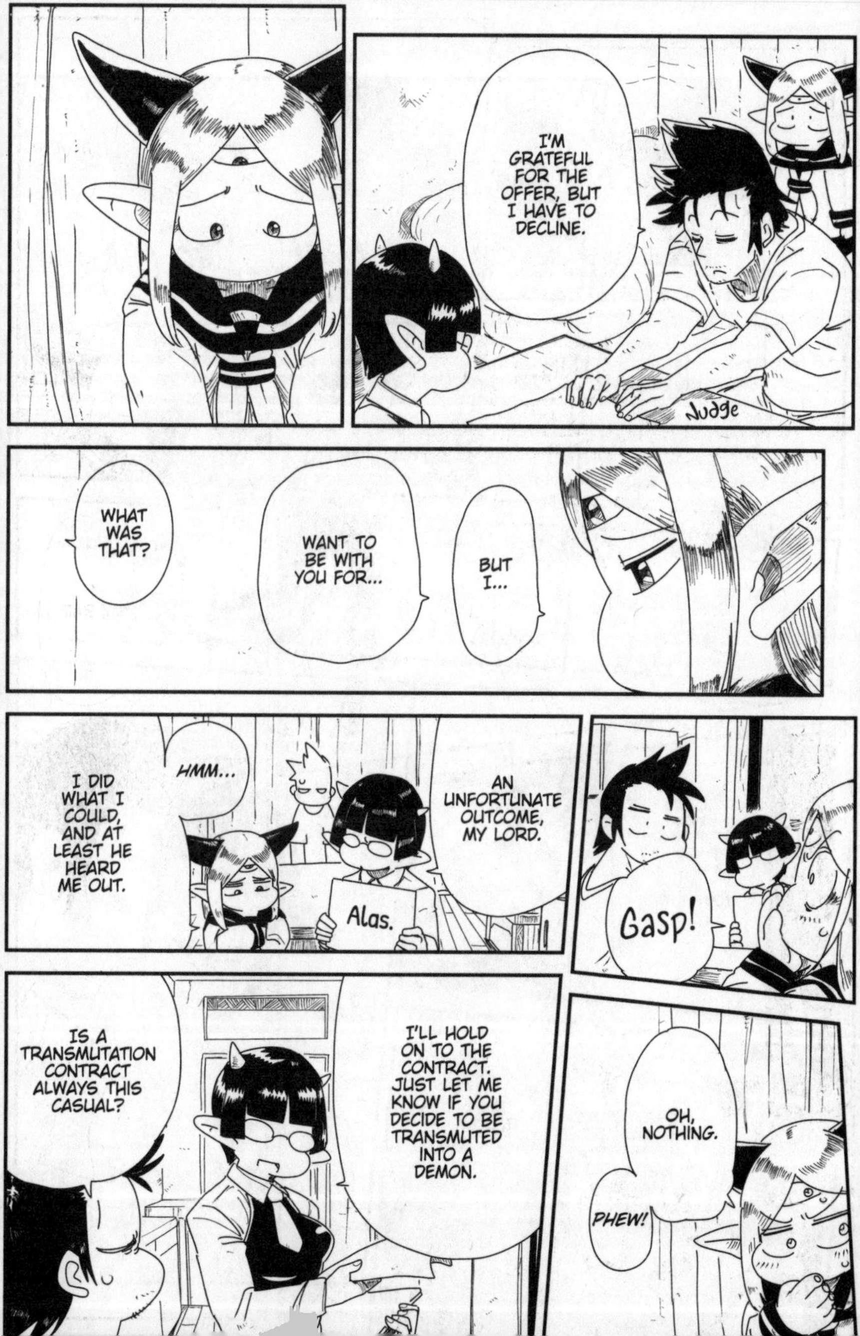
I'M GRATEFUL FOR THE OFFER, BUT I HAVE TO DECLINE.
Judge
BUT I...
WANT TO BE WITH YOU FOR...
WHAT WAS THAT?
Gasp!
AN UNFORTUNATE OUTCOME, MY LORD.
HMM...
I DID WHAT I COULD, AND AT LEAST HE HEARD ME OUT.
Alas.
OH, NOTHING.
PHEW!
I'LL HOLD ON TO THE CONTRACT. JUST LET ME KNOW IF YOU DECIDE TO BE TRANSMUTED INTO A DEMON.
IS A TRANSMUTATION CONTRACT ALWAYS THIS CASUAL?

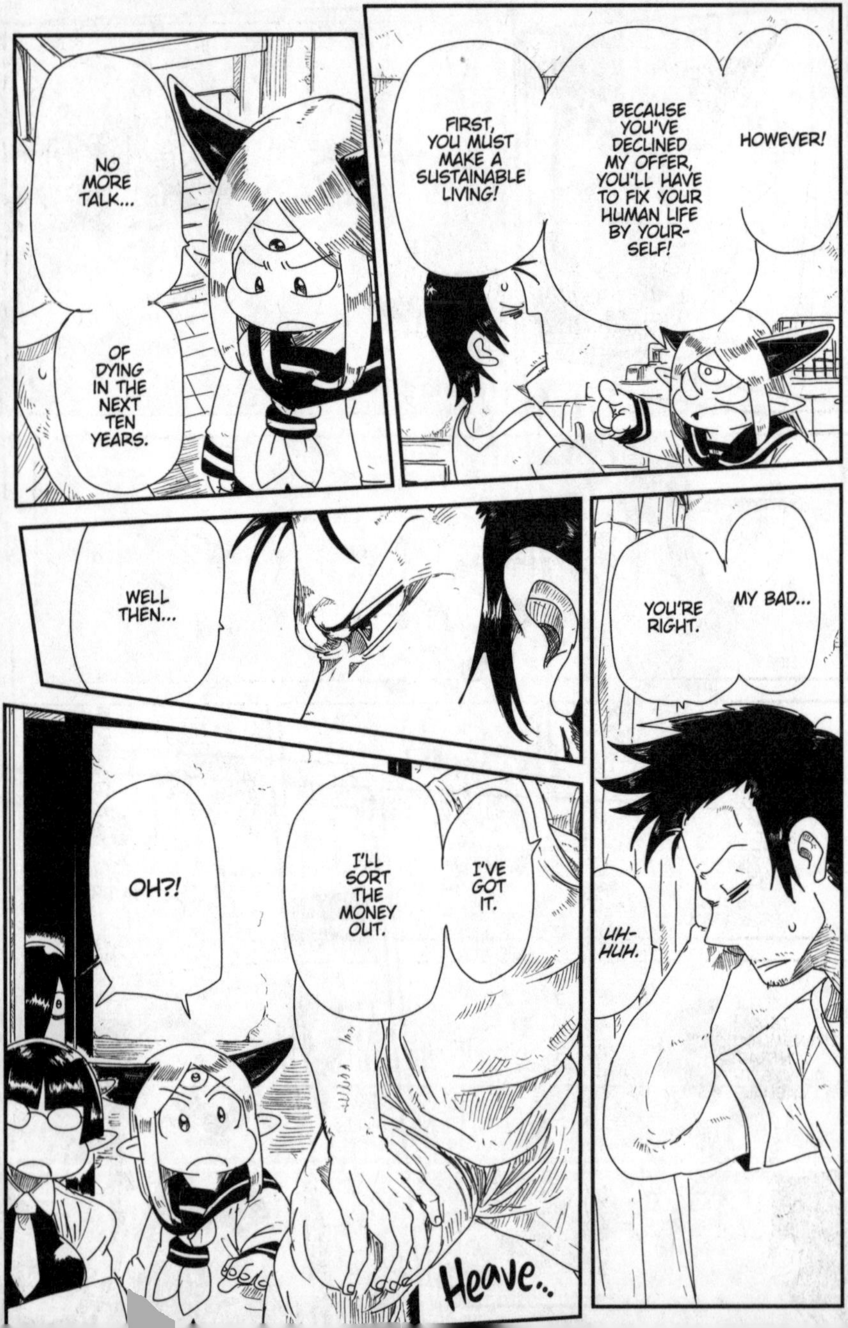
HOWEVER!
BECAUSE YOU'VE DECLINED MY OFFER, YOU'LL HAVE TO FIX YOUR HUMAN LIFE BY YOUR-SELF!
FIRST, YOU MUST MAKE A SUSTAINABLE LIVING!
NO MORE TALK...
OF DYING IN THE NEXT TEN YEARS.
MY BAD...
YOU'RE RIGHT.
UH-HUH.
WELL THEN...
I'VE GOT IT.
I'LL SORT THE MONEY OUT.
OH?!
Heave..

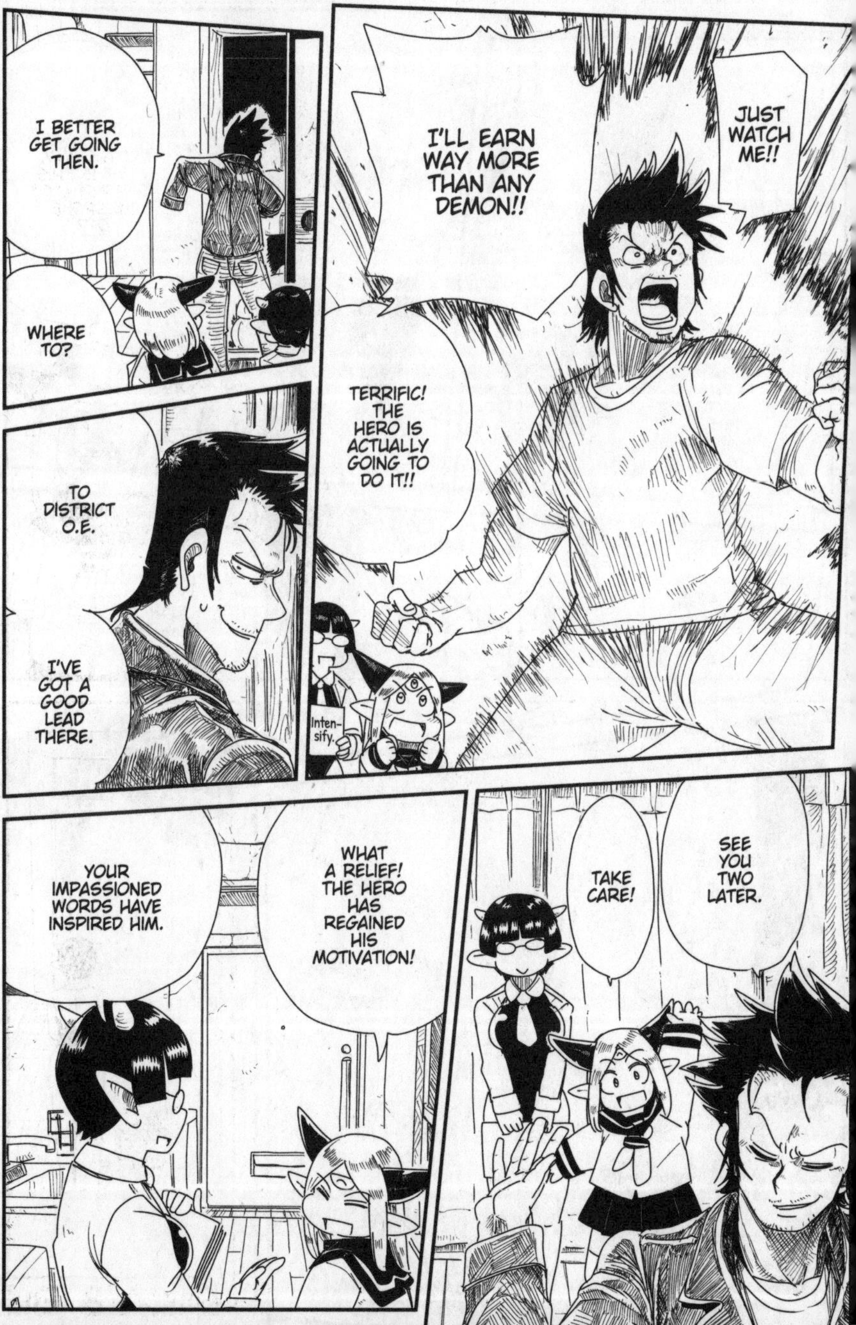
JUST WATCH ME!!
I'LL EARN WAY MORE THAN ANY DEMON!!
TERRIFIC! THE HERO IS ACTUALLY GOING TO DO IT!!
Inten-sify.
I BETTER GET GOING THEN.
WHERE TO?
TO DISTRICT O.E.
I'VE GOT A GOOD LEAD THERE.
SEE YOU TWO LATER.
TAKE CARE!
WHAT A RELIEF! THE HERO HAS REGAINED HIS MOTIVATION!
YOUR IMPASSIONED WORDS HAVE INSPIRED HIM.

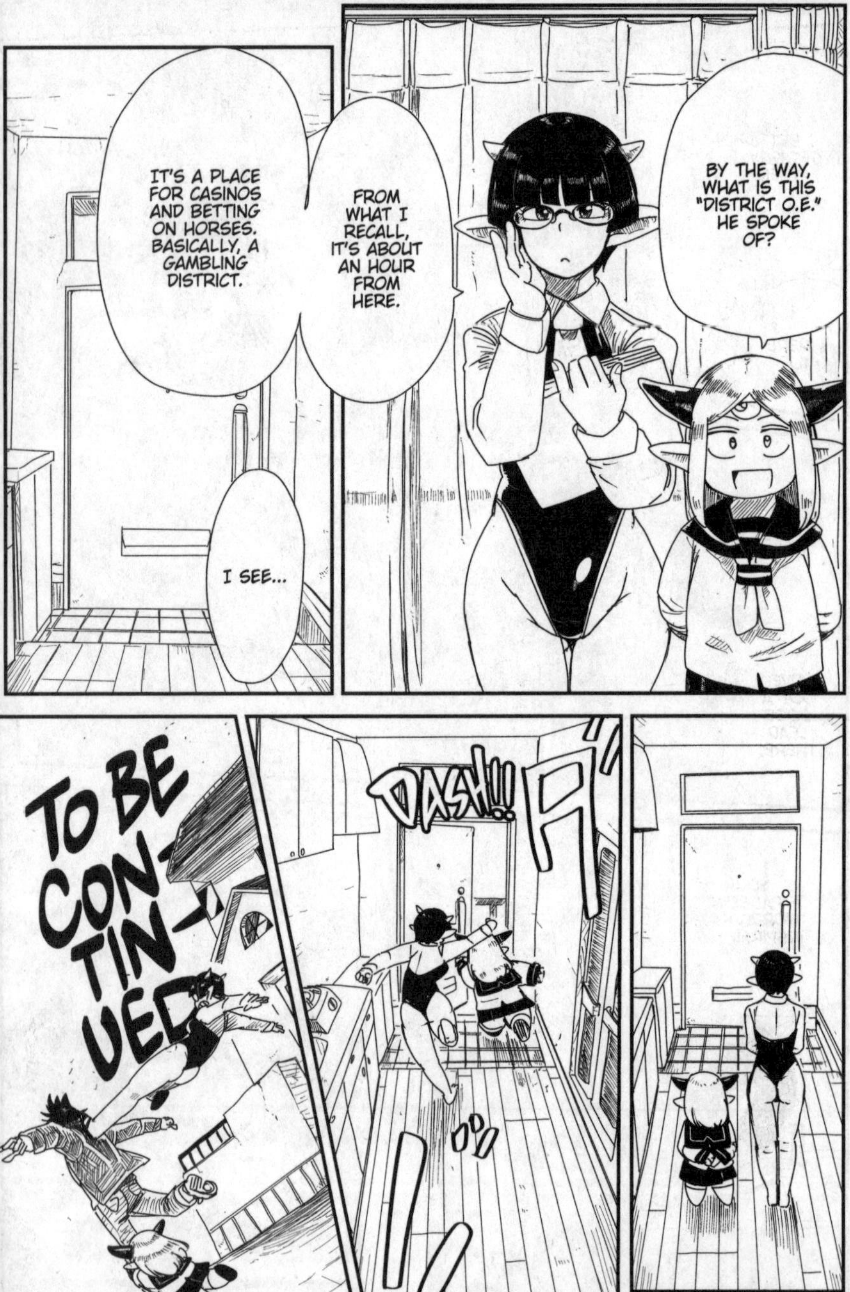
BY THE WAY, WHAT IS THIS "DISTRICT O.E." HE SPOKE OF?
FROM WHAT I RECALL, IT'S ABOUT AN HOUR FROM HERE.
IT'S A PLACE FOR CASINOS AND BETTING ON HORSES. BASICALLY, A GAMBLING DISTRICT.
I SEE...
DASH!!!
!!
TO BE CONTINUED

Episode 8 End

LEVEL 1 DEMON LORD & ONE ROOM HERO

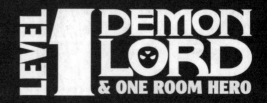

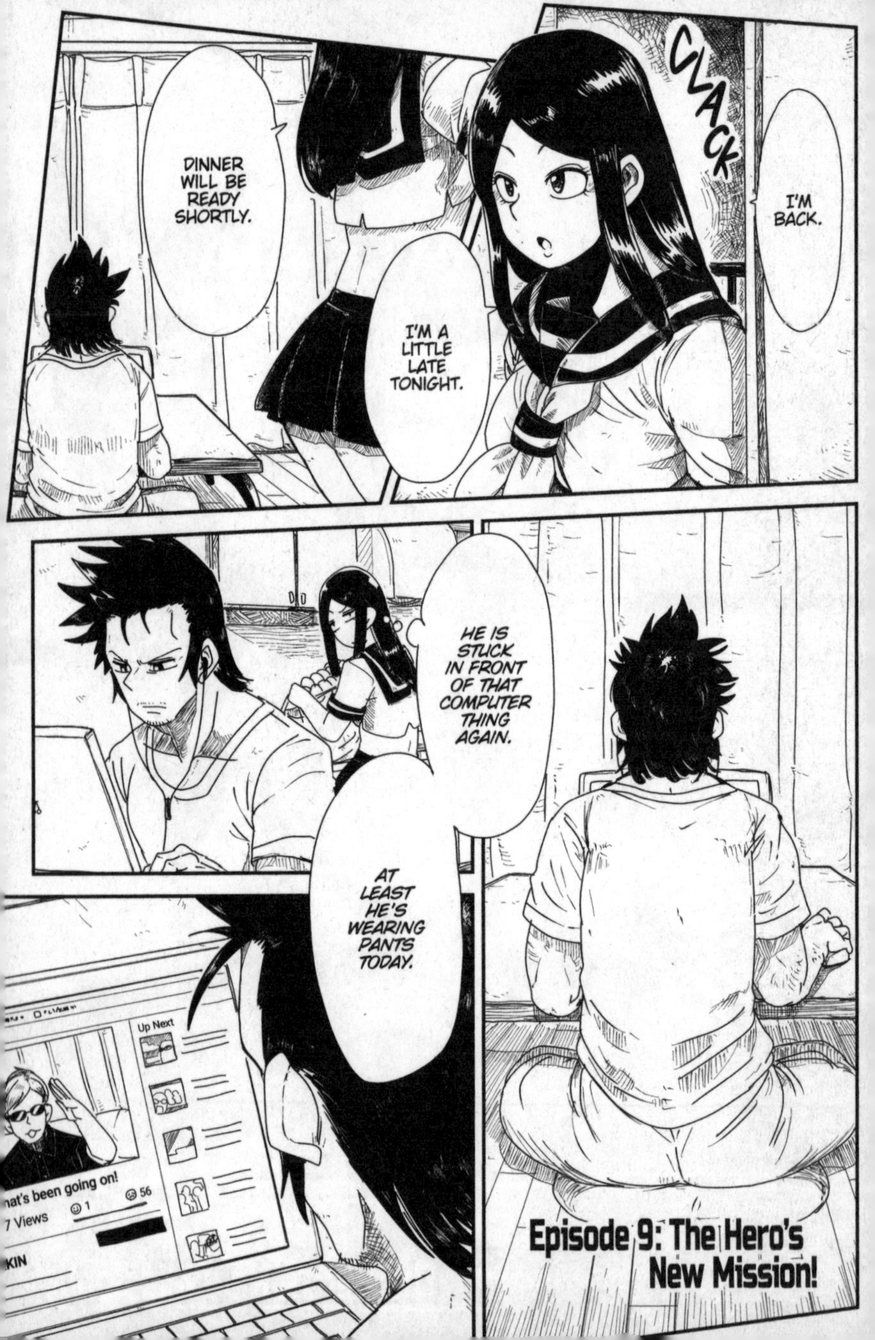
CLACK
I'M BACK.
I'M A LITTLE LATE TONIGHT.
DINNER WILL BE READY SHORTLY.
Episode 9: The Hero's New Mission!
HE IS STUCK IN FRONT OF THAT COMPUTER THING AGAIN.
AT LEAST HE'S WEARING PANTS TODAY.
Up Next
nat's been going on!
1
56
7 Views
[redacted]
KIN

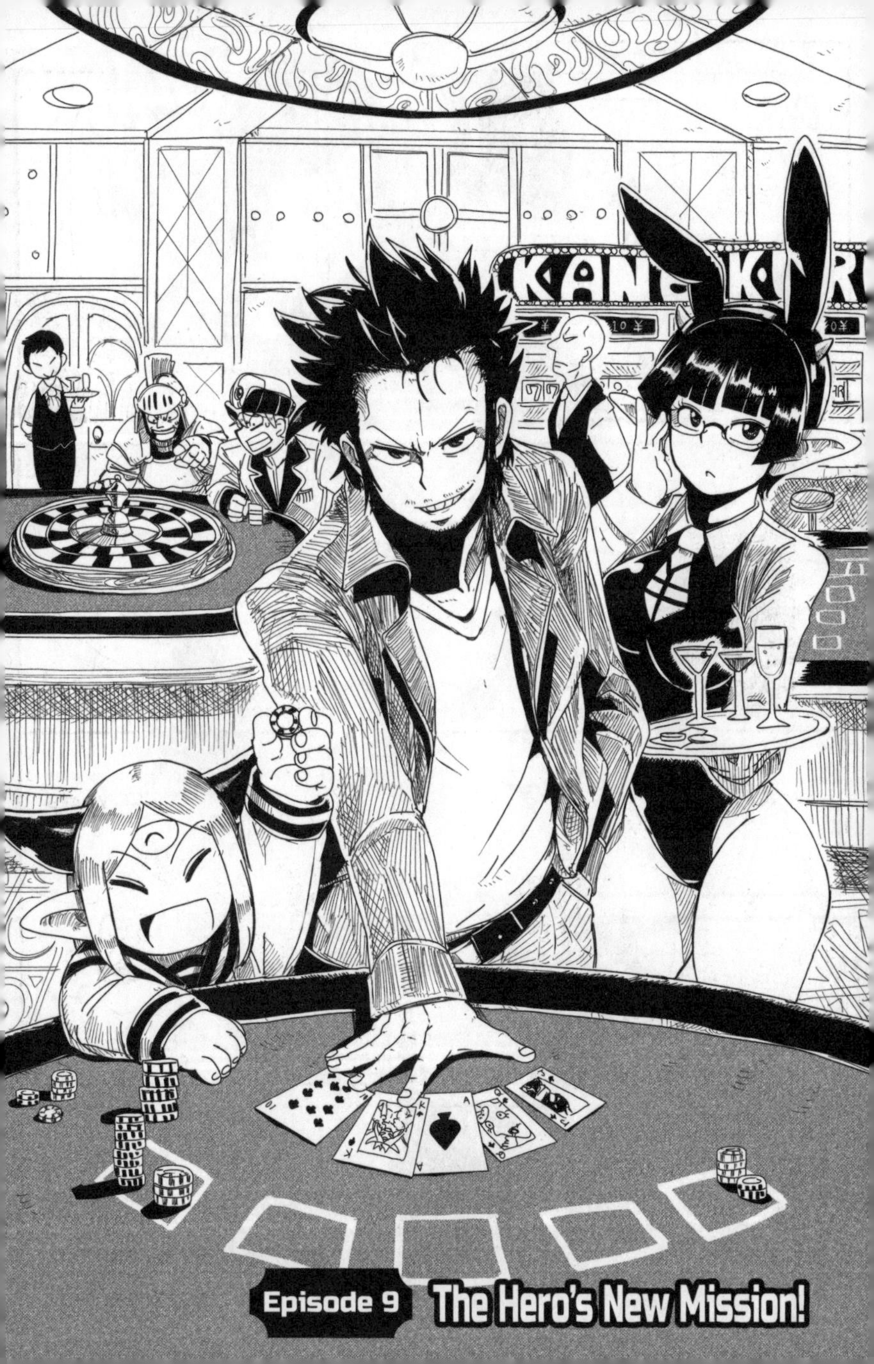

Episode 9 The Hero's New Mission!

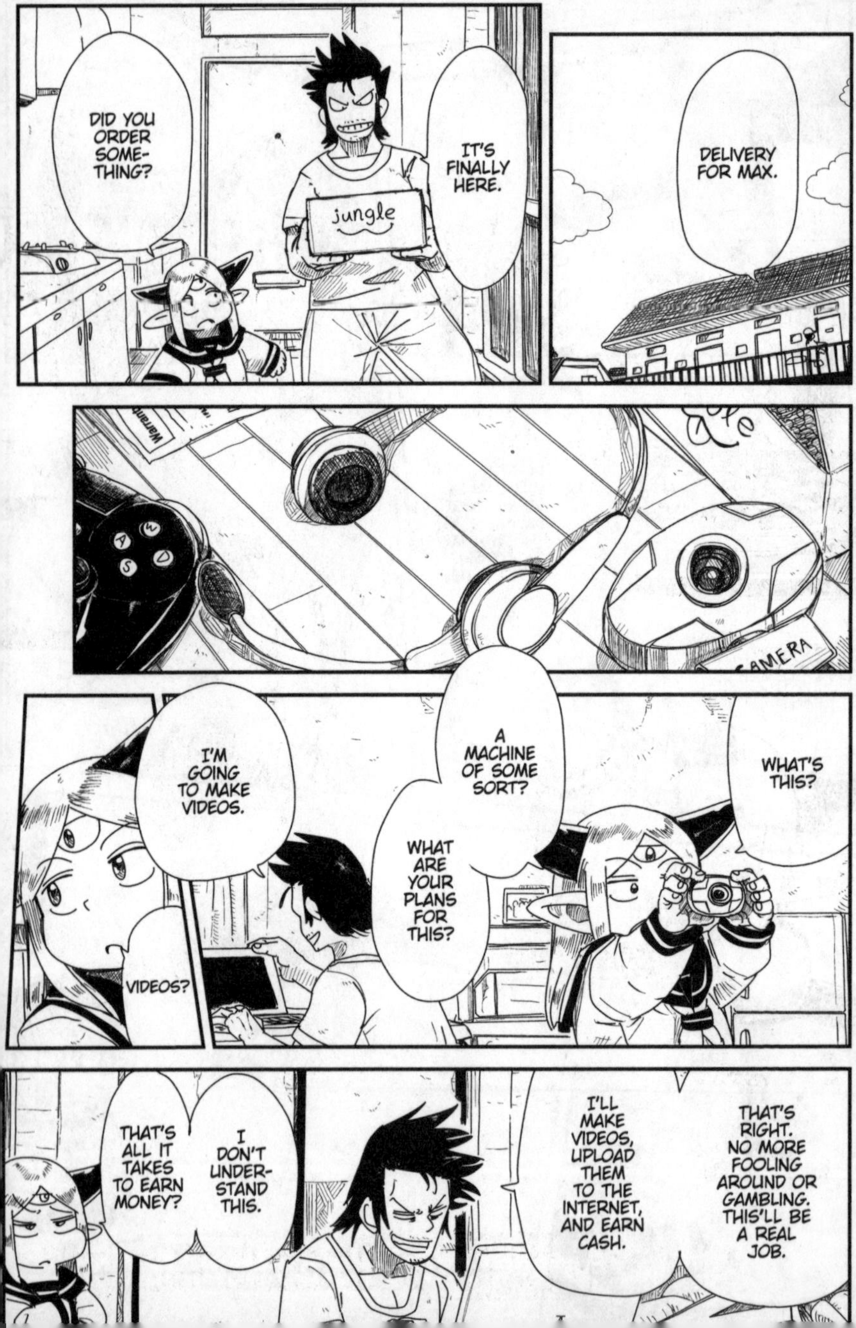
DELIVERY FOR MAX.
IT'S FINALLY HERE.
jungle
DID YOU ORDER SOME-THING?
CAMERA
WHAT'S THIS?
A MACHINE OF SOME SORT?
WHAT ARE YOUR PLANS FOR THIS?
I'M GOING TO MAKE VIDEOS.
VIDEOS?
THAT'S RIGHT. NO MORE FOOLING AROUND OR GAMBLING. THIS'LL BE A REAL JOB.
I'LL MAKE VIDEOS, UPLOAD THEM TO THE INTERNET, AND EARN CASH.
I DON'T UNDER-STAND THIS.
THAT'S ALL IT TAKES TO EARN MONEY?

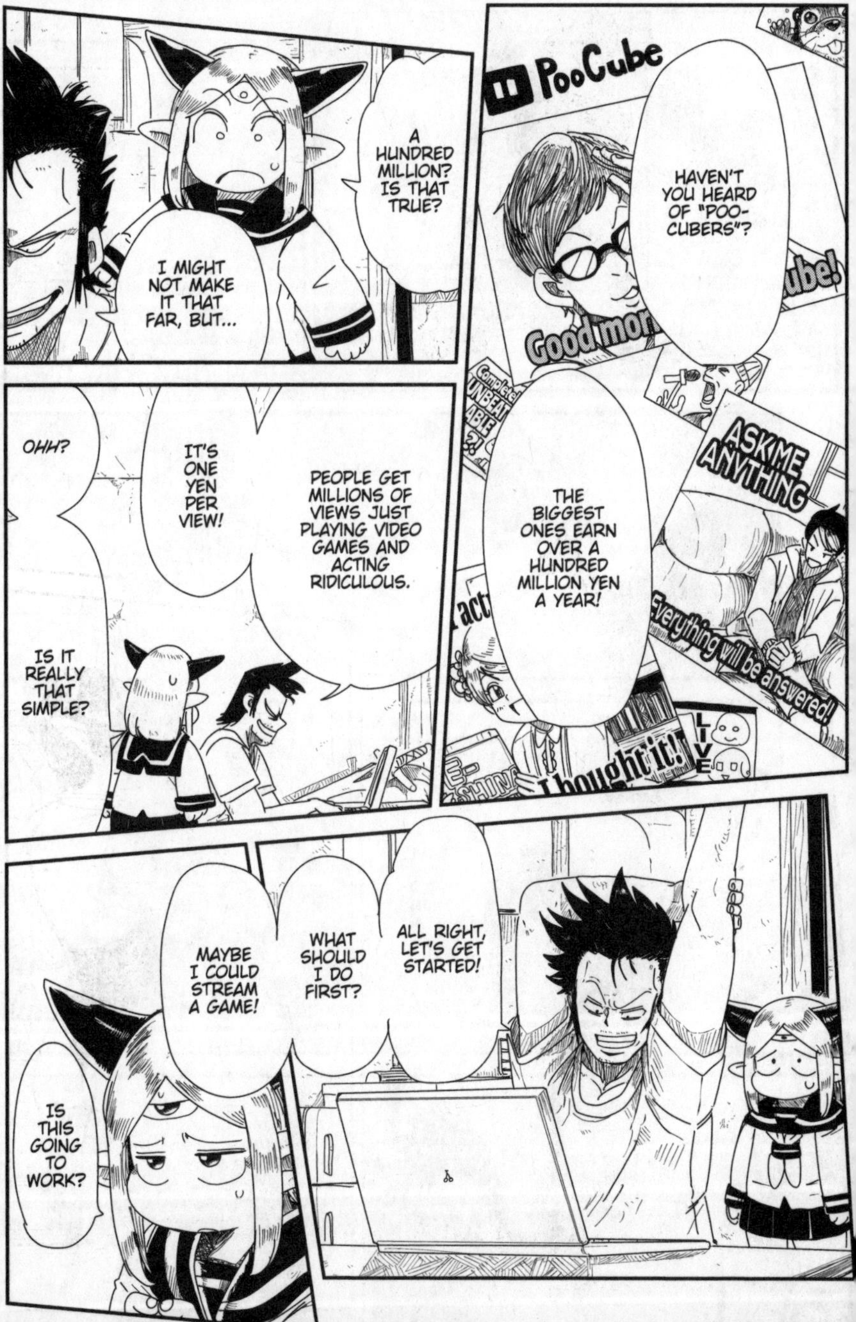
PooCube
HAVEN'T YOU HEARD OF "POO-CUBERS"?
Good mor
ube!
ASK ME ANYTHING
THE BIGGEST ONES EARN OVER A HUNDRED MILLION YEN A YEAR!
Everything will be answered!
LIVE
I thought it!
A HUNDRED MILLION? IS THAT TRUE?
I MIGHT NOT MAKE IT THAT FAR, BUT...
PEOPLE GET MILLIONS OF VIEWS JUST PLAYING VIDEO GAMES AND ACTING RIDICULOUS.
IT'S ONE YEN PER VIEW!
OHH?
IS IT REALLY THAT SIMPLE?
ALL RIGHT, LET'S GET STARTED!
WHAT SHOULD I DO FIRST?
MAYBE I COULD STREAM A GAME!
IS THIS GOING TO WORK?

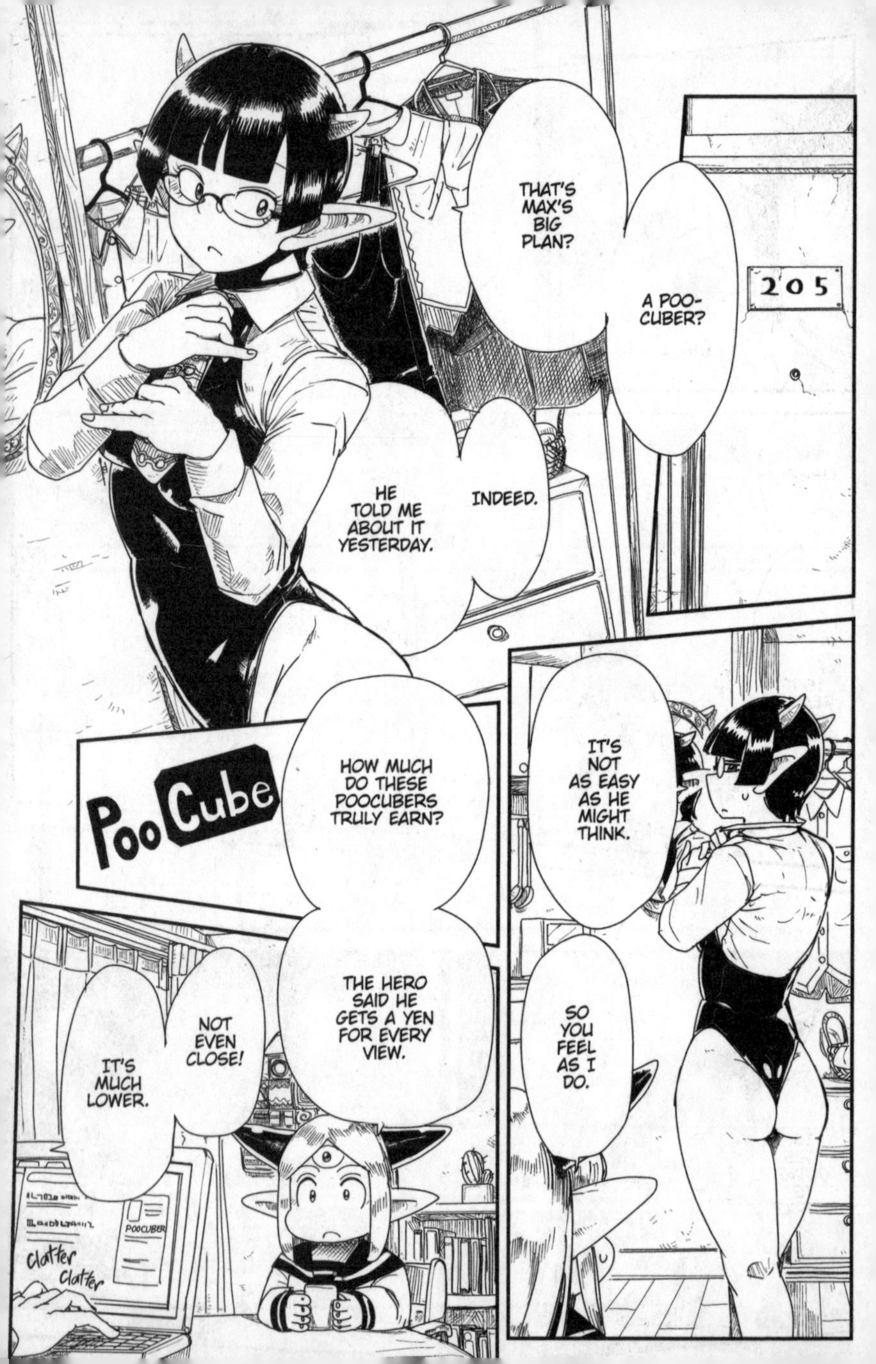
205
THAT'S MAX'S BIG PLAN?
A POO-CUBER?
INDEED.
HE TOLD ME ABOUT IT YESTERDAY.
IT'S NOT AS EASY AS HE MIGHT THINK.
SO YOU FEEL AS I DO.
PooCube
HOW MUCH DO THESE POOCUBERS TRULY EARN?
THE HERO SAID HE GETS A YEN FOR EVERY VIEW.
NOT EVEN CLOSE!
IT'S MUCH LOWER.
POOCUBER
Clatter
Clatter

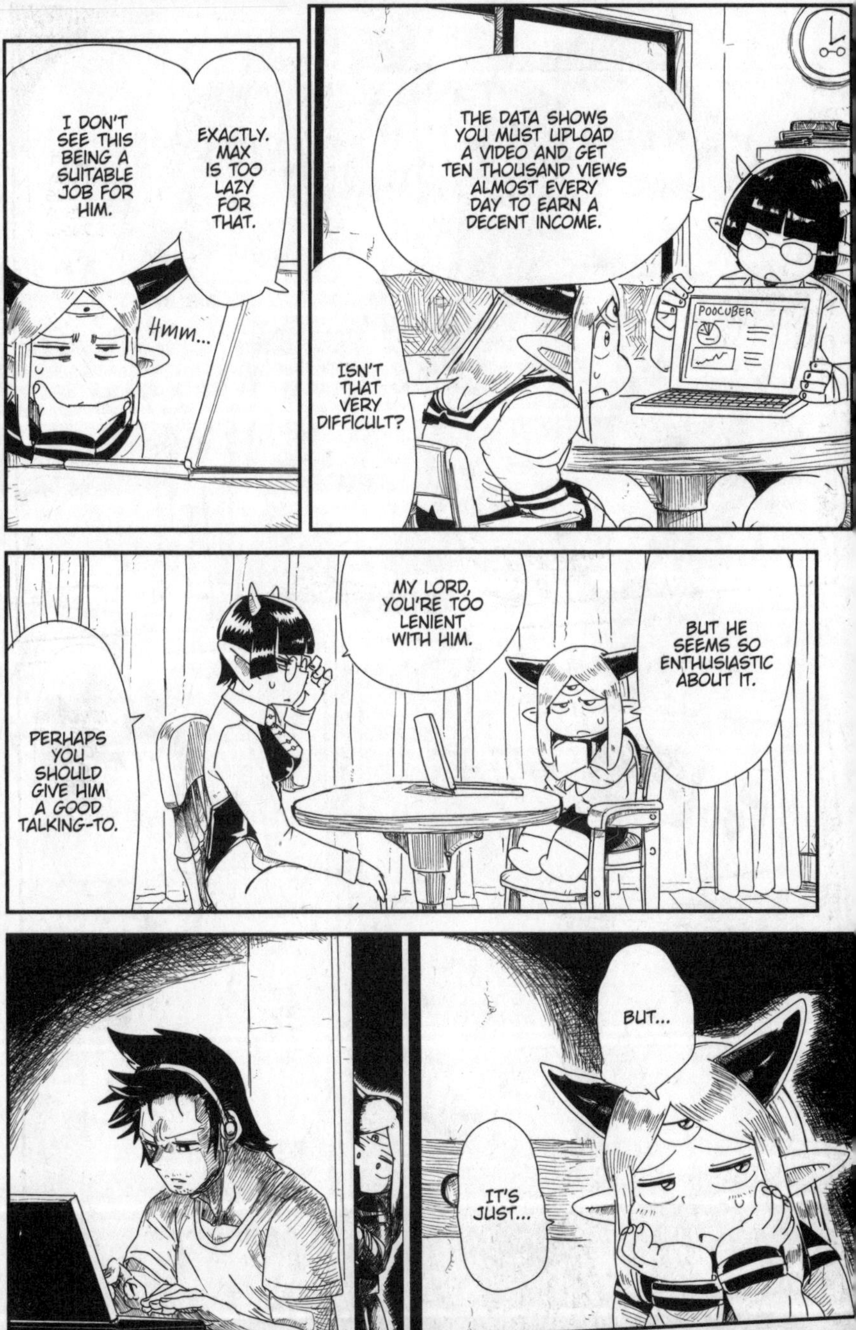
THE DATA SHOWS YOU MUST UPLOAD A VIDEO AND GET TEN THOUSAND VIEWS ALMOST EVERY DAY TO EARN A DECENT INCOME.
ISN'T THAT VERY DIFFICULT?
EXACTLY. MAX IS TOO LAZY FOR THAT.
I DON'T SEE THIS BEING A SUITABLE JOB FOR HIM.
Hmm...
POOCUBER
BUT HE SEEMS SO ENTHUSIASTIC ABOUT IT.
MY LORD, YOU'RE TOO LENIENT WITH HIM.
PERHAPS YOU SHOULD GIVE HIM A GOOD TALKING-TO.
BUT...
IT'S JUST...

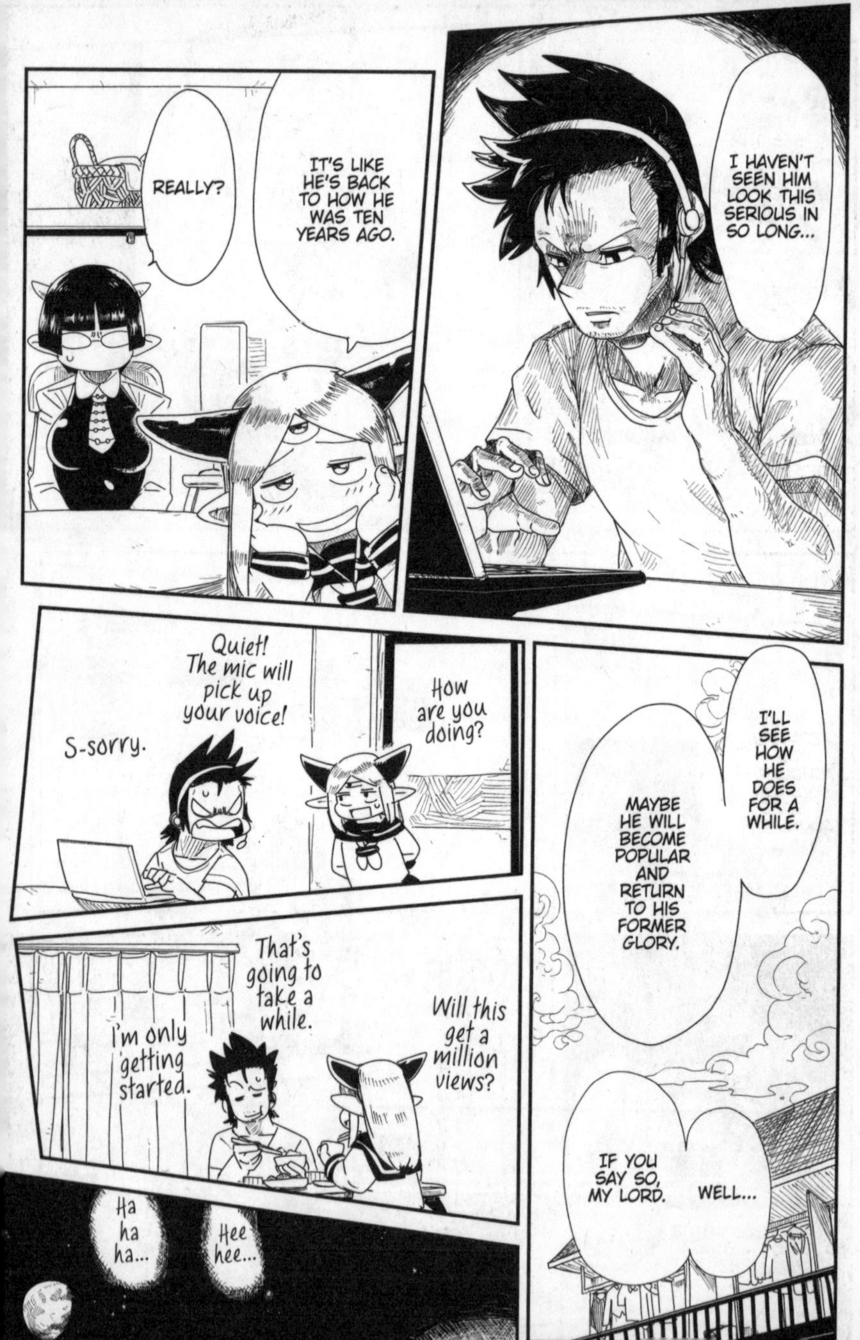
I HAVEN'T SEEN HIM LOOK THIS SERIOUS IN SO LONG...
IT'S LIKE HE'S BACK TO HOW HE WAS TEN YEARS AGO.
REALLY?
I'LL SEE HOW HE DOES FOR A WHILE.
MAYBE HE WILL BECOME POPULAR AND RETURN TO HIS FORMER GLORY.
WELL...
IF YOU SAY SO, MY LORD.
How are you doing?
Quiet! The mic will pick up your voice!
S-sorry.
Will this get a million views?
That's going to take a while.
I'm only getting started.
Hee hee...
Ha ha ha...

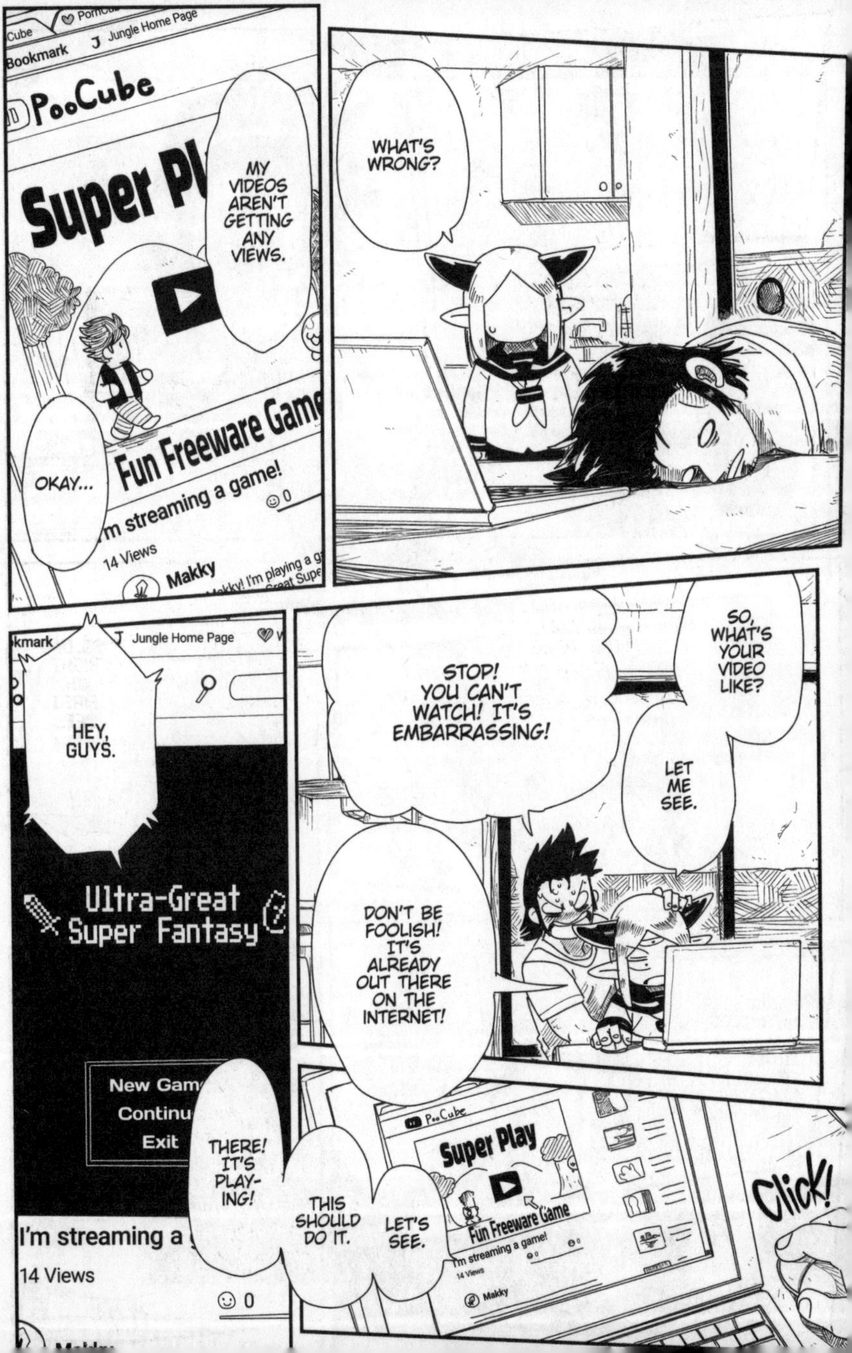
WHAT'S WRONG?
Cube
PornCube
Bookmark
Jungle Home Page
PooCube
Super Pl
MY VIDEOS AREN'T GETTING ANY VIEWS.
Fun Freeware Game
OKAY...
I'm streaming a game!
0
14 Views
Makky
Makky! I'm playing a g
Great Supe
SO, WHAT'S YOUR VIDEO LIKE?
STOP! YOU CAN'T WATCH! IT'S EMBARRASSING!
LET ME SEE.
DON'T BE FOOLISH! IT'S ALREADY OUT THERE ON THE INTERNET!
Click!
PooCube
Super Play
Fun Freeware Game
I'm streaming a game!
14 Views
Makky
LET'S SEE.
THIS SHOULD DO IT.
kmark
Jungle Home Page
HEY, GUYS.
Ultra-Great Super Fantasy
New Gam
Continu
Exit
THERE! IT'S PLAY-ING!
I'm streaming a
14 Views
0

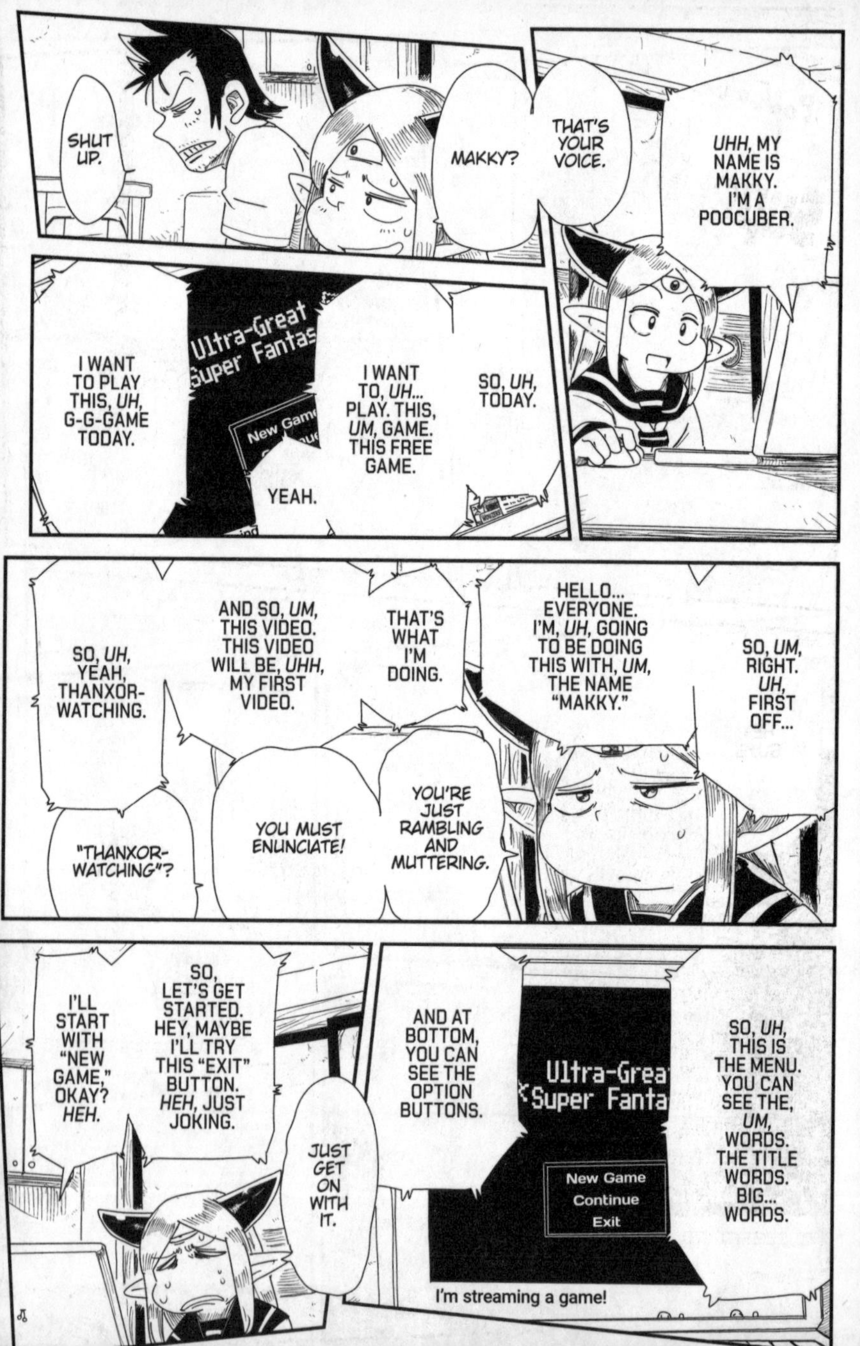
UHH, MY NAME IS MAKKY. I'M A POOCUBER.
THAT'S YOUR VOICE.
MAKKY?
SHUT UP.
SO, *UH*, TODAY.
I WANT TO, *UH*... PLAY. THIS, *UM*, GAME. THIS FREE GAME.
YEAH.
Ultra-Great Super Fantas
New Game
I WANT TO PLAY THIS, *UH*, G-G-GAME TODAY.
SO, *UM*, RIGHT. *UH*, FIRST OFF...
HELLO... EVERYONE. I'M, *UH*, GOING TO BE DOING THIS WITH, *UM*, THE NAME "MAKKY."
THAT'S WHAT I'M DOING.
AND SO, *UM*, THIS VIDEO. THIS VIDEO WILL BE, *UHH*, MY FIRST VIDEO.
SO, *UH*, YEAH, THANXOR-WATCHING.
YOU'RE JUST RAMBLING AND MUTTERING.
YOU MUST ENUNCIATE!
"THANXOR-WATCHING"?
SO, *UH*, THIS IS THE MENU. YOU CAN SEE THE, *UM*, WORDS. THE TITLE WORDS. BIG... WORDS.
Ultra-Grea Super Fanta
New Game
Continue
Exit
AND AT BOTTOM, YOU CAN SEE THE OPTION BUTTONS.
JUST GET ON WITH IT.
I'm streaming a game!
SO, LET'S GET STARTED. HEY, MAYBE I'LL TRY THIS "EXIT" BUTTON. *HEH*, JUST JOKING.
I'LL START WITH "NEW GAME," OKAY? *HEH*.

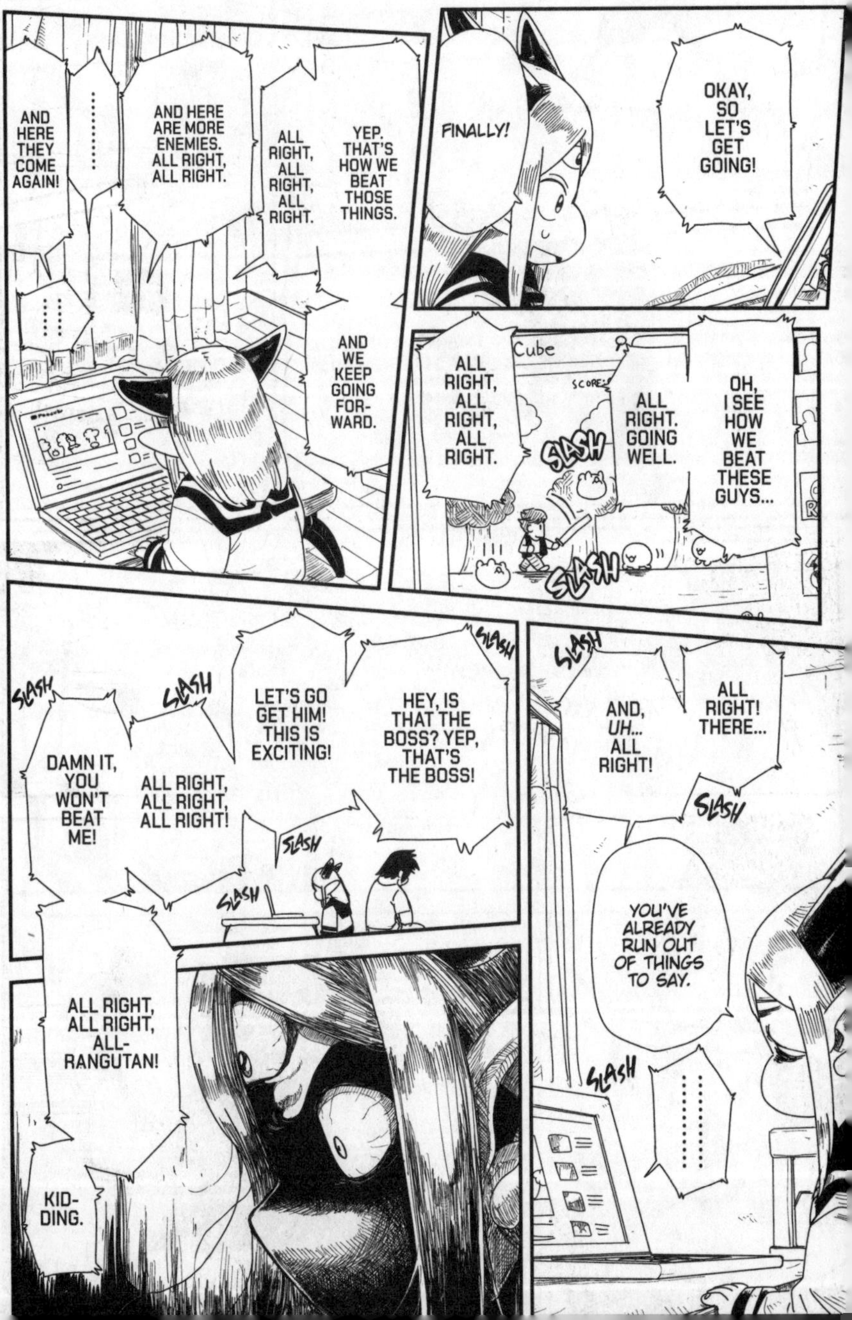

OKAY, SO LET'S GET GOING!
FINALLY!
Cube
OH, I SEE HOW WE BEAT THESE GUYS...
ALL RIGHT. GOING WELL.
SLASH
ALL RIGHT, ALL RIGHT, ALL RIGHT.
SLASH
YEP. THAT'S HOW WE BEAT THOSE THINGS.
ALL RIGHT, ALL RIGHT, ALL RIGHT.
AND HERE ARE MORE ENEMIES. ALL RIGHT, ALL RIGHT.
......
AND HERE THEY COME AGAIN!
AND WE KEEP GOING FORWARD.
......
SLASH
ALL RIGHT! THERE...
AND, *UH*... ALL RIGHT!
SLASH
YOU'VE ALREADY RUN OUT OF THINGS TO SAY.
SLASH
......
SLASH
HEY, IS THAT THE BOSS? YEP, THAT'S THE BOSS!
LET'S GO GET HIM! THIS IS EXCITING!
SLASH
ALL RIGHT, ALL RIGHT, ALL RIGHT!
SLASH
DAMN IT, YOU WON'T BEAT ME!
SLASH
SLASH
ALL RIGHT, ALL RIGHT, ALL-RANGUTAN!
KID-DING.

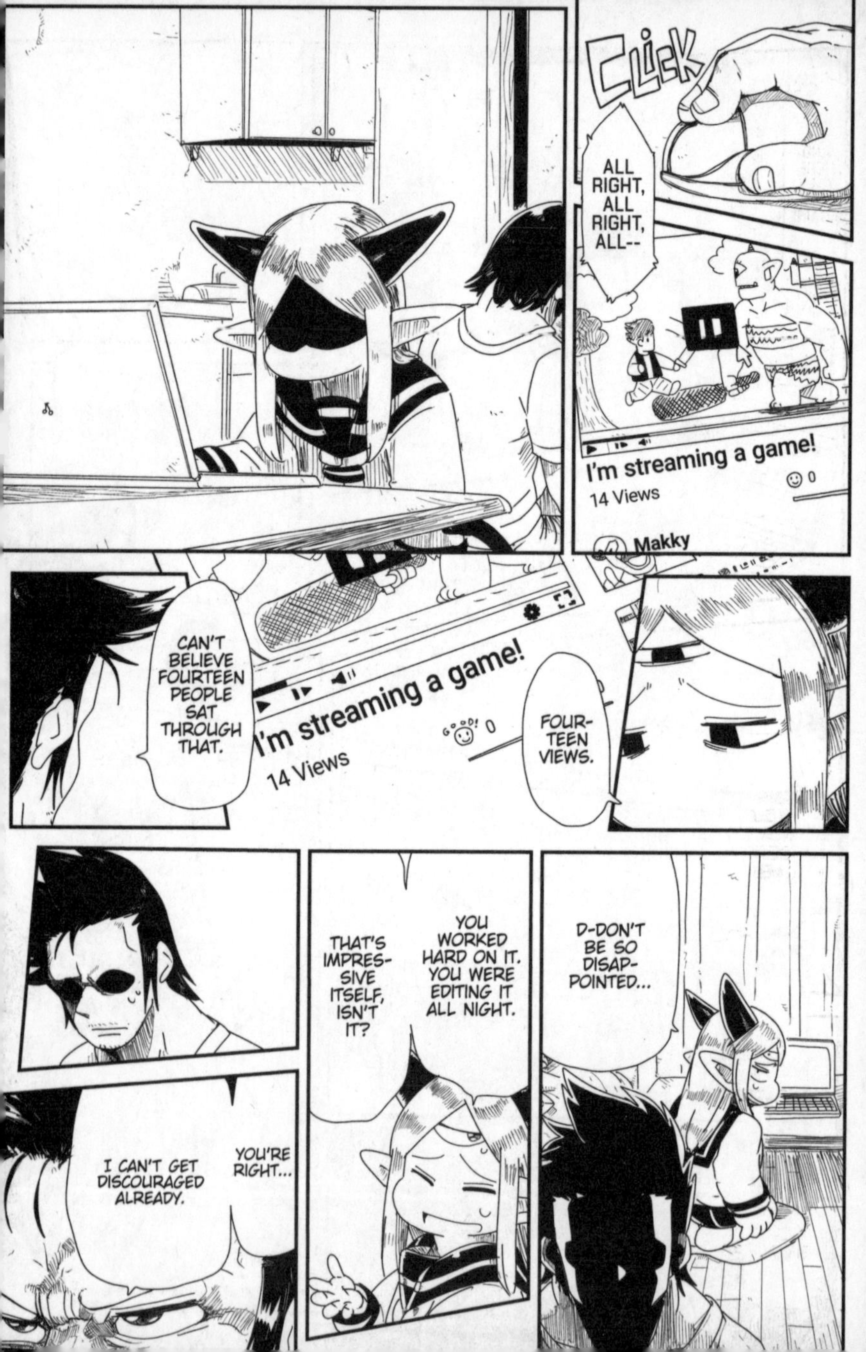
CLICK
ALL RIGHT, ALL RIGHT, ALL--
I'm streaming a game!
14 Views
0
Makky
FOUR-TEEN VIEWS.
I'm streaming a game!
14 Views
GOOD! 0
CAN'T BELIEVE FOURTEEN PEOPLE SAT THROUGH THAT.
D-DON'T BE SO DISAP-POINTED...
YOU WORKED HARD ON IT. YOU WERE EDITING IT ALL NIGHT.
THAT'S IMPRES-SIVE ITSELF, ISN'T IT?
YOU'RE RIGHT...
I CAN'T GET DISCOURAGED ALREADY.

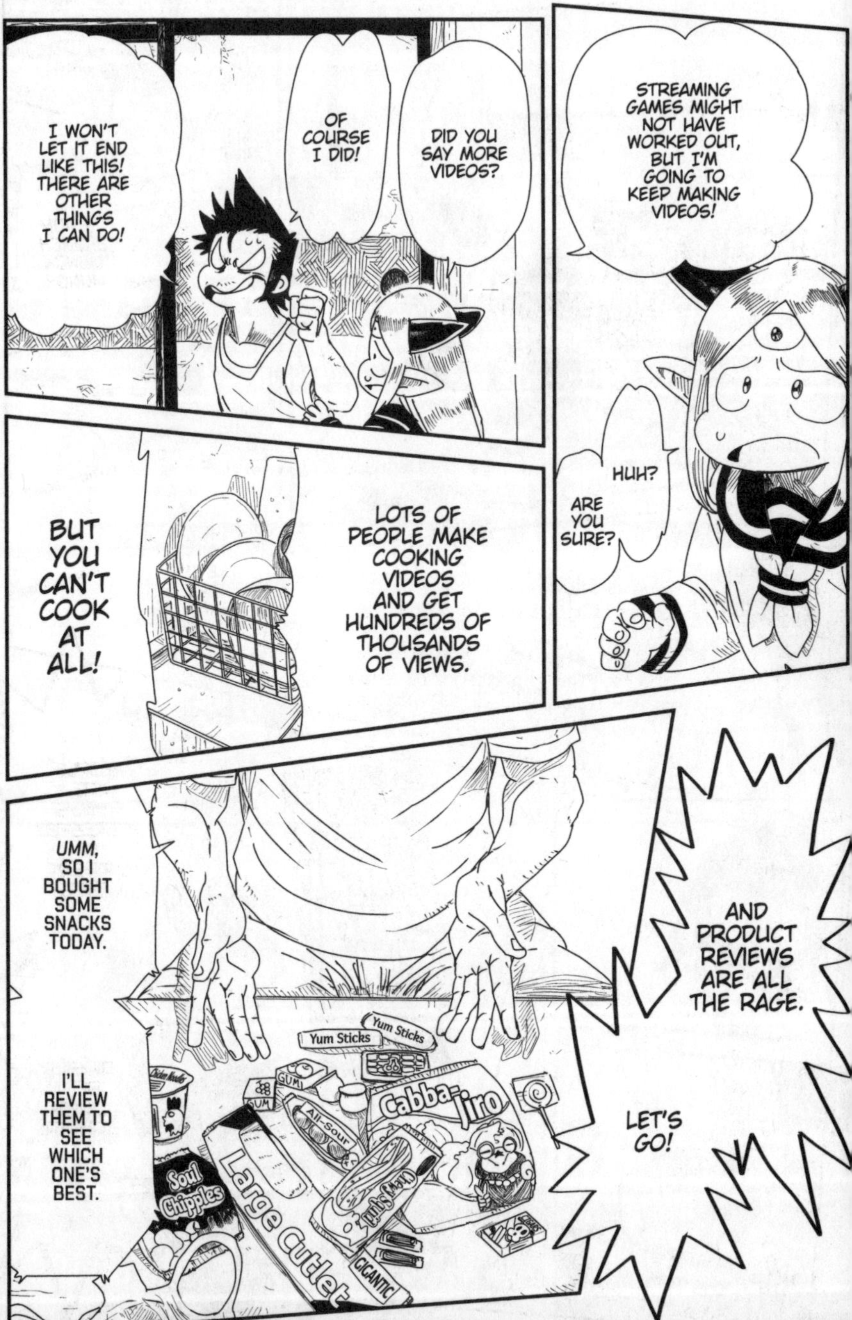
STREAMING GAMES MIGHT NOT HAVE WORKED OUT, BUT I'M GOING TO KEEP MAKING VIDEOS!
HUH?
ARE YOU SURE?
DID YOU SAY MORE VIDEOS?
OF COURSE I DID!
I WON'T LET IT END LIKE THIS! THERE ARE OTHER THINGS I CAN DO!
LOTS OF PEOPLE MAKE COOKING VIDEOS AND GET HUNDREDS OF THOUSANDS OF VIEWS.
BUT YOU CAN'T COOK AT ALL!
AND PRODUCT REVIEWS ARE ALL THE RAGE.
LET'S GO!
UMM, SO I BOUGHT SOME SNACKS TODAY.
I'LL REVIEW THEM TO SEE WHICH ONE'S BEST.
Yum Sticks
Yum Sticks
GUMI
All-Sour
Cabba-jiro
Soul Chipples
Large Cutlet
GIGANTIC

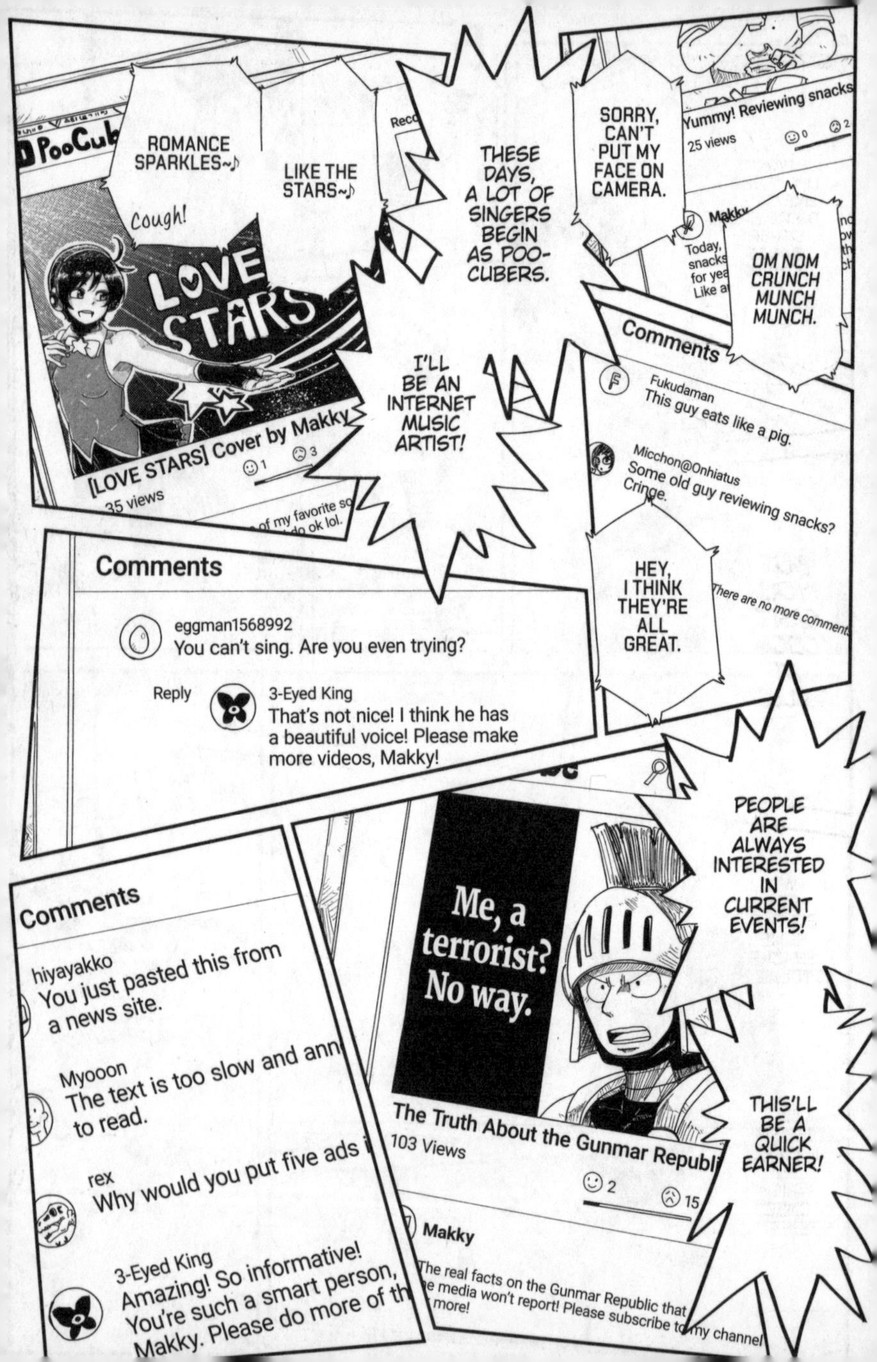
Yummy! Reviewing snacks
25 views
0
2
SORRY, CAN'T PUT MY FACE ON CAMERA.
Makky
OM NOM CRUNCH MUNCH MUNCH.
Comments
Fukudaman
This guy eats like a pig.
Micchon@Onhiatus
Some old guy reviewing snacks? Cringe.
HEY, I THINK THEY'RE ALL GREAT.
There are no more comments
THESE DAYS, A LOT OF SINGERS BEGIN AS POO-CUBERS.
I'LL BE AN INTERNET MUSIC ARTIST!
ROMANCE SPARKLES~♪
LIKE THE STARS~♪
Cough!
LOVE STARS
[LOVE STARS] Cover by Makky
1
3
35 views
Comments
eggman1568992
You can't sing. Are you even trying?
Reply
3-Eyed King
That's not nice! I think he has a beautiful voice! Please make more videos, Makky!
PEOPLE ARE ALWAYS INTERESTED IN CURRENT EVENTS!
Me, a terrorist? No way.
THIS'LL BE A QUICK EARNER!
103 Views
2
15
Makky
Comments
hiyayakko
You just pasted this from a news site.
Myooon
to read.
rex
3-Eyed King
Amazing! So informative!

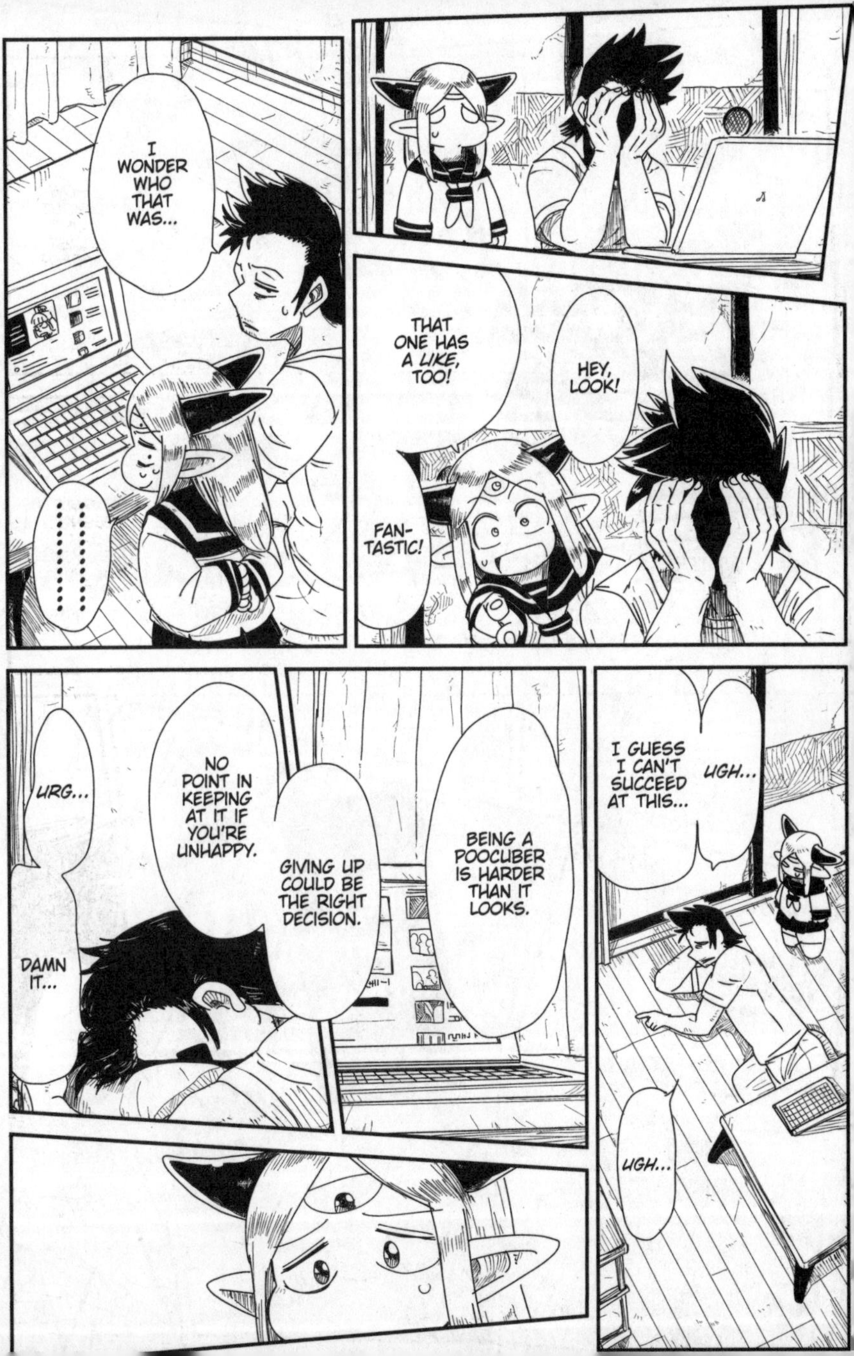
HEY, LOOK!
THAT ONE HAS A *LIKE*, TOO!
FAN-TASTIC!
I WONDER WHO THAT WAS...
......
UGH...
I GUESS I CAN'T SUCCEED AT THIS...
UGH...
BEING A POOCUBER IS HARDER THAN IT LOOKS.
GIVING UP COULD BE THE RIGHT DECISION.
NO POINT IN KEEPING AT IT IF YOU'RE UNHAPPY.
URG...
DAMN IT...

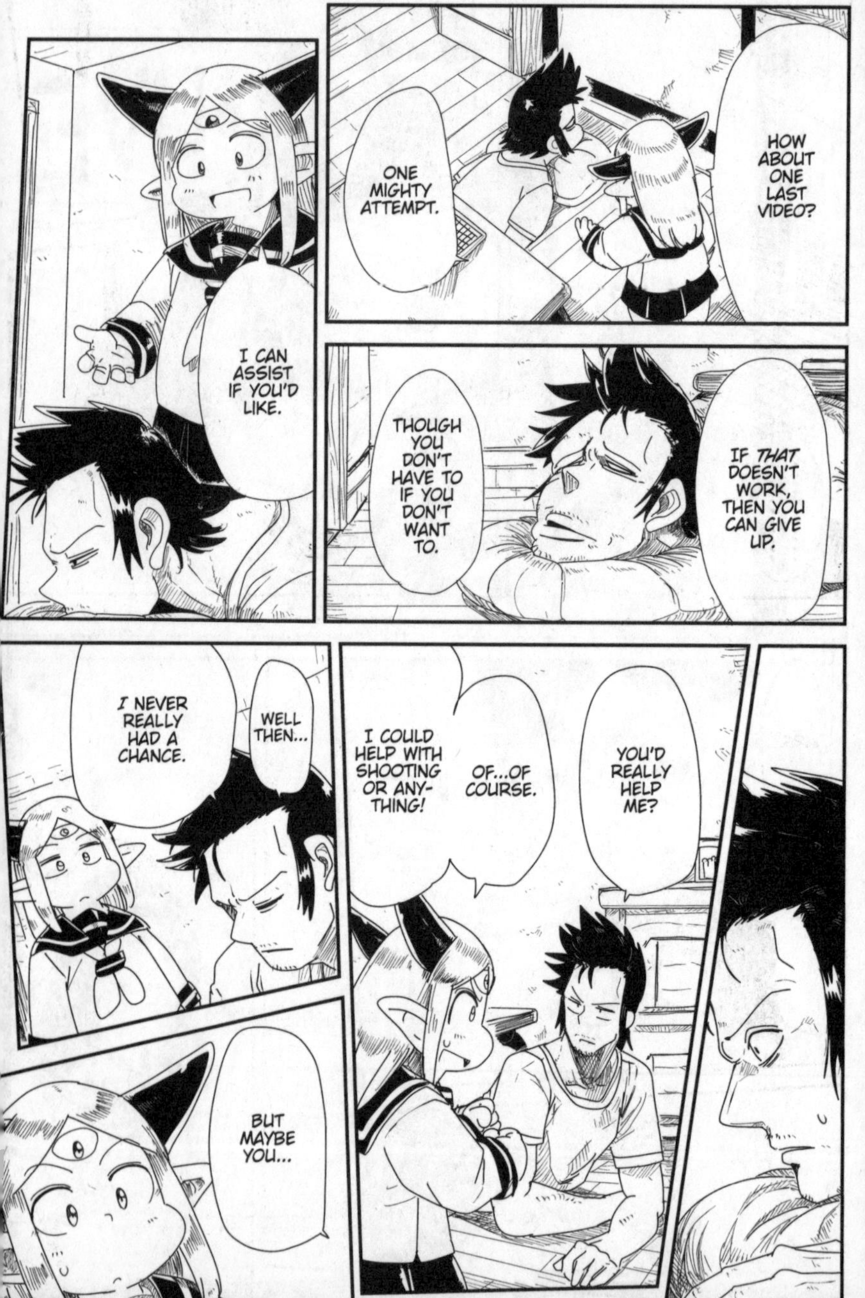
HOW ABOUT ONE LAST VIDEO?
ONE MIGHTY ATTEMPT.
IF *THAT* DOESN'T WORK, THEN YOU CAN GIVE UP.
THOUGH YOU DON'T HAVE TO IF YOU DON'T WANT TO.
I CAN ASSIST IF YOU'D LIKE.
YOU'D REALLY HELP ME?
OF...OF COURSE.
I COULD HELP WITH SHOOTING OR ANY-THING!
WELL THEN...
I NEVER REALLY HAD A CHANCE.
BUT MAYBE YOU...

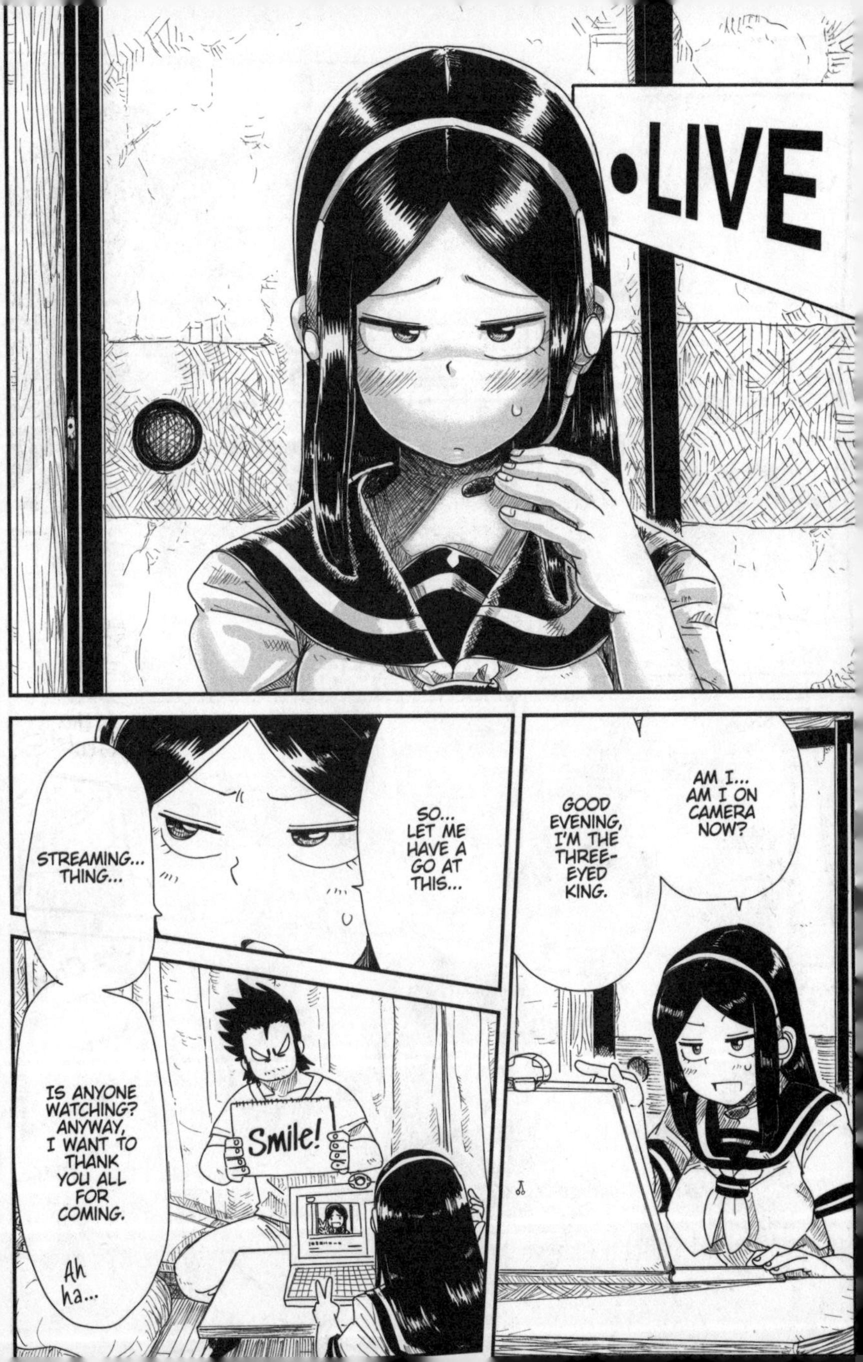
•LIVE
AM I... AM I ON CAMERA NOW?
GOOD EVENING, I'M THE THREE-EYED KING.
SO... LET ME HAVE A GO AT THIS...
STREAMING... THING...
IS ANYONE WATCHING? ANYWAY, I WANT TO THANK YOU ALL FOR COMING.
Ah ha...
Smile!

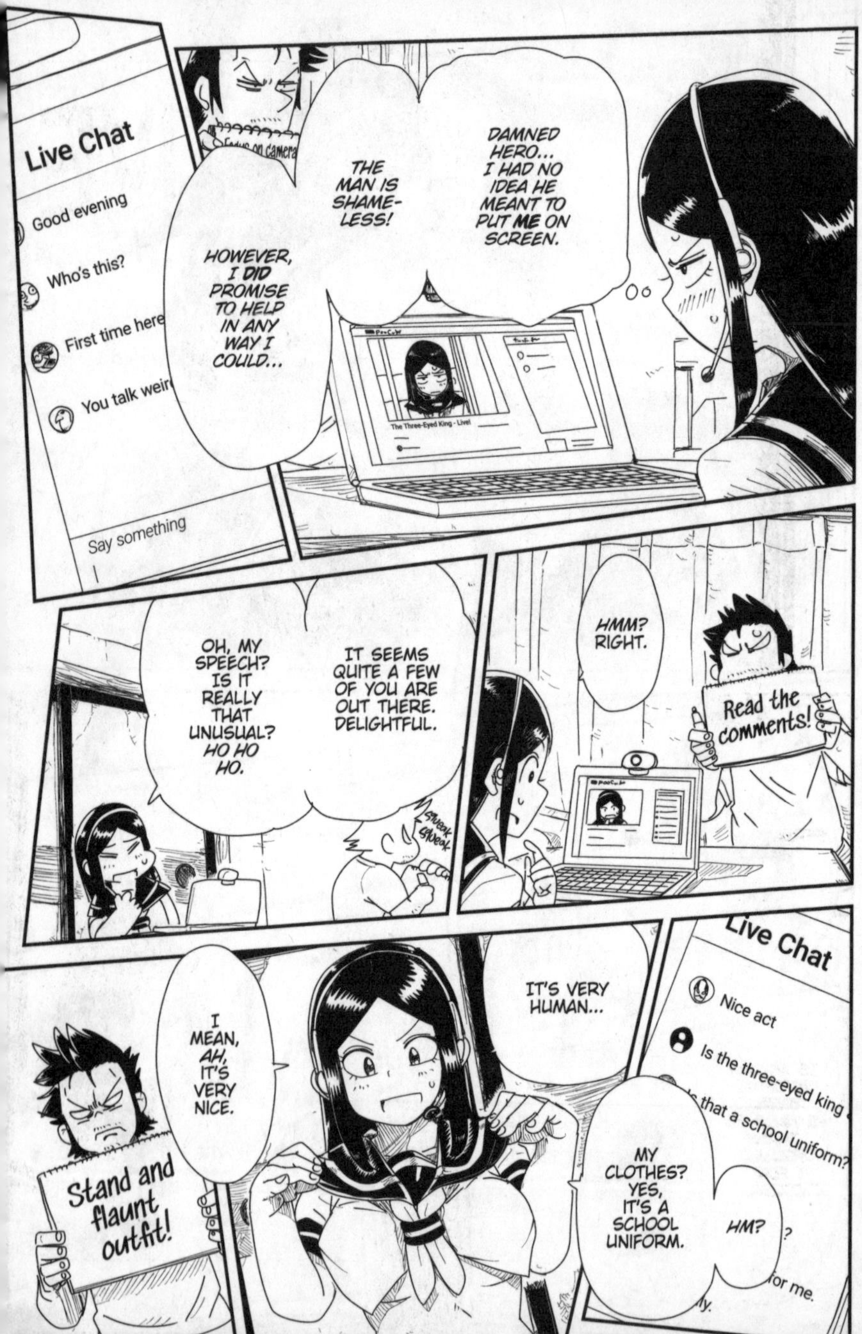
Focus on camera
DAMNED HERO... I HAD NO IDEA HE MEANT TO PUT ME ON SCREEN.
THE MAN IS SHAMELESS!
HOWEVER, I DID PROMISE TO HELP IN ANY WAY I COULD...
The Three-Eyed King - Live!
Live Chat
Good evening
Who's this?
First time here
You talk weir
Say something
HMM? RIGHT.
Read the comments!
IT SEEMS QUITE A FEW OF YOU ARE OUT THERE. DELIGHTFUL.
OH, MY SPEECH? IS IT REALLY THAT UNUSUAL? HO HO HO.
SQUEAK SQUEAK
Live Chat
Nice act
Is the three-eyed king
that a school uniform?
for me.
HM?
MY CLOTHES? YES, IT'S A SCHOOL UNIFORM.
IT'S VERY HUMAN...
I MEAN, AH, IT'S VERY NICE.
Stand and flaunt outfit!

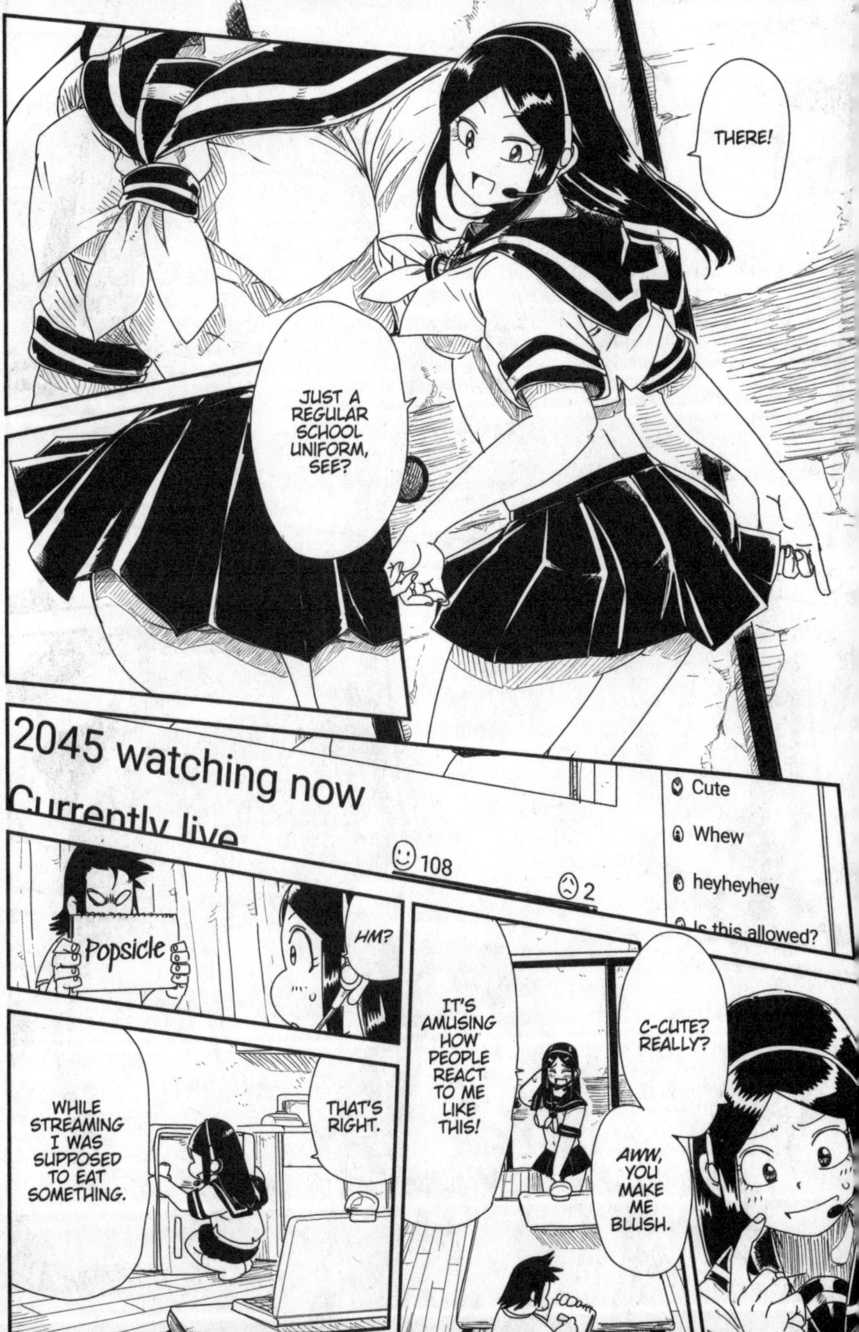
THERE!
JUST A REGULAR SCHOOL UNIFORM, SEE?
2045 watching now
Currently live
108
2
Cute
Whew
heyheyhey
Is this allowed?
C-CUTE? REALLY?
AWW, YOU MAKE ME BLUSH.
IT'S AMUSING HOW PEOPLE REACT TO ME LIKE THIS!
HM?
Popsicle
THAT'S RIGHT.
WHILE STREAMING I WAS SUPPOSED TO EAT SOMETHING.

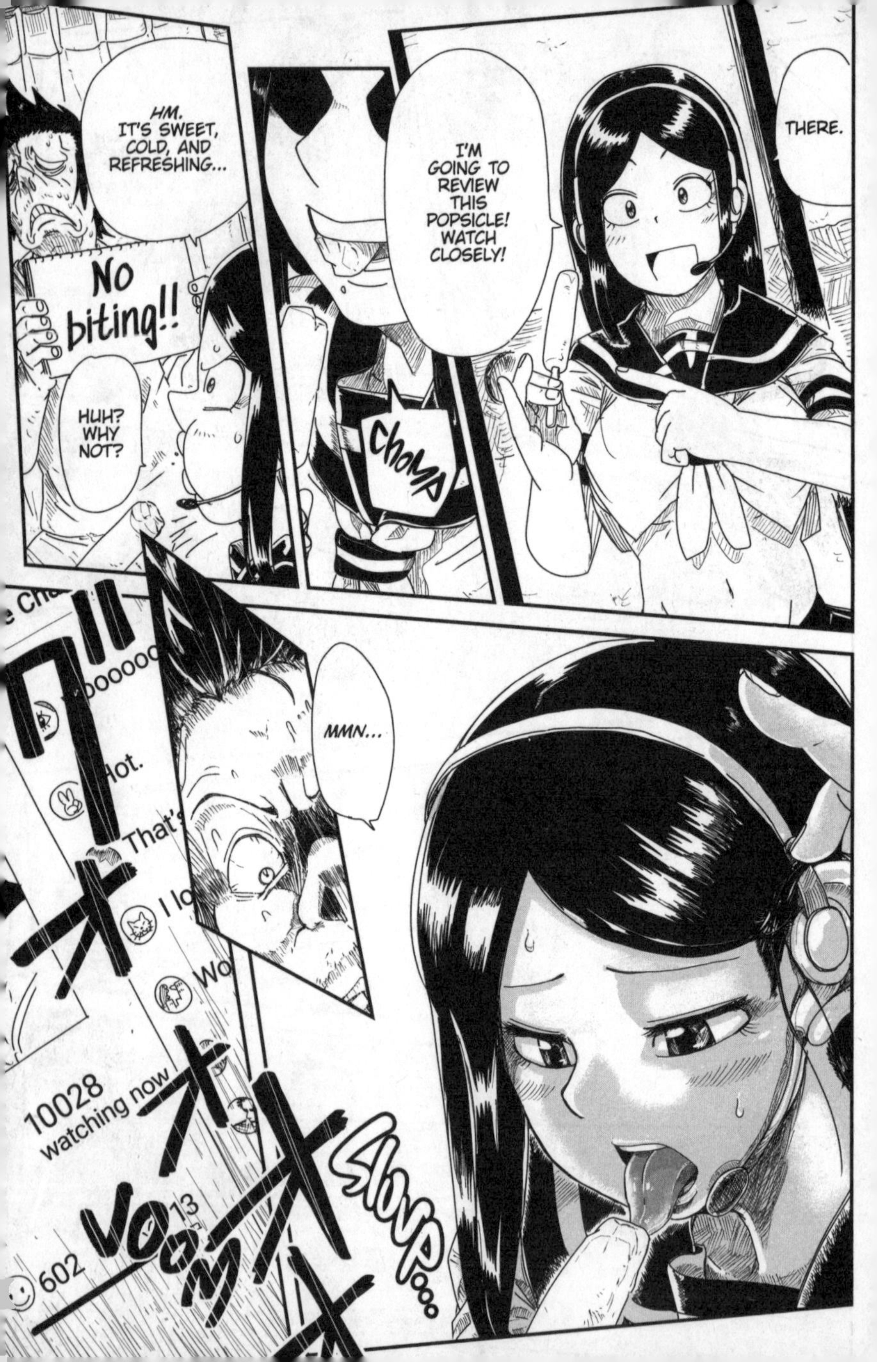
THERE.
I'M GOING TO REVIEW THIS POPSICLE! WATCH CLOSELY!
CHOMP
HM. IT'S SWEET, COLD, AND REFRESHING...
No biting!!
HUH? WHY NOT?
SLURP...
MMN...
Hot.
10028 watching now
602

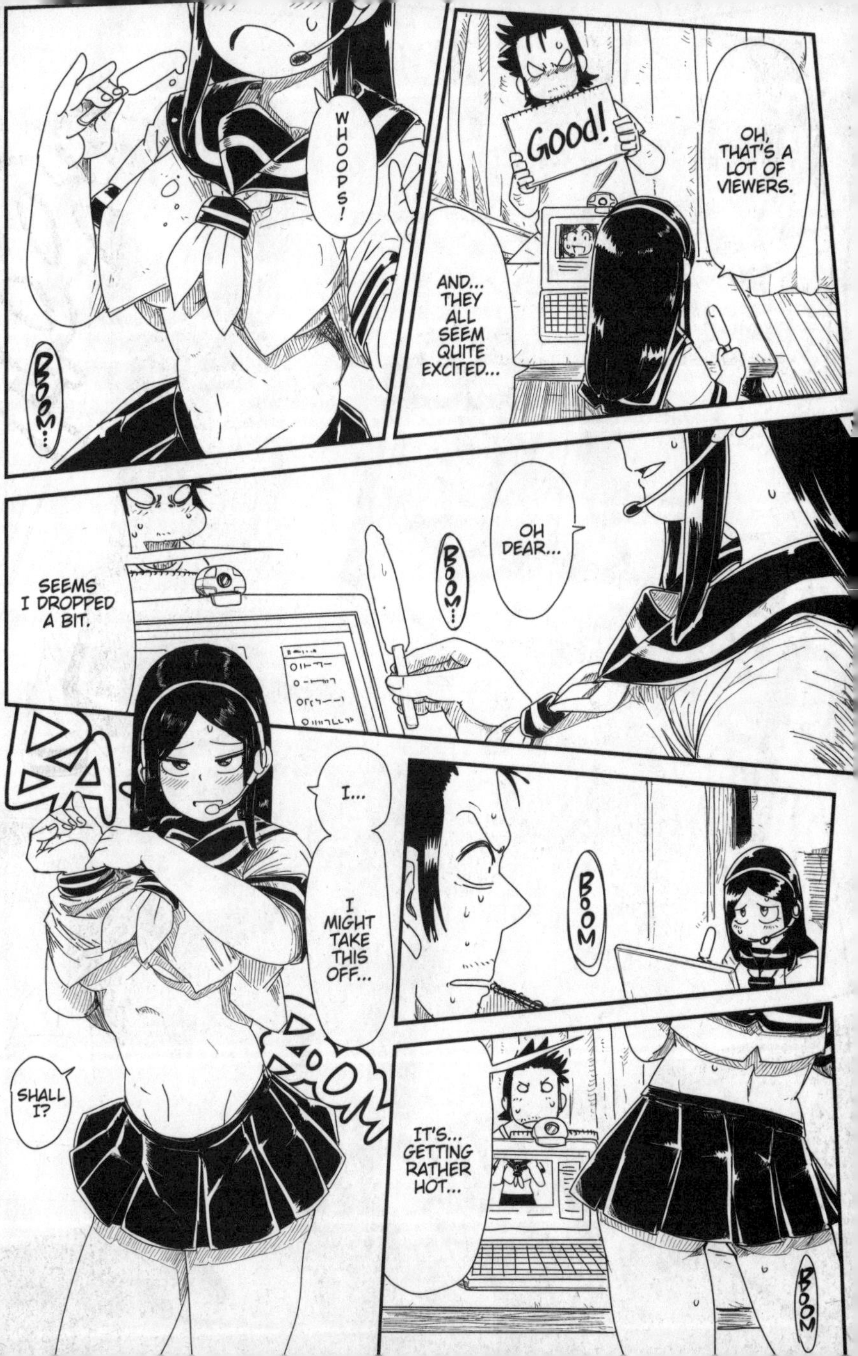
OH, THAT'S A LOT OF VIEWERS.
Good!
AND... THEY ALL SEEM QUITE EXCITED...
WHOOPS!
BOOM...
OH DEAR...
BOOM...
SEEMS I DROPPED A BIT.
BOOM
IT'S... GETTING RATHER HOT...
BOOM
BA
I...
I MIGHT TAKE THIS OFF...
SHALL I?
DOOM

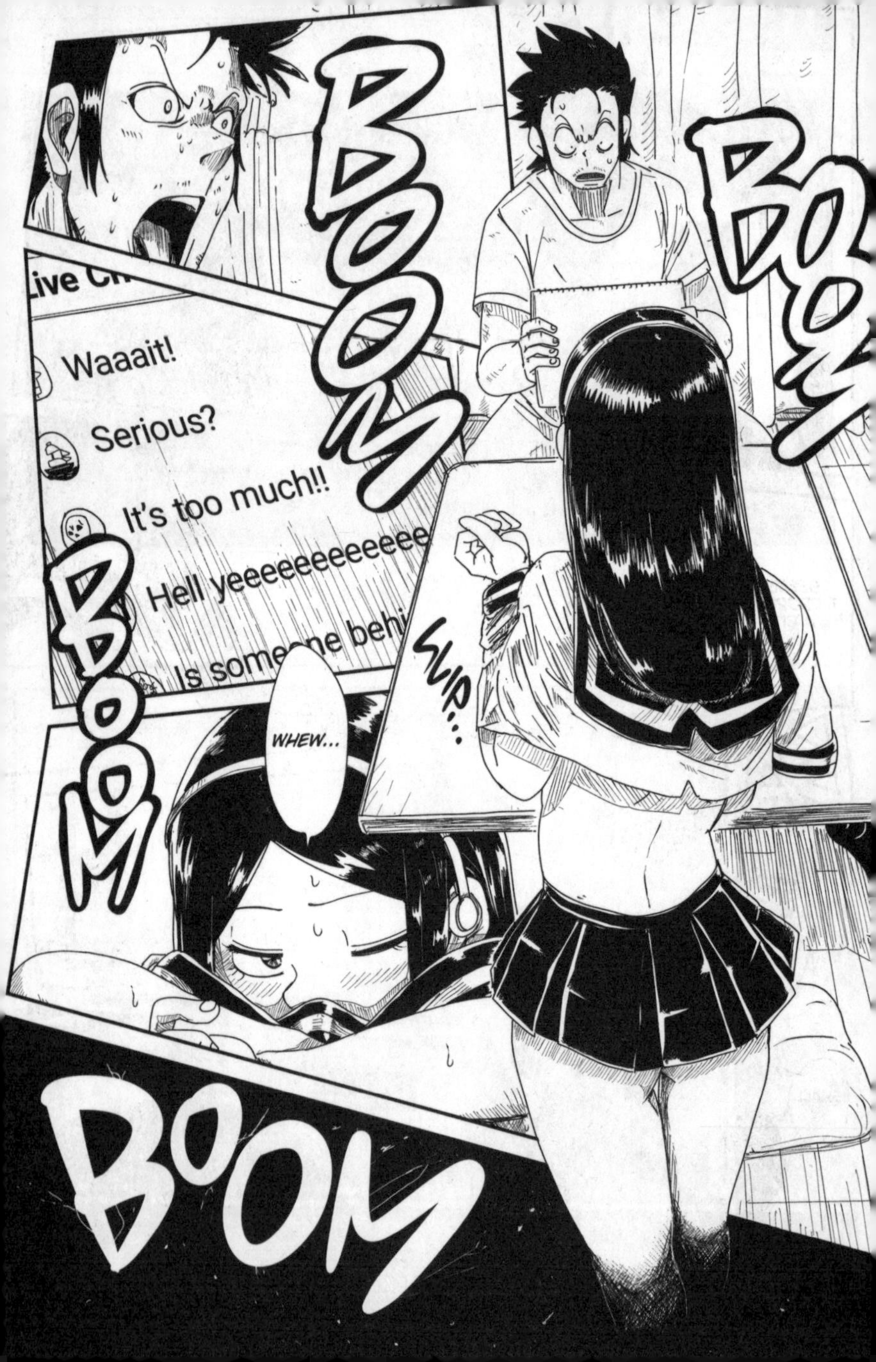

BOOM
SLIP...
BOOM
Live Ch
Waaait!
Serious?
It's too much!!
Hell yeeeeeeeeeeee
Is someone behi
BOOM
WHEW...
BOOM

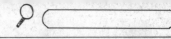

Your account has been suspended for violating PooCube's Terms of Service.

Reason: Video or stream containing objectionable content.

HOW
FOOLISH
WE ARE.

Episode 9　End

LEVEL 1 DEMON LORD
& ONE ROOM HERO

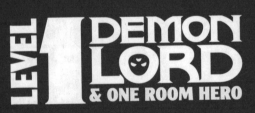

LEVEL 1 DEMON LORD
& ONE ROOM HERO

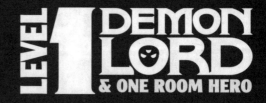

Episode 10: With the Demon Lord!

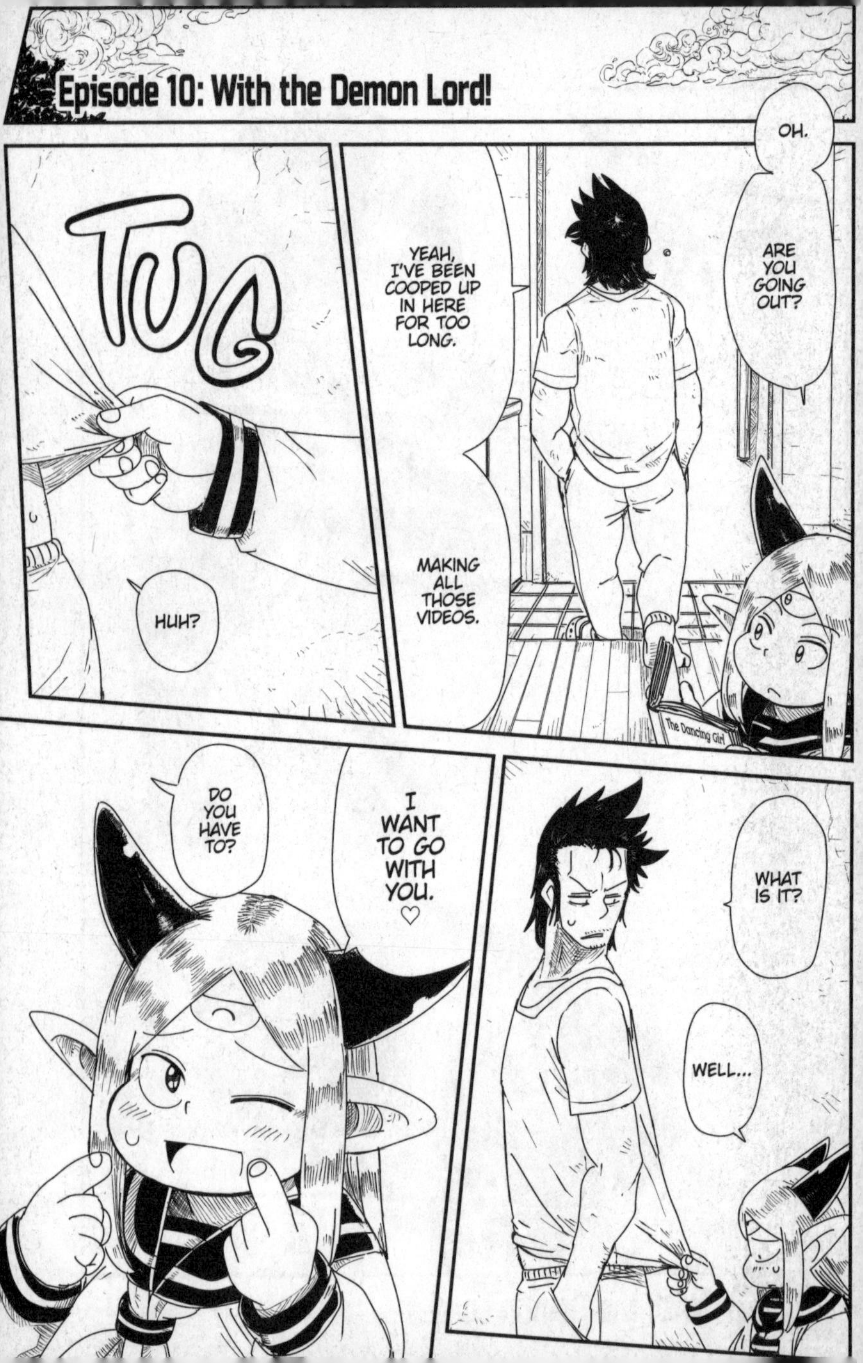
OH.
ARE YOU GOING OUT?
YEAH, I'VE BEEN COOPED UP IN HERE FOR TOO LONG.
MAKING ALL THOSE VIDEOS.
The Dancing Girl
TUG
HUH?
WHAT IS IT?
WELL...
DO YOU HAVE TO?
I WANT TO GO WITH YOU. ♡

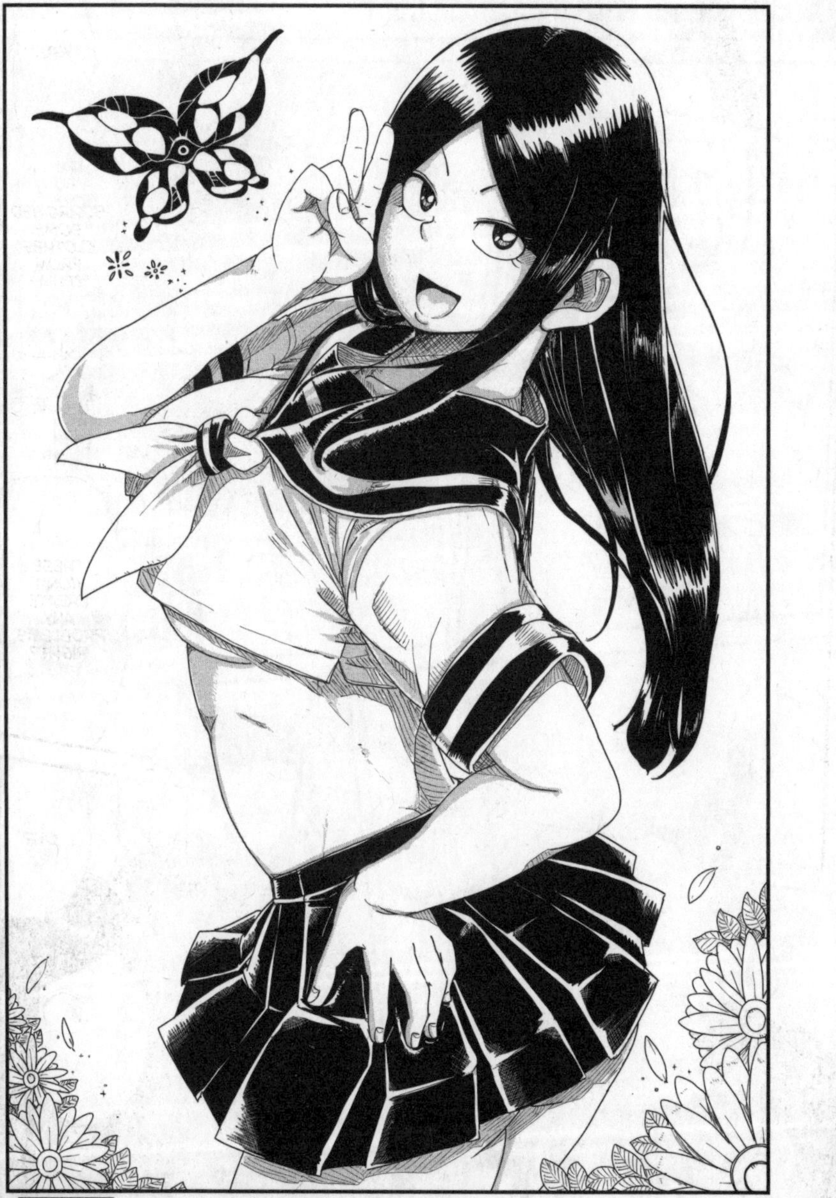

Episode 10 With the Demon Lord!

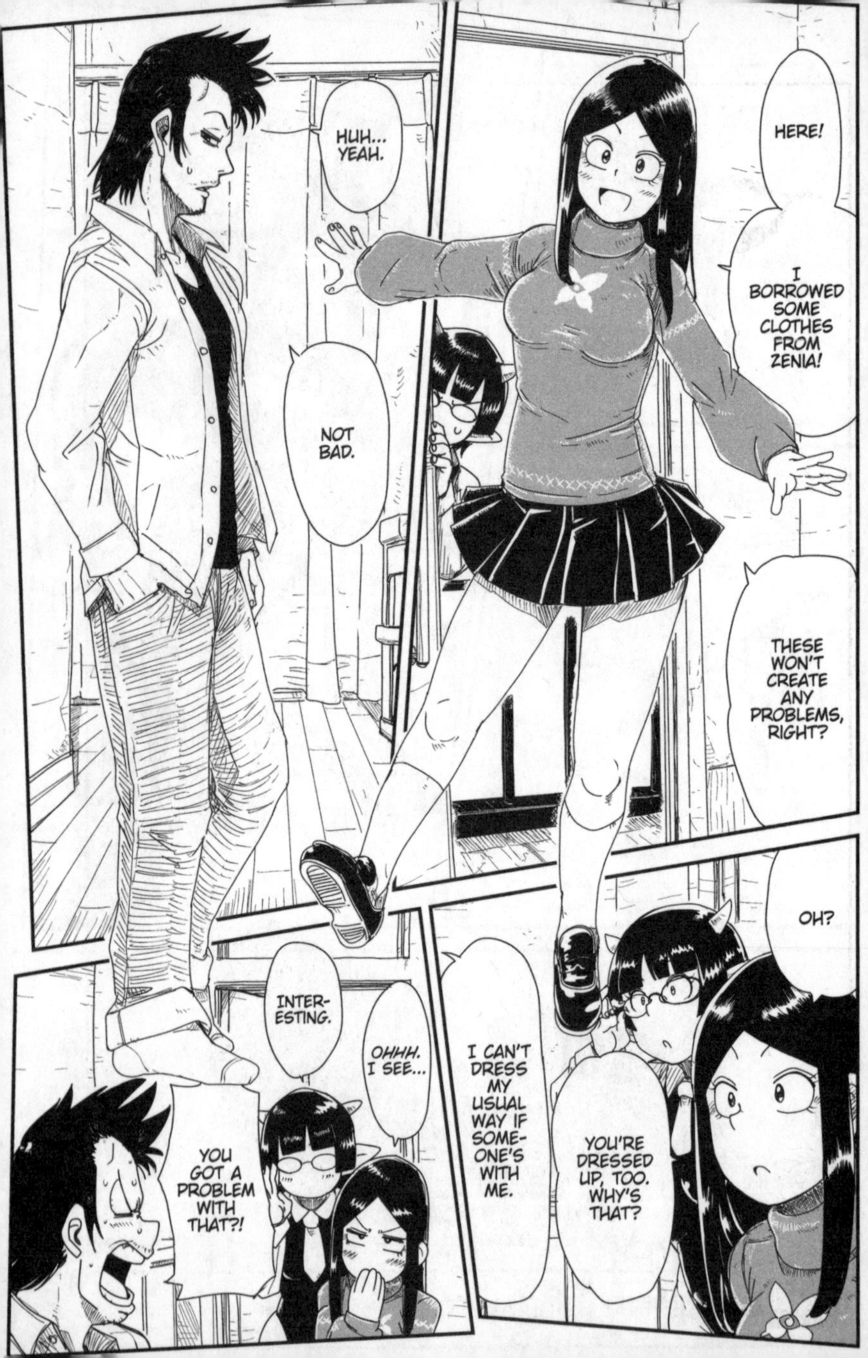
HERE!
I BORROWED SOME CLOTHES FROM ZENIA!
THESE WON'T CREATE ANY PROBLEMS, RIGHT?
HUH... YEAH.
NOT BAD.
OH?
YOU'RE DRESSED UP, TOO. WHY'S THAT?
I CAN'T DRESS MY USUAL WAY IF SOME-ONE'S WITH ME.
OHHH. I SEE...
INTER-ESTING.
YOU GOT A PROBLEM WITH THAT?!

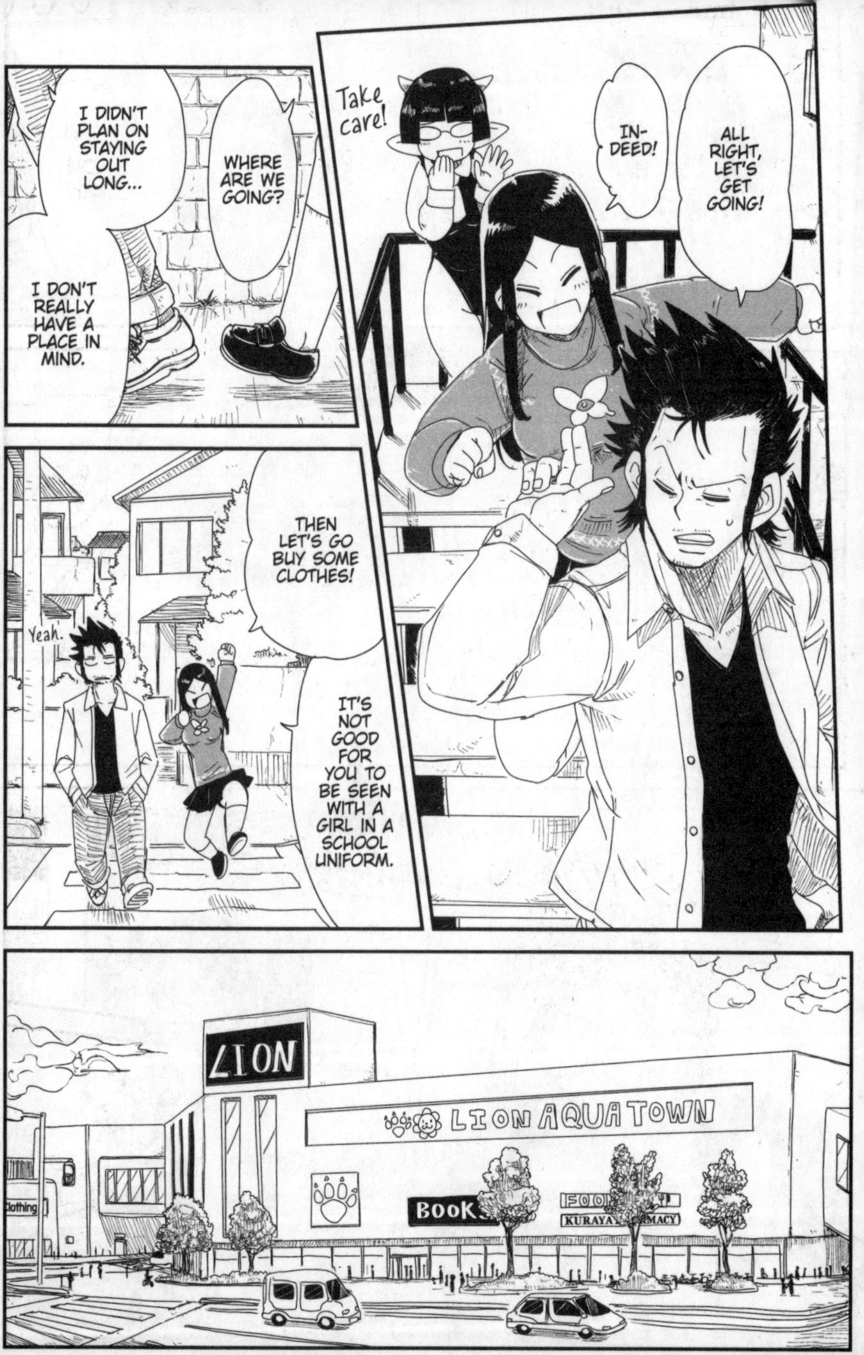
ALL RIGHT, LET'S GET GOING!
IN-DEED!
Take care!
WHERE ARE WE GOING?
I DIDN'T PLAN ON STAYING OUT LONG...
I DON'T REALLY HAVE A PLACE IN MIND.
THEN LET'S GO BUY SOME CLOTHES!
Yeah.
IT'S NOT GOOD FOR YOU TO BE SEEN WITH A GIRL IN A SCHOOL UNIFORM.
LION
LION AQUA TOWN
Clothing

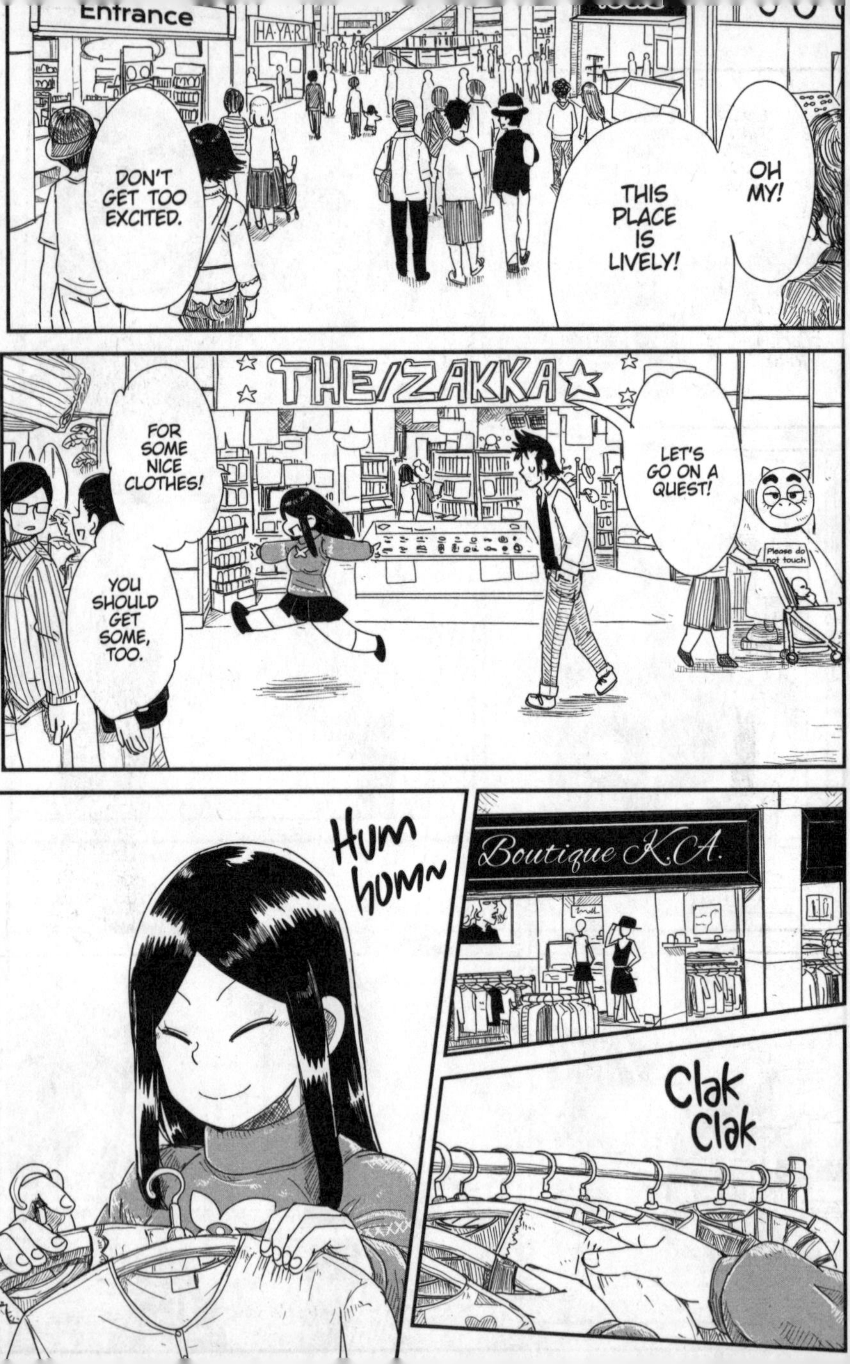
Entrance
HA-YA-RI
OH MY!
THIS PLACE IS LIVELY!
DON'T GET TOO EXCITED.
THE/ZAKKA
LET'S GO ON A QUEST!
Please do not touch
FOR SOME NICE CLOTHES!
YOU SHOULD GET SOME, TOO.
Boutique K.CA.
Clak Clak
Hum hom~

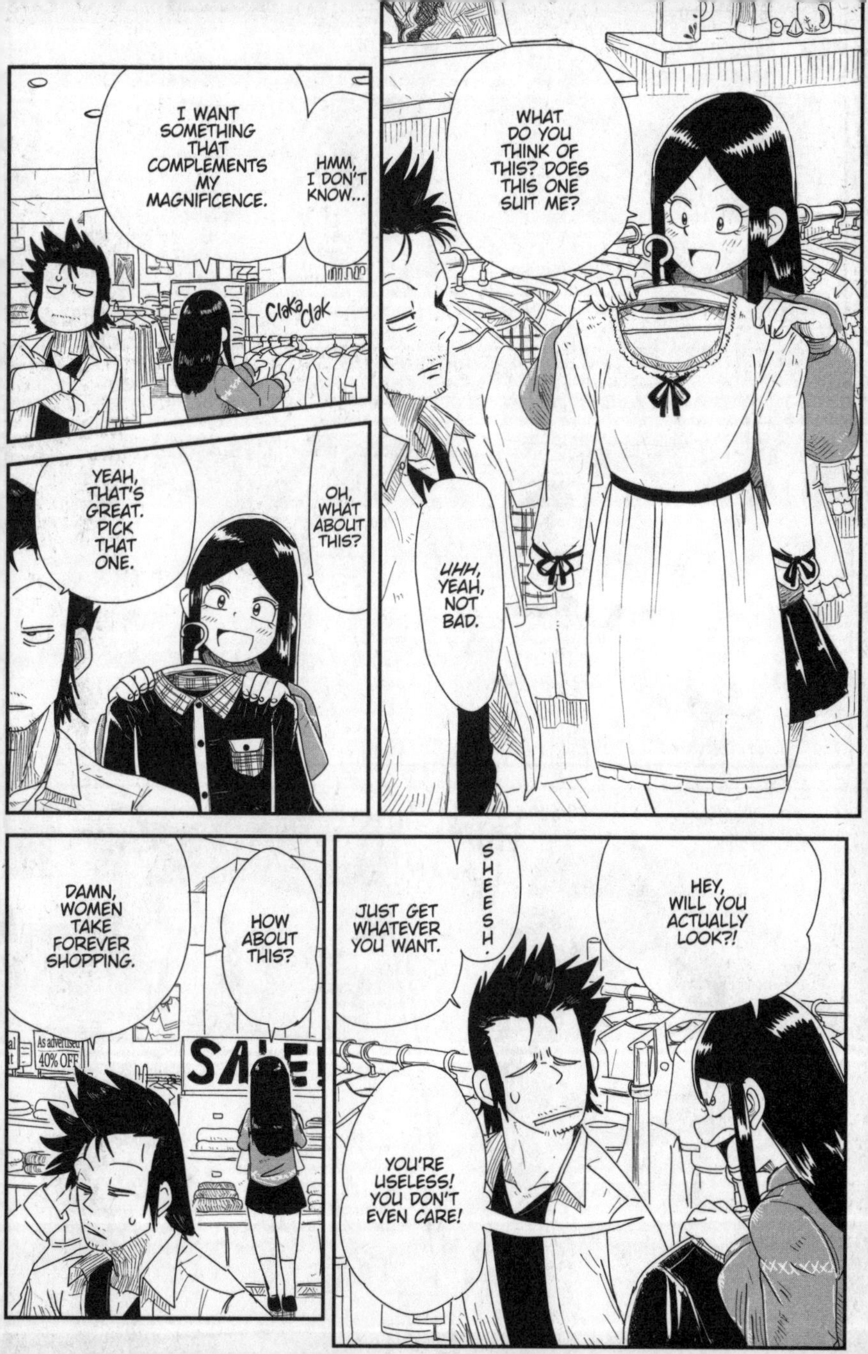
WHAT DO YOU THINK OF THIS? DOES THIS ONE SUIT ME?
UHH, YEAH, NOT BAD.
HMM, I DON'T KNOW...
I WANT SOMETHING THAT COMPLEMENTS MY MAGNIFICENCE.
CLAKA CLAK
OH, WHAT ABOUT THIS?
YEAH, THAT'S GREAT. PICK THAT ONE.
HEY, WILL YOU ACTUALLY LOOK?!
SHEESH.
JUST GET WHATEVER YOU WANT.
YOU'RE USELESS! YOU DON'T EVEN CARE!
HOW ABOUT THIS?
DAMN, WOMEN TAKE FOREVER SHOPPING.
As advertised 40% OFF
SALE!

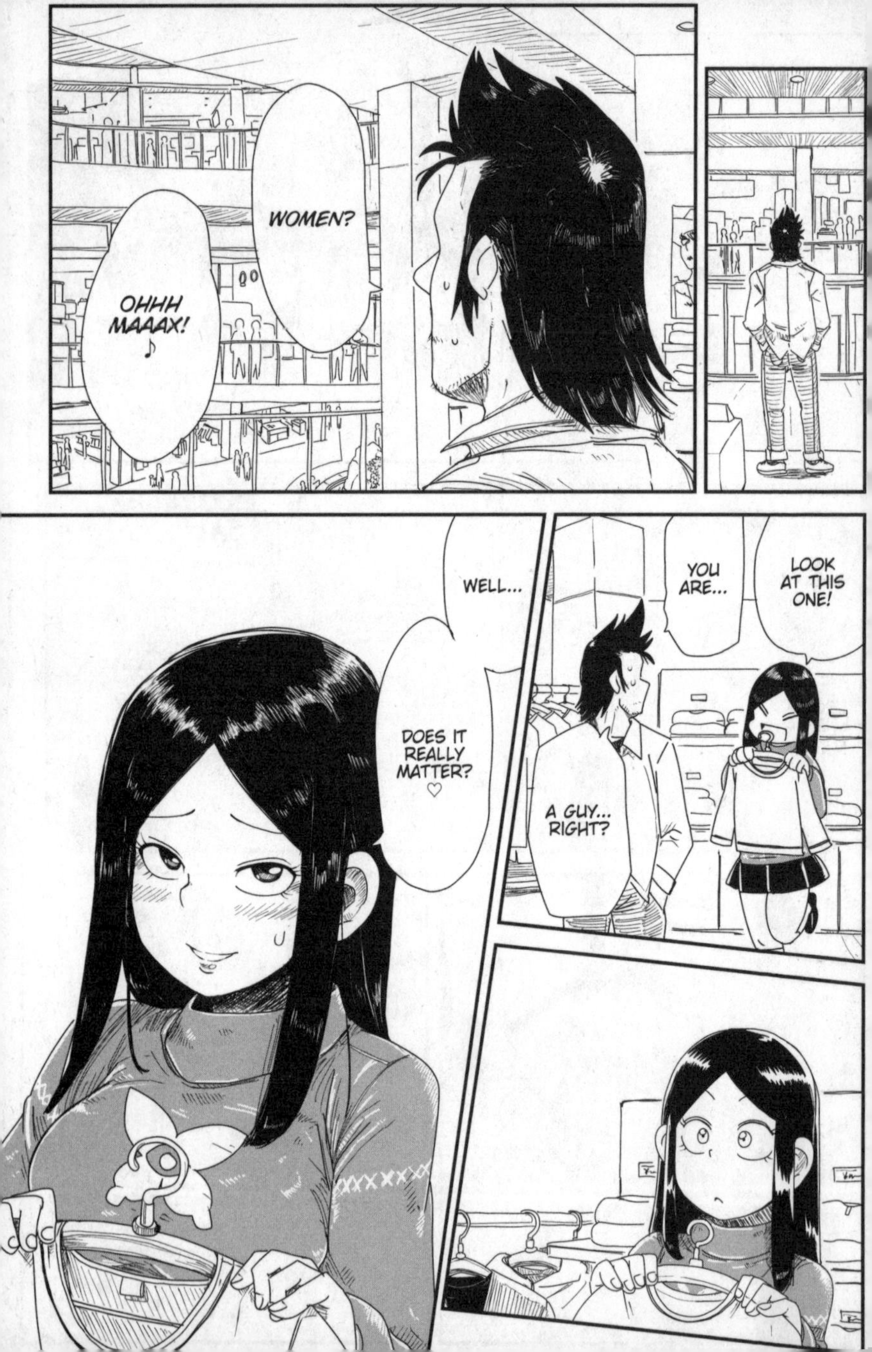
WOMEN?
OHHH MAAAX! ♪
LOOK AT THIS ONE!
YOU ARE...
A GUY... RIGHT?
WELL...
DOES IT REALLY MATTER? ♡

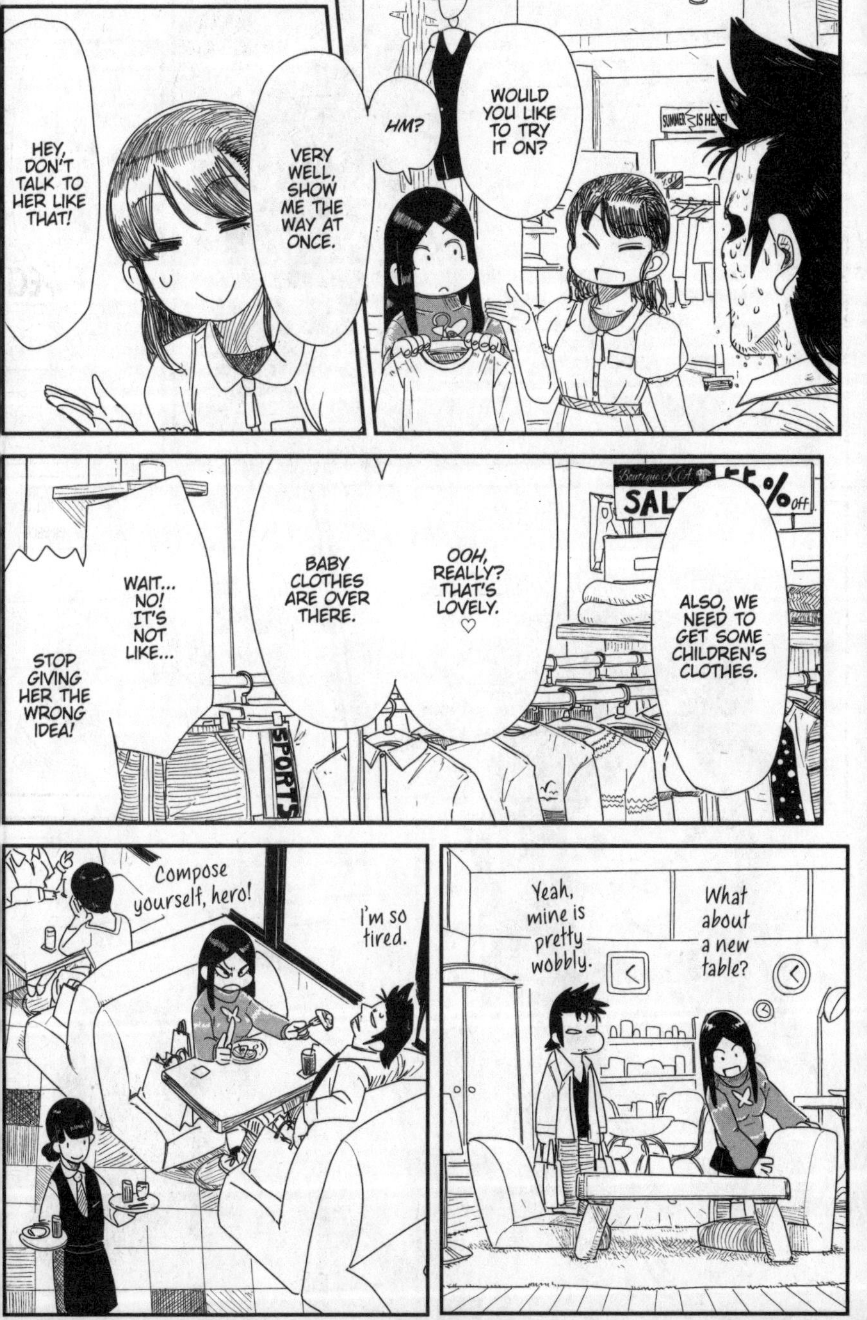
SUMMER
WOULD YOU LIKE TO TRY IT ON?
HM?
VERY WELL, SHOW ME THE WAY AT ONCE.
HEY, DON'T TALK TO HER LIKE THAT!
ALSO, WE NEED TO GET SOME CHILDREN'S CLOTHES.
OOH, REALLY? THAT'S LOVELY. ♡
BABY CLOTHES ARE OVER THERE.
WAIT... NO! IT'S NOT LIKE...
STOP GIVING HER THE WRONG IDEA!
SPORTS
What about a new table?
Yeah, mine is pretty wobbly.
I'm so tired.
Compose yourself, hero!

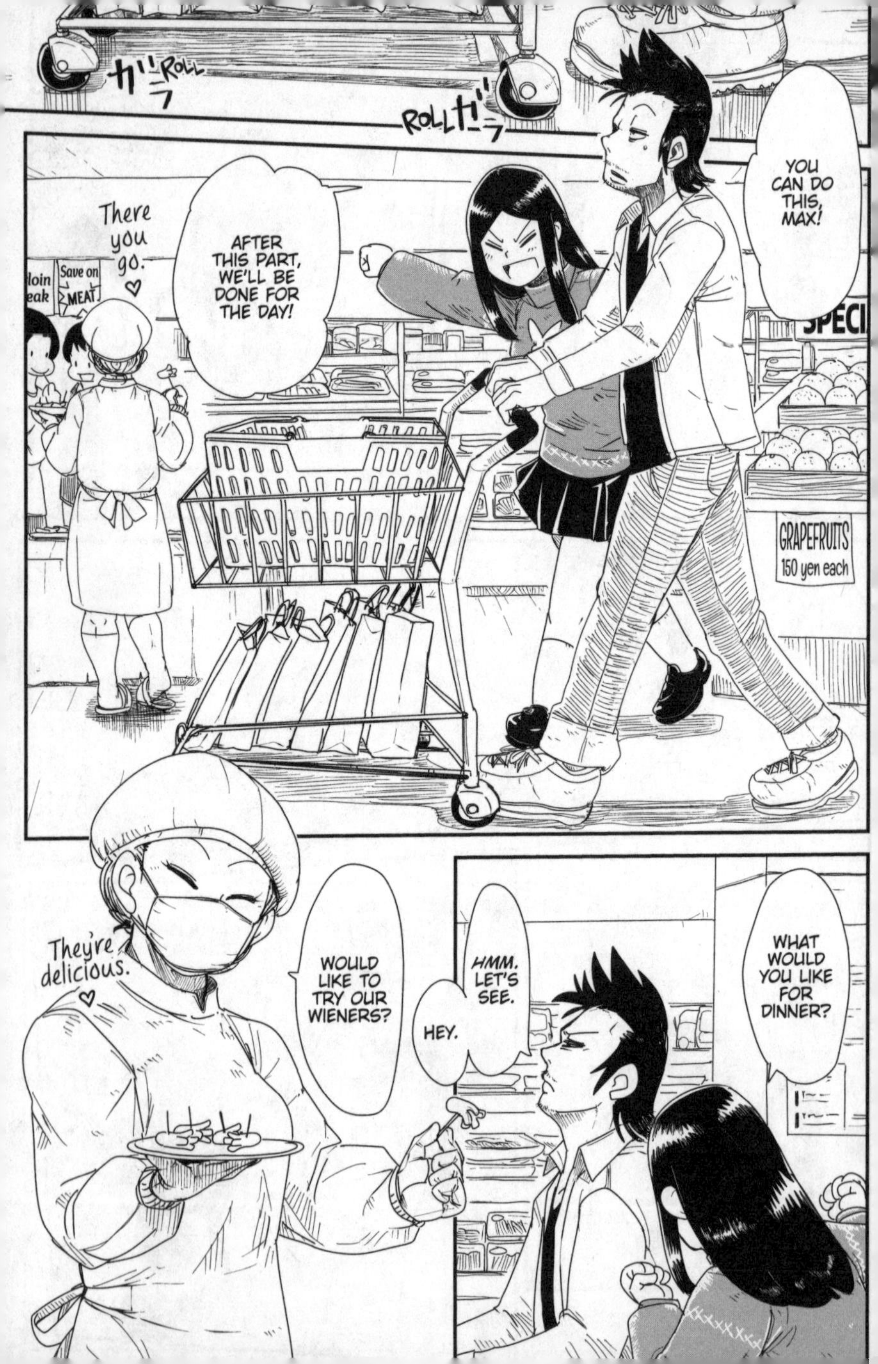

ROLL
ROLL
GRAPEFRUITS 150 yen each
SPECI
YOU CAN DO THIS, MAX!
AFTER THIS PART, WE'LL BE DONE FOR THE DAY!
There you go. ♡
Save on MEAT
WHAT WOULD YOU LIKE FOR DINNER?
HMM. LET'S SEE.
HEY.
WOULD LIKE TO TRY OUR WIENERS?
They're delicious. ♡

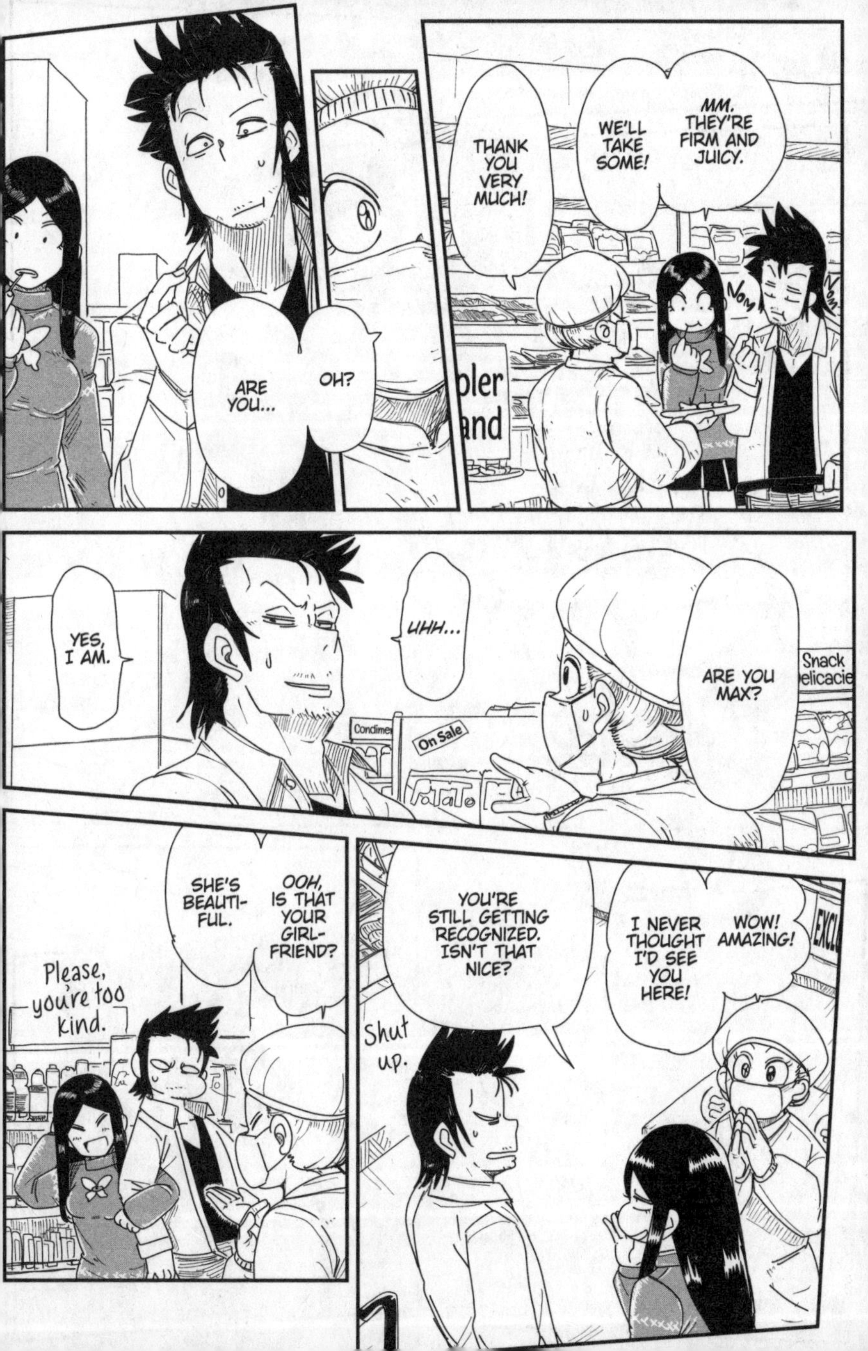
MM. THEY'RE FIRM AND JUICY.
WE'LL TAKE SOME!
NOM
NOM
THANK YOU VERY MUCH!
OH?
ARE YOU...
ARE YOU MAX?
UHH...
YES, I AM.
On Sale
WOW! AMAZING!
I NEVER THOUGHT I'D SEE YOU HERE!
YOU'RE STILL GETTING RECOGNIZED. ISN'T THAT NICE?
Shut up.
OOH, IS THAT YOUR GIRL-FRIEND?
SHE'S BEAUTI-FUL.
Please, you're too kind.

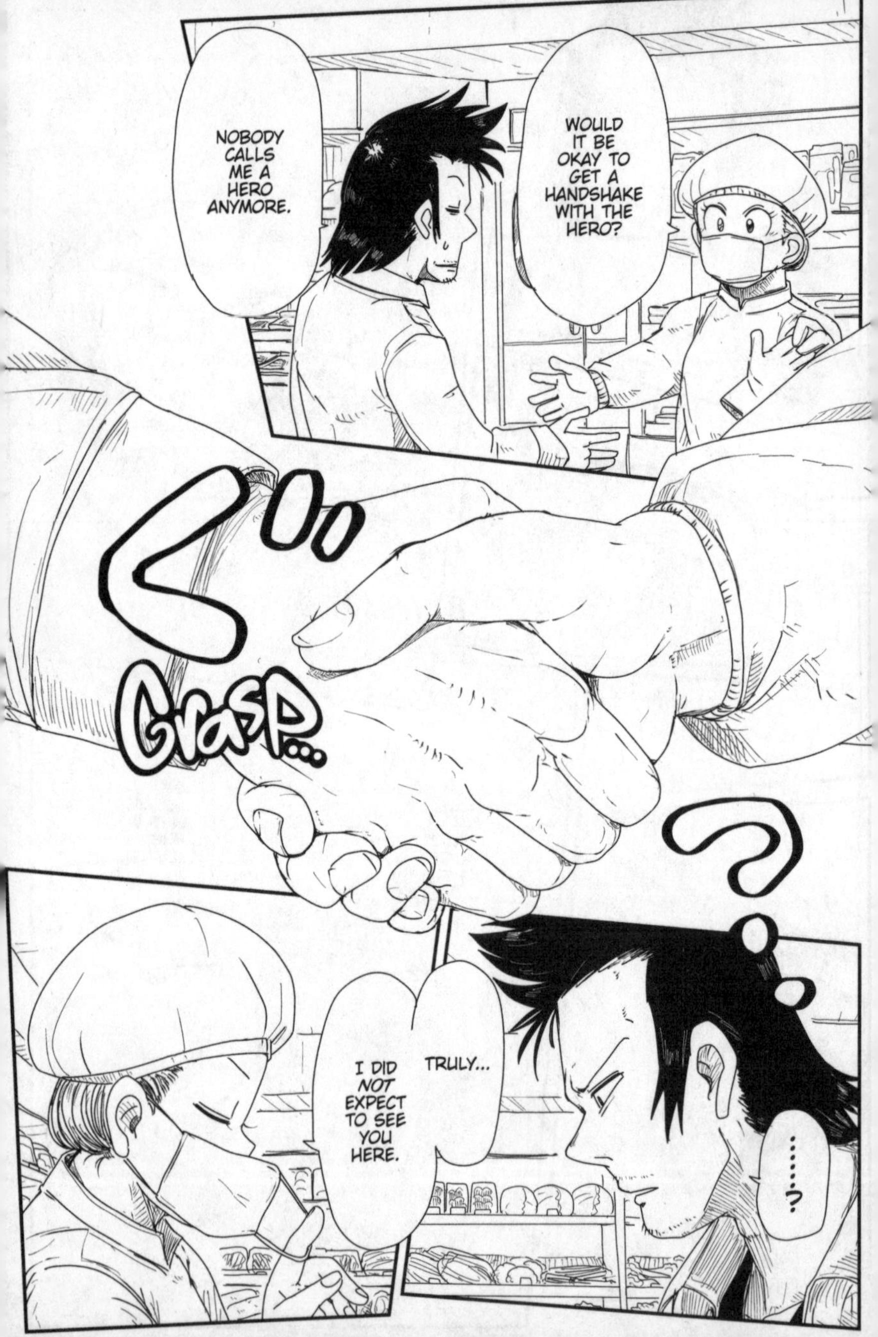
WOULD IT BE OKAY TO GET A HANDSHAKE WITH THE HERO?
NOBODY CALLS ME A HERO ANYMORE.
GRASP...
......?
TRULY...
I DID *NOT* EXPECT TO SEE YOU HERE.

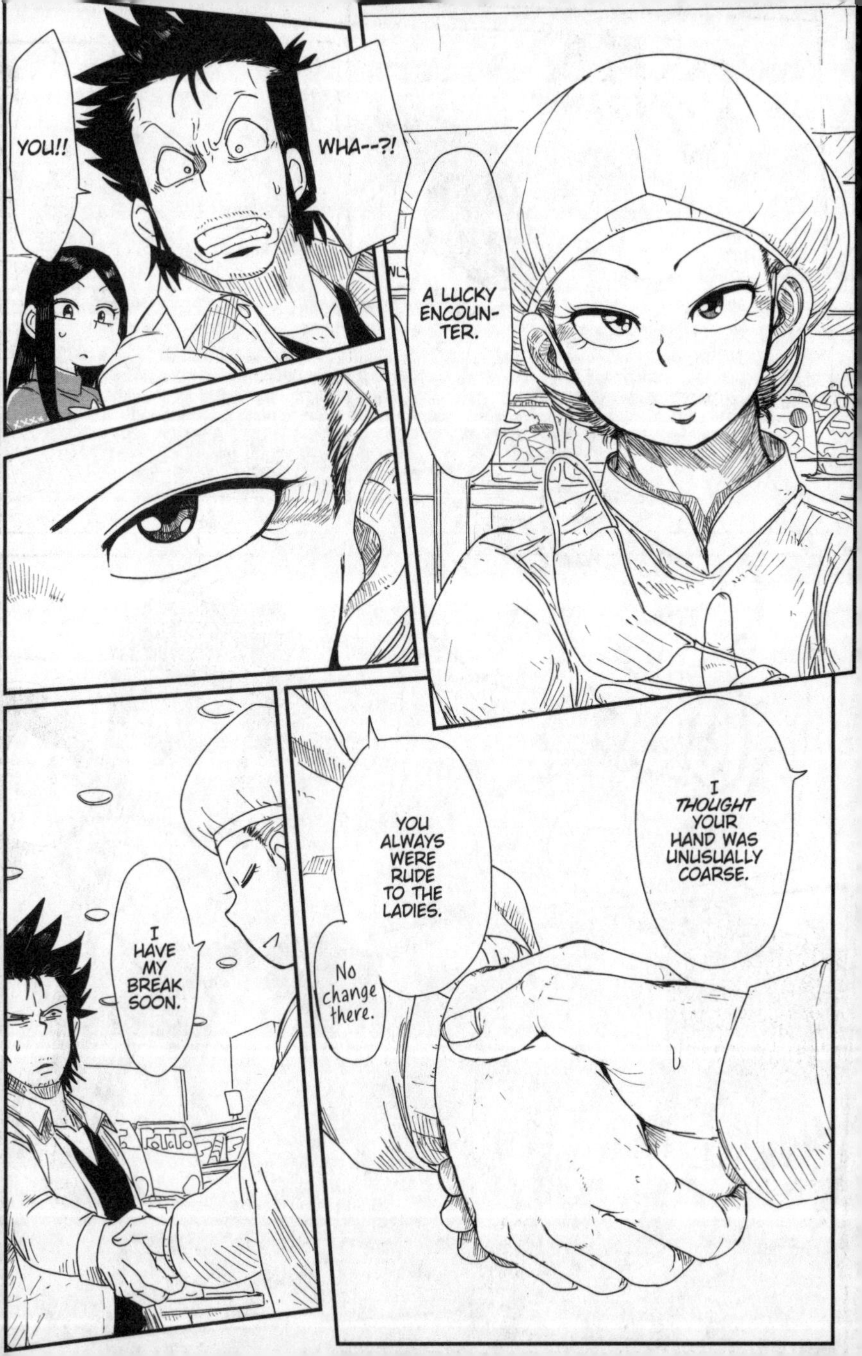
A LUCKY ENCOUNTER.
WHA--?!
YOU!!
I *THOUGHT* YOUR HAND WAS UNUSUALLY COARSE.
YOU ALWAYS WERE RUDE TO THE LADIES.
No change there.
I HAVE MY BREAK SOON.

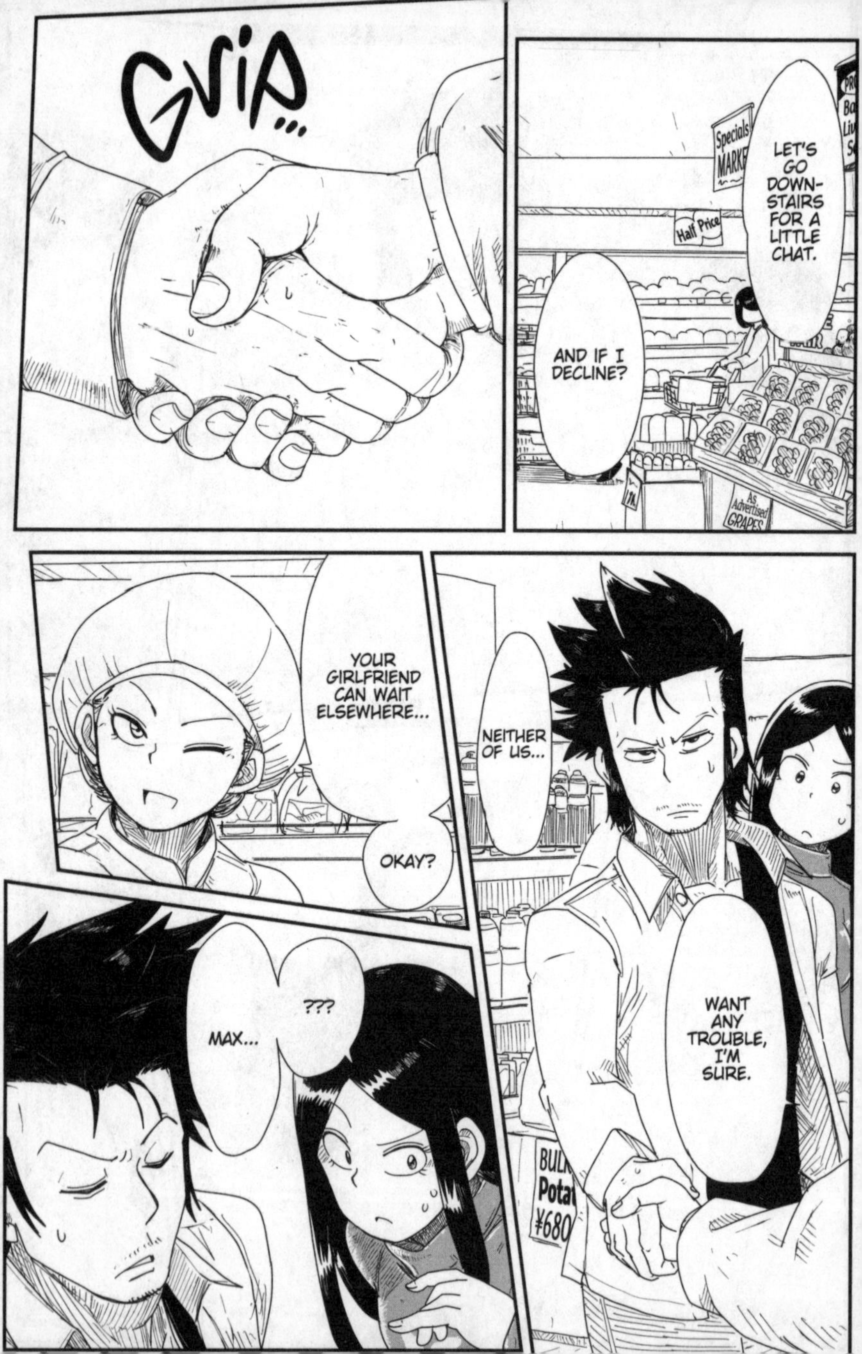
LET'S GO DOWN-STAIRS FOR A LITTLE CHAT.
Specials
Half Price
AND IF I DECLINE?
As Advertised GRAPES
GRIP...
NEITHER OF US...
WANT ANY TROUBLE, I'M SURE.
YOUR GIRLFRIEND CAN WAIT ELSEWHERE...
OKAY?
???
MAX...

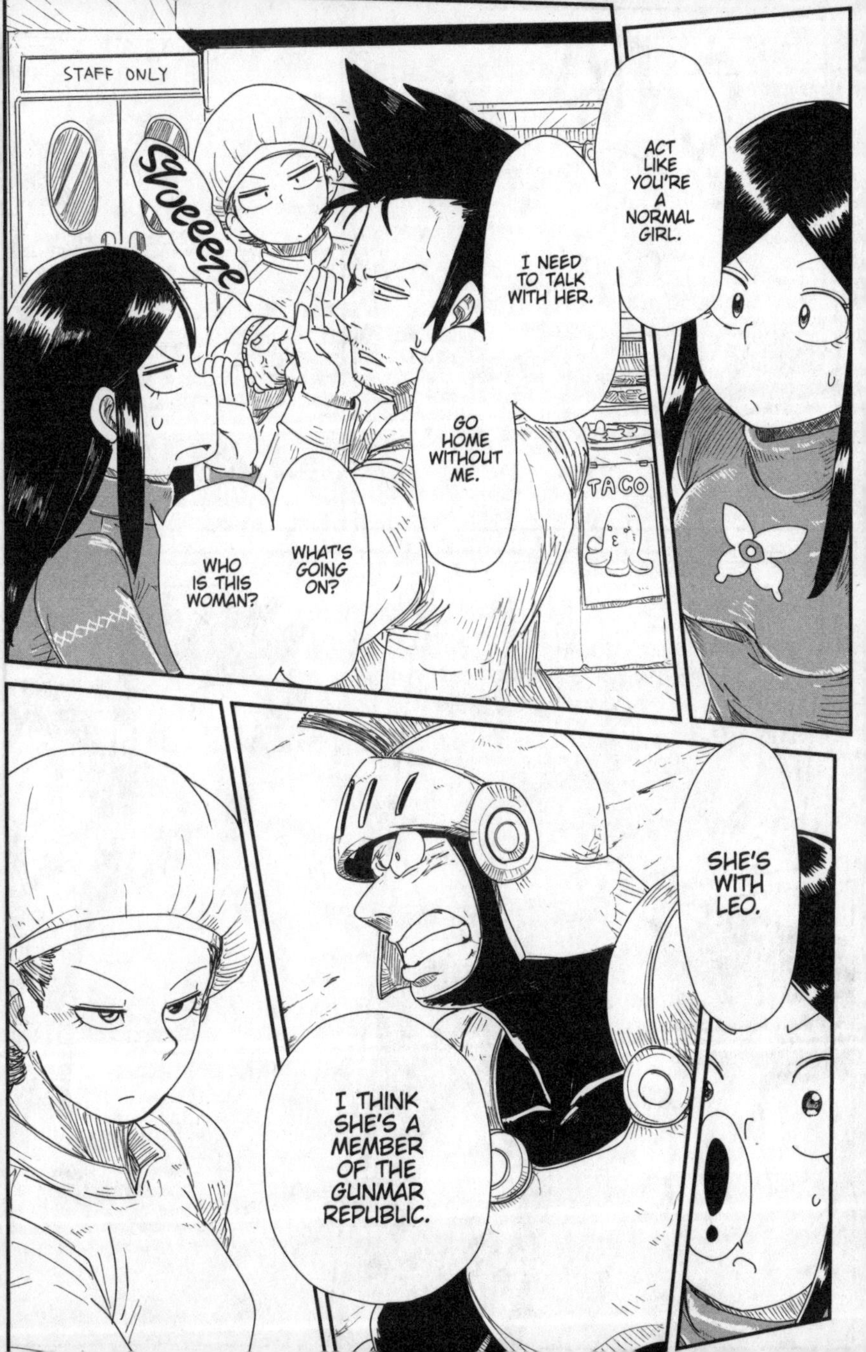
ACT LIKE YOU'RE A NORMAL GIRL.
I NEED TO TALK WITH HER.
STAFF ONLY
squeeeze
GO HOME WITHOUT ME.
TACO
WHAT'S GOING ON?
WHO IS THIS WOMAN?
SHE'S WITH LEO.
I THINK SHE'S A MEMBER OF THE GUNMAR REPUBLIC.

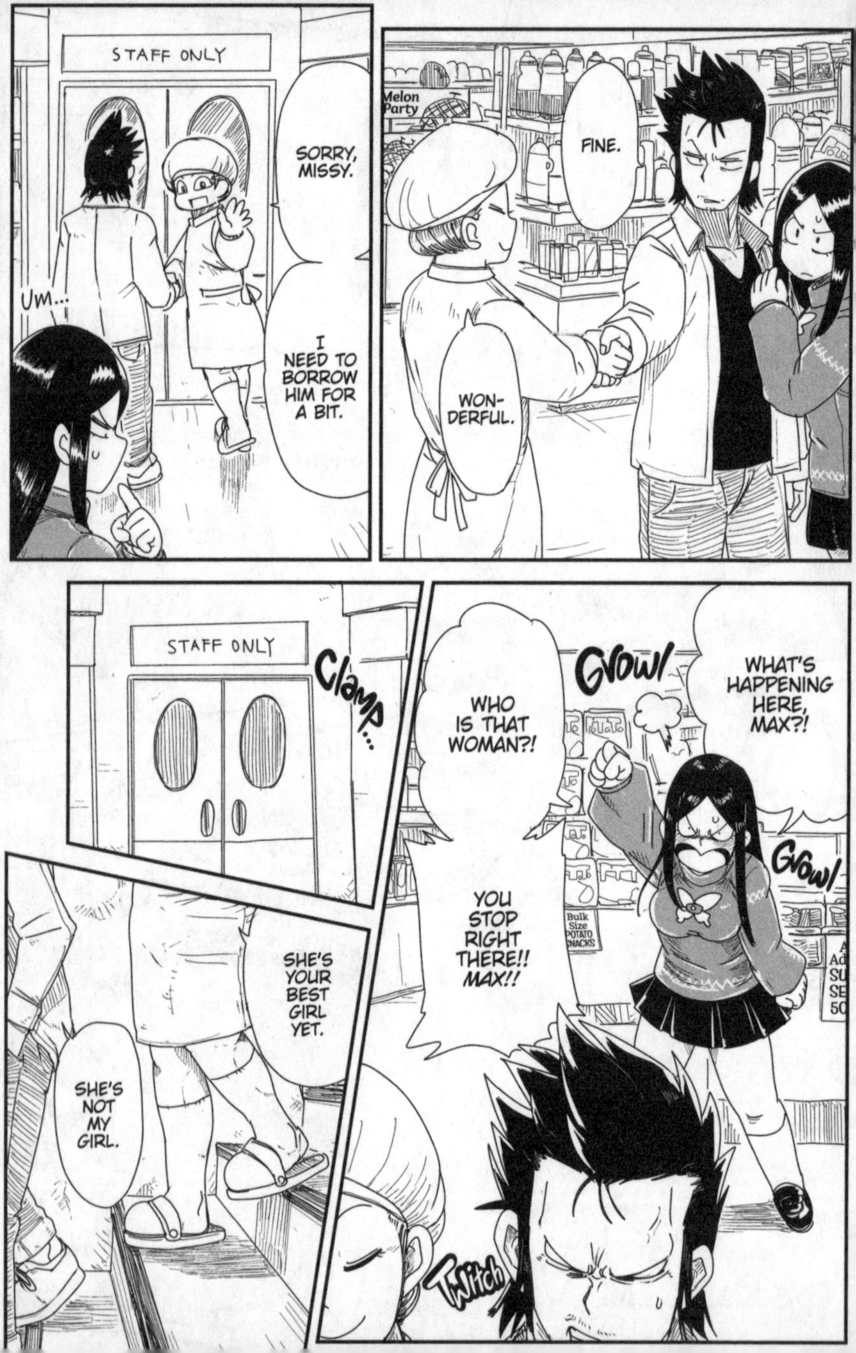
Melon Party
FINE.
WON-DERFUL.
STAFF ONLY
SORRY, MISSY.
I NEED TO BORROW HIM FOR A BIT.
UM...
WHAT'S HAPPENING HERE, MAX?!
GROWL
WHO IS THAT WOMAN?!
GROWL
Bulk Size POTATO SNACKS
YOU STOP RIGHT THERE!! MAX!!
TWITCH
STAFF ONLY
CLAMP...
SHE'S YOUR BEST GIRL YET.
SHE'S NOT MY GIRL.

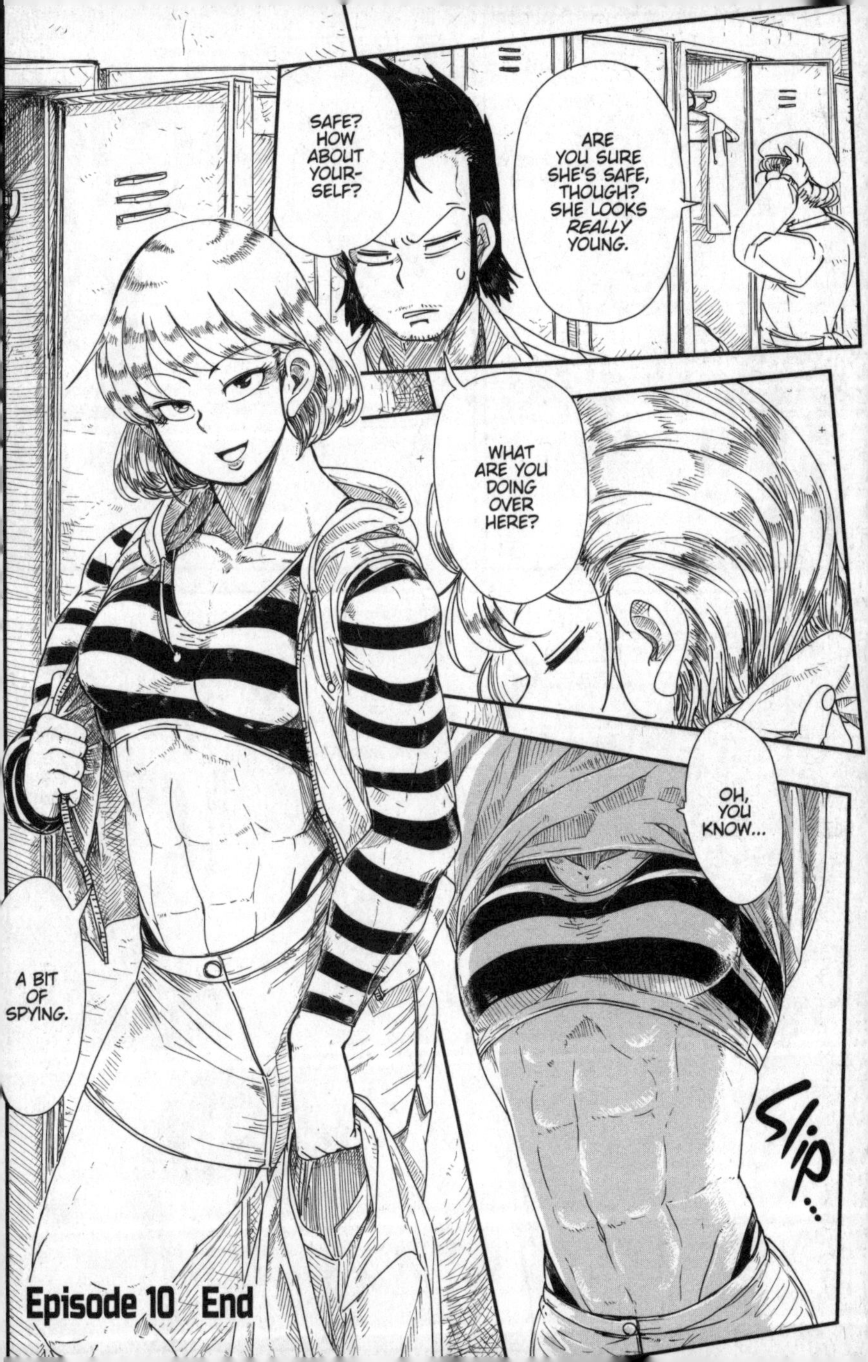
ARE YOU SURE SHE'S SAFE, THOUGH? SHE LOOKS *REALLY* YOUNG.
SAFE? HOW ABOUT YOURSELF?
WHAT ARE YOU DOING OVER HERE?
OH, YOU KNOW...
Slip...
A BIT OF SPYING.

Episode 10 End

LEVEL 1 DEMON LORD & ONE ROOM HERO

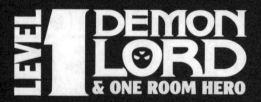

LEVEL 1 DEMON LORD & ONE ROOM HERO

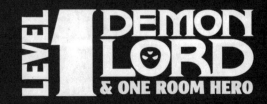

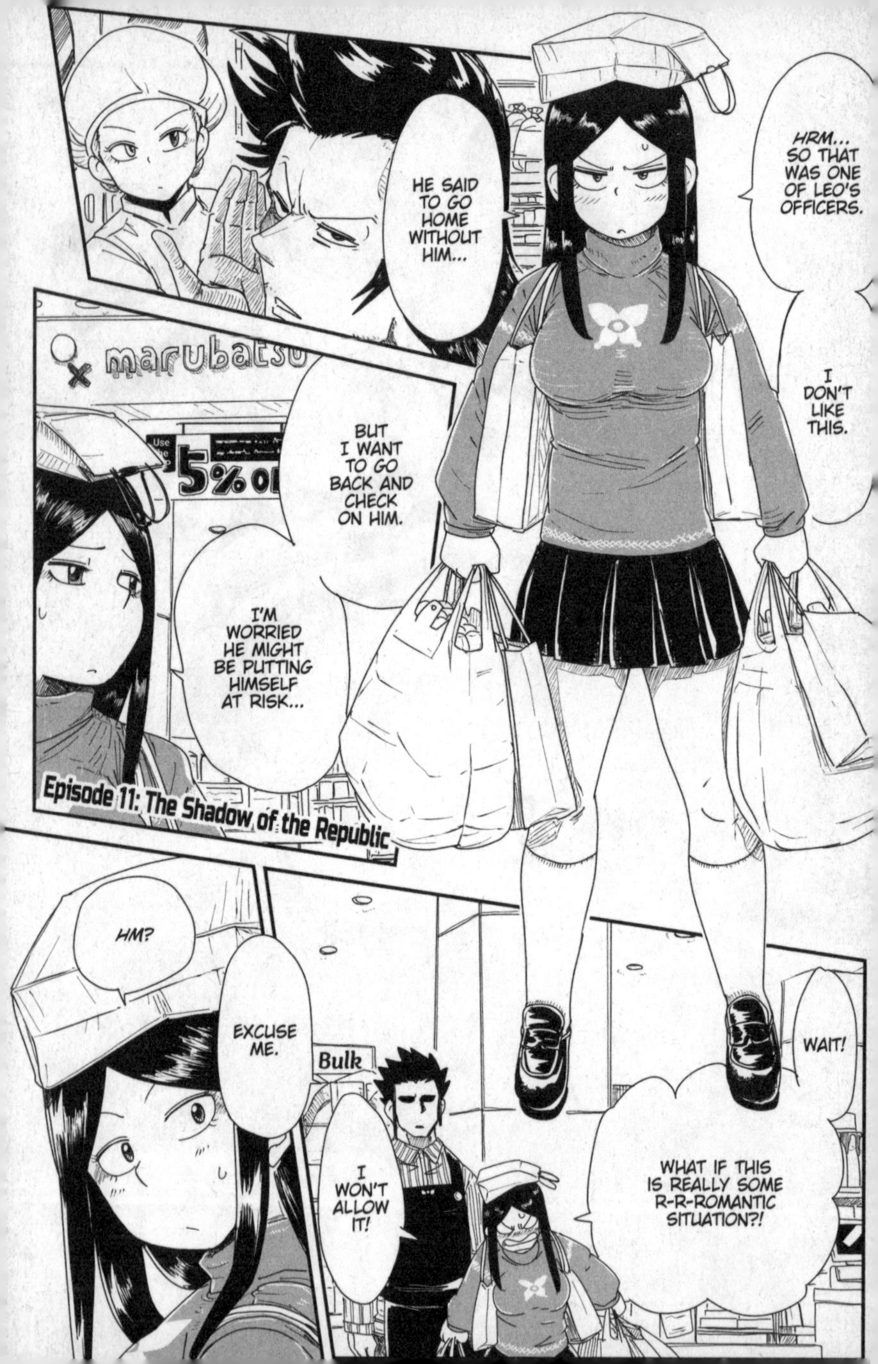
HRM... SO THAT WAS ONE OF LEO'S OFFICERS.
I DON'T LIKE THIS.
HE SAID TO GO HOME WITHOUT HIM...
marubatsu
BUT I WANT TO GO BACK AND CHECK ON HIM.
I'M WORRIED HE MIGHT BE PUTTING HIMSELF AT RISK...
Episode 11: The Shadow of the Republic
WAIT!
WHAT IF THIS IS REALLY SOME R-R-ROMANTIC SITUATION?!
I WON'T ALLOW IT!
Bulk
EXCUSE ME.
HM?

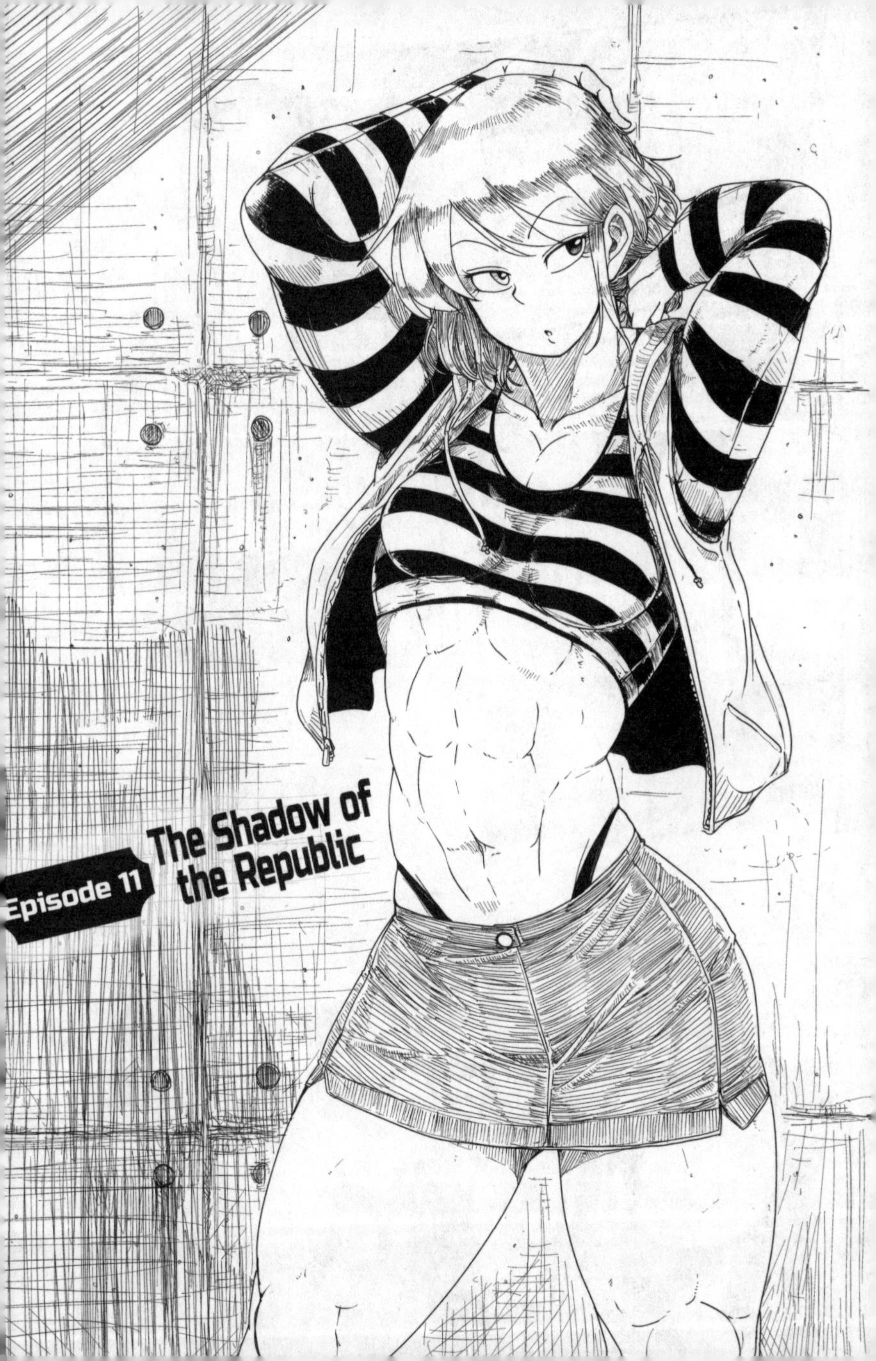
Episode 11
The Shadow of the Republic

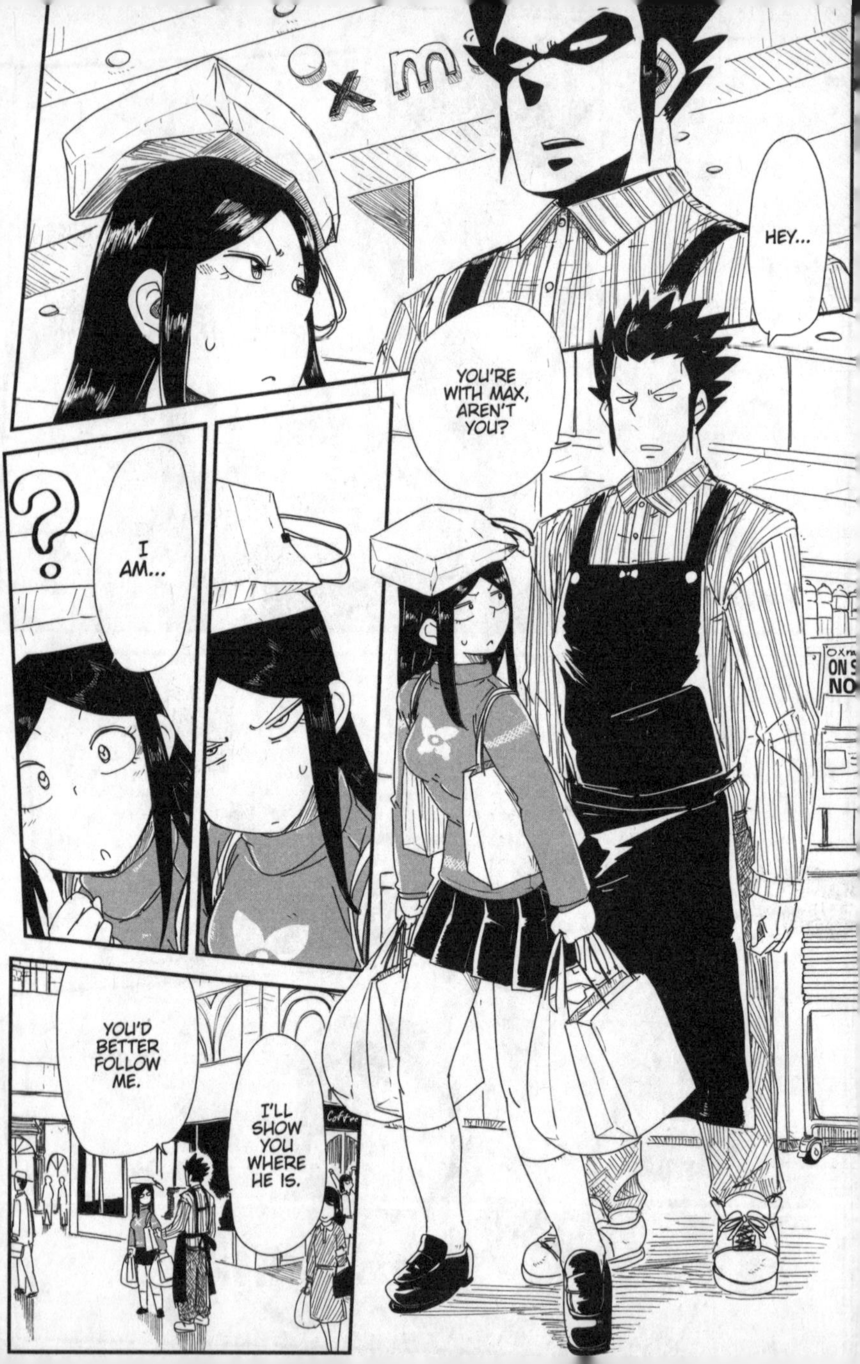
HEY...
YOU'RE WITH MAX, AREN'T YOU?
I AM...
YOU'D BETTER FOLLOW ME.
I'LL SHOW YOU WHERE HE IS.

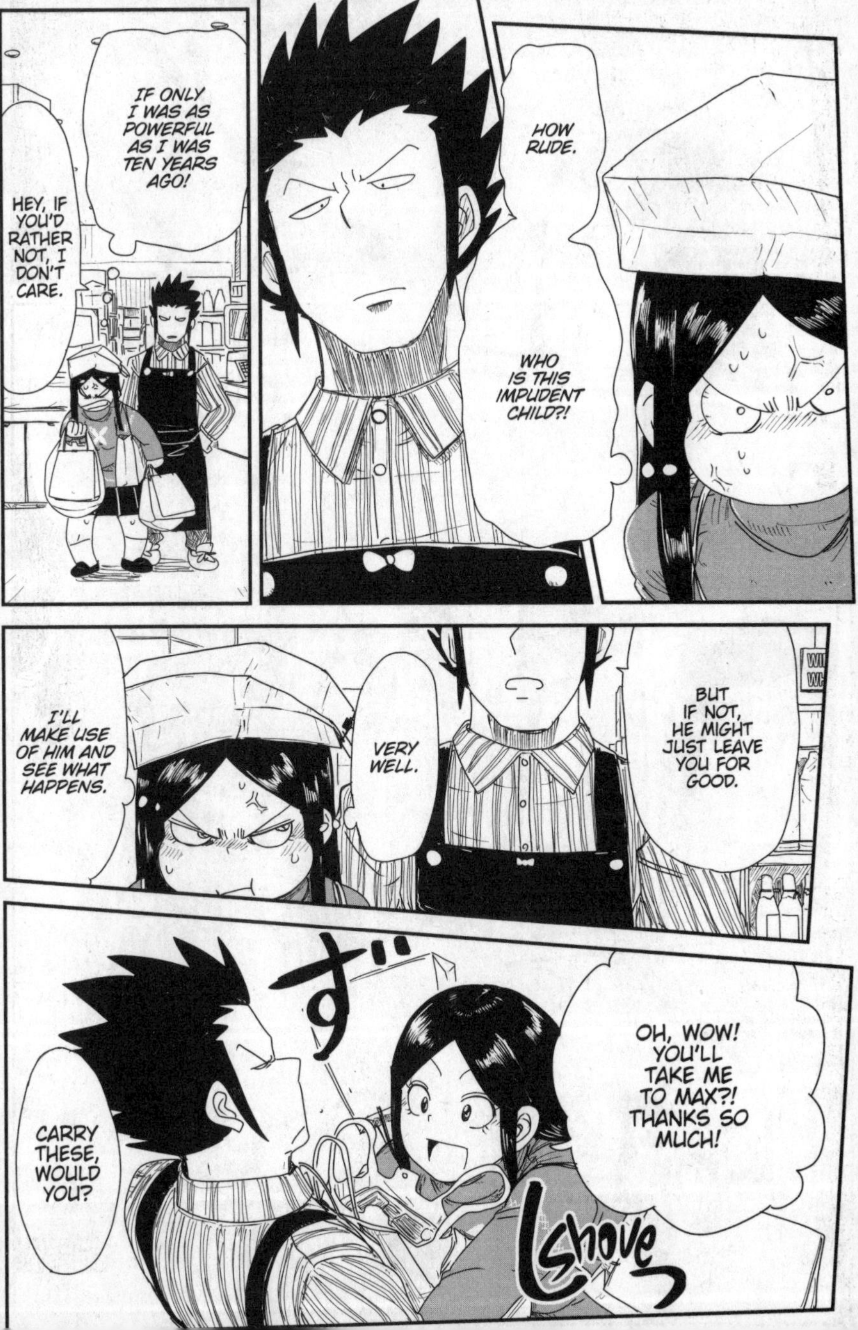
HOW RUDE.
WHO IS THIS IMPUDENT CHILD?!
IF ONLY I WAS AS POWERFUL AS I WAS TEN YEARS AGO!
HEY, IF YOU'D RATHER NOT, I DON'T CARE.
BUT IF NOT, HE MIGHT JUST LEAVE YOU FOR GOOD.
VERY WELL.
I'LL MAKE USE OF HIM AND SEE WHAT HAPPENS.
OH, WOW! YOU'LL TAKE ME TO MAX?! THANKS SO MUCH!
ず
shove
CARRY THESE, WOULD YOU?

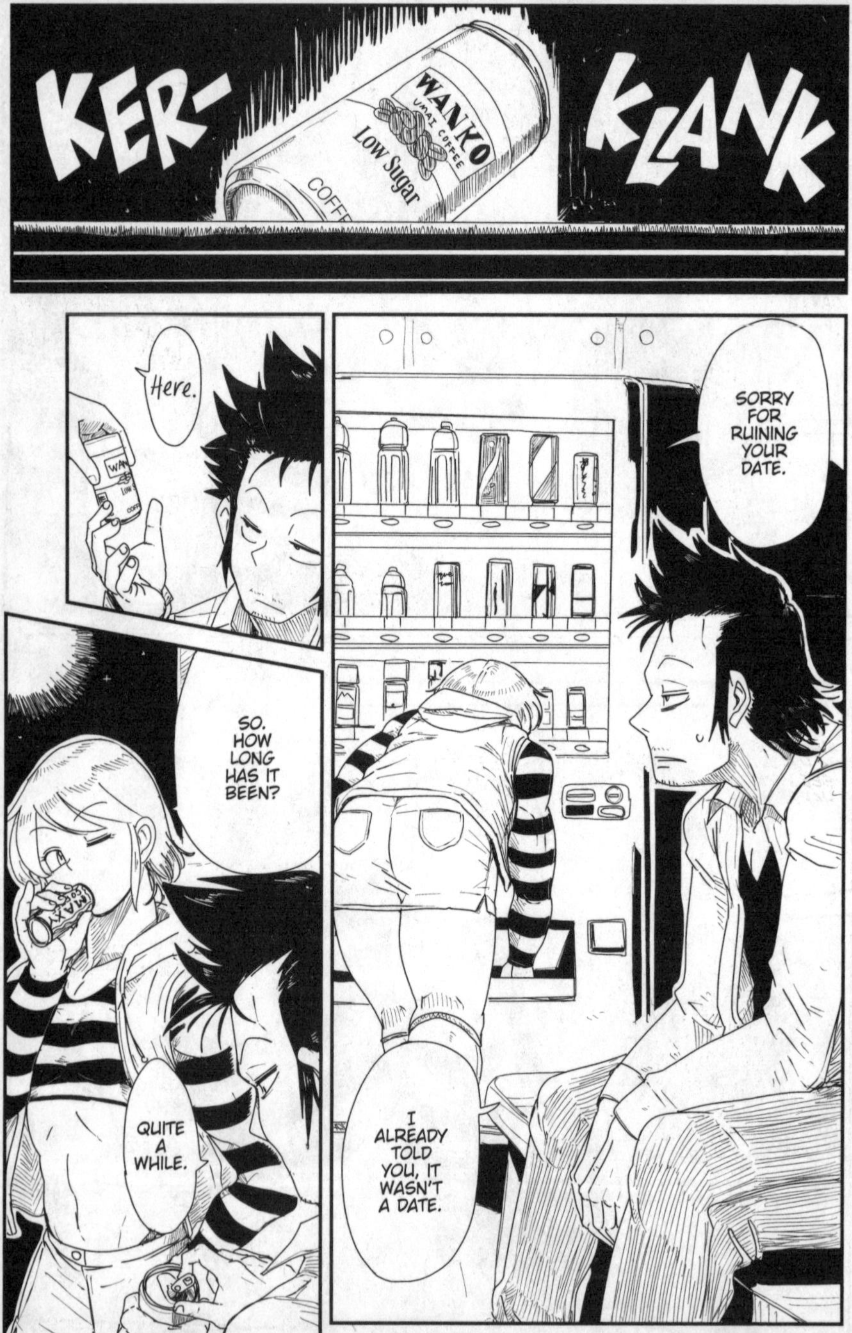
KER-
KLANK
WANKO
UMAI COFFEE
Low Sugar
SORRY FOR RUINING YOUR DATE.
I ALREADY TOLD YOU, IT WASN'T A DATE.
Here.
SO. HOW LONG HAS IT BEEN?
QUITE A WHILE.

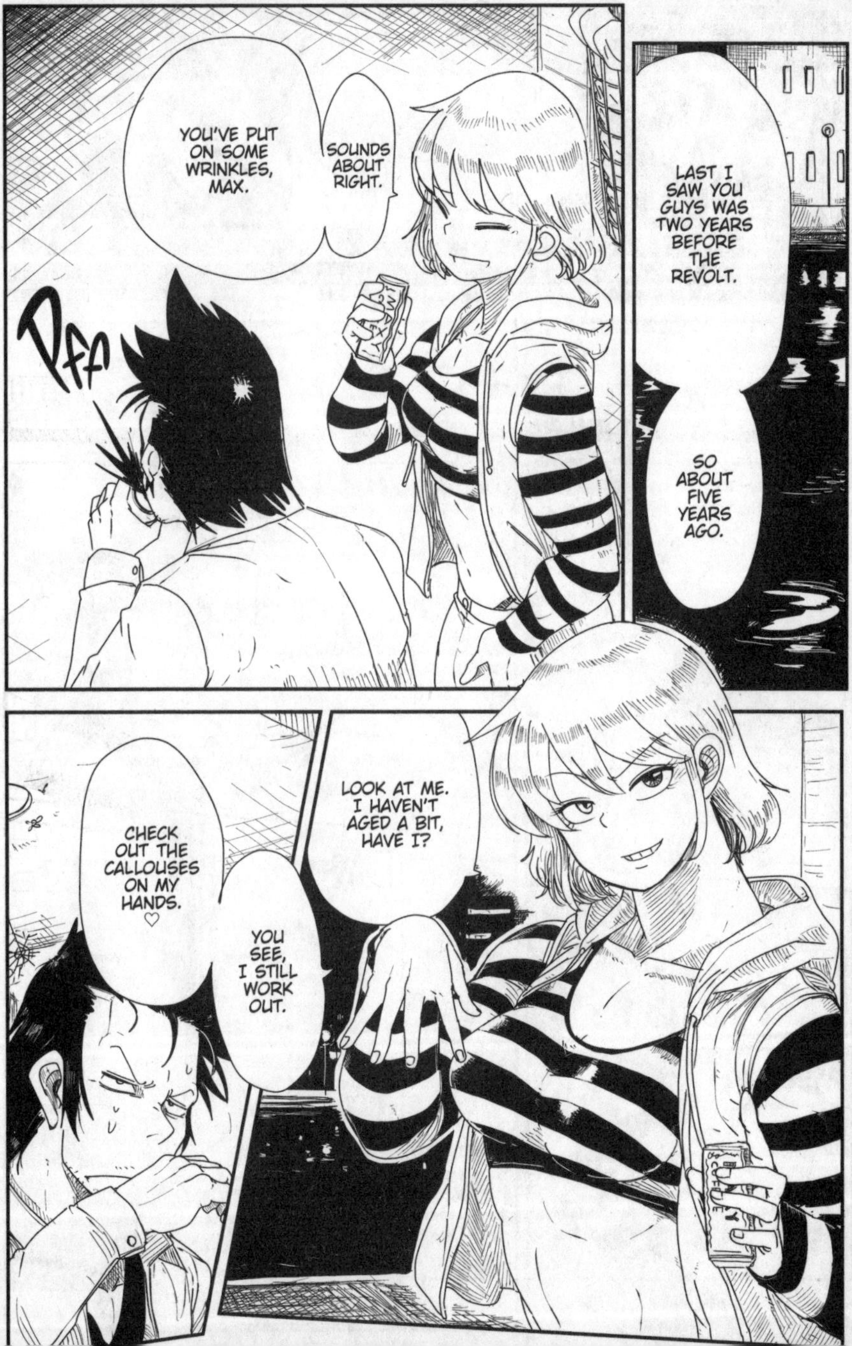
YOU'VE PUT ON SOME WRINKLES, MAX.
SOUNDS ABOUT RIGHT.
Pff
LAST I SAW YOU GUYS WAS TWO YEARS BEFORE THE REVOLT.
SO ABOUT FIVE YEARS AGO.
CHECK OUT THE CALLOUSES ON MY HANDS. ♡
LOOK AT ME. I HAVEN'T AGED A BIT, HAVE I?
YOU SEE, I STILL WORK OUT.

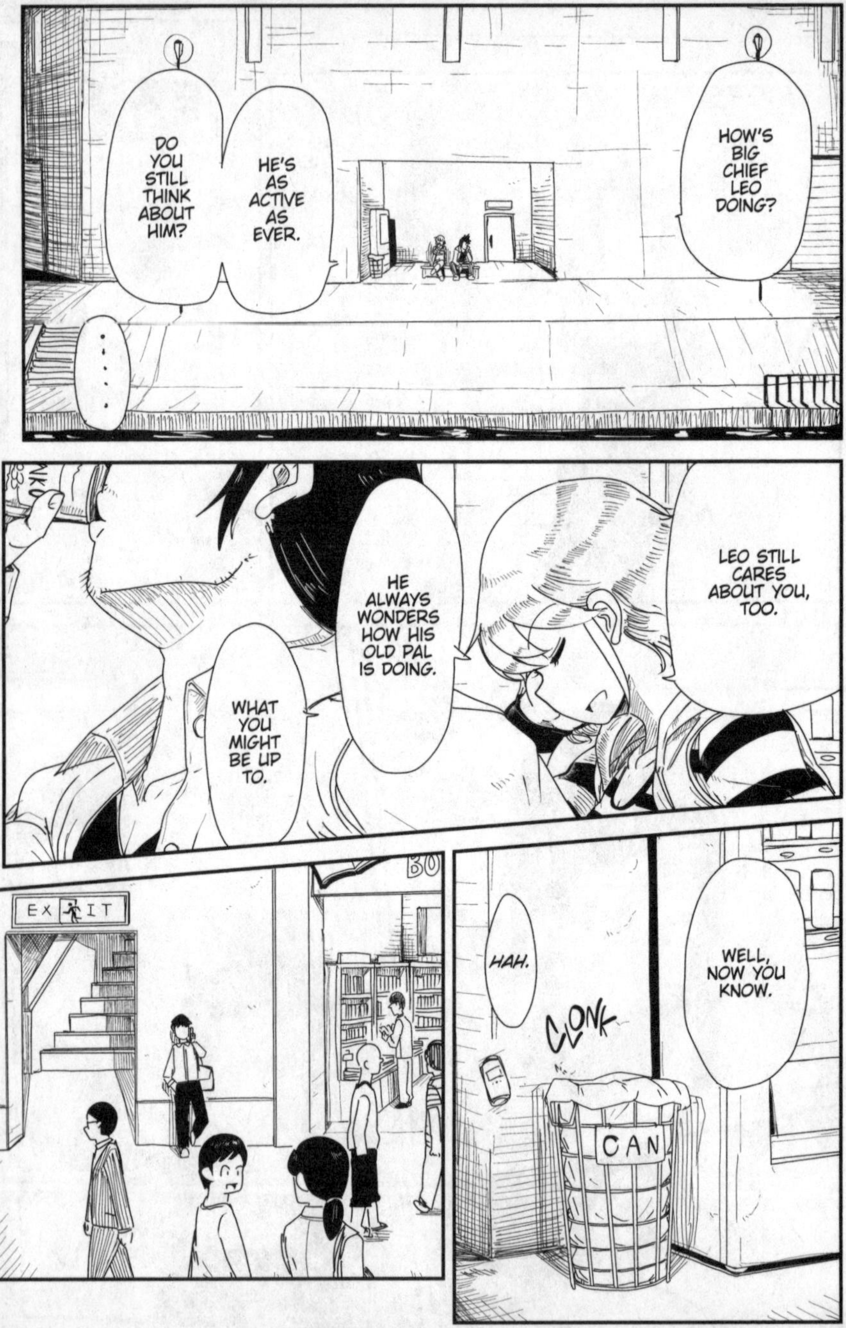
HOW'S BIG CHIEF LEO DOING?
HE'S AS ACTIVE AS EVER.
DO YOU STILL THINK ABOUT HIM?
......
LEO STILL CARES ABOUT YOU, TOO.
HE ALWAYS WONDERS HOW HIS OLD PAL IS DOING.
WHAT YOU MIGHT BE UP TO.
WELL, NOW YOU KNOW.
HAH.
CLONK
CAN
EXIT

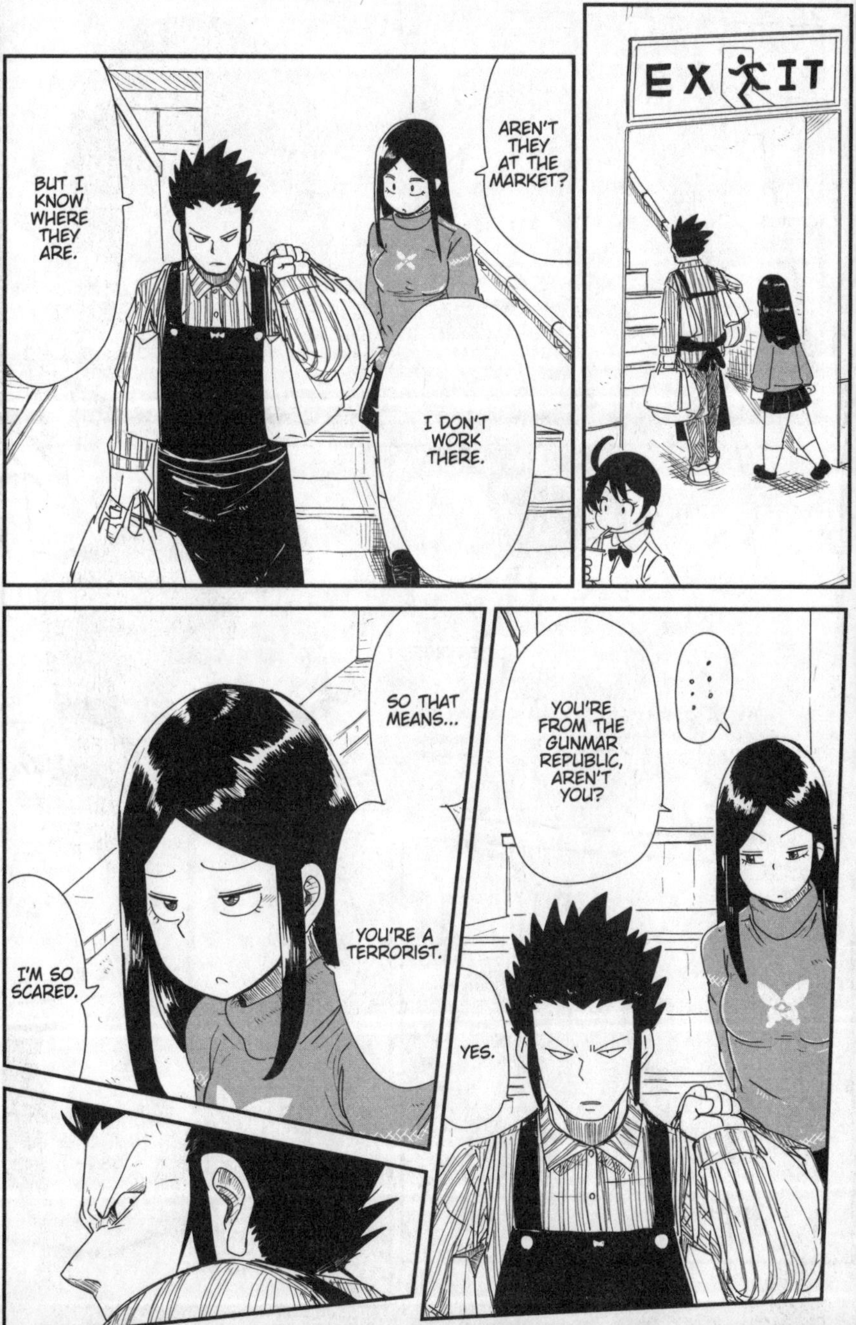
EXIT
AREN'T THEY AT THE MARKET?
I DON'T WORK THERE.
BUT I KNOW WHERE THEY ARE.
...
YOU'RE FROM THE GUNMAR REPUBLIC, AREN'T YOU?
YES.
SO THAT MEANS...
YOU'RE A TERRORIST.
I'M SO SCARED.

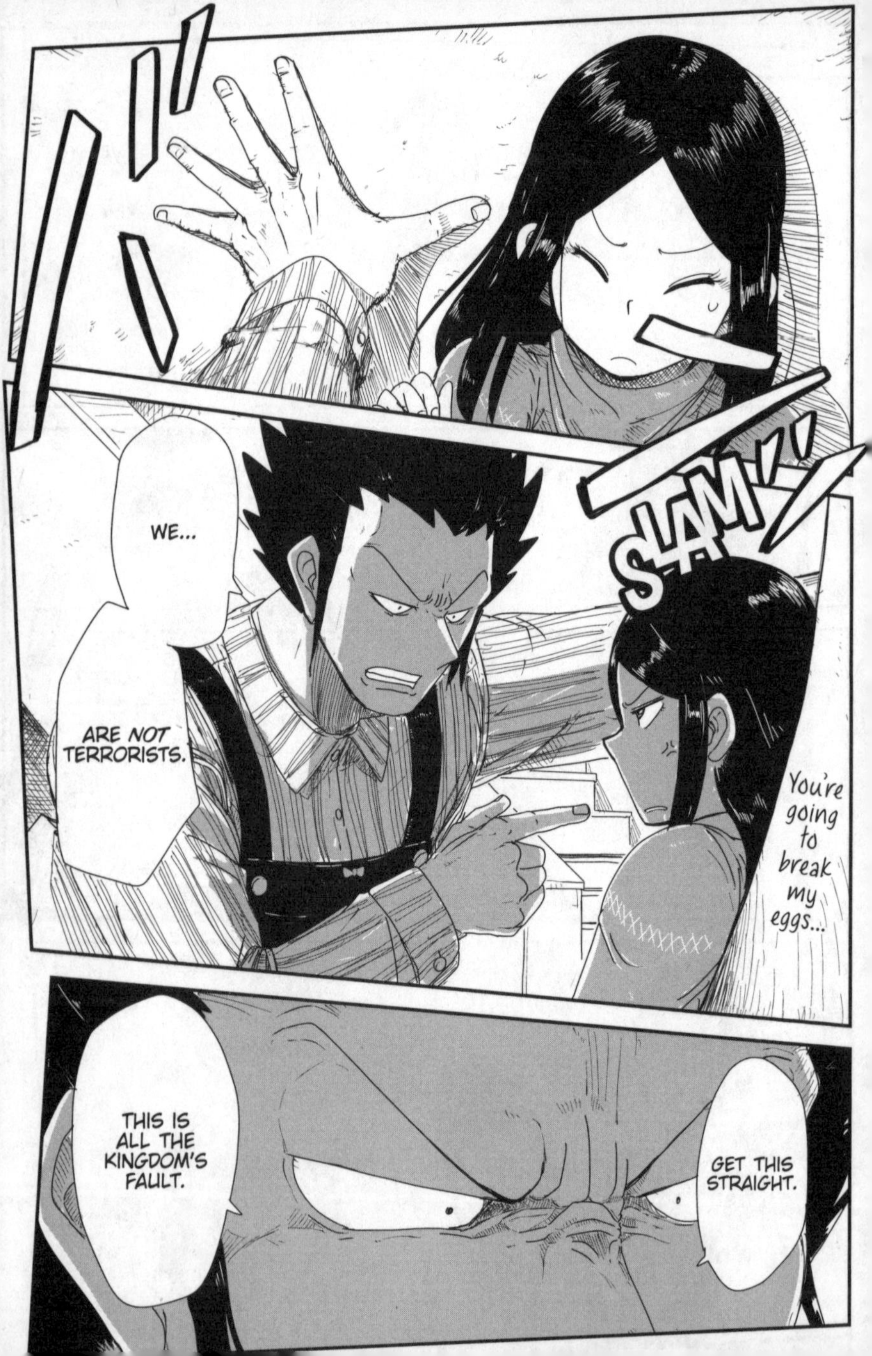
SLAM
You're going to break my eggs...
WE...
ARE *NOT* TERRORISTS.
GET THIS STRAIGHT.
THIS IS ALL THE KINGDOM'S FAULT.

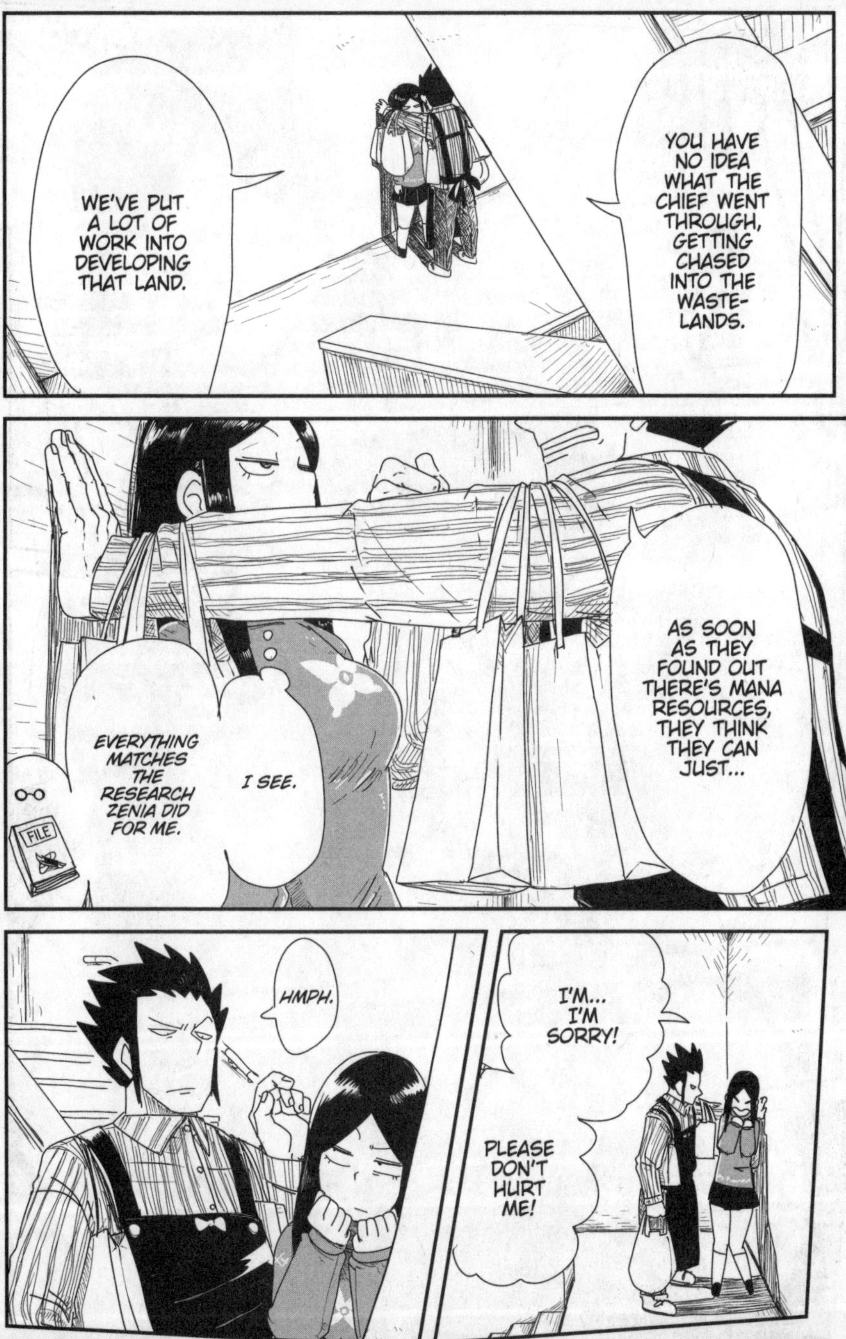
YOU HAVE NO IDEA WHAT THE CHIEF WENT THROUGH, GETTING CHASED INTO THE WASTE-LANDS.
WE'VE PUT A LOT OF WORK INTO DEVELOPING THAT LAND.
AS SOON AS THEY FOUND OUT THERE'S MANA RESOURCES, THEY THINK THEY CAN JUST...
I SEE.
EVERYTHING MATCHES THE RESEARCH ZENIA DID FOR ME.
FILE
I'M... I'M SORRY!
PLEASE DON'T HURT ME!
HMPH.

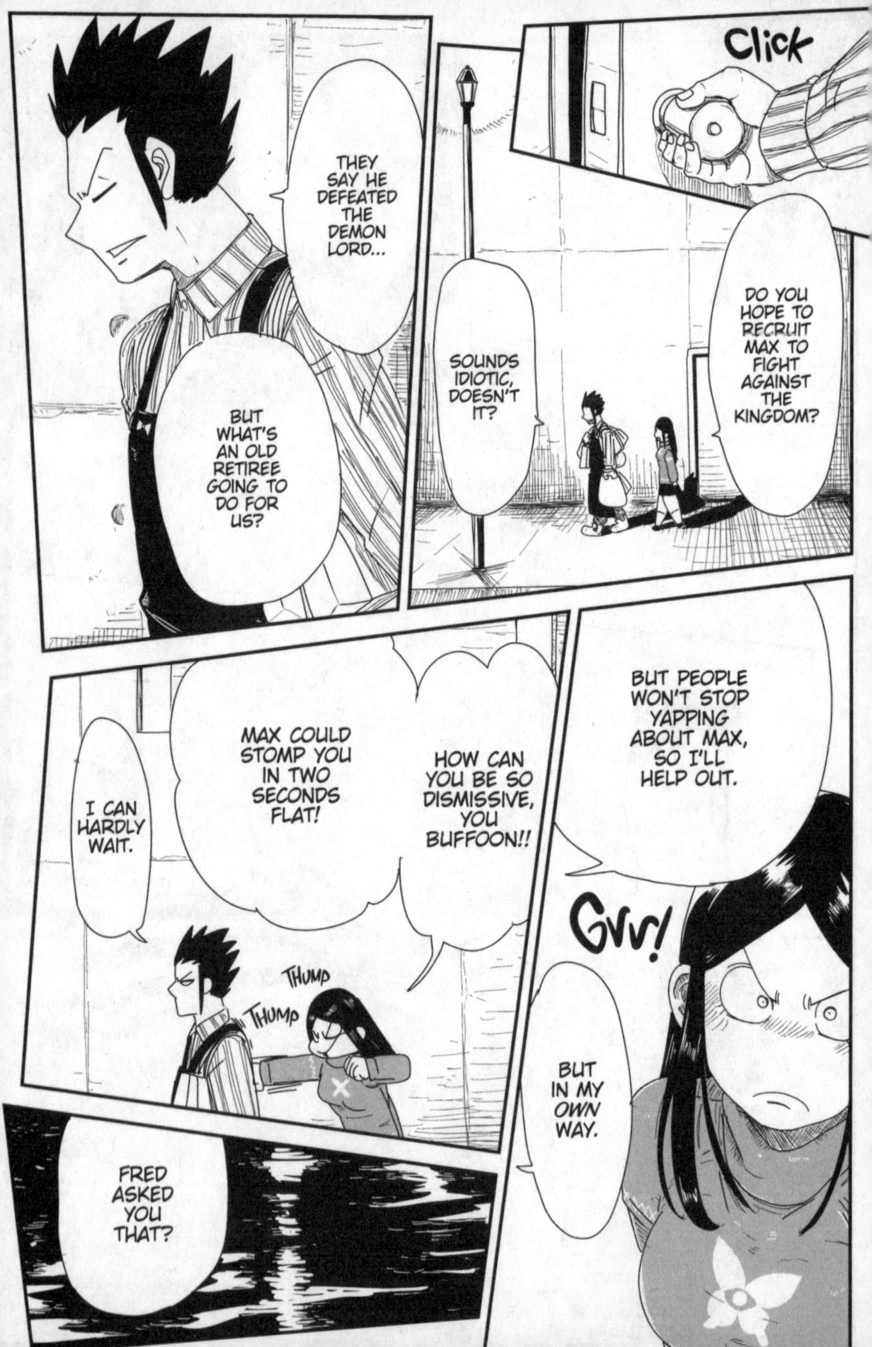
Click
DO YOU HOPE TO RECRUIT MAX TO FIGHT AGAINST THE KINGDOM?
SOUNDS IDIOTIC, DOESN'T IT?
THEY SAY HE DEFEATED THE DEMON LORD...
BUT WHAT'S AN OLD RETIREE GOING TO DO FOR US?
BUT PEOPLE WON'T STOP YAPPING ABOUT MAX, SO I'LL HELP OUT.
Gvv!
BUT IN MY OWN WAY.
HOW CAN YOU BE SO DISMISSIVE, YOU BUFFOON!!
MAX COULD STOMP YOU IN TWO SECONDS FLAT!
I CAN HARDLY WAIT.
THUMP
THUMP
FRED ASKED YOU THAT?

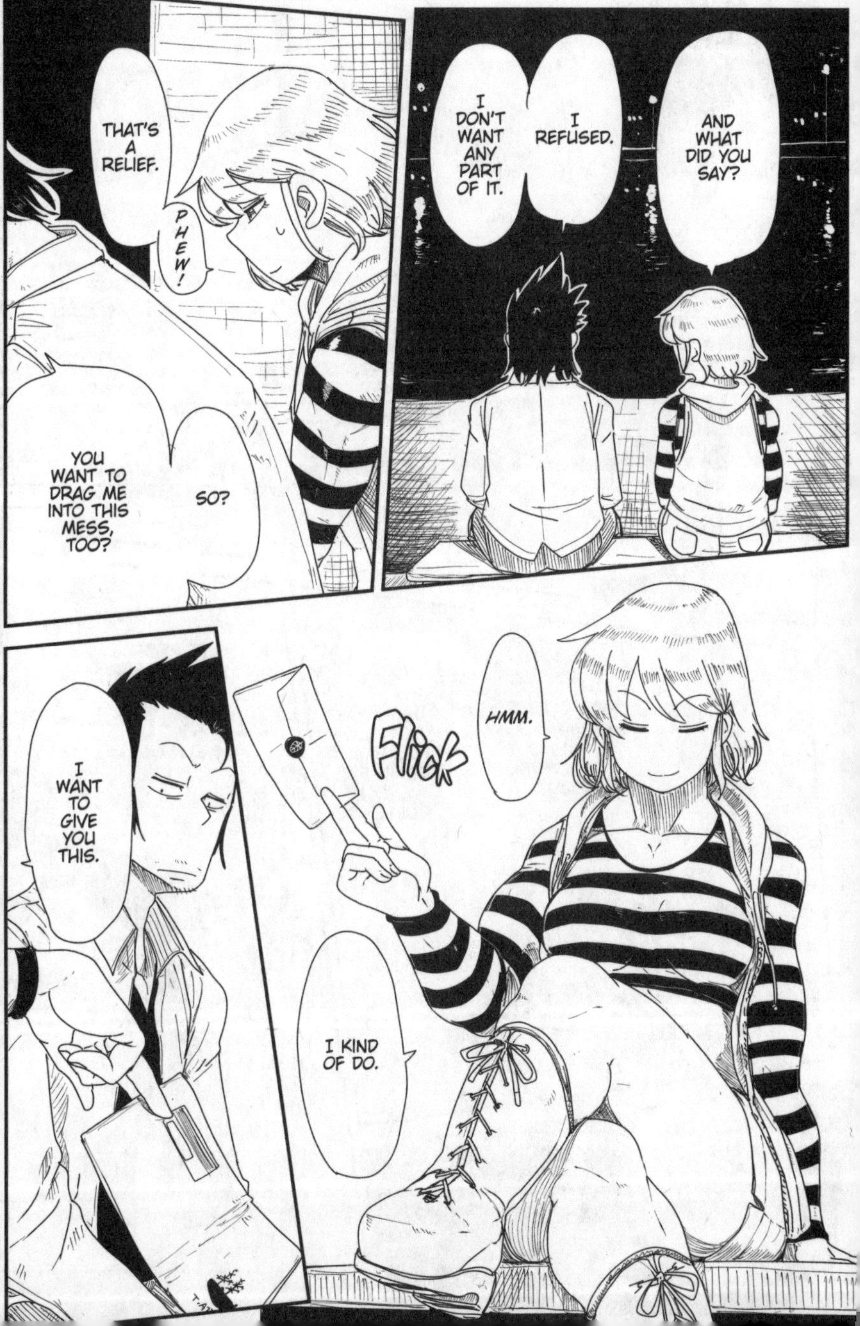
AND WHAT DID YOU SAY?
I REFUSED.
I DON'T WANT ANY PART OF IT.
THAT'S A RELIEF.
PHEW!
SO?
YOU WANT TO DRAG ME INTO THIS MESS, TOO?
HMM.
Flick
I KIND OF DO.
I WANT TO GIVE YOU THIS.

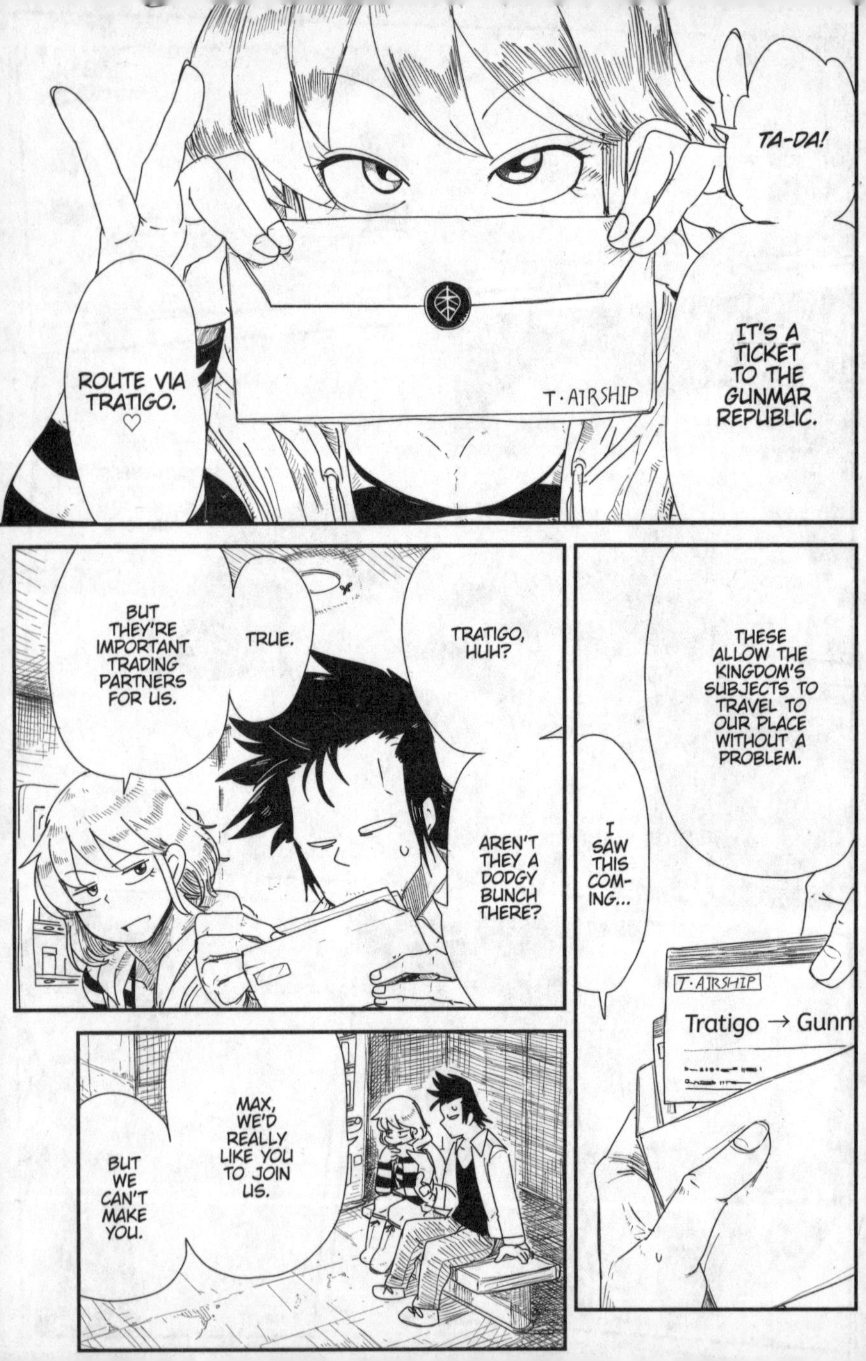
TA-DA!
IT'S A TICKET TO THE GUNMAR REPUBLIC.
T · AIRSHIP
ROUTE VIA TRATIGO. ♡
THESE ALLOW THE KINGDOM'S SUBJECTS TO TRAVEL TO OUR PLACE WITHOUT A PROBLEM.
I SAW THIS COM-ING...
T · AIRSHIP
Tratigo → Gunm
TRATIGO, HUH?
AREN'T THEY A DODGY BUNCH THERE?
TRUE.
BUT THEY'RE IMPORTANT TRADING PARTNERS FOR US.
MAX, WE'D REALLY LIKE YOU TO JOIN US.
BUT WE CAN'T MAKE YOU.

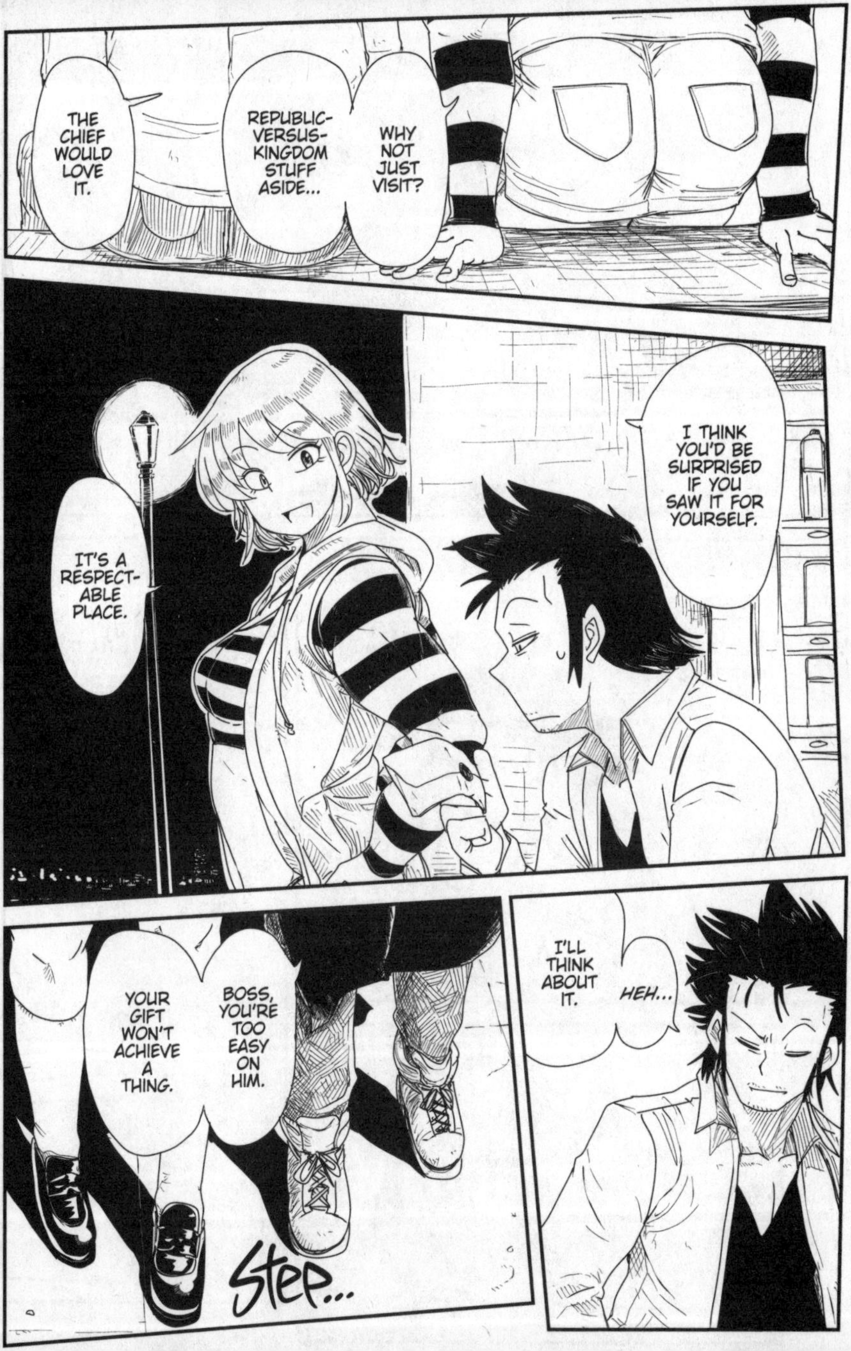
WHY NOT JUST VISIT?
REPUBLIC-VERSUS-KINGDOM STUFF ASIDE...
THE CHIEF WOULD LOVE IT.
I THINK YOU'D BE SURPRISED IF YOU SAW IT FOR YOURSELF.
IT'S A RESPECTABLE PLACE.
HEH...
I'LL THINK ABOUT IT.
BOSS, YOU'RE TOO EASY ON HIM.
YOUR GIFT WON'T ACHIEVE A THING.
Step...

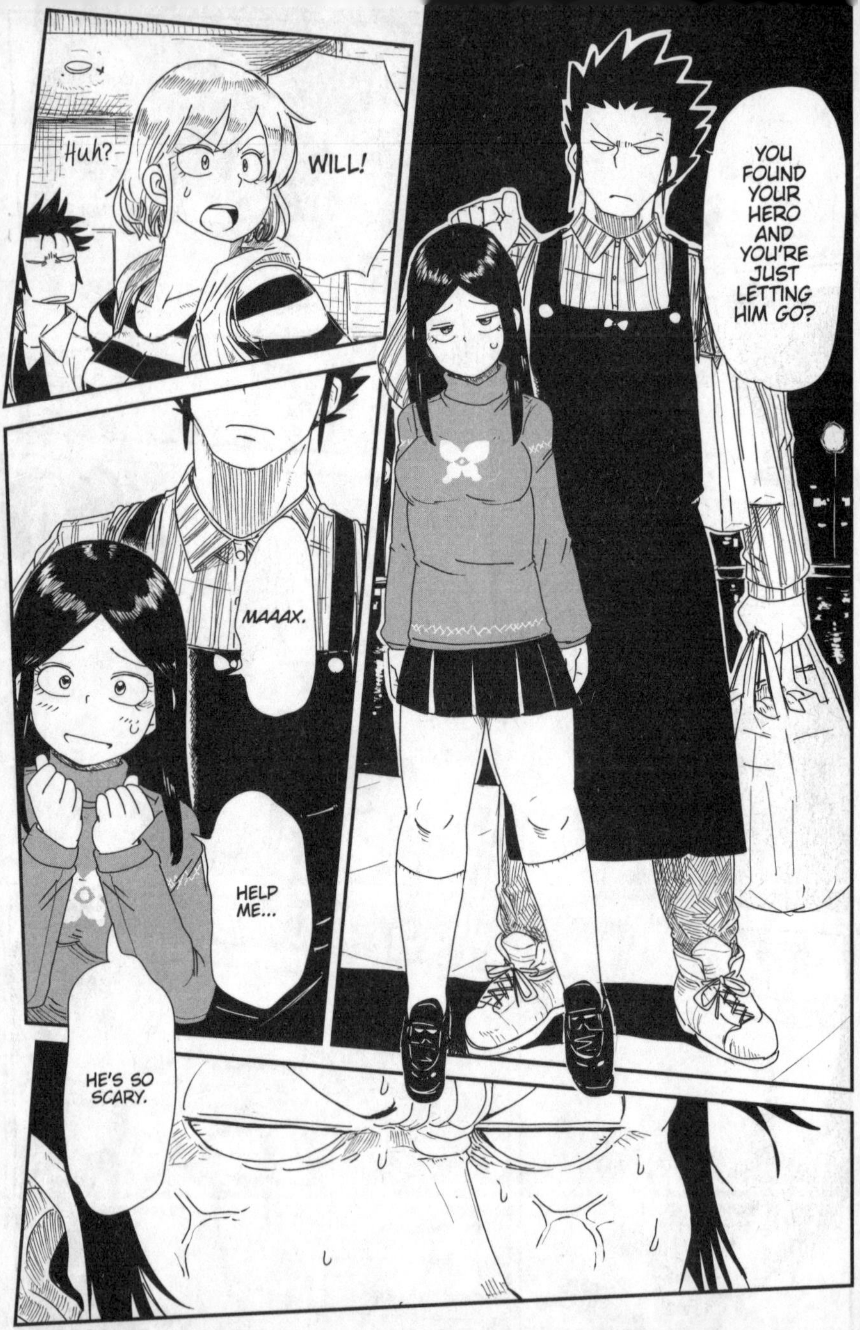
YOU FOUND YOUR HERO AND YOU'RE JUST LETTING HIM GO?
WILL!
Huh?
MAAAX.
HELP ME...
HE'S SO SCARY.

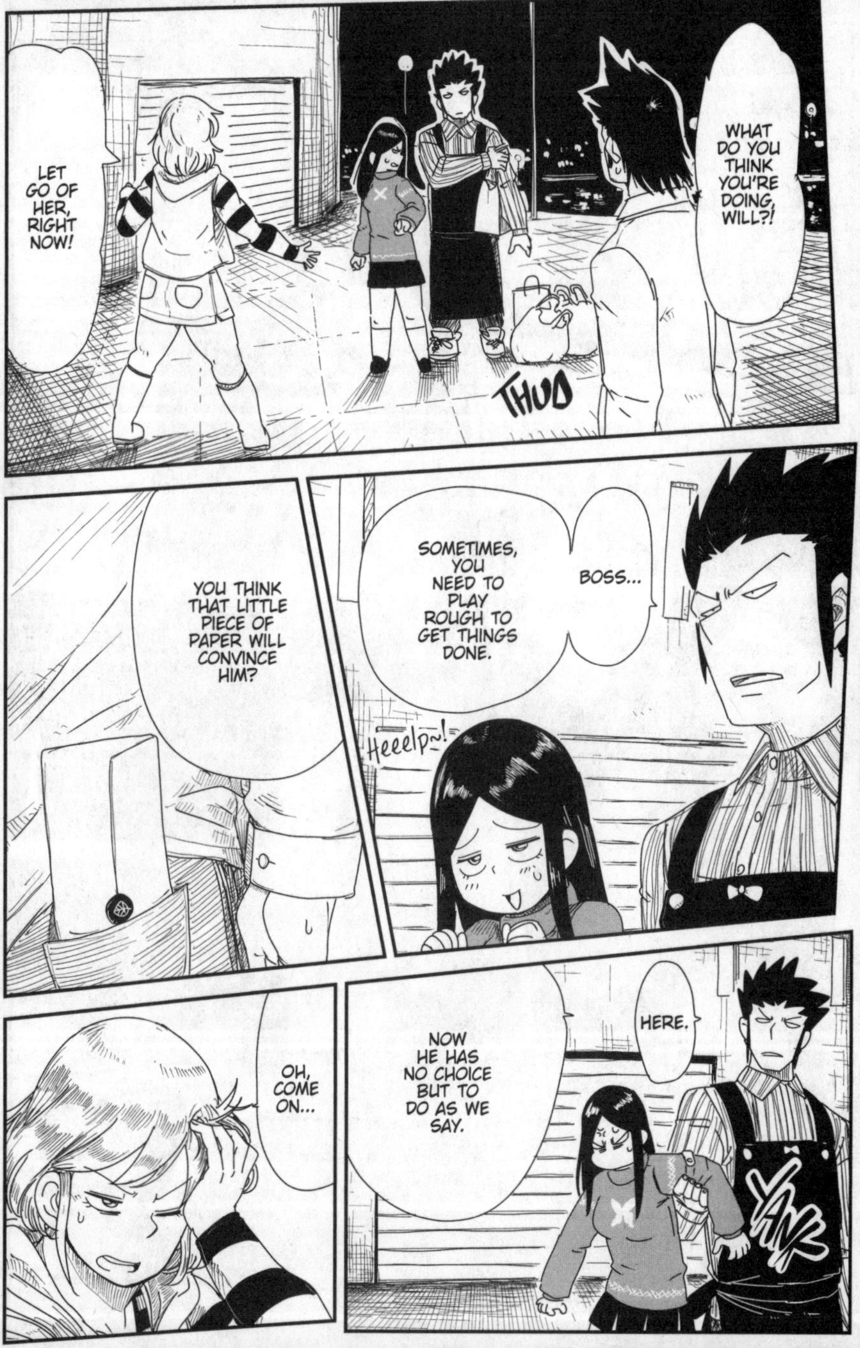
WHAT DO YOU THINK YOU'RE DOING, WILL?!
LET GO OF HER, RIGHT NOW!
THUD
BOSS...
SOMETIMES, YOU NEED TO PLAY ROUGH TO GET THINGS DONE.
Heeelp~!
YOU THINK THAT LITTLE PIECE OF PAPER WILL CONVINCE HIM?
HERE.
NOW HE HAS NO CHOICE BUT TO DO AS WE SAY.
YANK
OH, COME ON...

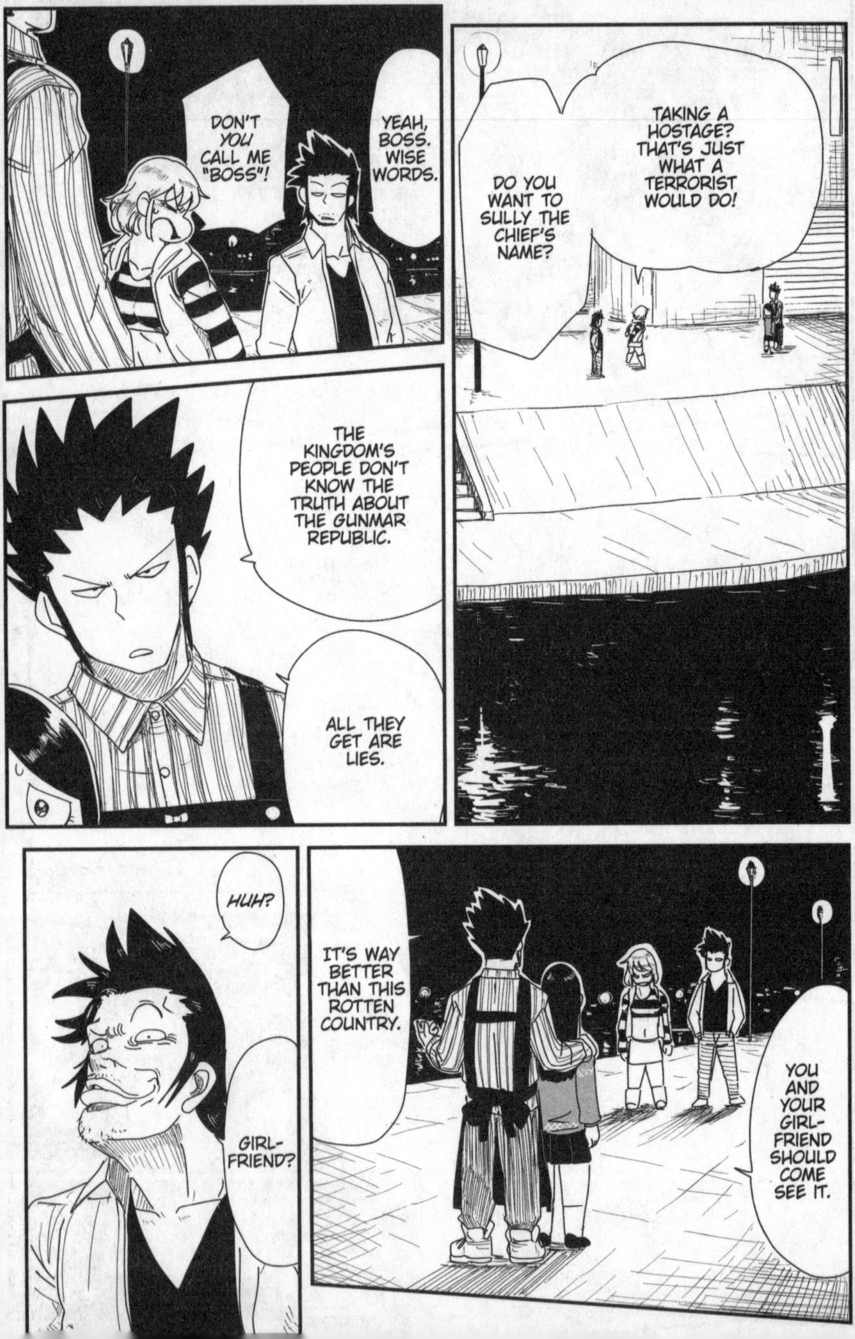
TAKING A HOSTAGE? THAT'S JUST WHAT A TERRORIST WOULD DO!
DO YOU WANT TO SULLY THE CHIEF'S NAME?
YEAH, BOSS. WISE WORDS.
DON'T *YOU* CALL ME "BOSS"!
THE KINGDOM'S PEOPLE DON'T KNOW THE TRUTH ABOUT THE GUNMAR REPUBLIC.
ALL THEY GET ARE LIES.
IT'S WAY BETTER THAN THIS ROTTEN COUNTRY.
YOU AND YOUR GIRL-FRIEND SHOULD COME SEE IT.
HUH?
GIRL-FRIEND?

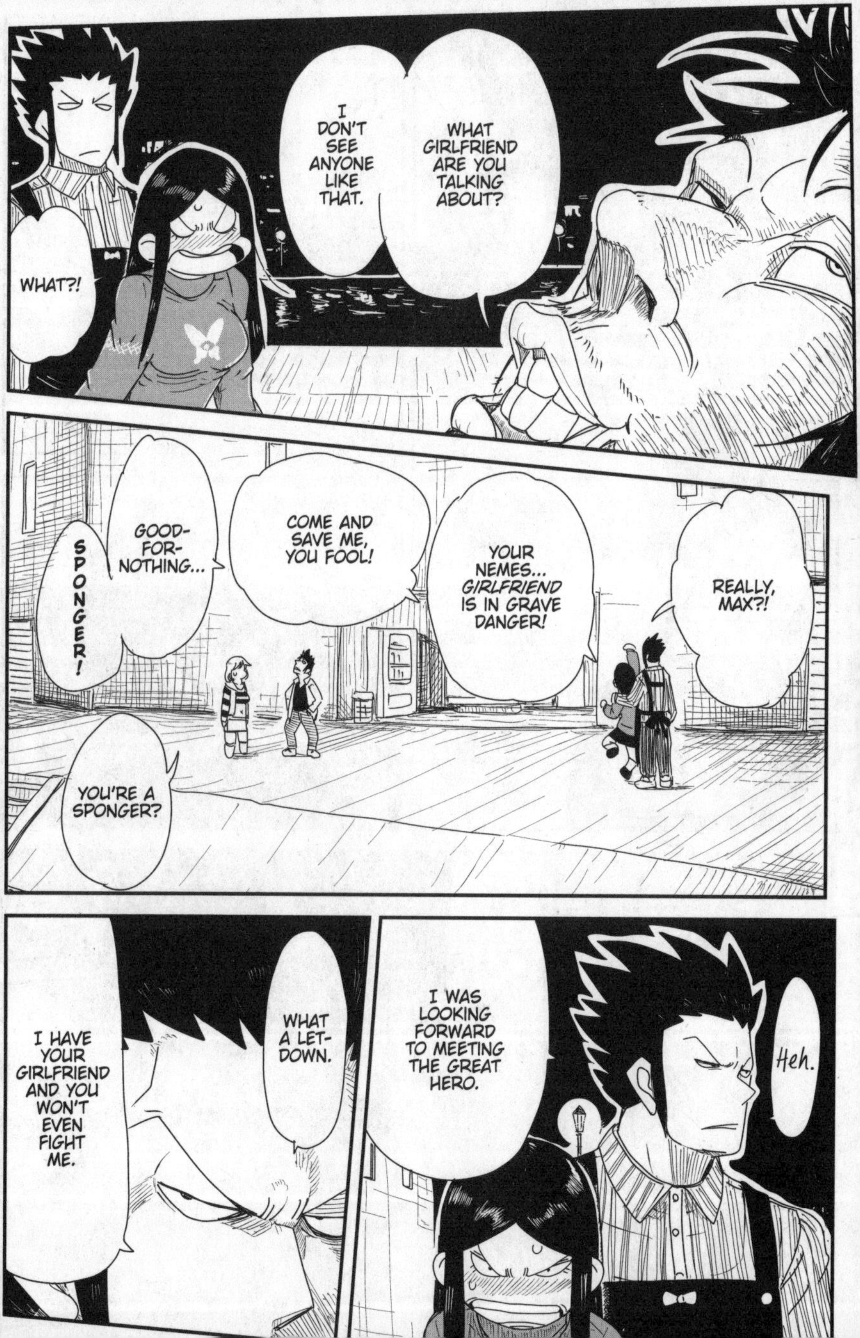
WHAT GIRLFRIEND ARE YOU TALKING ABOUT?
I DON'T SEE ANYONE LIKE THAT.
WHAT?!
REALLY, MAX?!
YOUR NEMES... *GIRLFRIEND* IS IN GRAVE DANGER!
COME AND SAVE ME, YOU FOOL!
GOOD-FOR-NOTHING...
SPONGER!
YOU'RE A SPONGER?
Heh.
I WAS LOOKING FORWARD TO MEETING THE GREAT HERO.
WHAT A LET-DOWN.
I HAVE YOUR GIRLFRIEND AND YOU WON'T EVEN FIGHT ME.

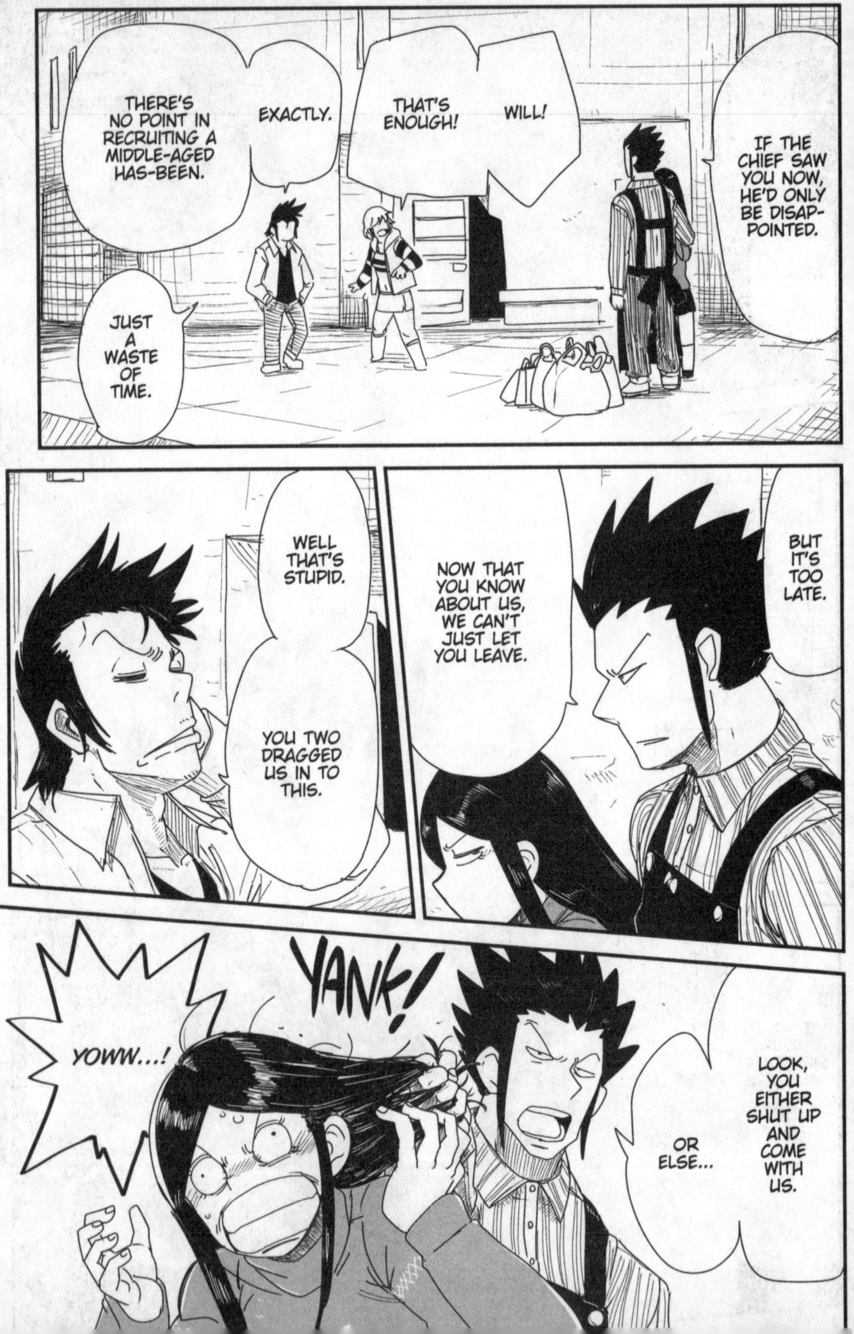
IF THE CHIEF SAW YOU NOW, HE'D ONLY BE DISAPPOINTED.
WILL!
THAT'S ENOUGH!
EXACTLY.
THERE'S NO POINT IN RECRUITING A MIDDLE-AGED HAS-BEEN.
JUST A WASTE OF TIME.
BUT IT'S TOO LATE.
NOW THAT YOU KNOW ABOUT US, WE CAN'T JUST LET YOU LEAVE.
WELL THAT'S STUPID.
YOU TWO DRAGGED US IN TO THIS.
LOOK, YOU EITHER SHUT UP AND COME WITH US.
OR ELSE...
YANK!
YOWW...!

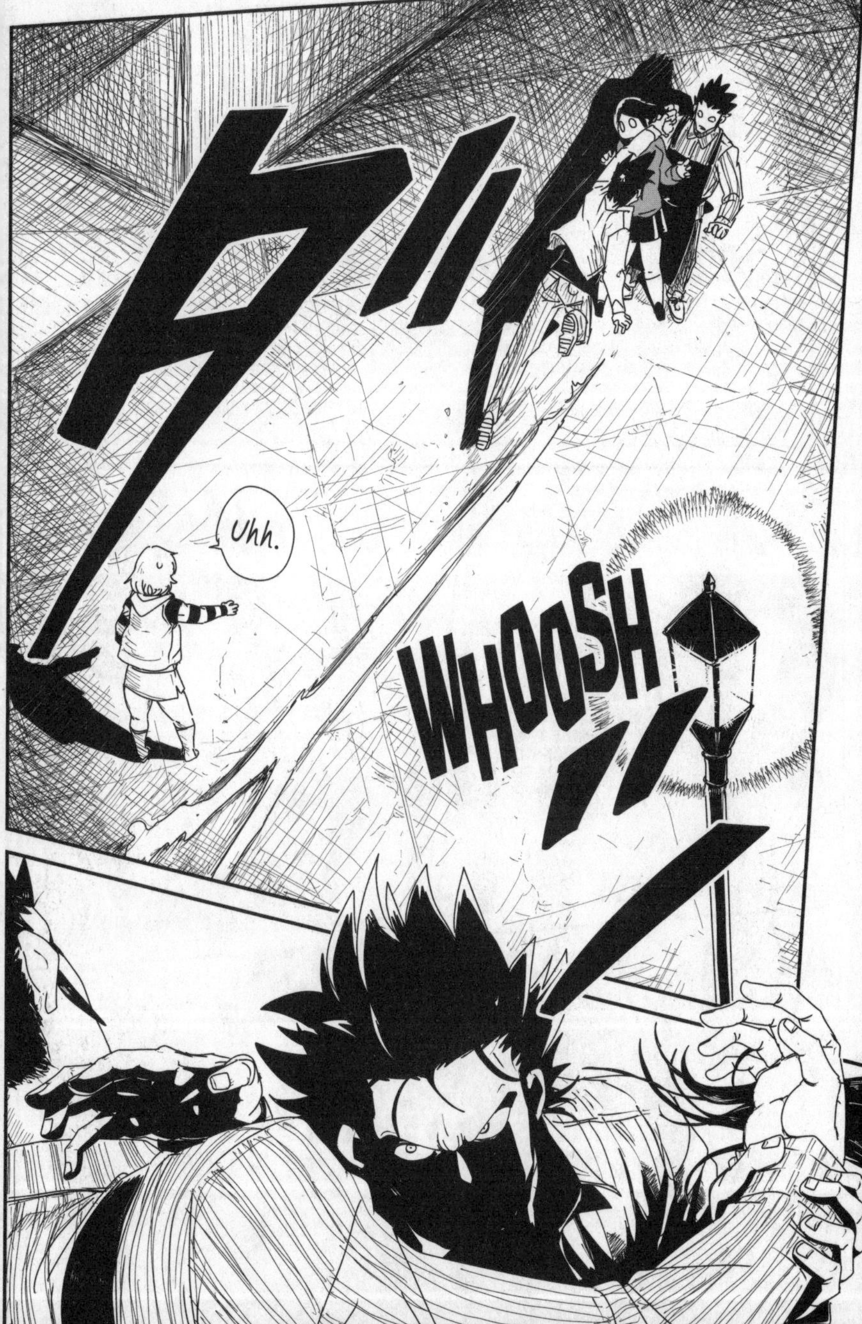
Uhh.
WHOOSH

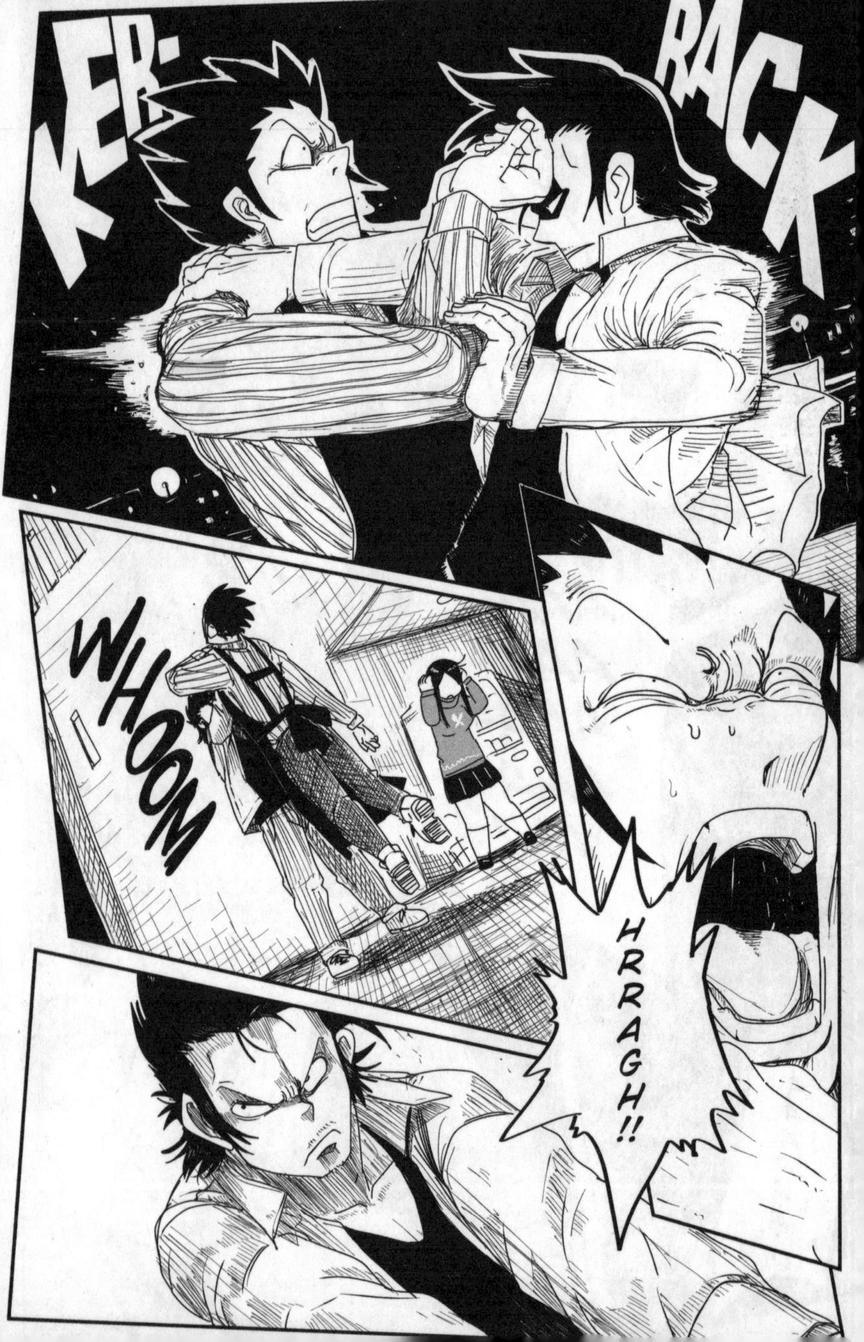
KER-RACK
HRRAGH!!
WHOOM

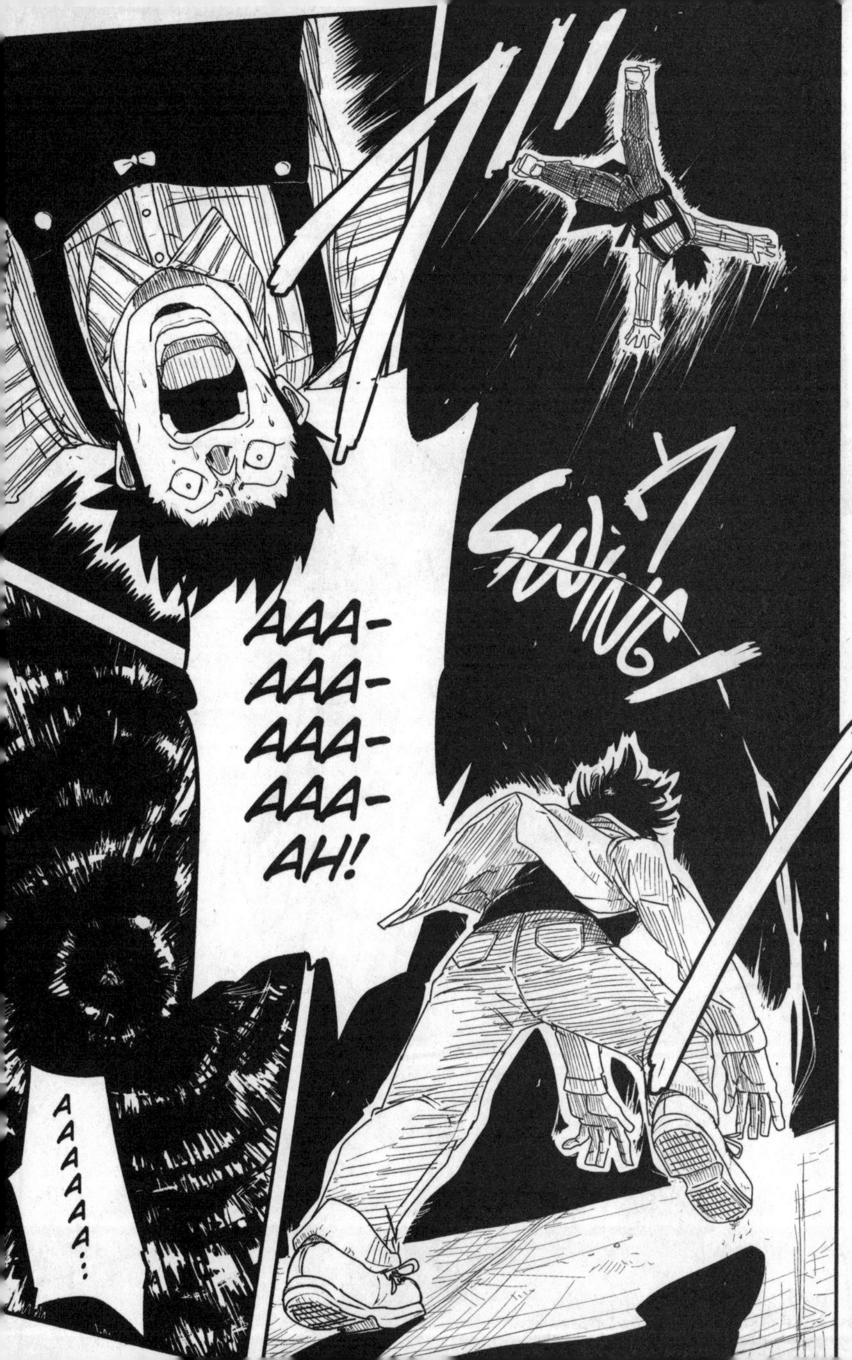
SWING!
AAA-AAA-AAA-AAA-AH!
AAAAAA...

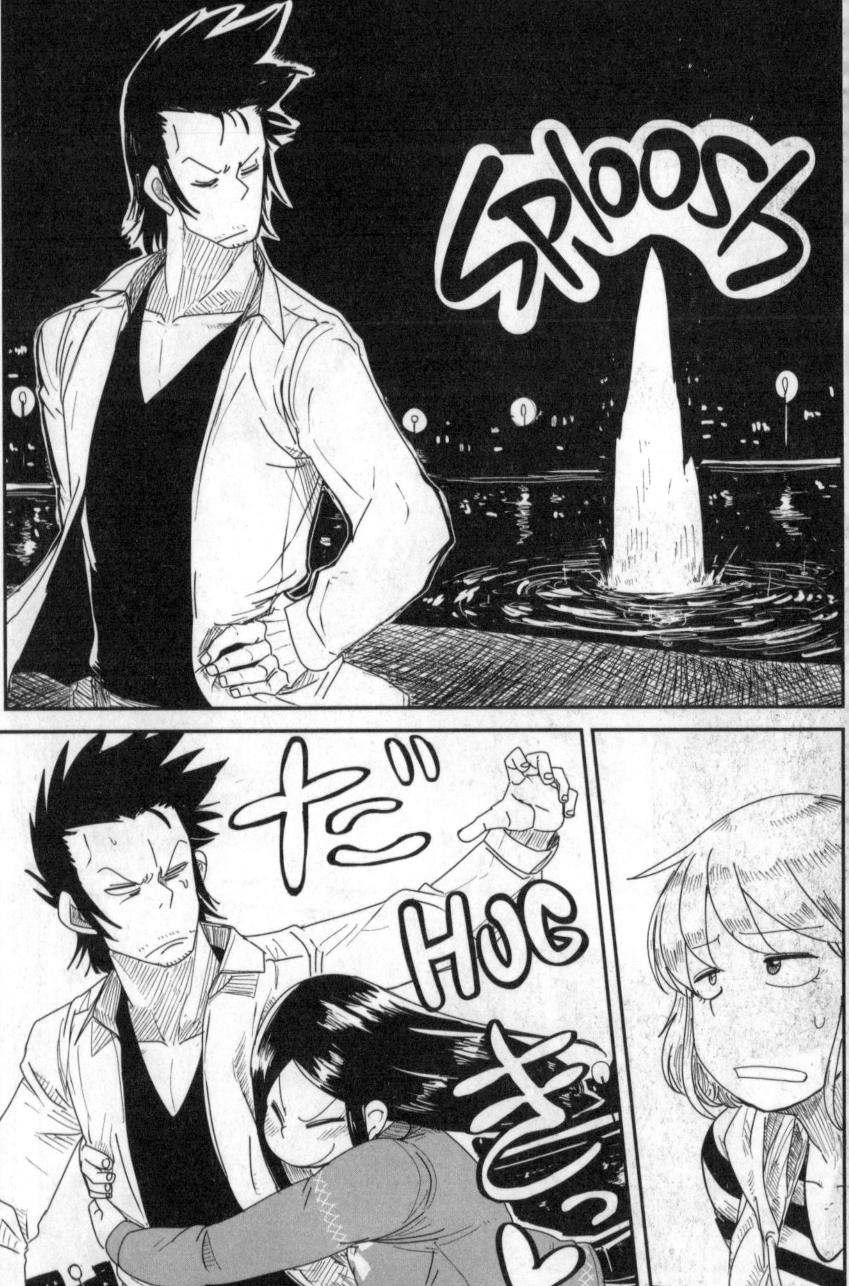

SPLOOSH
だ
HUG
ぎゅっ

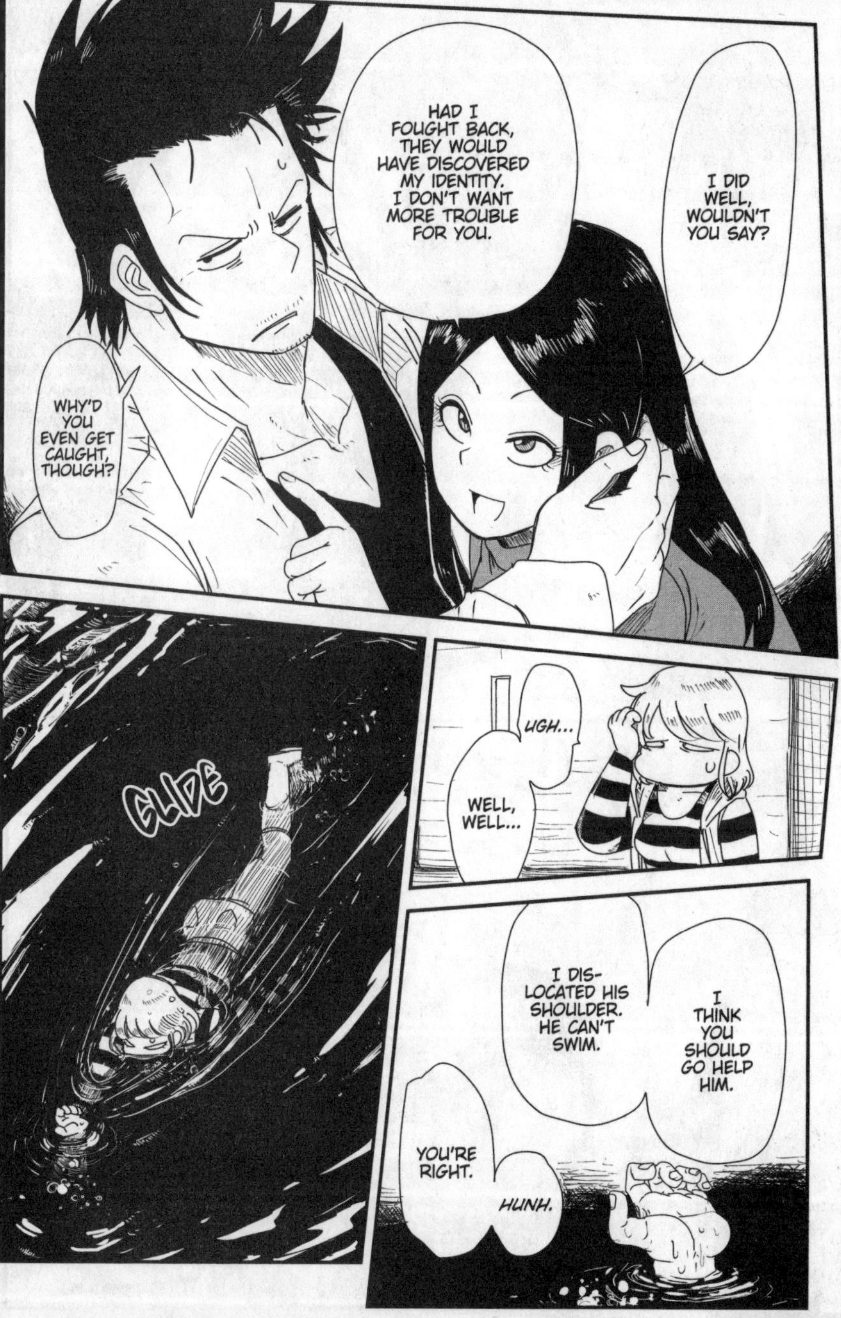
I DID WELL, WOULDN'T YOU SAY?
HAD I FOUGHT BACK, THEY WOULD HAVE DISCOVERED MY IDENTITY. I DON'T WANT MORE TROUBLE FOR YOU.
WHY'D YOU EVEN GET CAUGHT, THOUGH?
UGH...
WELL, WELL...
I THINK YOU SHOULD GO HELP HIM.
I DIS-LOCATED HIS SHOULDER. HE CAN'T SWIM.
YOU'RE RIGHT.
HUNH.
GLIDE

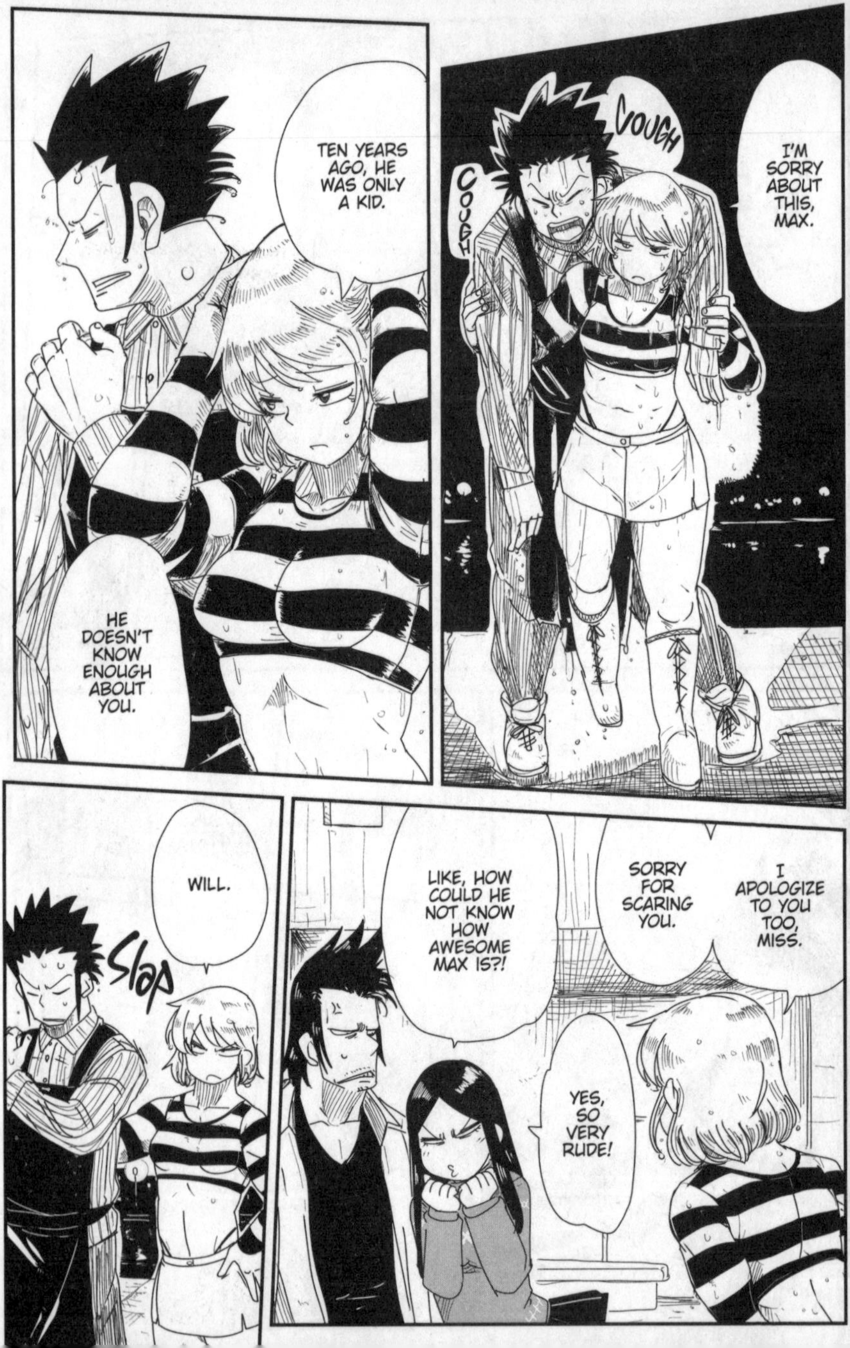
I'M SORRY ABOUT THIS, MAX.
COUGH
COUGH
TEN YEARS AGO, HE WAS ONLY A KID.
HE DOESN'T KNOW ENOUGH ABOUT YOU.
I APOLOGIZE TO YOU TOO, MISS.
SORRY FOR SCARING YOU.
LIKE, HOW COULD HE NOT KNOW HOW AWESOME MAX IS?!
YES, SO VERY RUDE!
WILL.
Slap

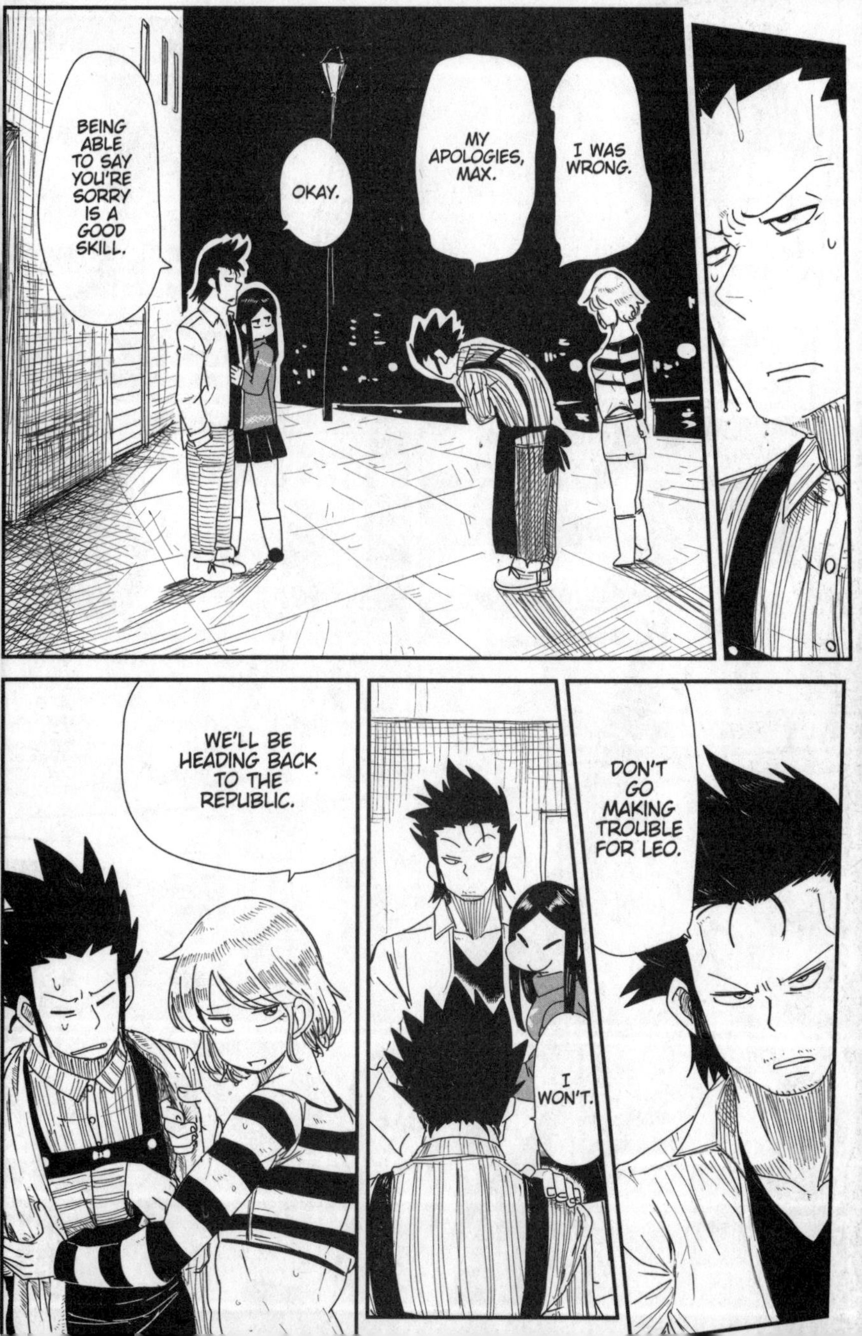
I WAS WRONG.
MY APOLOGIES, MAX.
OKAY.
BEING ABLE TO SAY YOU'RE SORRY IS A GOOD SKILL.
DON'T GO MAKING TROUBLE FOR LEO.
I WON'T.
WE'LL BE HEADING BACK TO THE REPUBLIC.

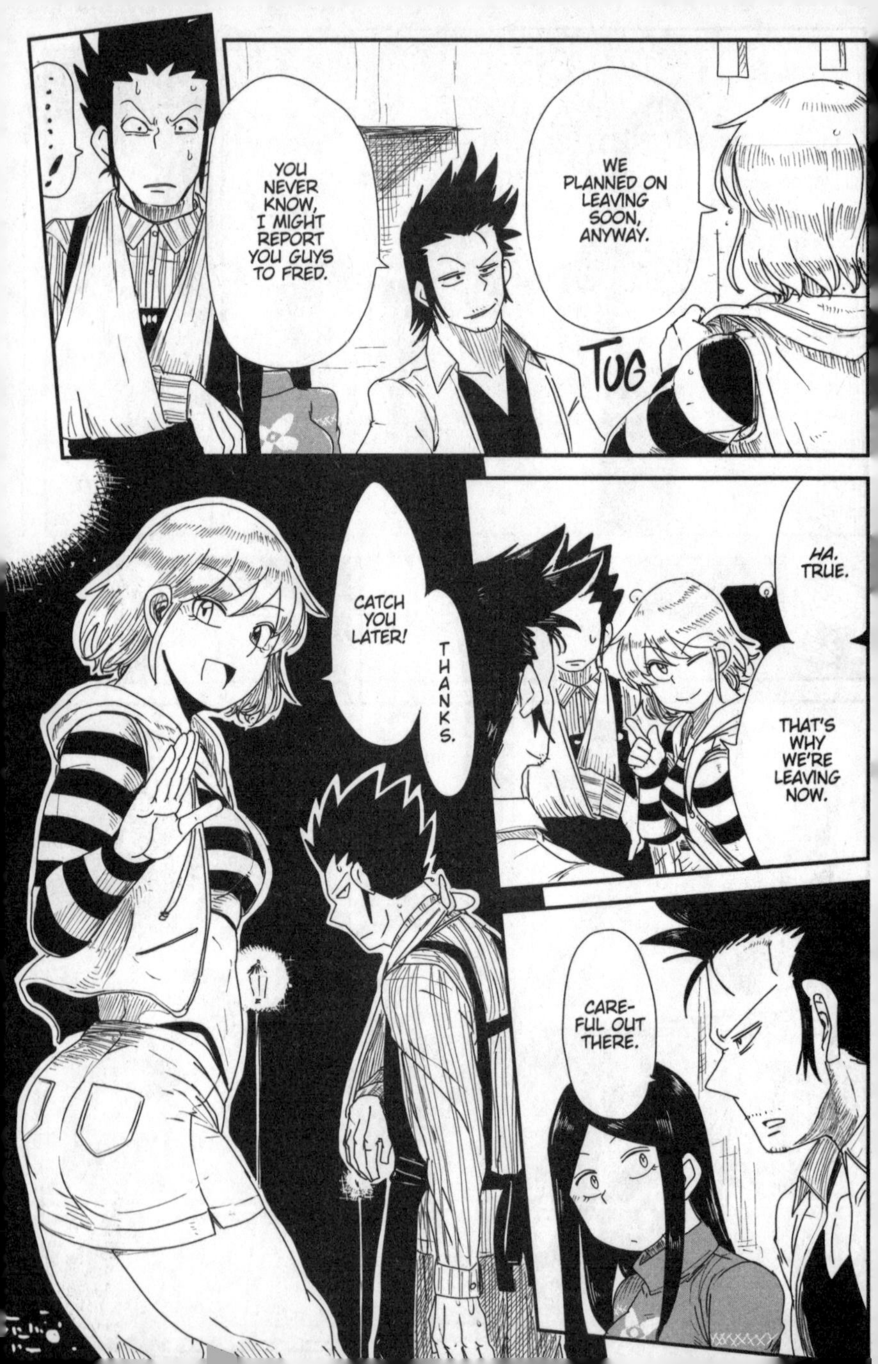
WE PLANNED ON LEAVING SOON, ANYWAY.
TUG
YOU NEVER KNOW, I MIGHT REPORT YOU GUYS TO FRED.
......!
HA. TRUE.
THAT'S WHY WE'RE LEAVING NOW.
CARE-FUL OUT THERE.
CATCH YOU LATER!
THANKS.

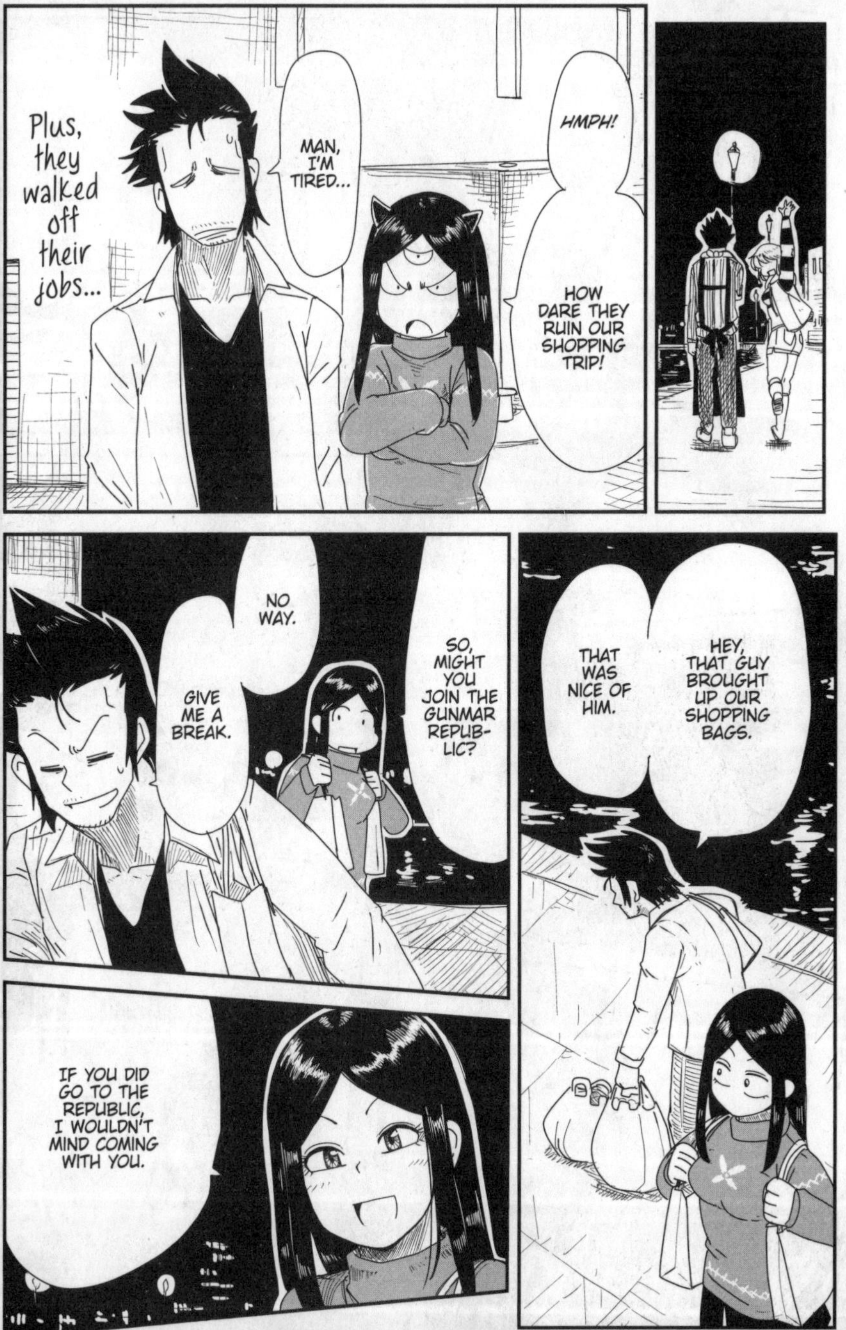
HMPH!
HOW DARE THEY RUIN OUR SHOPPING TRIP!
MAN, I'M TIRED...
Plus, they walked off their jobs...
HEY, THAT GUY BROUGHT UP OUR SHOPPING BAGS.
THAT WAS NICE OF HIM.
SO, MIGHT YOU JOIN THE GUNMAR REPUB-LIC?
NO WAY.
GIVE ME A BREAK.
IF YOU DID GO TO THE REPUBLIC, I WOULDN'T MIND COMING WITH YOU.

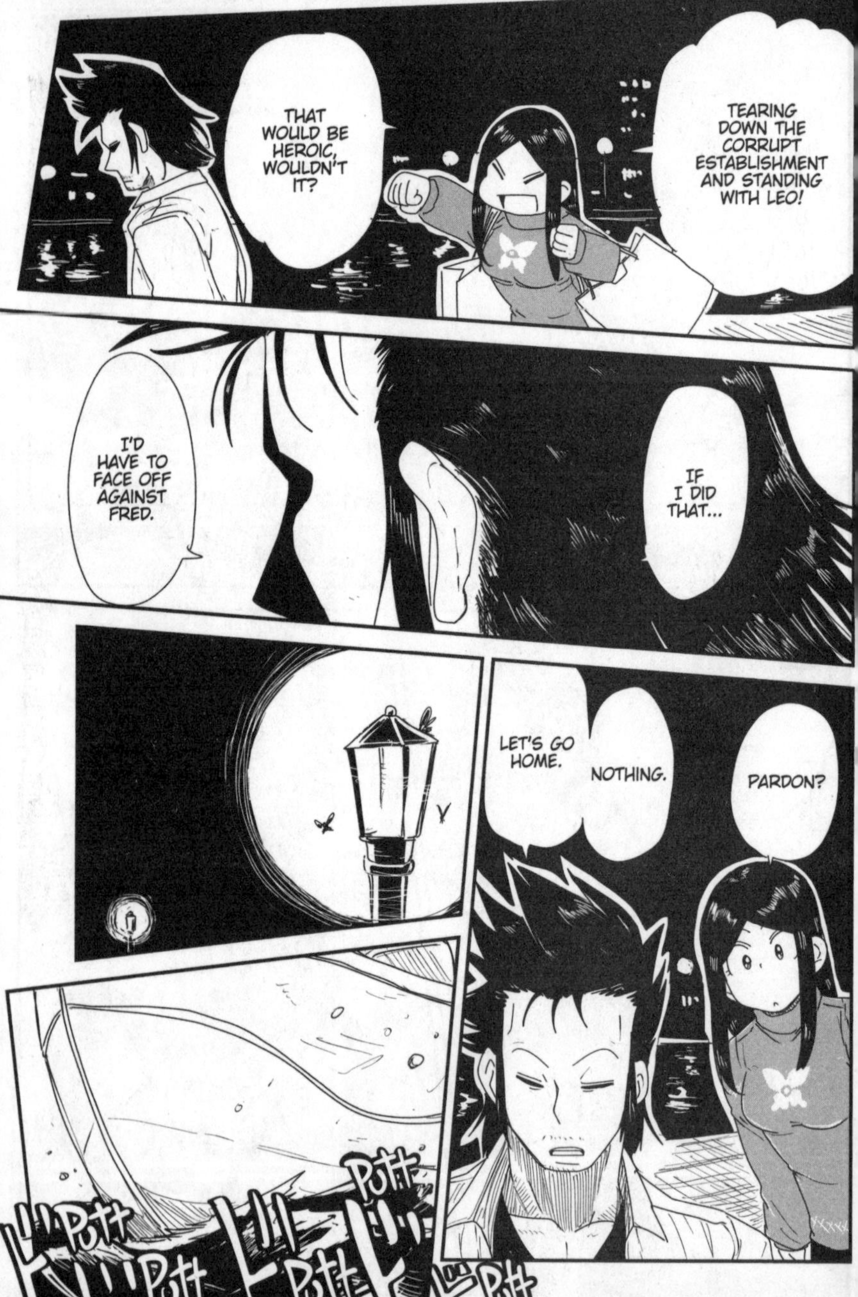
TEARING DOWN THE CORRUPT ESTABLISHMENT AND STANDING WITH LEO!
THAT WOULD BE HEROIC, WOULDN'T IT?
IF I DID THAT...
I'D HAVE TO FACE OFF AGAINST FRED.
PARDON?
NOTHING.
LET'S GO HOME.
Putt
Putt
Putt
Putt
Putt
Putt

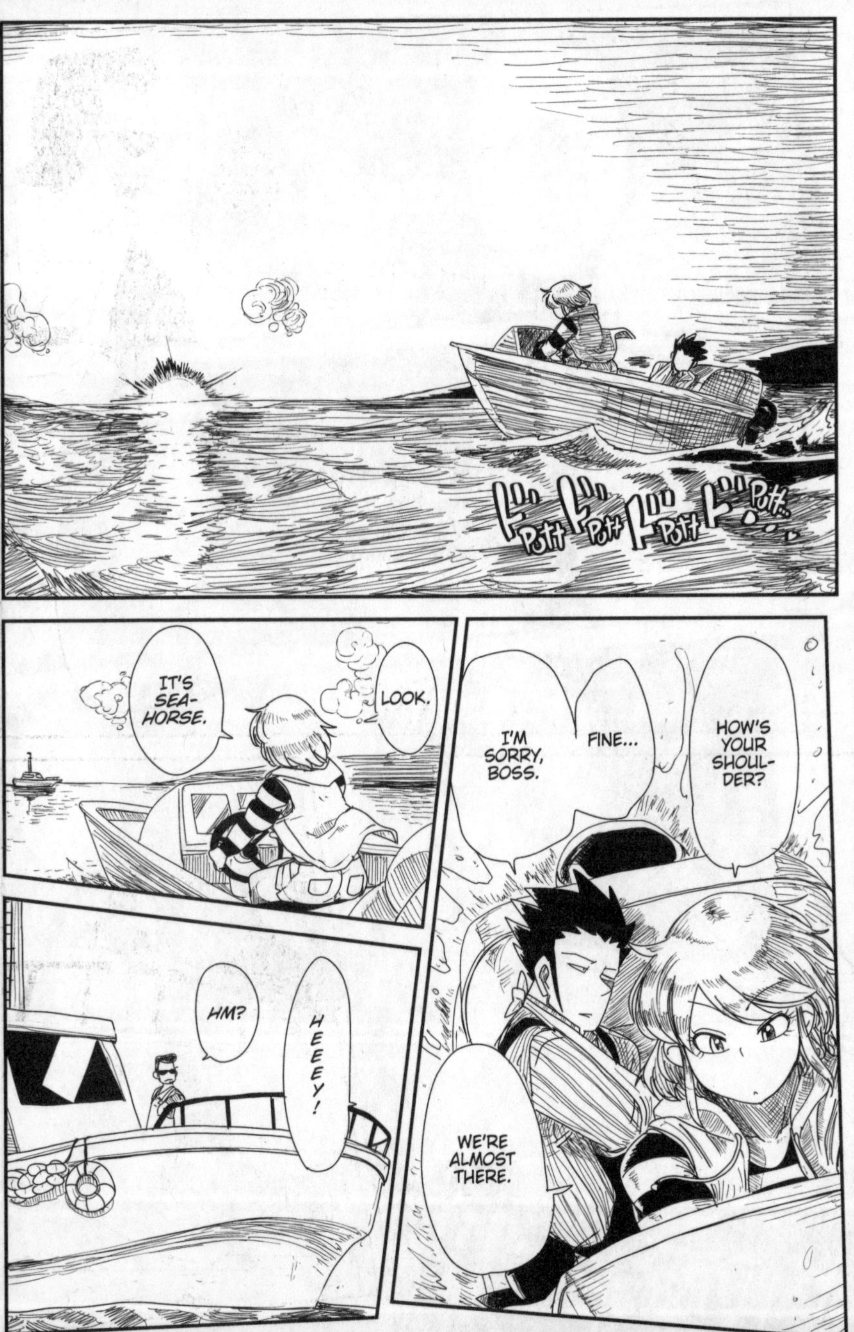
Putt Putt Putt Putt
HOW'S YOUR SHOULDER?
FINE...
I'M SORRY, BOSS.
WE'RE ALMOST THERE.
LOOK.
IT'S SEA-HORSE.
HEEEEY!
HM?

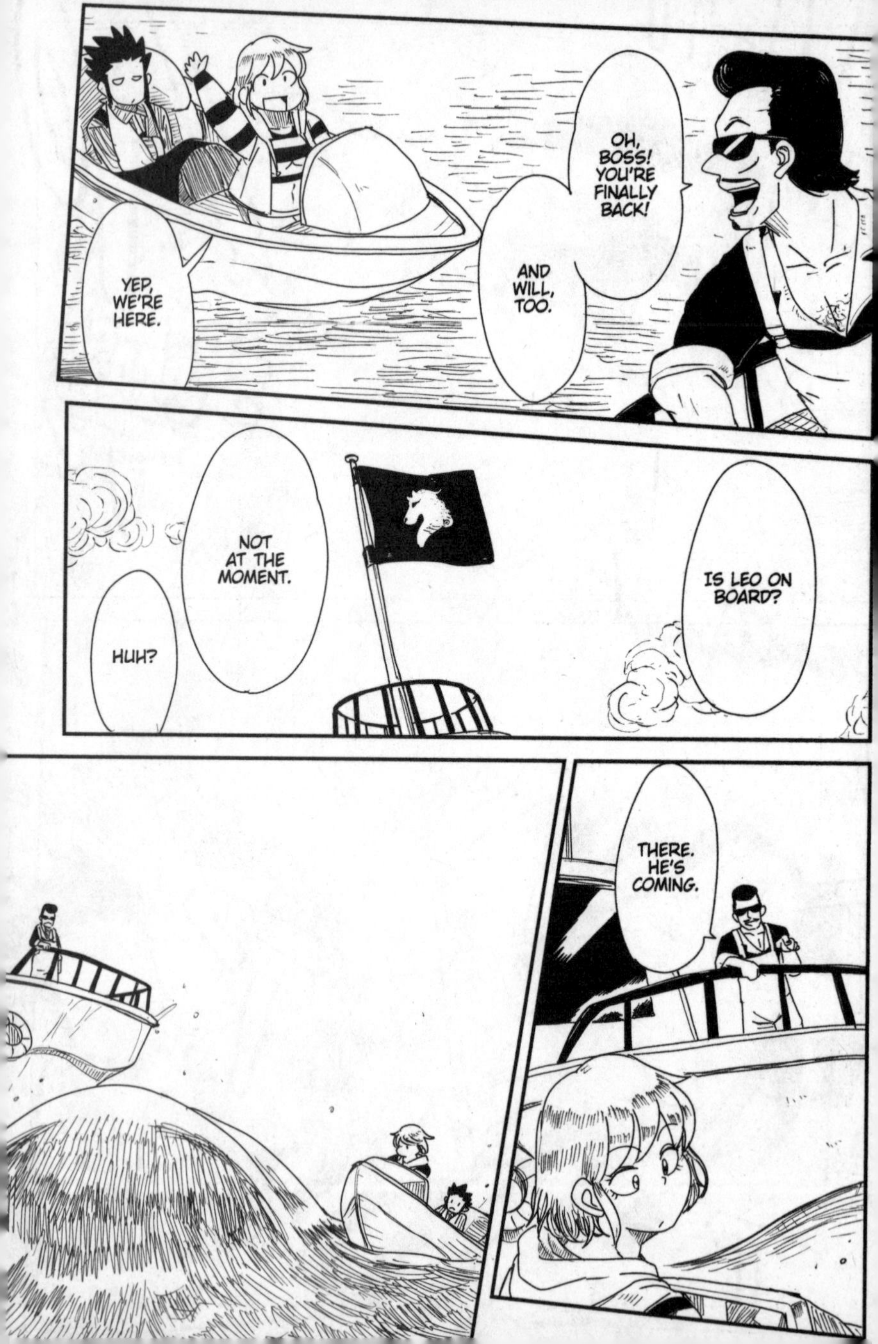
OH, BOSS! YOU'RE FINALLY BACK!
AND WILL, TOO.
YEP, WE'RE HERE.
IS LEO ON BOARD?
NOT AT THE MOMENT.
HUH?
THERE. HE'S COMING.

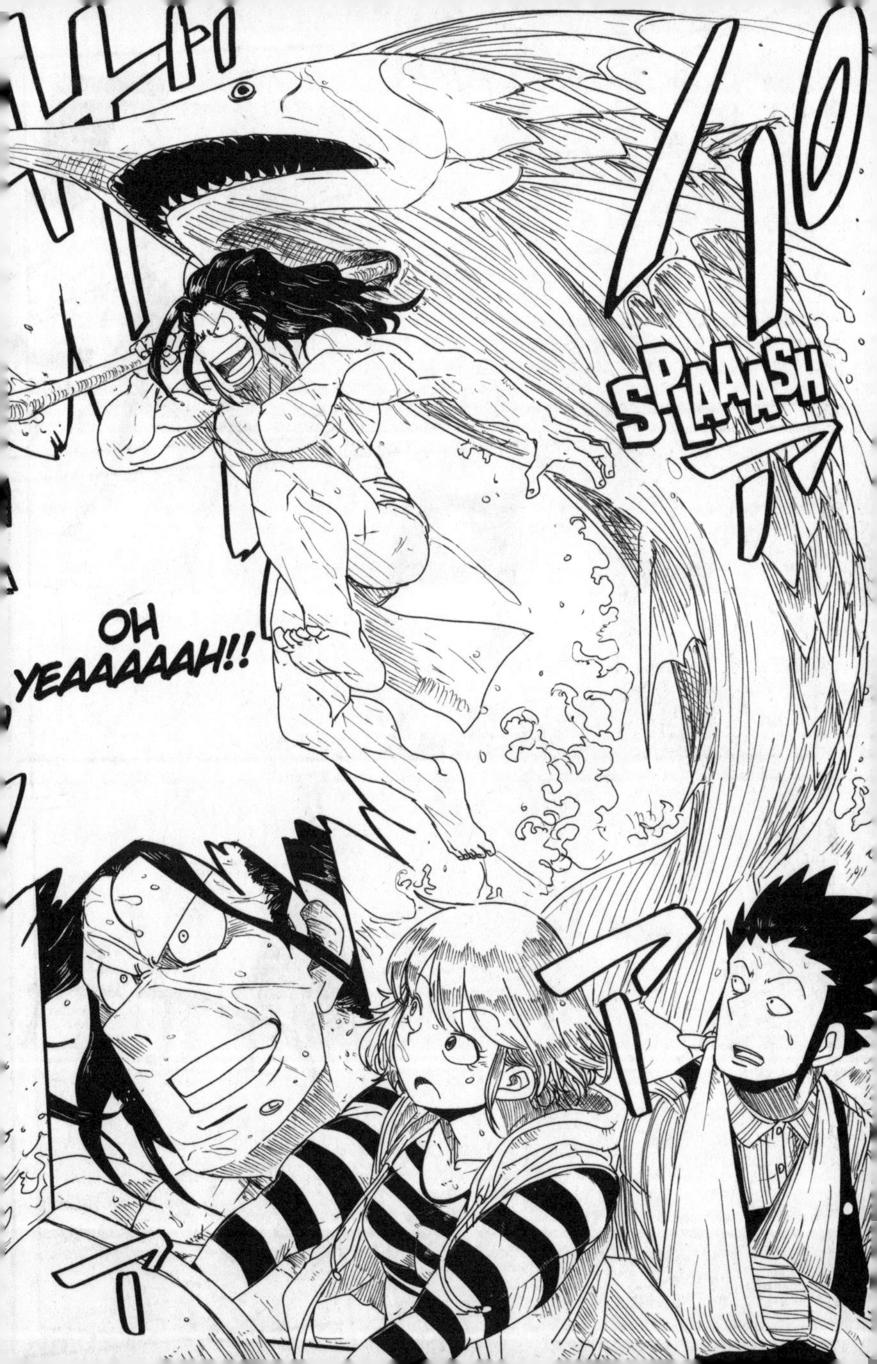
SPLAAASH
OH YEAAAAAH!!

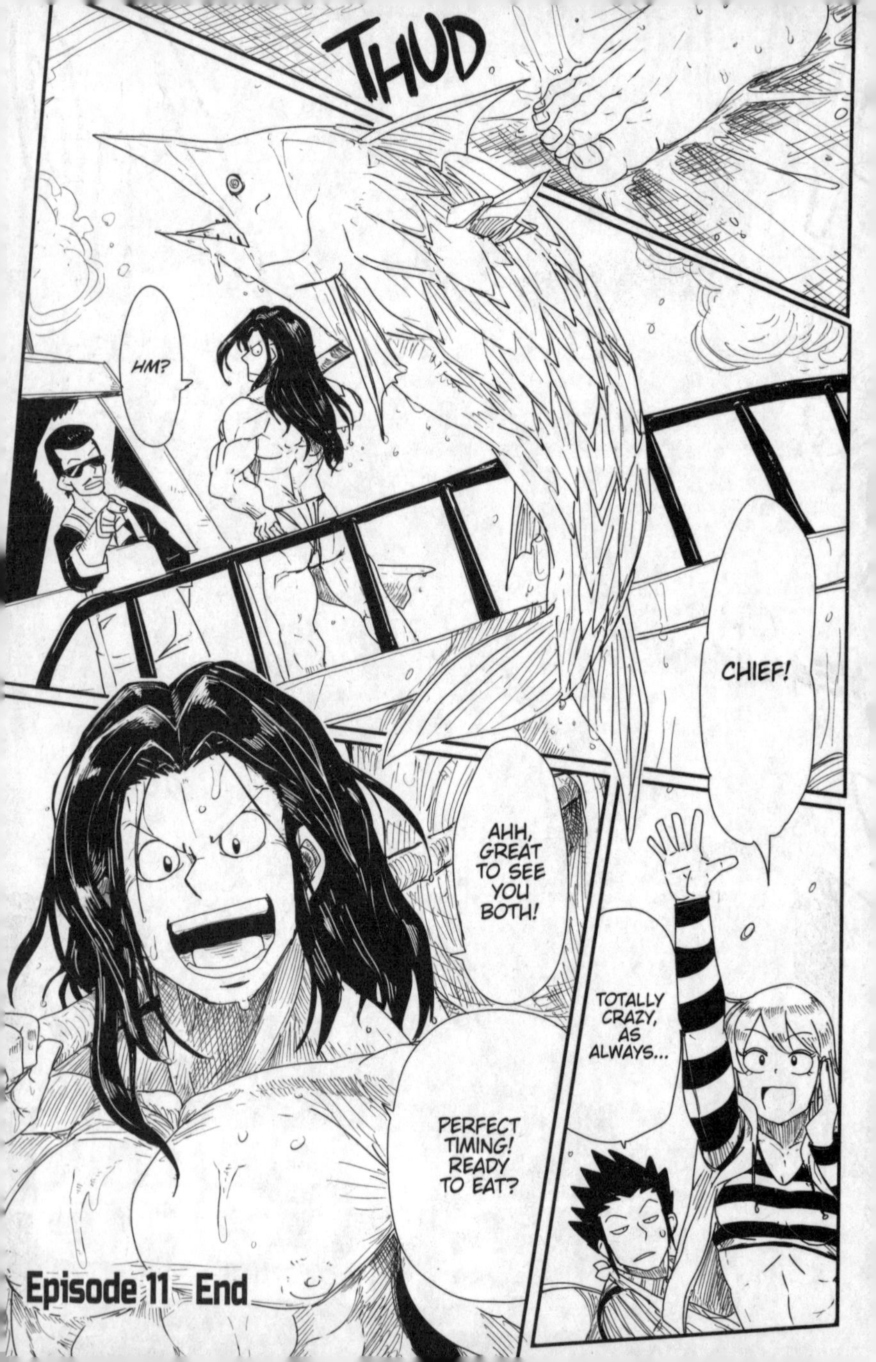
THUD
HM?
CHIEF!
TOTALLY CRAZY, AS ALWAYS...
AHH, GREAT TO SEE YOU BOTH!
PERFECT TIMING! READY TO EAT?
Episode 11 End

LEVEL 1 DEMON LORD & ONE ROOM HERO

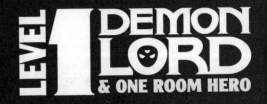

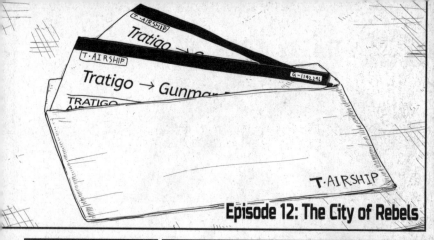

T·AIRSHIP
Tratigo
T·AIRSHIP
Tratigo → Gunmar
T·AIRSHIP
Episode 12: The City of Rebels
ARE THESE THE TICKETS THAT LADY GAVE YOU?
SNAP
TO GO TO THE GUNMAR REPUBLIC?
WHY TAKE PICTURES OF THEM?
BECAUSE YOU CAN'T GET THEM IN THIS COUNTRY.
Auction points
I'M GOING TO SELL THEM ONLINE.
I BET I CAN GET A GOOD PRICE.
Your item
Tratigo → Gunmar
T·AIRSHIP
Crypto Currency
We won't scam you!
Gunmar via Tratigo (2)
From 99,800 Yen
YOU SPONGER!!
COUPONS

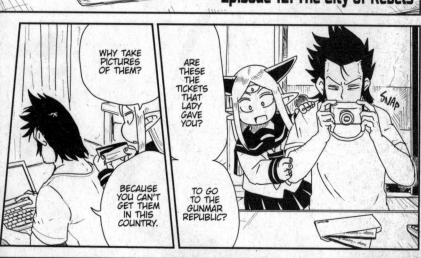

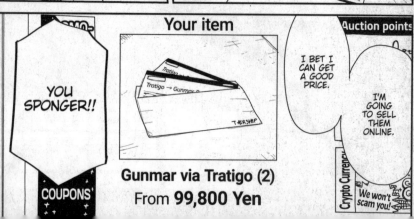

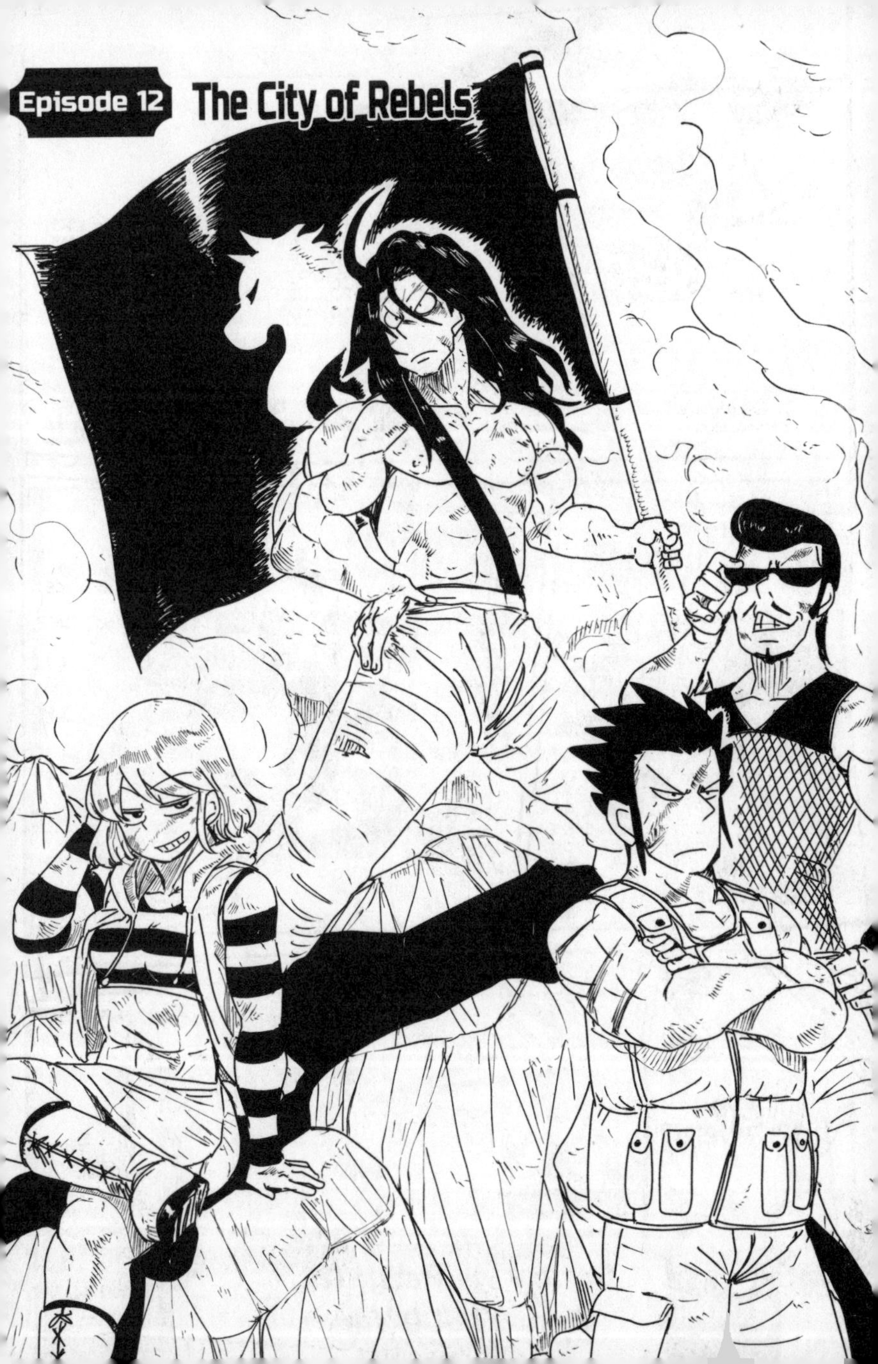
Episode 12
The City of Rebels

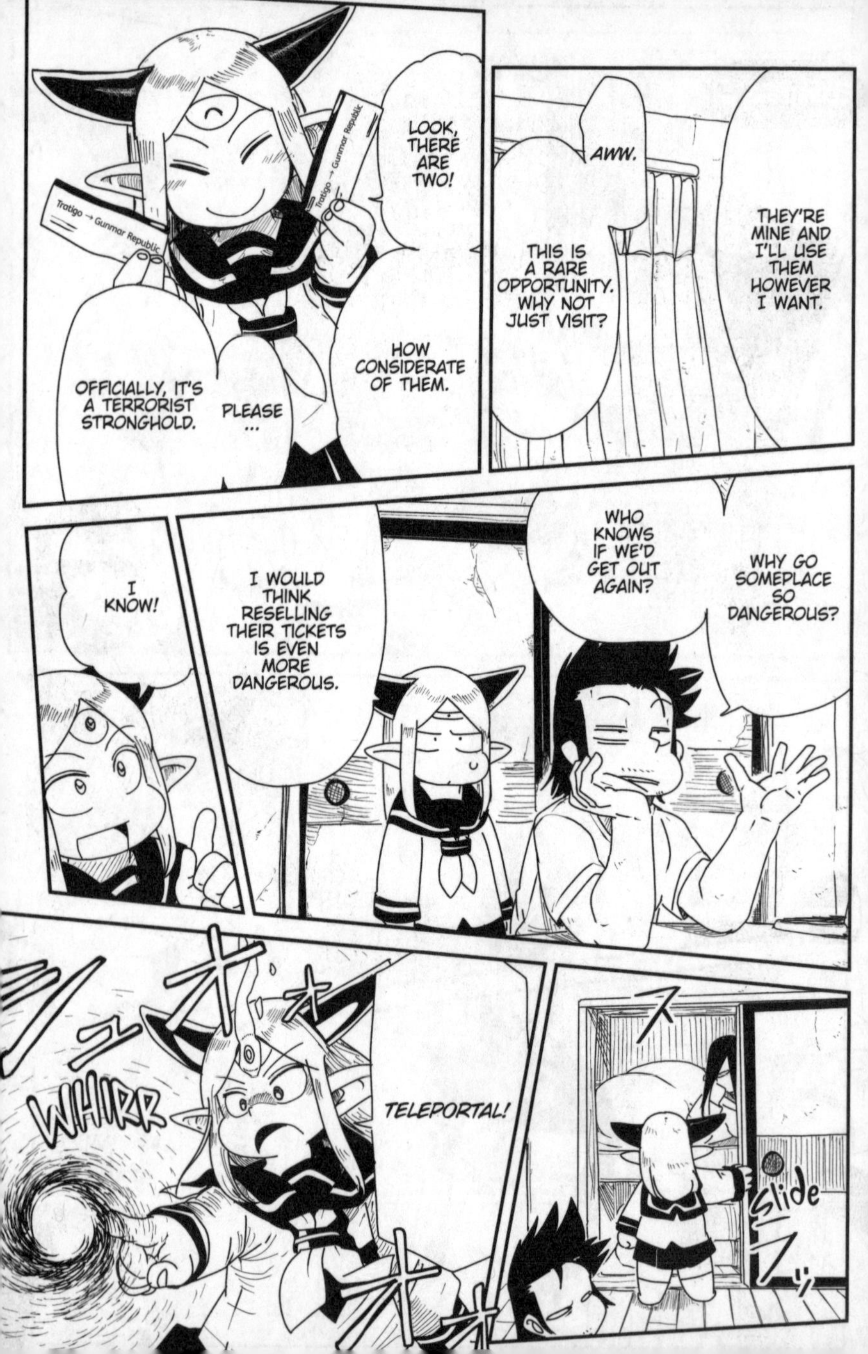
THEY'RE MINE AND I'LL USE THEM HOWEVER I WANT.
AWW.
THIS IS A RARE OPPORTUNITY. WHY NOT JUST VISIT?
LOOK, THERE ARE TWO!
Tratigo → Gunmar Republic
Tratigo → Gunmar Republic
HOW CONSIDERATE OF THEM.
PLEASE ...
OFFICIALLY, IT'S A TERRORIST STRONGHOLD.
WHY GO SOMEPLACE SO DANGEROUS?
WHO KNOWS IF WE'D GET OUT AGAIN?
I WOULD THINK RESELLING THEIR TICKETS IS EVEN MORE DANGEROUS.
I KNOW!
Slide
TELEPORTAL!
WHIRR

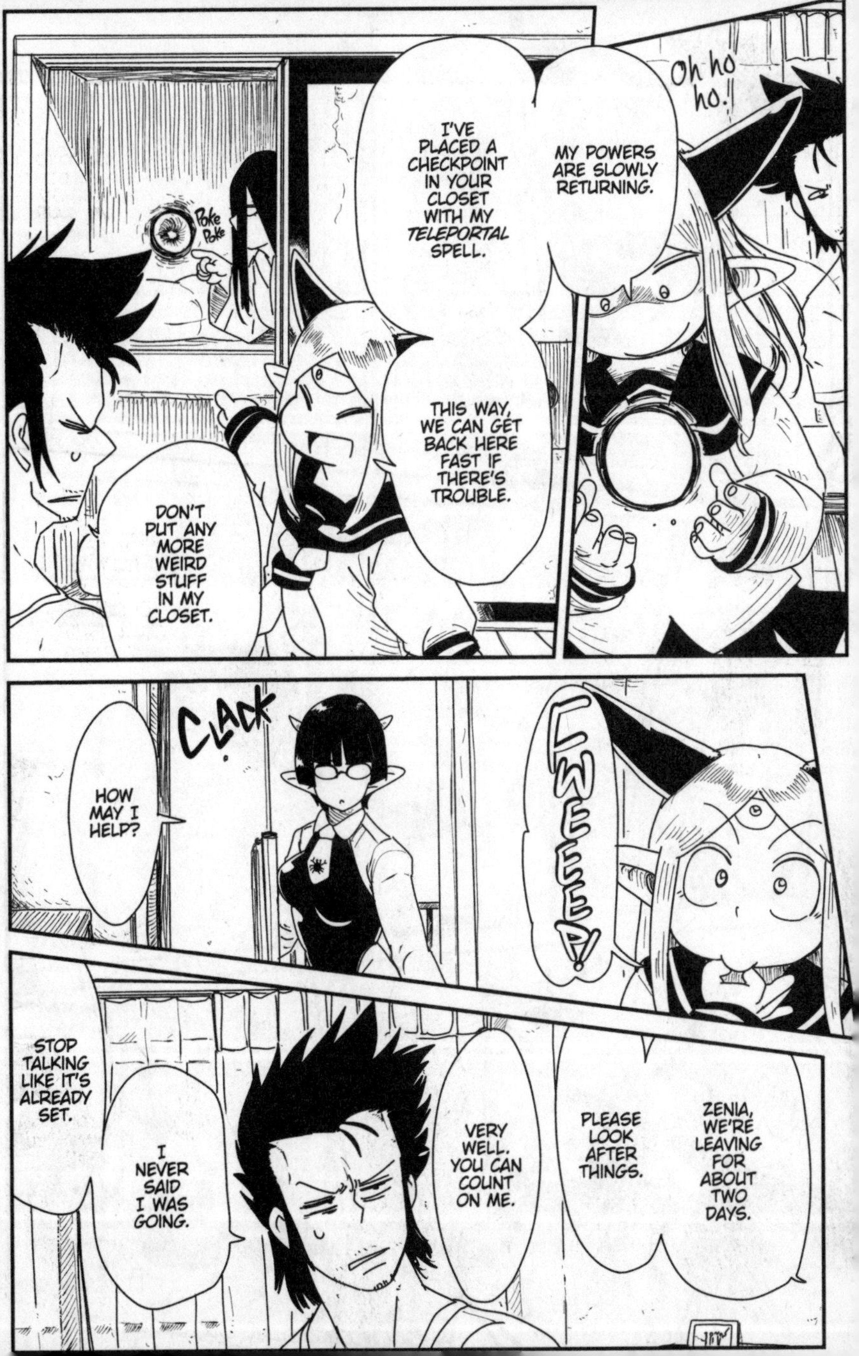
Oh ho ho.!
MY POWERS ARE SLOWLY RETURNING.
I'VE PLACED A CHECKPOINT IN YOUR CLOSET WITH MY *TELEPORTAL* SPELL.
THIS WAY, WE CAN GET BACK HERE FAST IF THERE'S TROUBLE.
Poke Poke
DON'T PUT ANY MORE WEIRD STUFF IN MY CLOSET.
CWEEEEP!
CLACK
HOW MAY I HELP?
ZENIA, WE'RE LEAVING FOR ABOUT TWO DAYS.
PLEASE LOOK AFTER THINGS.
VERY WELL. YOU CAN COUNT ON ME.
I NEVER SAID I WAS GOING.
STOP TALKING LIKE IT'S ALREADY SET.

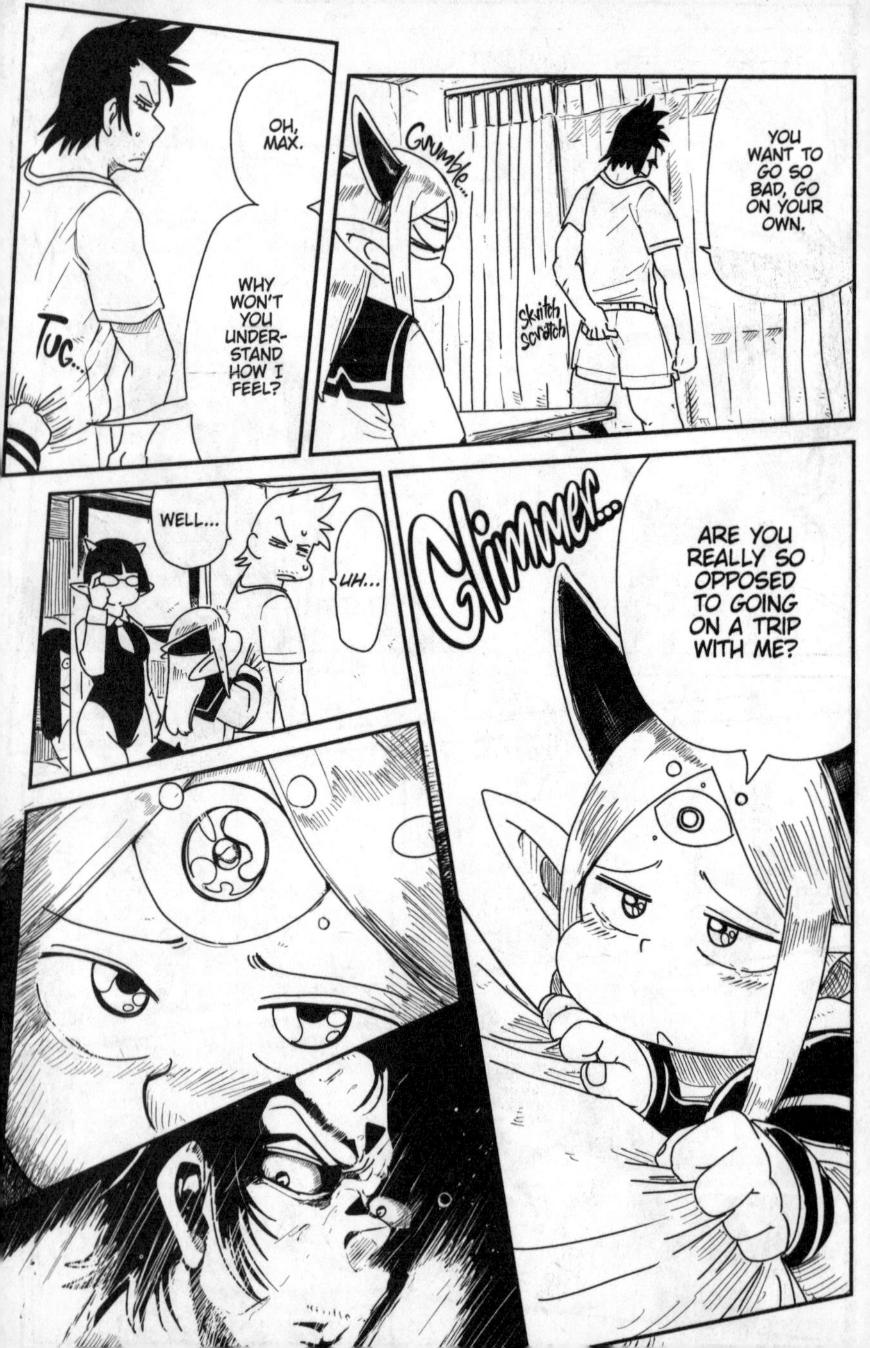
YOU WANT TO GO SO BAD, GO ON YOUR OWN.
Skritch scratch
Grumble...
OH, MAX.
WHY WON'T YOU UNDERSTAND HOW I FEEL?
TUG...
ARE YOU REALLY SO OPPOSED TO GOING ON A TRIP WITH ME?
Glimmer...
UH...
WELL...

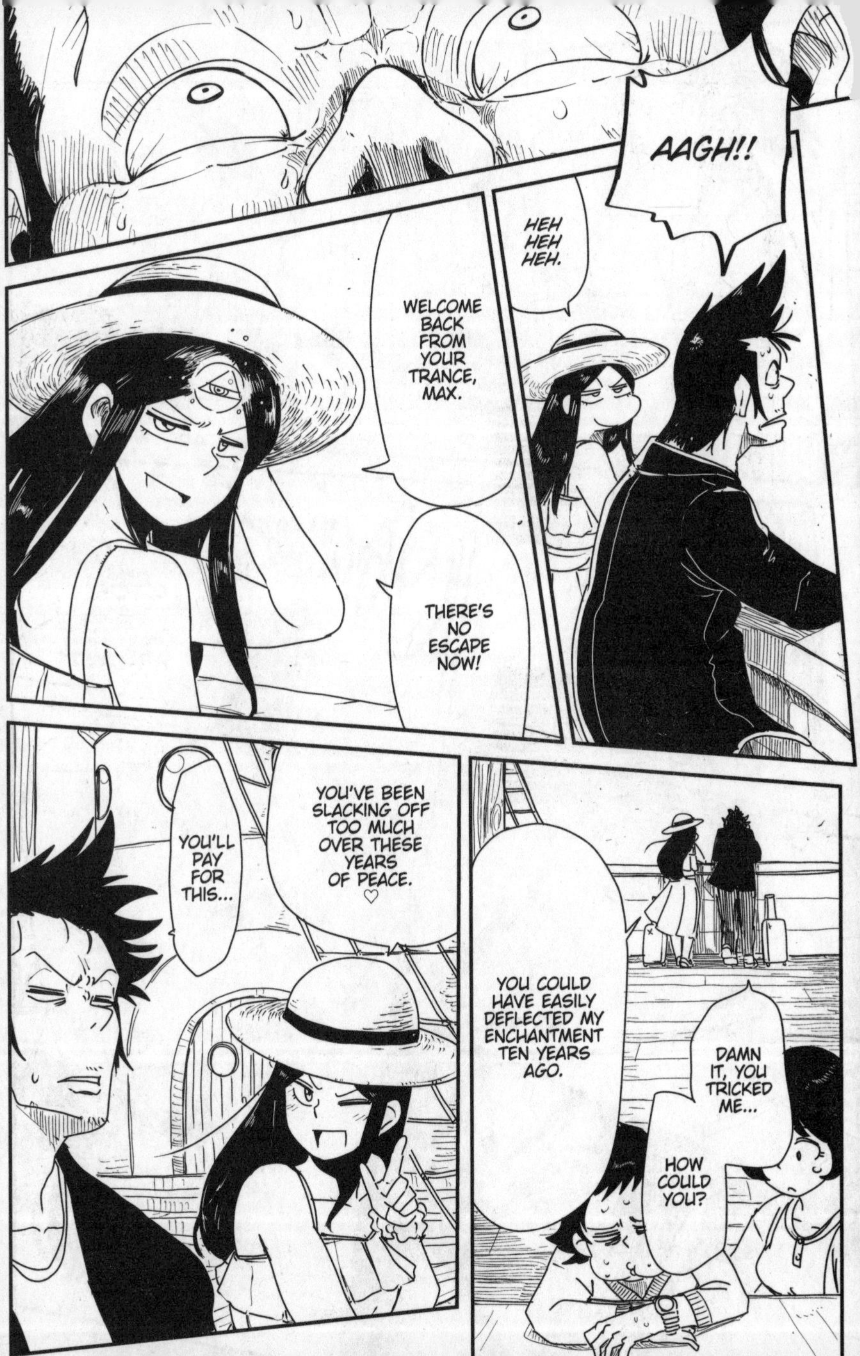
AAGH!!
HEH HEH HEH.
WELCOME BACK FROM YOUR TRANCE, MAX.
THERE'S NO ESCAPE NOW!
DAMN IT, YOU TRICKED ME...
HOW COULD YOU?
YOU COULD HAVE EASILY DEFLECTED MY ENCHANTMENT TEN YEARS AGO.
YOU'VE BEEN SLACKING OFF TOO MUCH OVER THESE YEARS OF PEACE. ♡
YOU'LL PAY FOR THIS...

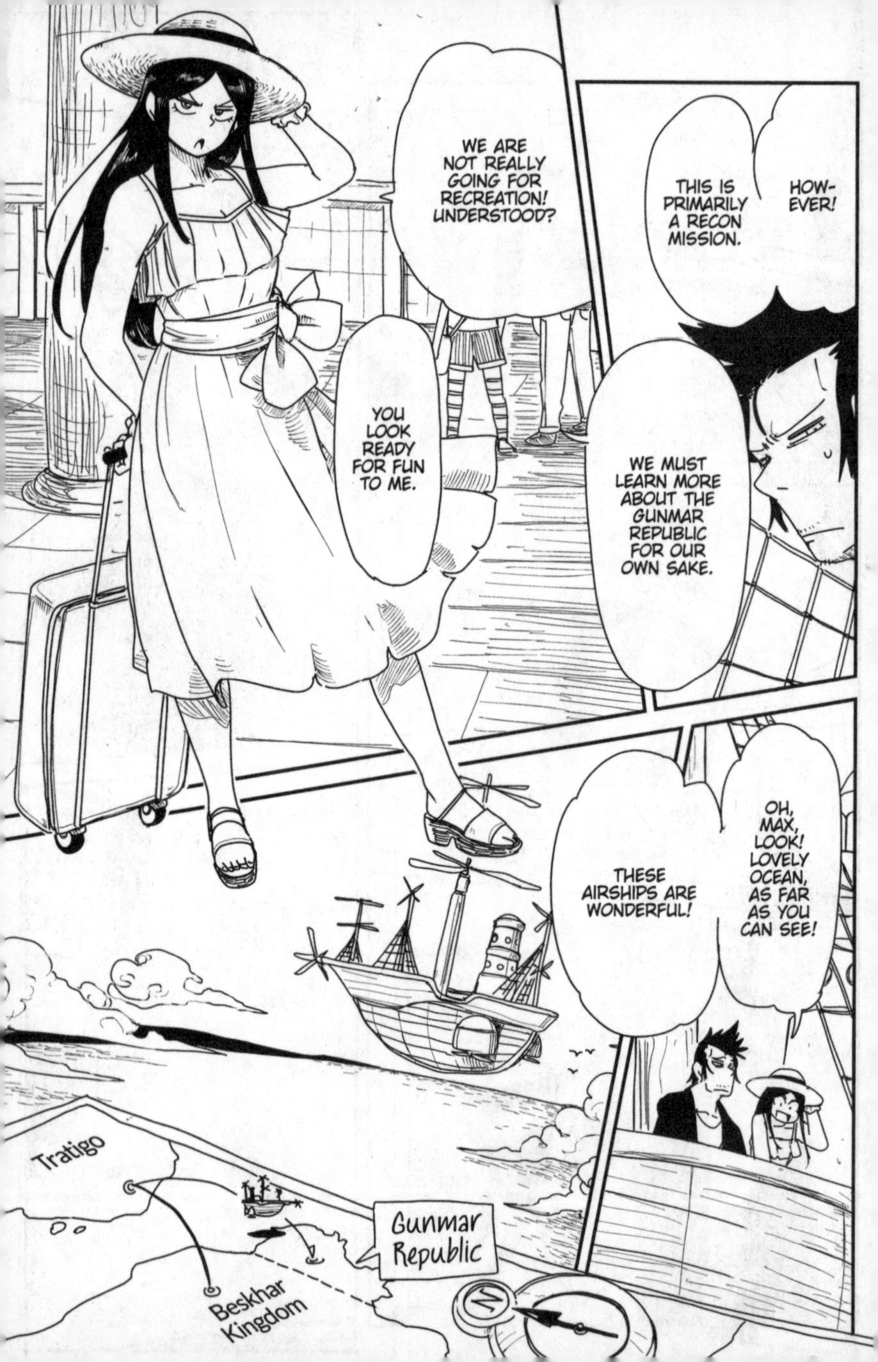
HOW-EVER!
THIS IS PRIMARILY A RECON MISSION.
WE MUST LEARN MORE ABOUT THE GUNMAR REPUBLIC FOR OUR OWN SAKE.
WE ARE NOT REALLY GOING FOR RECREATION! UNDERSTOOD?
YOU LOOK READY FOR FUN TO ME.
OH, MAX, LOOK! LOVELY OCEAN, AS FAR AS YOU CAN SEE!
THESE AIRSHIPS ARE WONDERFUL!
Gunmar Republic
Tratigo
Beskhar Kingdom

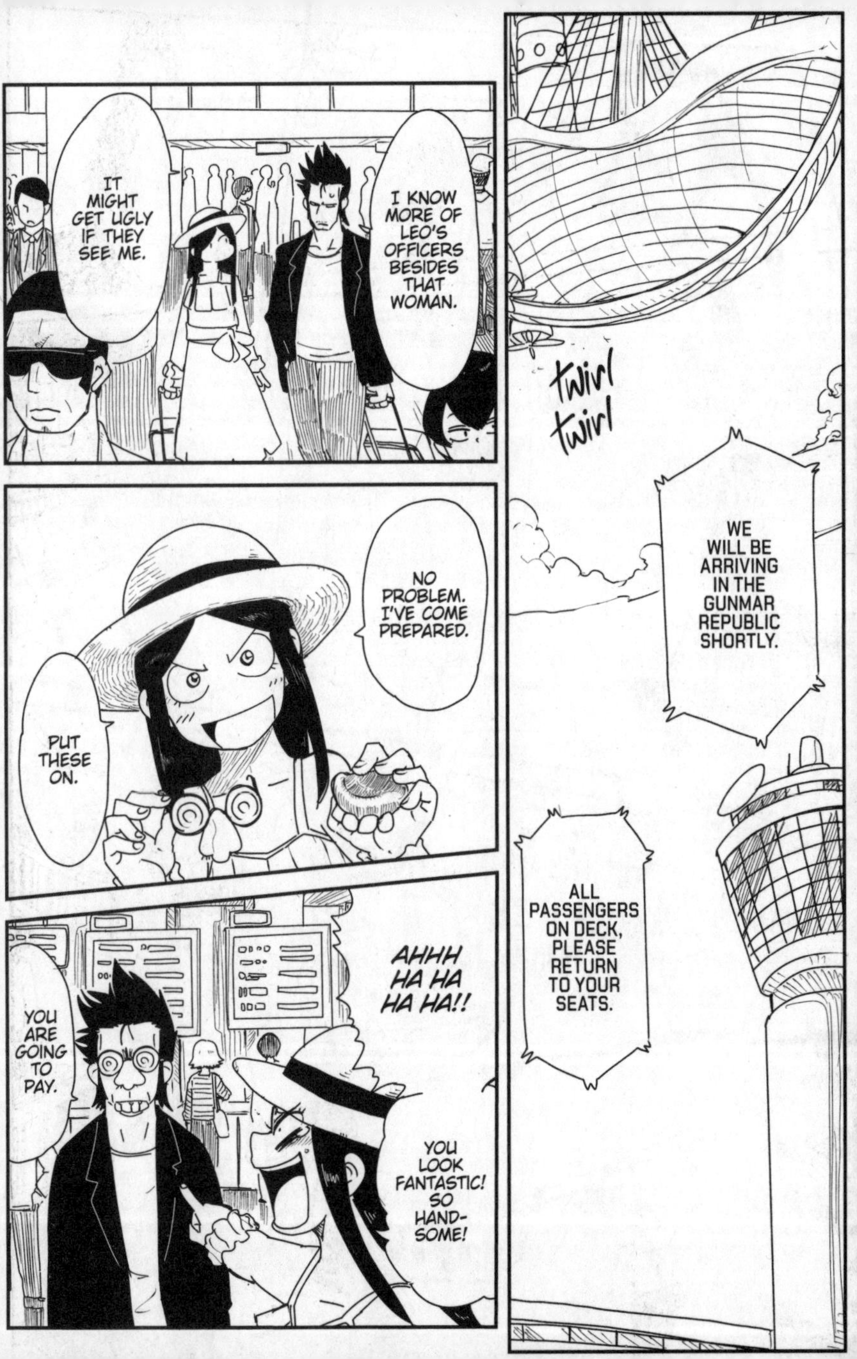
twirl twirl
WE WILL BE ARRIVING IN THE GUNMAR REPUBLIC SHORTLY.
ALL PASSENGERS ON DECK, PLEASE RETURN TO YOUR SEATS.
I KNOW MORE OF LEO'S OFFICERS BESIDES THAT WOMAN.
IT MIGHT GET UGLY IF THEY SEE ME.
NO PROBLEM. I'VE COME PREPARED.
PUT THESE ON.
AHHH HA HA HA HA!!
YOU LOOK FANTASTIC! SO HAND-SOME!
YOU ARE GOING TO PAY.

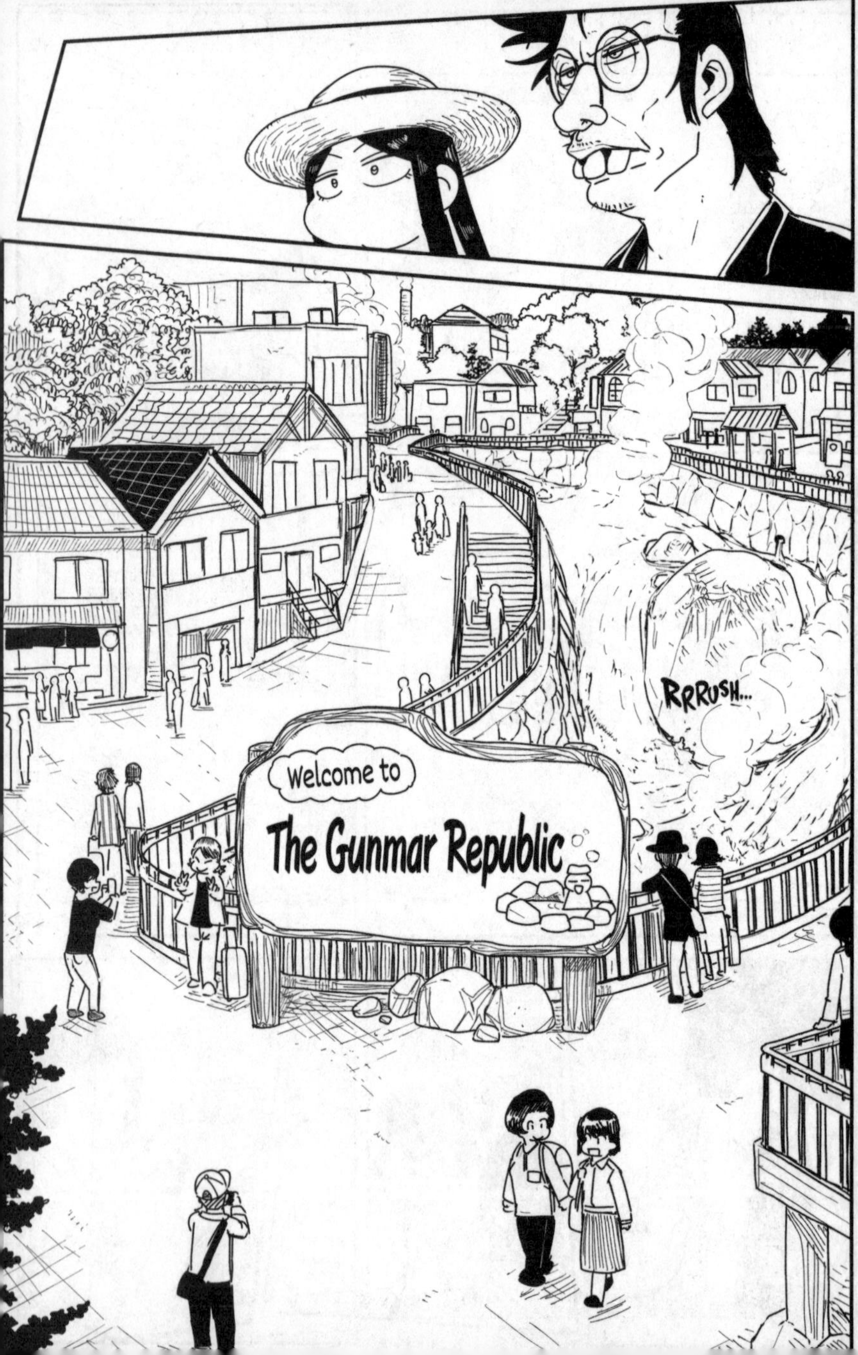
RRRUSH...
Welcome to
The Gunmar Republic

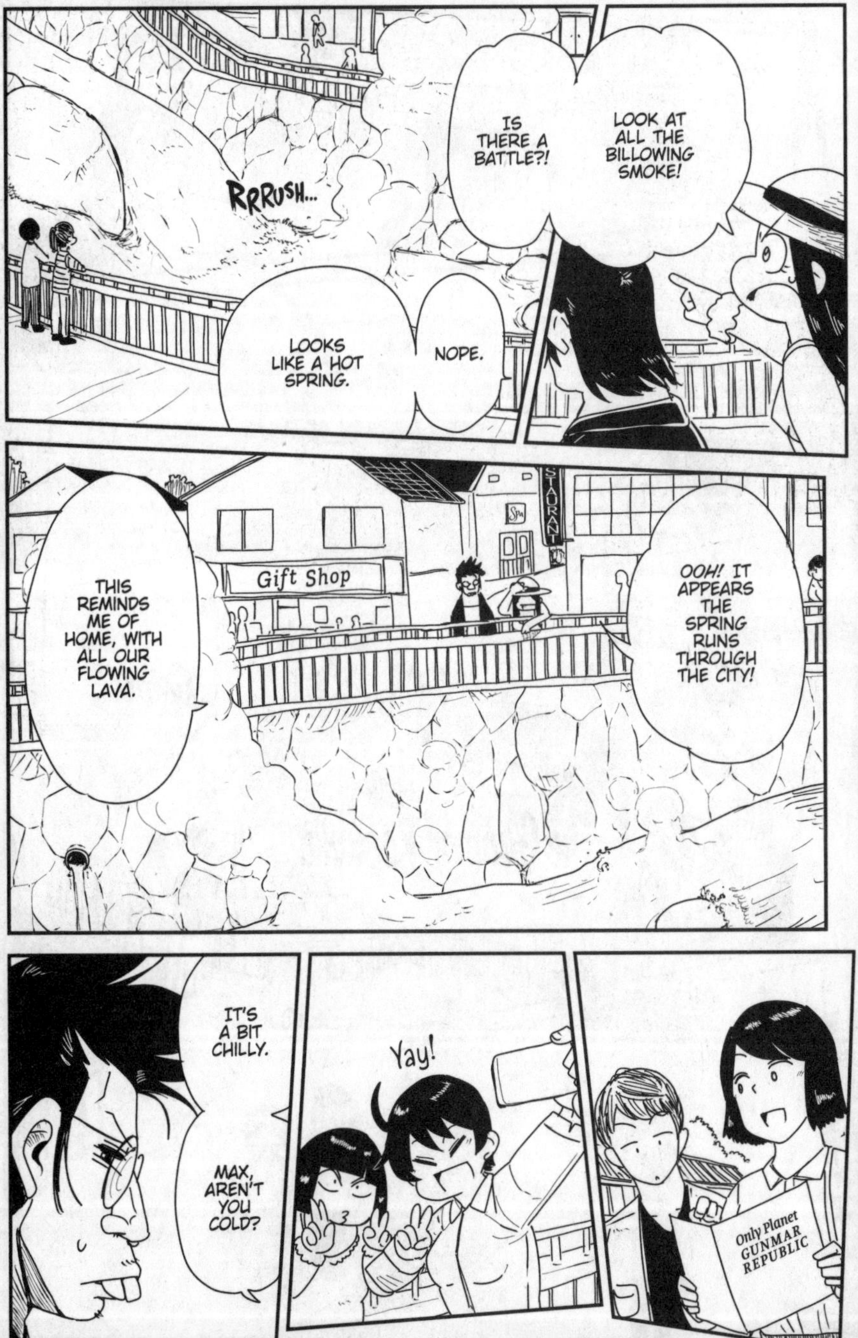
LOOK AT ALL THE BILLOWING SMOKE!
IS THERE A BATTLE?!
NOPE.
LOOKS LIKE A HOT SPRING.
RRRUSH...
OOH! IT APPEARS THE SPRING RUNS THROUGH THE CITY!
STAURANT
Spa
Gift Shop
THIS REMINDS ME OF HOME, WITH ALL OUR FLOWING LAVA.
Only Planet GUNMAR REPUBLIC
Yay!
IT'S A BIT CHILLY.
MAX, AREN'T YOU COLD?

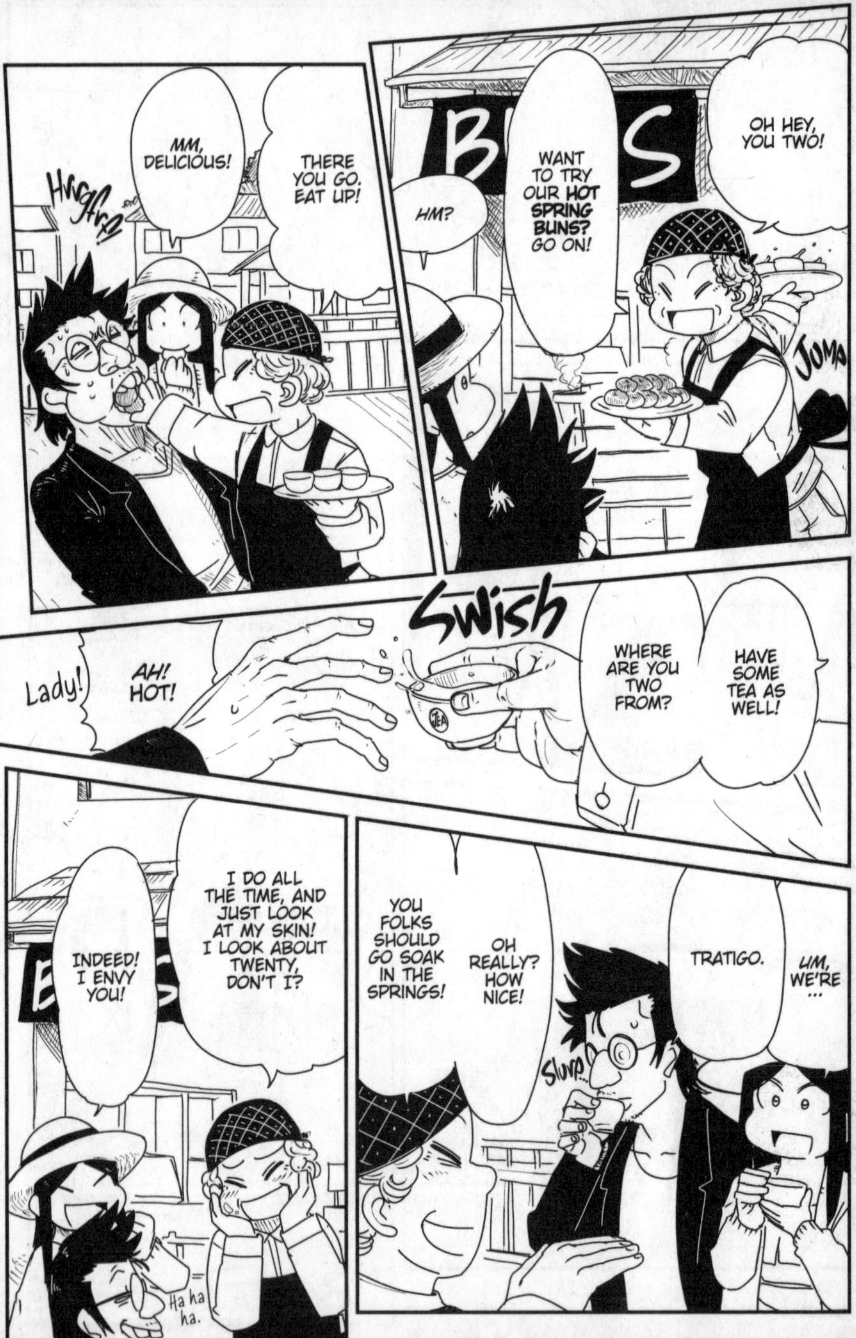
OH HEY, YOU TWO!
WANT TO TRY OUR HOT SPRING BUNS? GO ON!
HM?
THERE YOU GO. EAT UP!
MM, DELICIOUS!
Swish
HAVE SOME TEA AS WELL!
WHERE ARE YOU TWO FROM?
AH! HOT!
Lady!
UM, WE'RE ...
TRATIGO.
Slurp...
OH REALLY? HOW NICE!
YOU FOLKS SHOULD GO SOAK IN THE SPRINGS!
I DO ALL THE TIME, AND JUST LOOK AT MY SKIN! I LOOK ABOUT TWENTY, DON'T I?
INDEED! I ENVY YOU!
Ha ha ha.

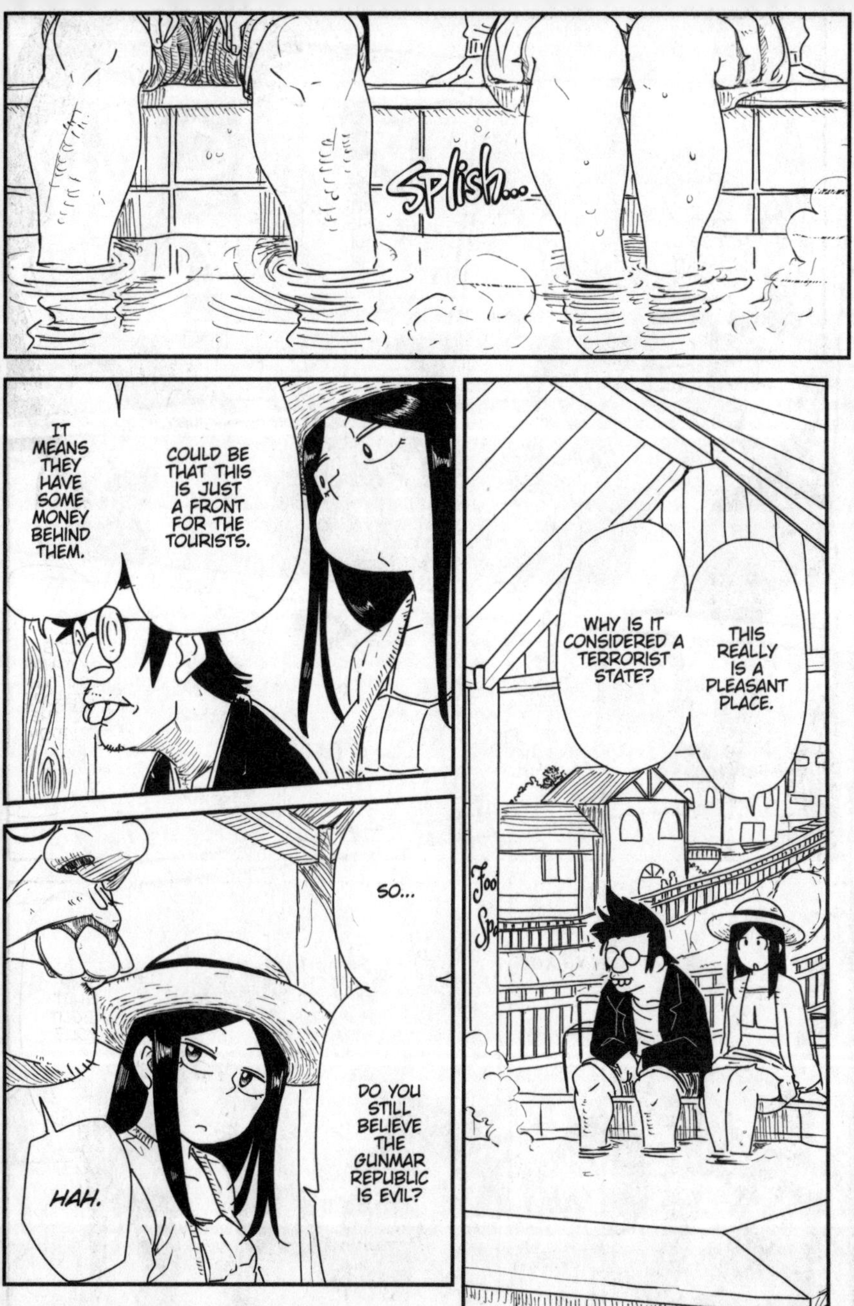
Splish...
THIS REALLY IS A PLEASANT PLACE.
WHY IS IT CONSIDERED A TERRORIST STATE?
COULD BE THAT THIS IS JUST A FRONT FOR THE TOURISTS.
IT MEANS THEY HAVE SOME MONEY BEHIND THEM.
SO...
DO YOU STILL BELIEVE THE GUNMAR REPUBLIC IS EVIL?
HAH.

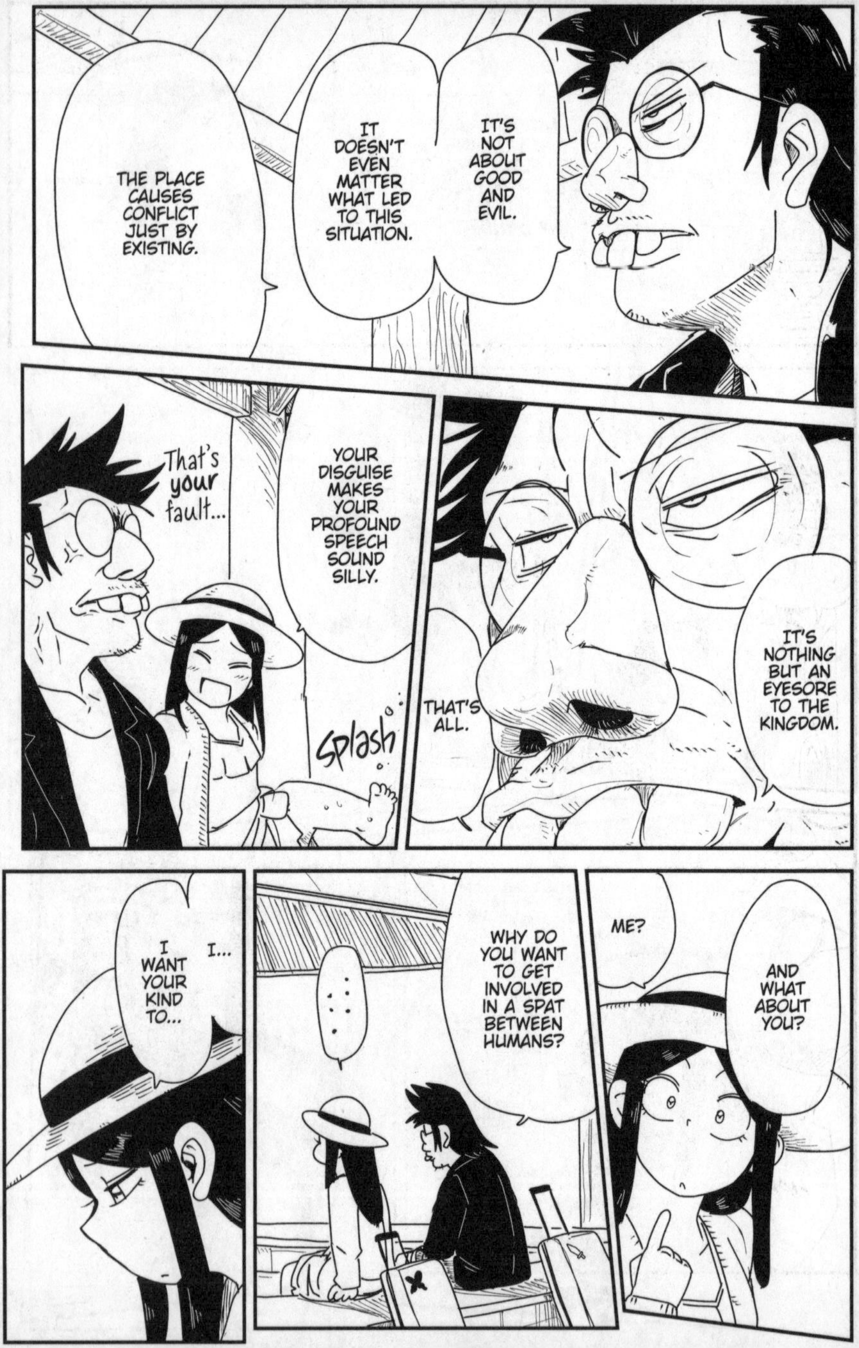
IT'S NOT ABOUT GOOD AND EVIL.
IT DOESN'T EVEN MATTER WHAT LED TO THIS SITUATION.
THE PLACE CAUSES CONFLICT JUST BY EXISTING.
IT'S NOTHING BUT AN EYESORE TO THE KINGDOM.
THAT'S ALL.
YOUR DISGUISE MAKES YOUR PROFOUND SPEECH SOUND SILLY.
Splash
That's your fault...
AND WHAT ABOUT YOU?
ME?
WHY DO YOU WANT TO GET INVOLVED IN A SPAT BETWEEN HUMANS?
...
I...
I WANT YOUR KIND TO...

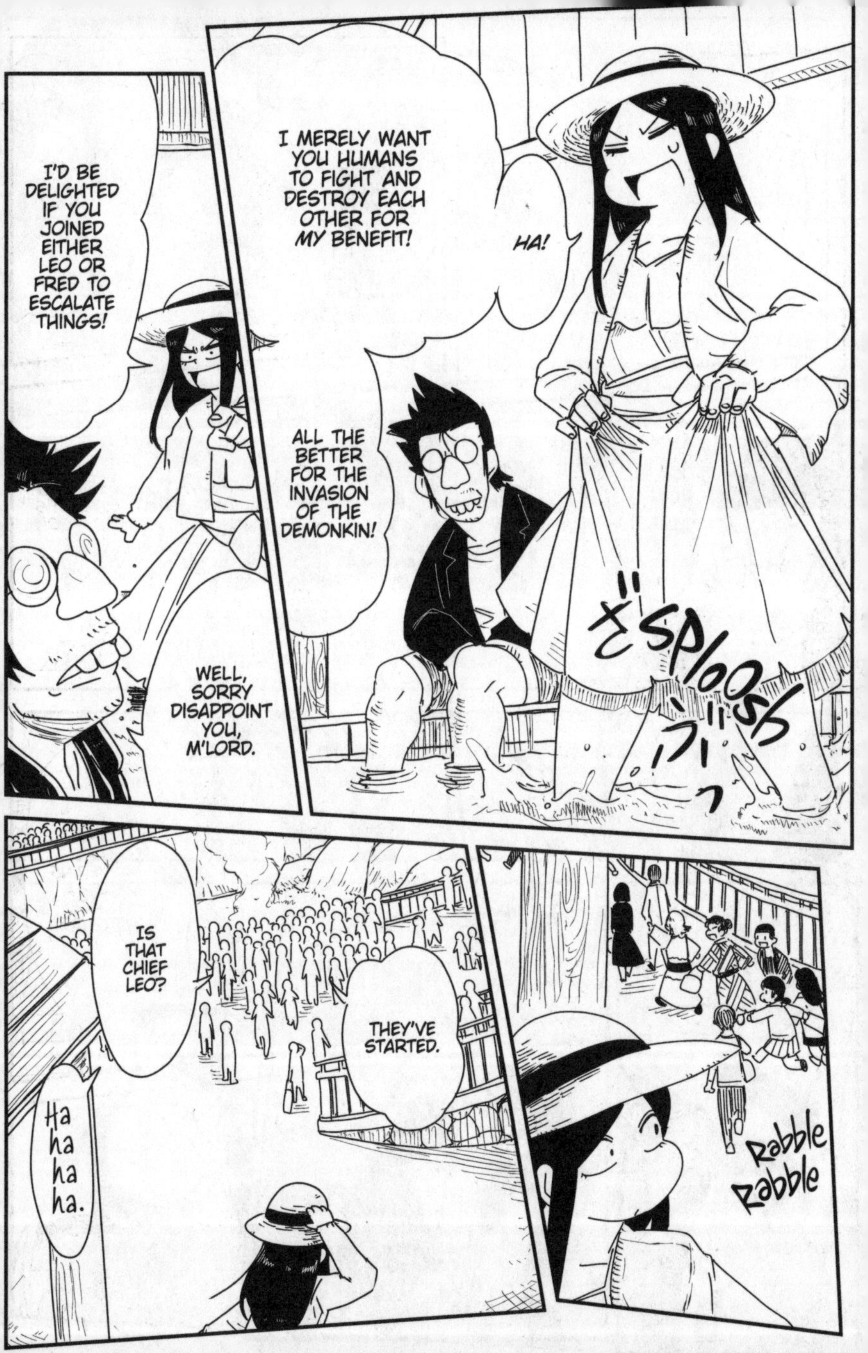
I MERELY WANT YOU HUMANS TO FIGHT AND DESTROY EACH OTHER FOR MY BENEFIT!
HA!
ALL THE BETTER FOR THE INVASION OF THE DEMONKIN!
splOOsh
I'D BE DELIGHTED IF YOU JOINED EITHER LEO OR FRED TO ESCALATE THINGS!
WELL, SORRY DISAPPOINT YOU, M'LORD.
Rabble Rabble
THEY'VE STARTED.
IS THAT CHIEF LEO?
Ha ha ha ha.

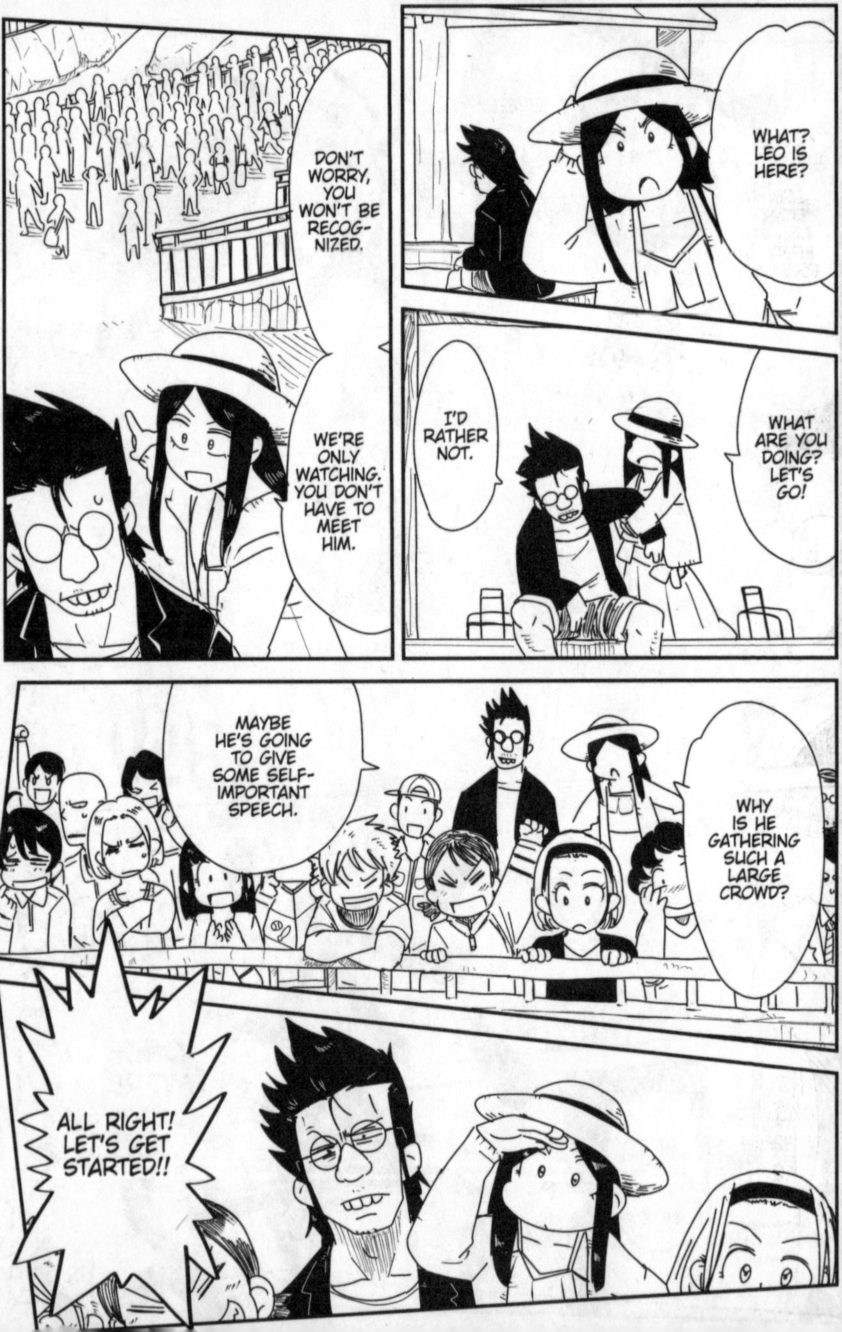
WHAT? LEO IS HERE?
WHAT ARE YOU DOING? LET'S GO!
I'D RATHER NOT.
DON'T WORRY, YOU WON'T BE RECOG-NIZED.
WE'RE ONLY WATCHING. YOU DON'T HAVE TO MEET HIM.
WHY IS HE GATHERING SUCH A LARGE CROWD?
MAYBE HE'S GOING TO GIVE SOME SELF-IMPORTANT SPEECH.
ALL RIGHT! LET'S GET STARTED!!

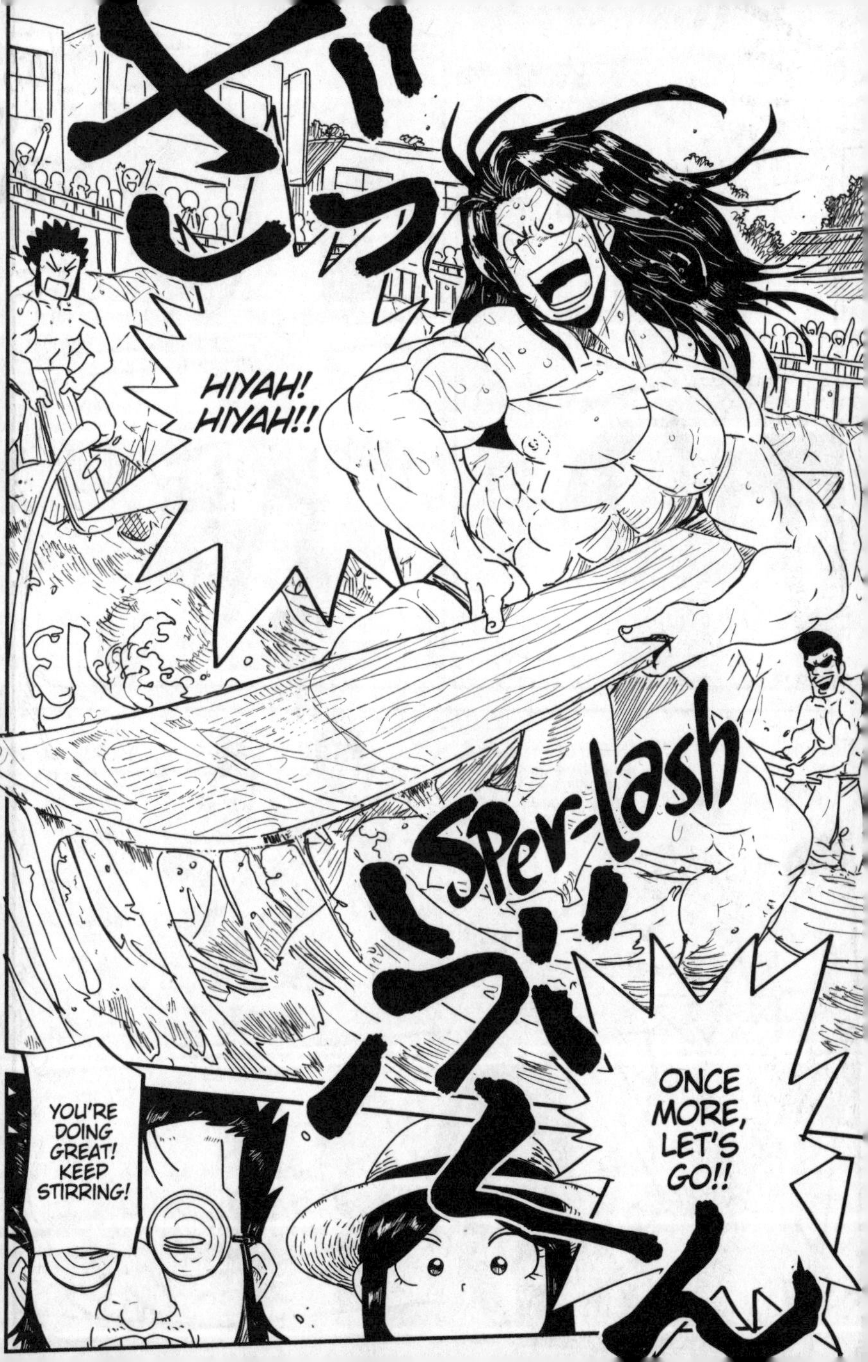
HIYAH! HIYAH!!
SPER-LASH
ONCE MORE, LET'S GO!!
YOU'RE DOING GREAT! KEEP STIRRING!

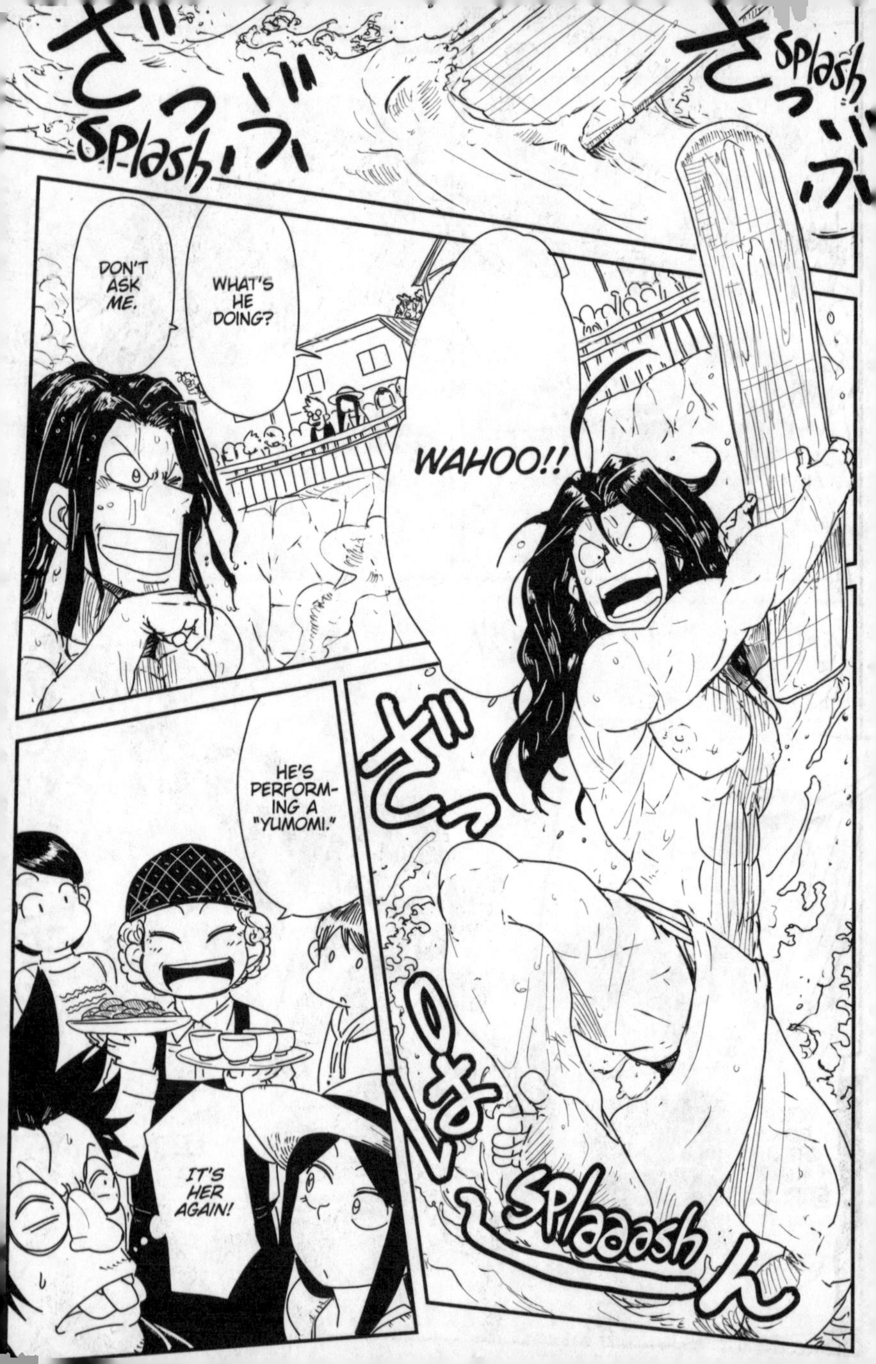
ざっぶ
Splash
ざっぶ
Splash
WAHOO!!
ざっぱ〜ん
Splaaash
WHAT'S HE DOING?
DON'T ASK ME.
HE'S PERFORMING A "YUMOMI."
IT'S HER AGAIN!

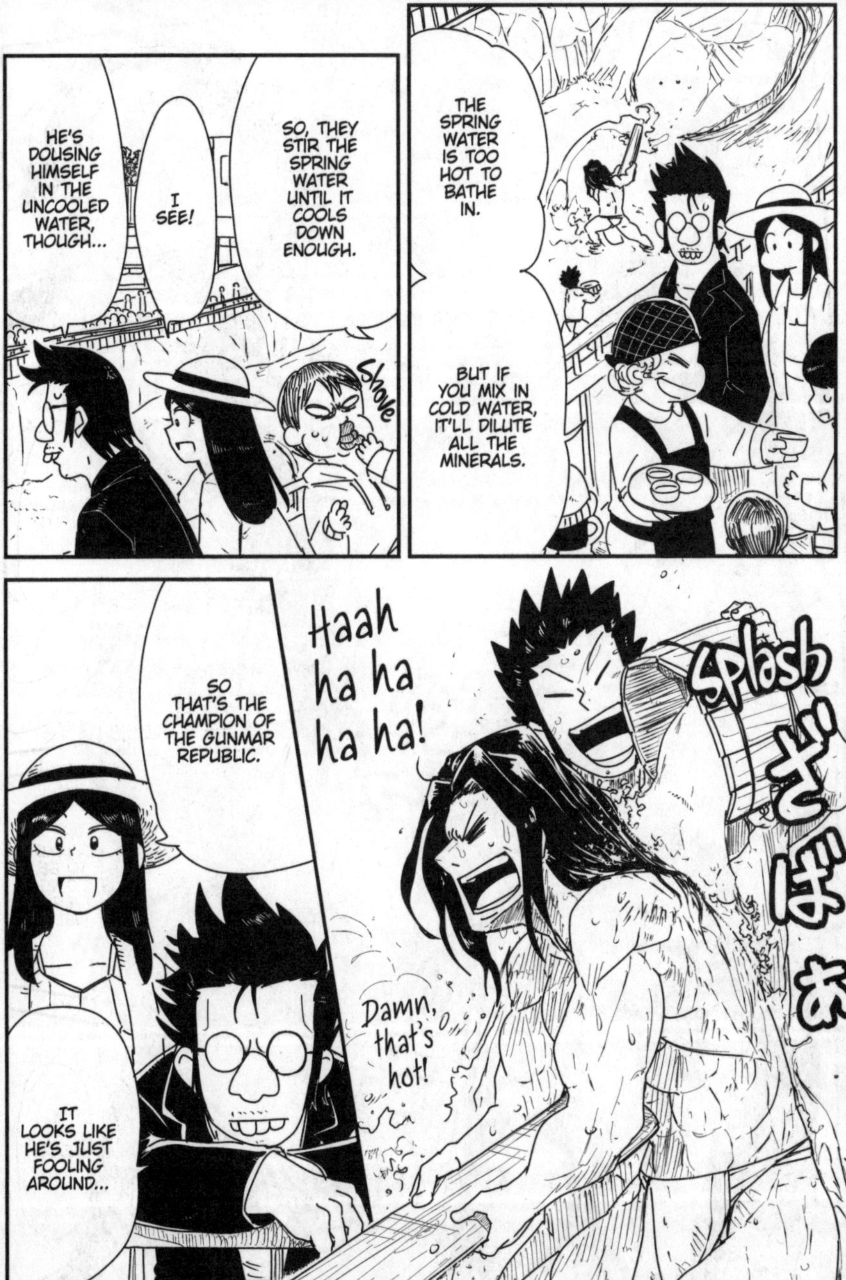
THE SPRING WATER IS TOO HOT TO BATHE IN.
BUT IF YOU MIX IN COLD WATER, IT'LL DILUTE ALL THE MINERALS.
SO, THEY STIR THE SPRING WATER UNTIL IT COOLS DOWN ENOUGH.
I SEE!
HE'S DOUSING HIMSELF IN THE UNCOOLED WATER, THOUGH...
Shove
splash
ざぼぁ
Haah ha ha ha ha!
Damn, that's hot!
SO THAT'S THE CHAMPION OF THE GUNMAR REPUBLIC.
IT LOOKS LIKE HE'S JUST FOOLING AROUND...

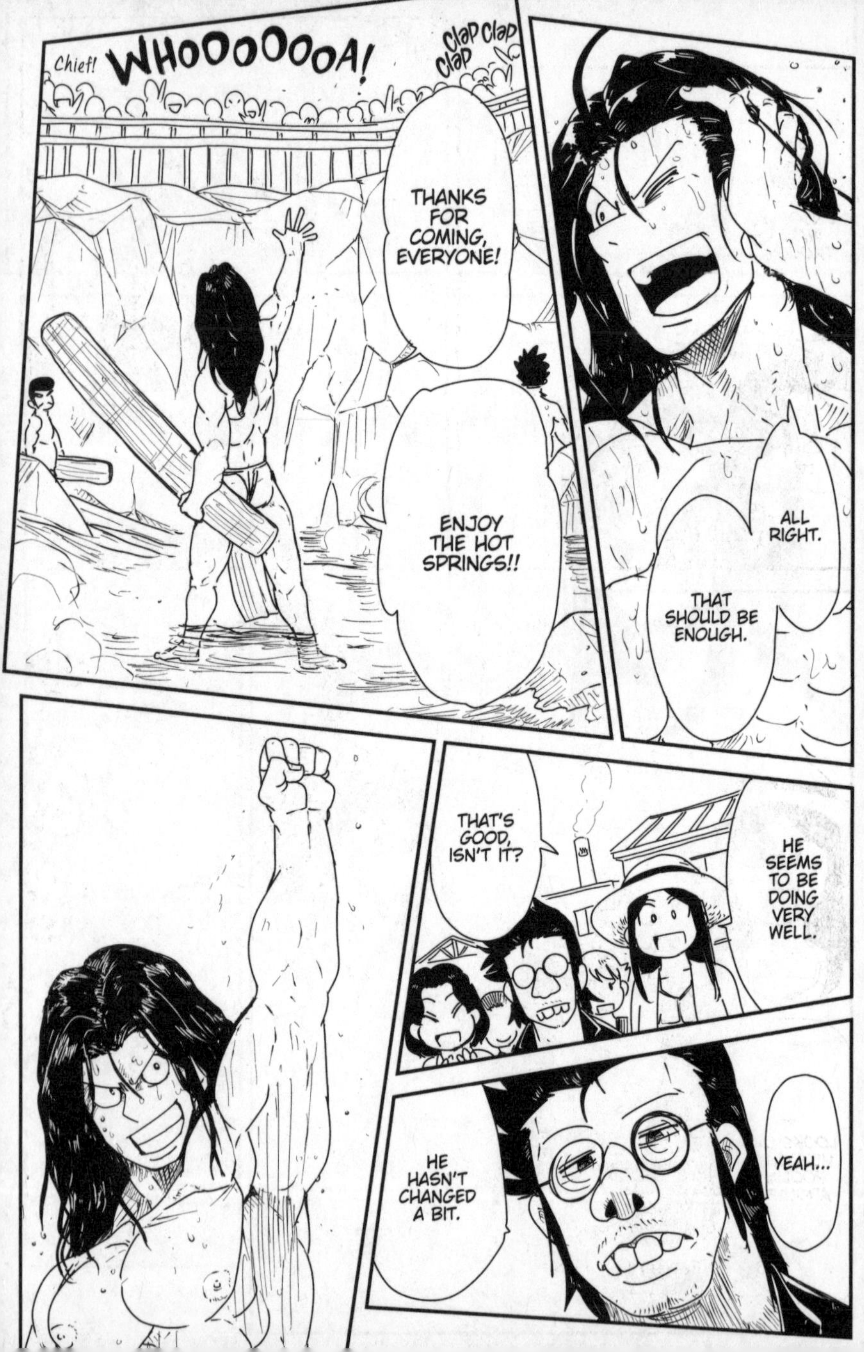
ALL RIGHT.
THAT SHOULD BE ENOUGH.
Chief!
WHOOOOOOA!
Clap Clap Clap
THANKS FOR COMING, EVERYONE!
ENJOY THE HOT SPRINGS!!
HE SEEMS TO BE DOING VERY WELL.
THAT'S GOOD, ISN'T IT?
YEAH...
HE HASN'T CHANGED A BIT.

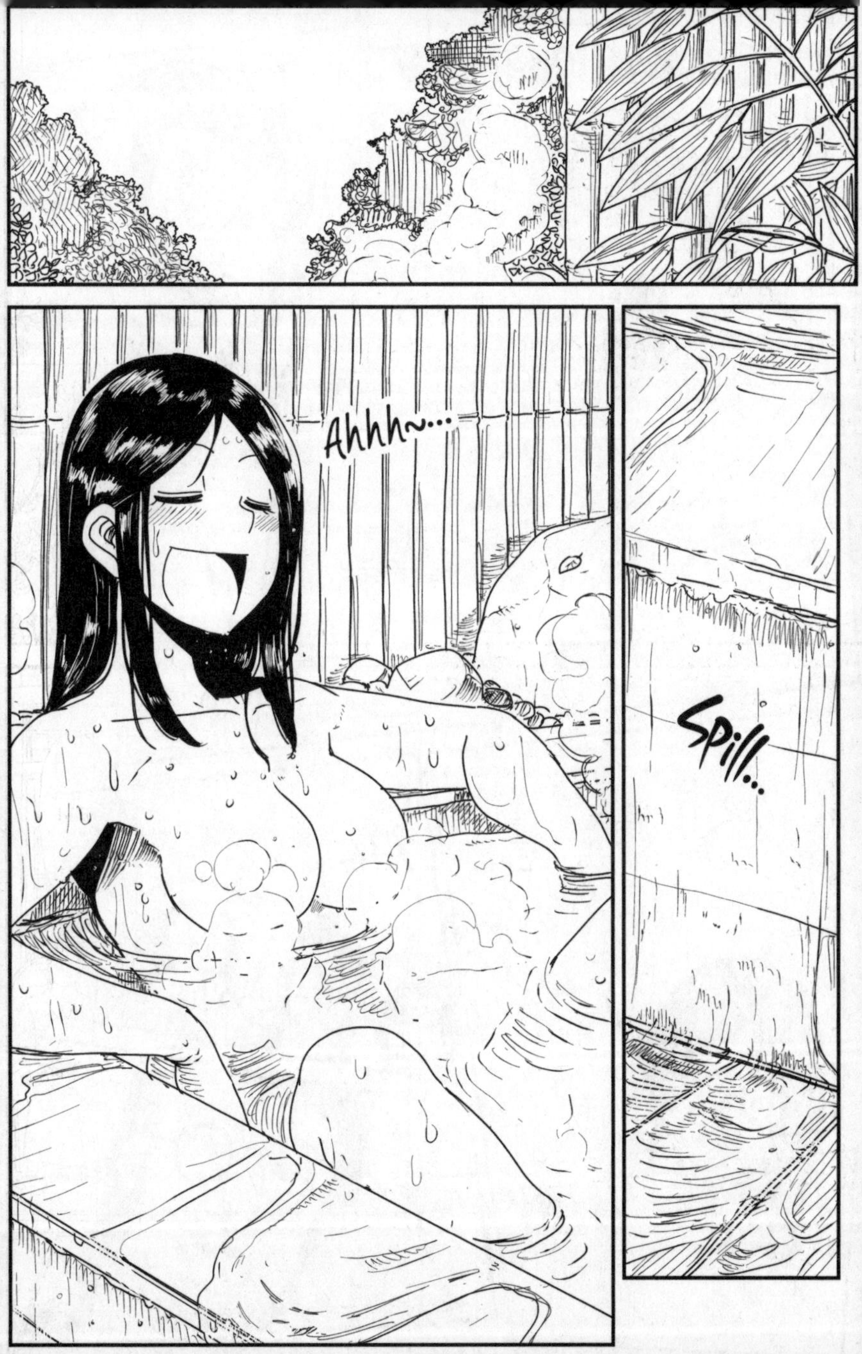
Spill...
Ahhh~...

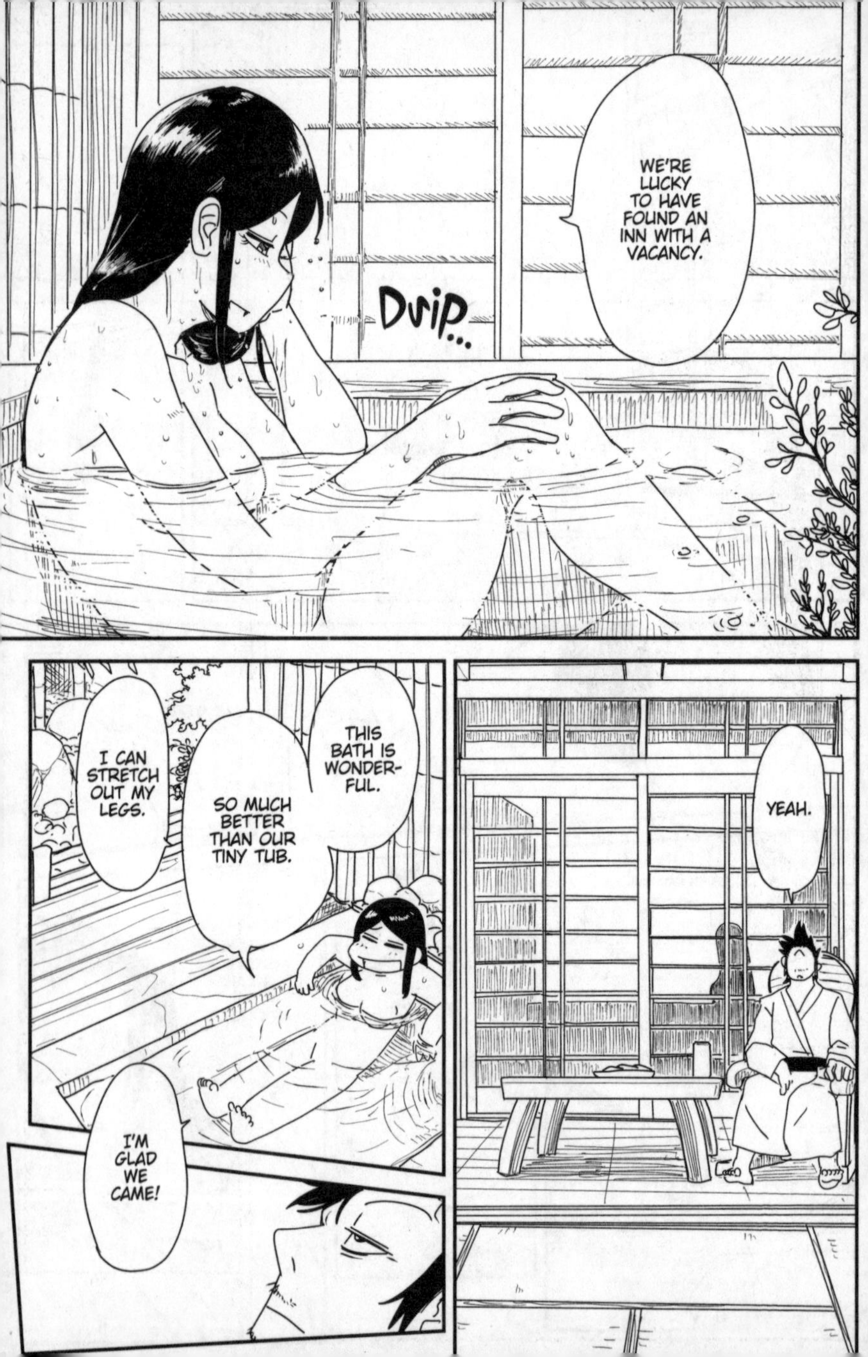
WE'RE LUCKY TO HAVE FOUND AN INN WITH A VACANCY.
Drip...
YEAH.
THIS BATH IS WONDERFUL.
SO MUCH BETTER THAN OUR TINY TUB.
I CAN STRETCH OUT MY LEGS.
I'M GLAD WE CAME!

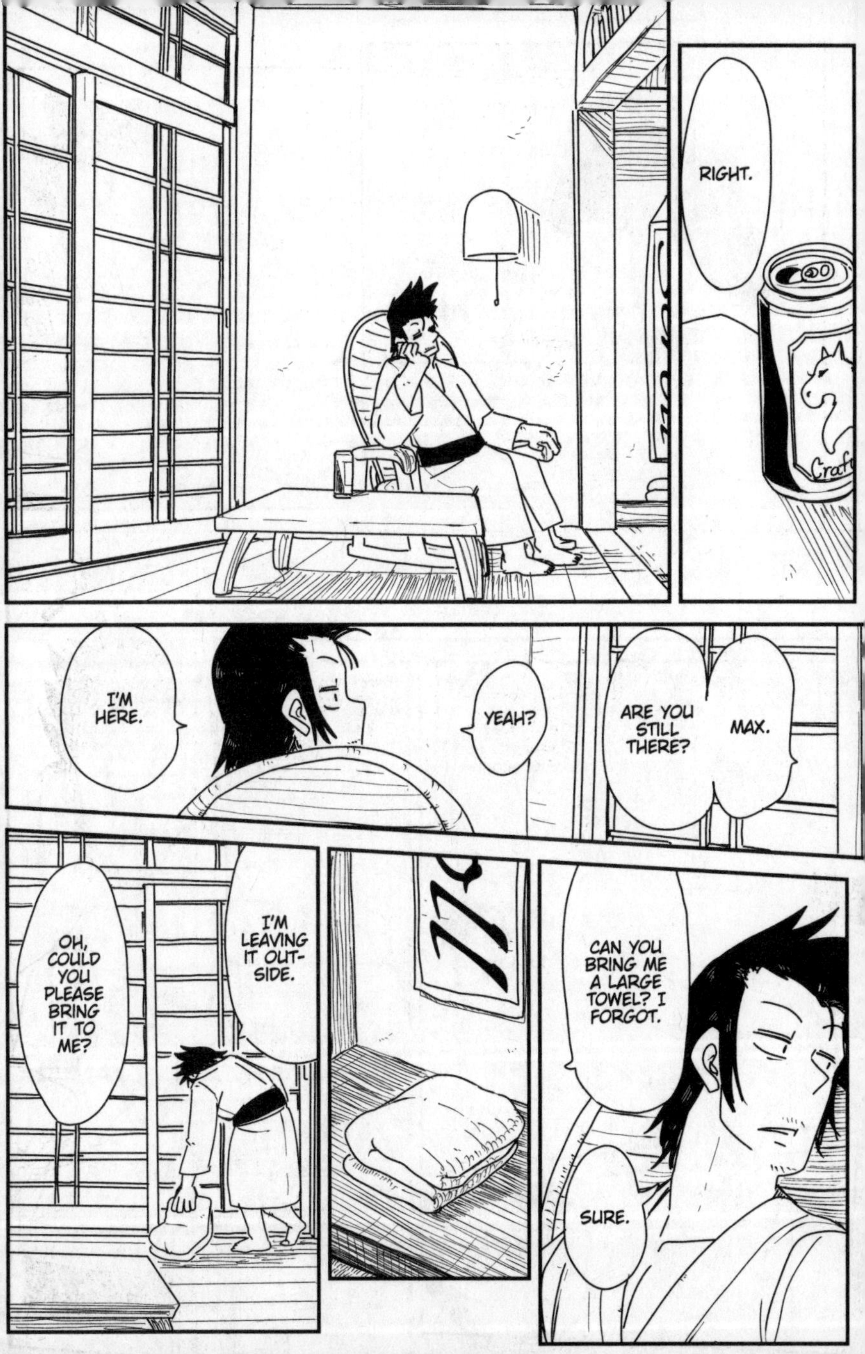
RIGHT.
MAX.
ARE YOU STILL THERE?
YEAH?
I'M HERE.
CAN YOU BRING ME A LARGE TOWEL? I FORGOT.
SURE.
I'M LEAVING IT OUT-SIDE.
OH, COULD YOU PLEASE BRING IT TO ME?

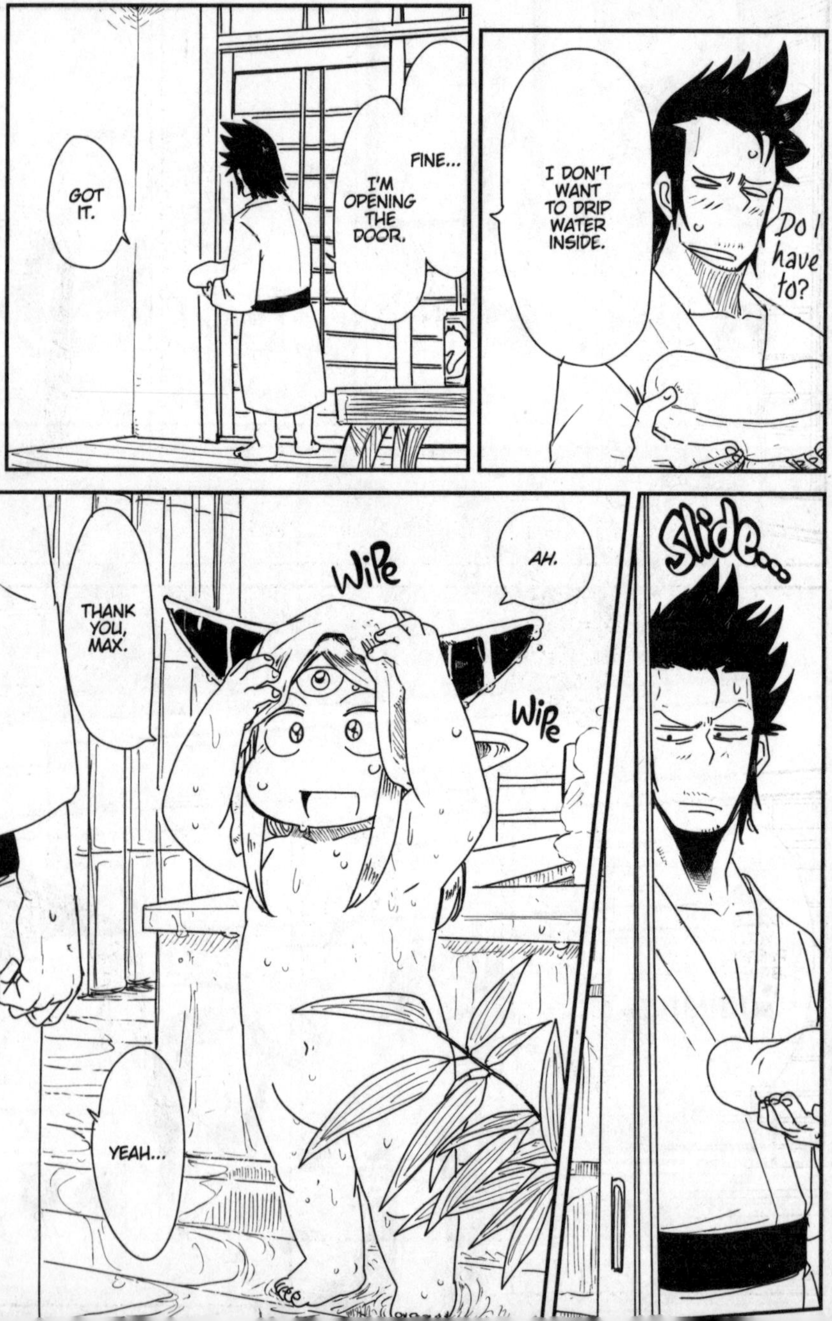
I DON'T WANT TO DRIP WATER INSIDE.
Do I have to?
FINE... I'M OPENING THE DOOR.
GOT IT.
Slide...
AH.
Wipe
Wipe
THANK YOU, MAX.
YEAH...

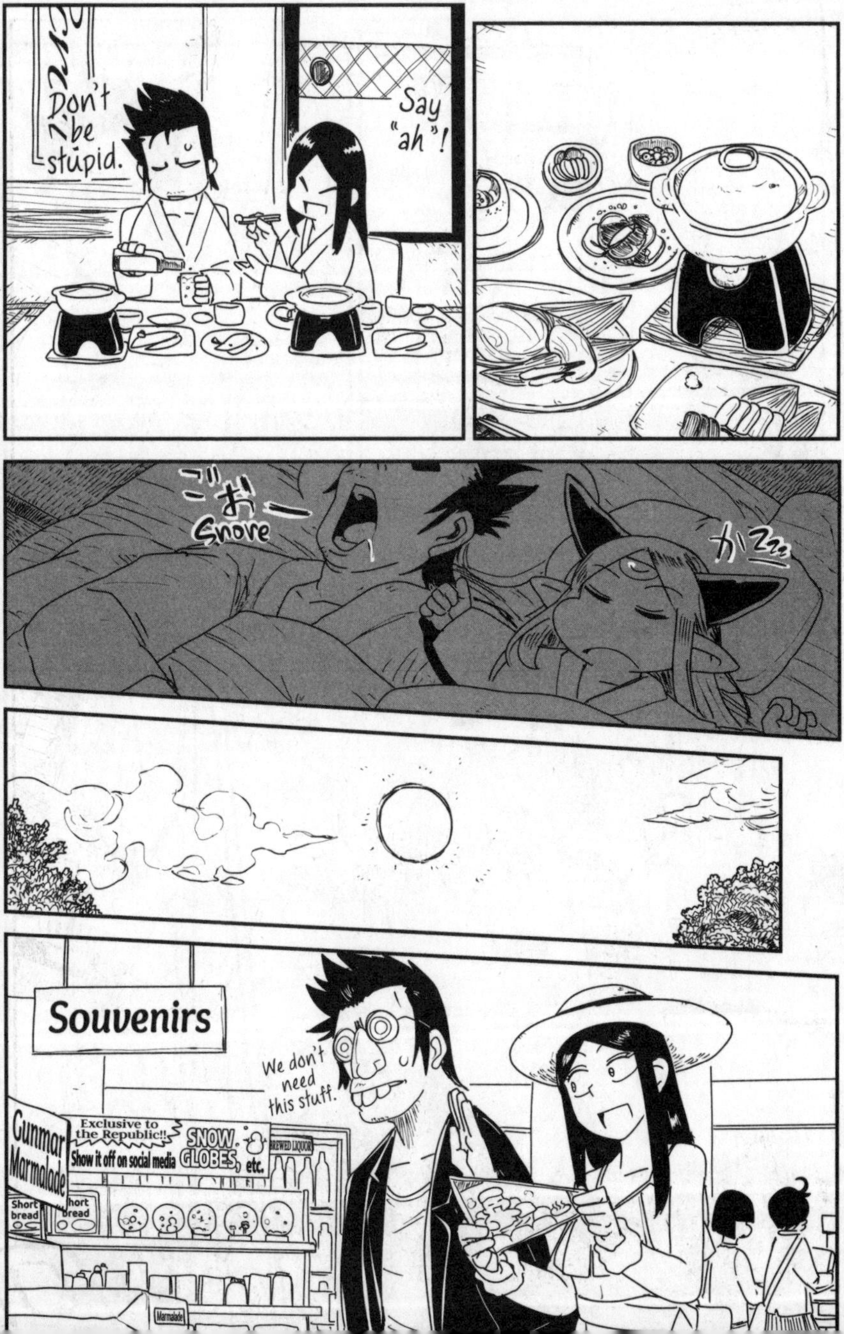
Say "ah"!
Don't be stupid.
ごおー
Snore
かzzz
Souvenirs
We don't need this stuff.
BREWED LIQUOR
Exclusive to the Republic!!
Show it off on social media
SNOW GLOBES, etc.
Gunmar Marmalade
Short bread
Short bread
Marmalade

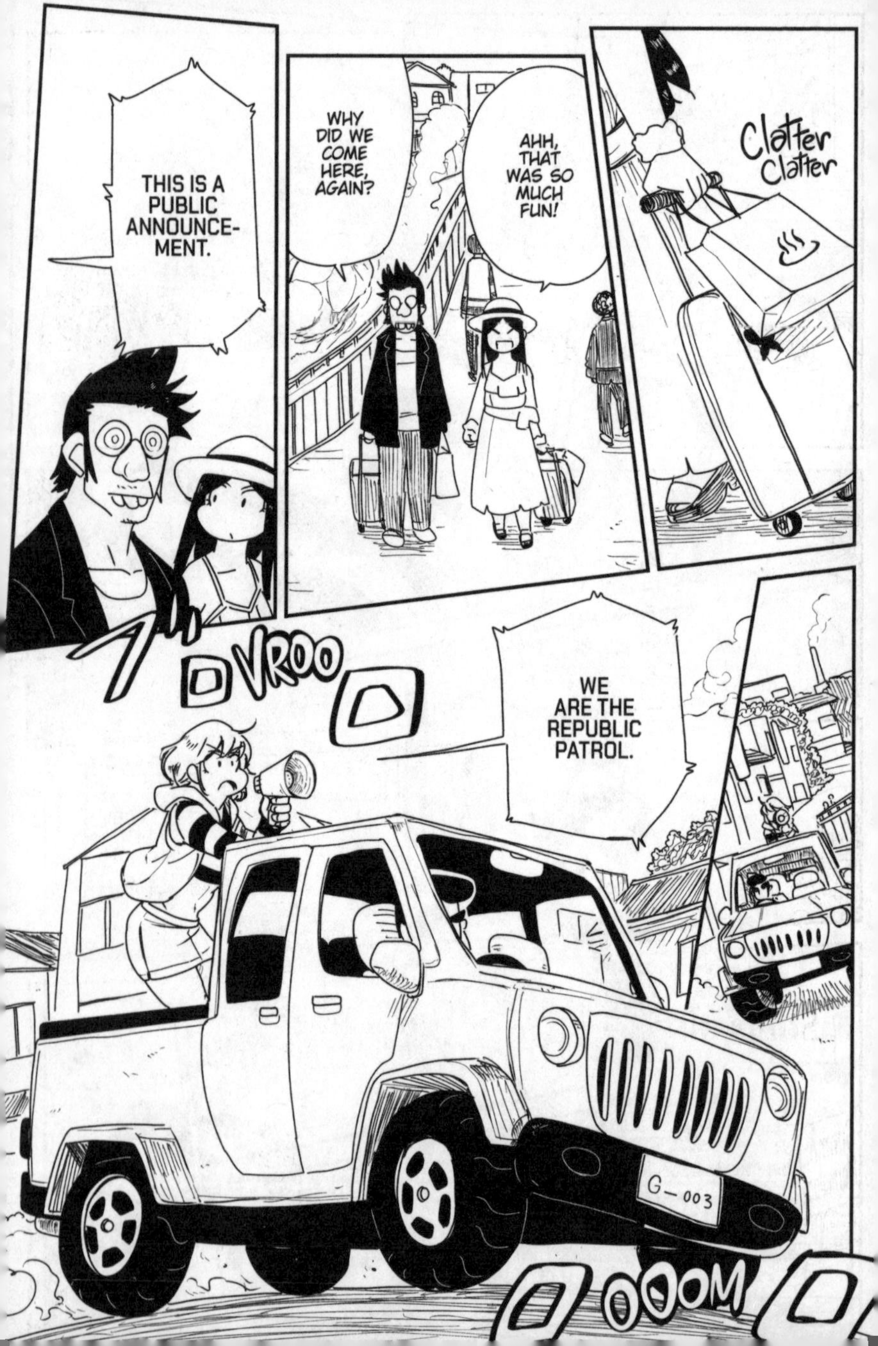
Clatter Clatter
AHH, THAT WAS SO MUCH FUN!
WHY DID WE COME HERE, AGAIN?
THIS IS A PUBLIC ANNOUNCEMENT.
WE ARE THE REPUBLIC PATROL.
VROO
OOOM
G-003

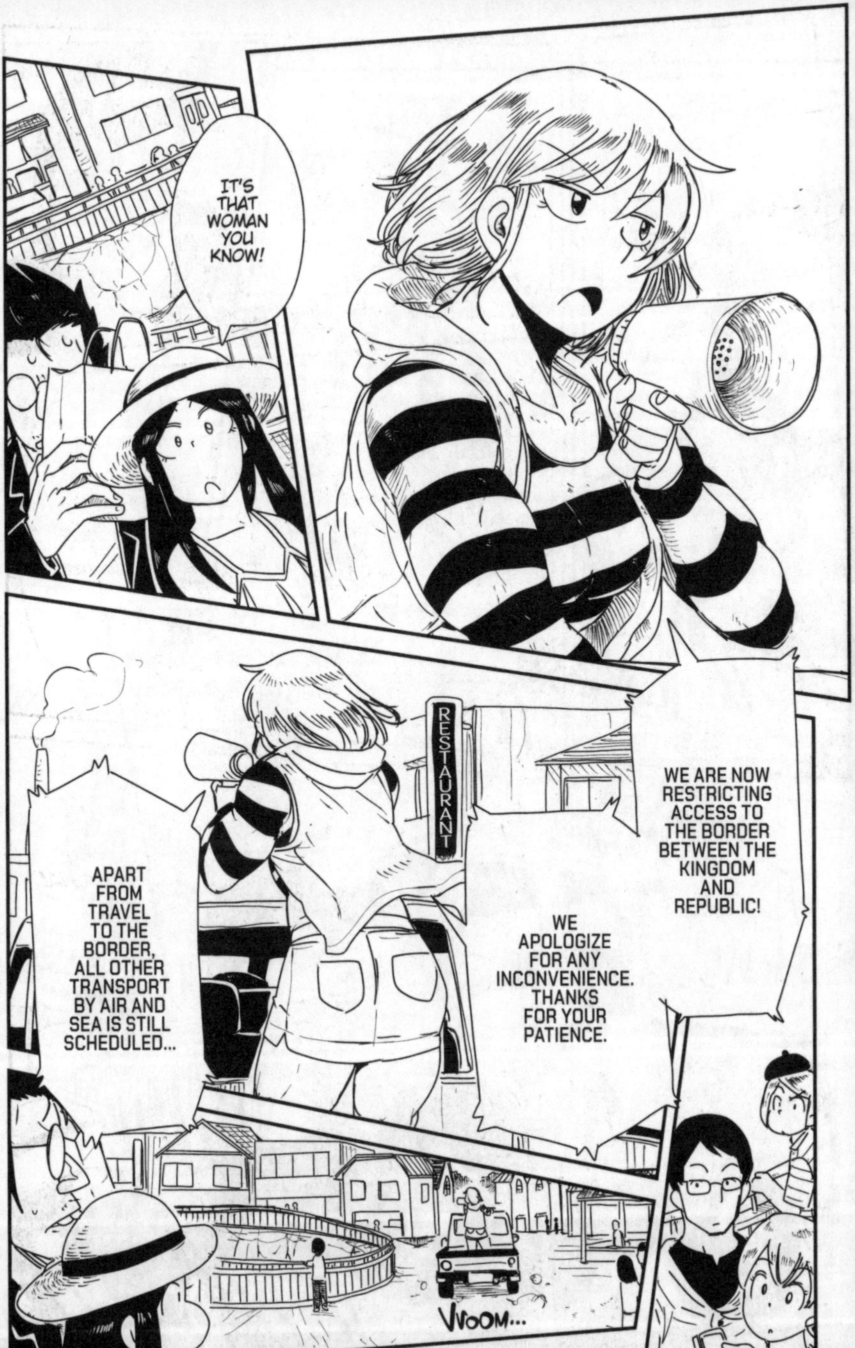
IT'S THAT WOMAN YOU KNOW!
WE ARE NOW RESTRICTING ACCESS TO THE BORDER BETWEEN THE KINGDOM AND REPUBLIC!
RESTAURANT
WE APOLOGIZE FOR ANY INCONVENIENCE. THANKS FOR YOUR PATIENCE.
APART FROM TRAVEL TO THE BORDER, ALL OTHER TRANSPORT BY AIR AND SEA IS STILL SCHEDULED...
VROOM...

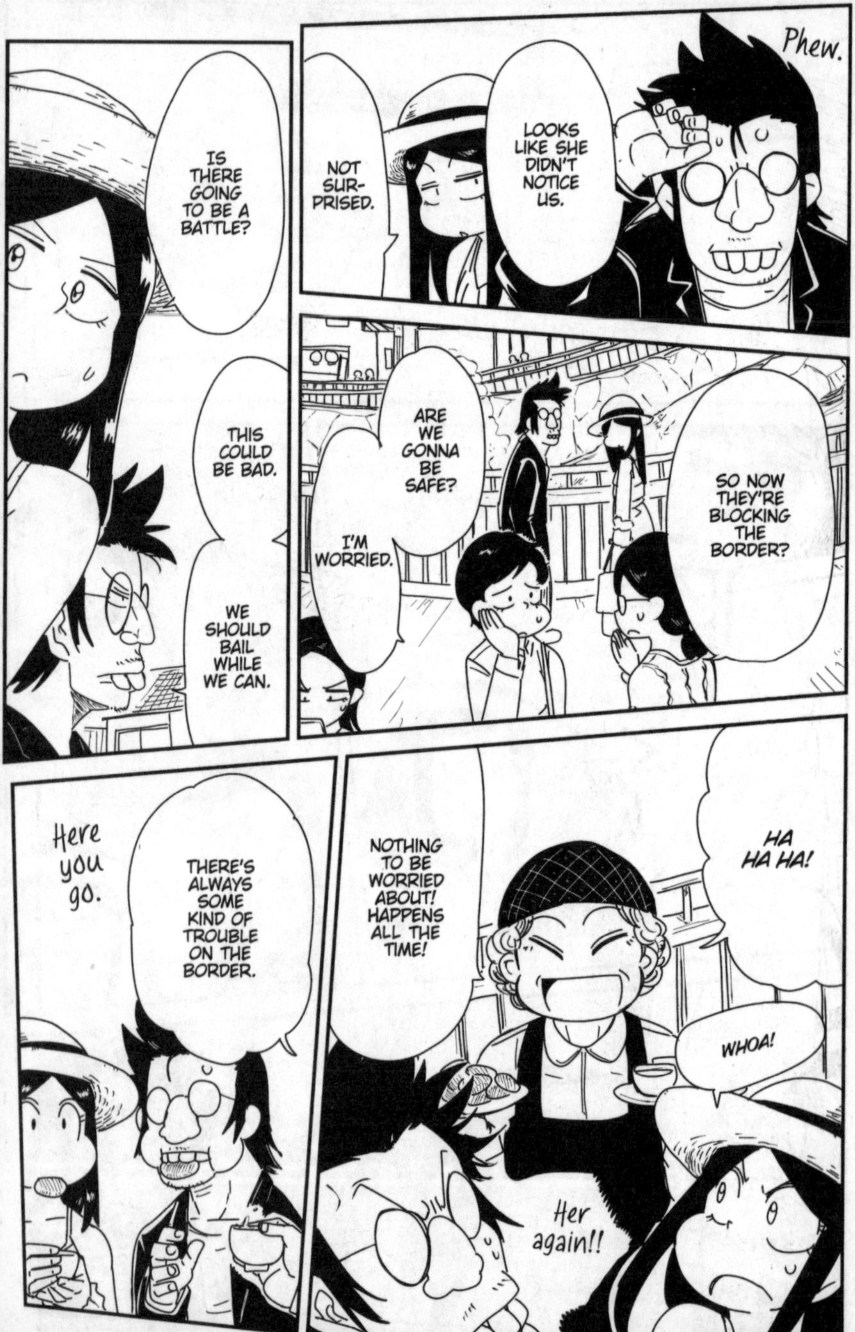
Phew.
LOOKS LIKE SHE DIDN'T NOTICE US.
NOT SURPRISED.
SO NOW THEY'RE BLOCKING THE BORDER?
ARE WE GONNA BE SAFE?
I'M WORRIED.
IS THERE GOING TO BE A BATTLE?
THIS COULD BE BAD.
WE SHOULD BAIL WHILE WE CAN.
HA HA HA!
WHOA!
NOTHING TO BE WORRIED ABOUT! HAPPENS ALL THE TIME!
Her again!!
THERE'S ALWAYS SOME KIND OF TROUBLE ON THE BORDER.
Here you go.

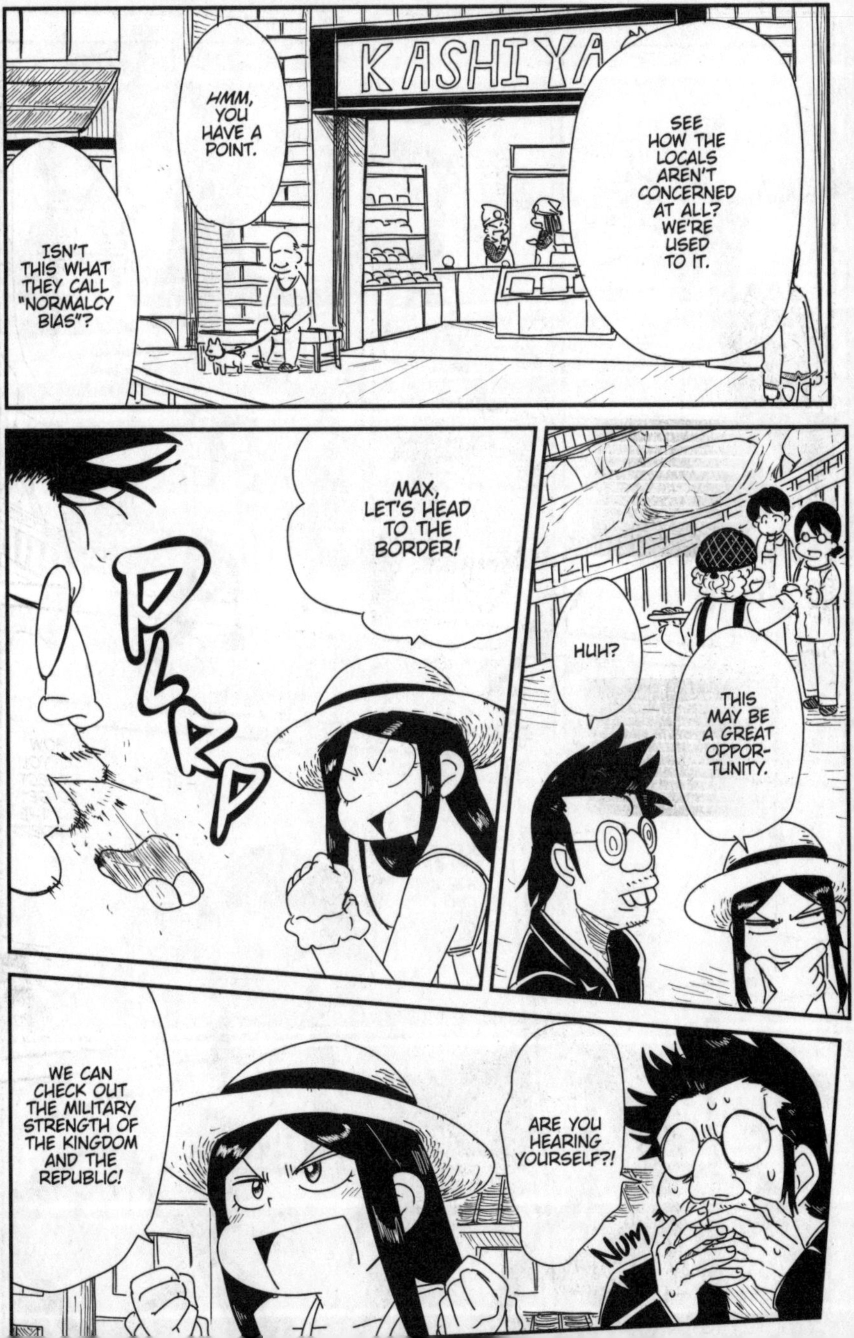
KASHIYA
SEE HOW THE LOCALS AREN'T CONCERNED AT ALL? WE'RE USED TO IT.
HMM, YOU HAVE A POINT.
ISN'T THIS WHAT THEY CALL "NORMALCY BIAS"?
THIS MAY BE A GREAT OPPORTUNITY.
HUH?
MAX, LET'S HEAD TO THE BORDER!
PLRP
WE CAN CHECK OUT THE MILITARY STRENGTH OF THE KINGDOM AND THE REPUBLIC!
ARE YOU HEARING YOURSELF?!
NUM

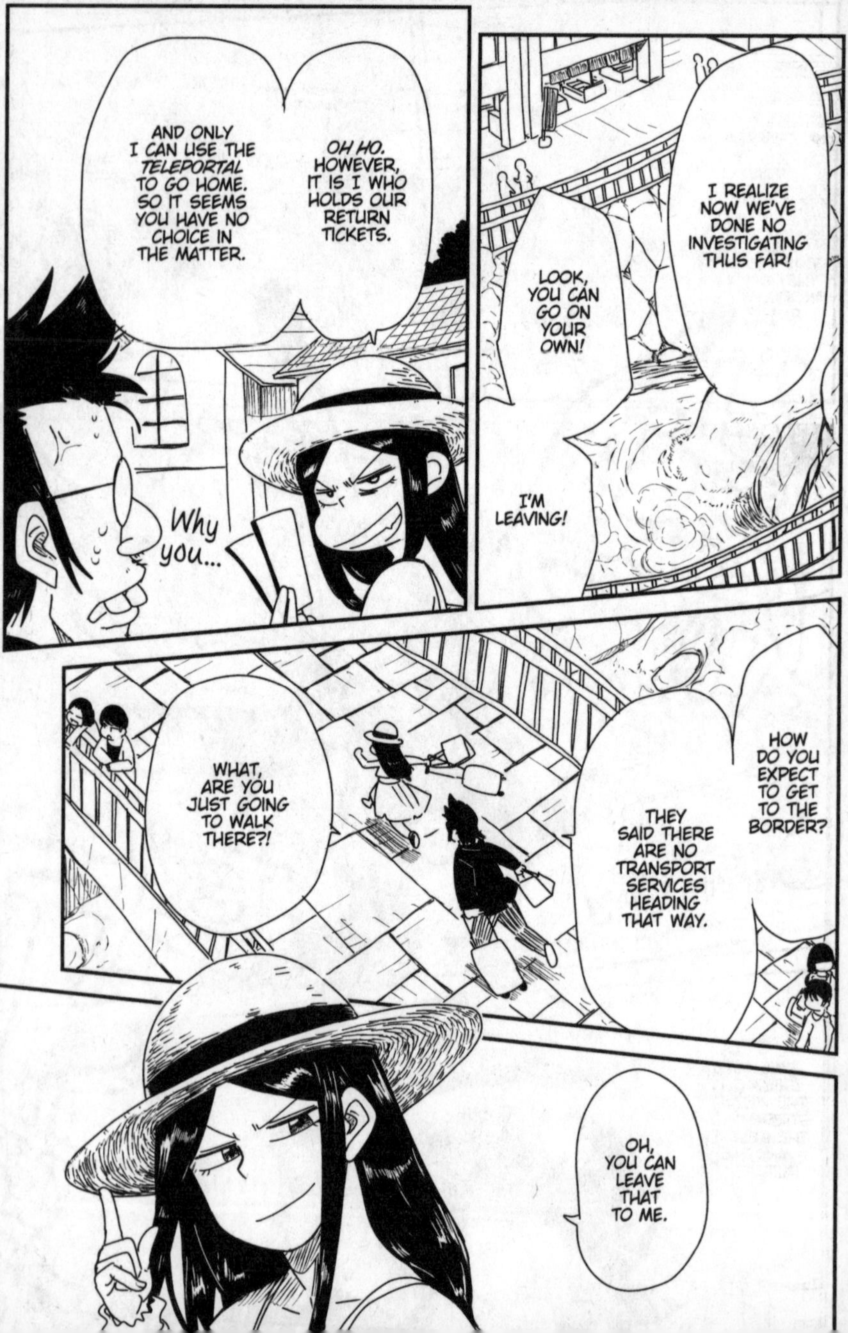
I REALIZE NOW WE'VE DONE NO INVESTIGATING THUS FAR!
LOOK, YOU CAN GO ON YOUR OWN!
I'M LEAVING!
OH HO. HOWEVER, IT IS I WHO HOLDS OUR RETURN TICKETS.
AND ONLY I CAN USE THE *TELEPORTAL* TO GO HOME. SO IT SEEMS YOU HAVE NO CHOICE IN THE MATTER.
Why you...
HOW DO YOU EXPECT TO GET TO THE BORDER?
THEY SAID THERE ARE NO TRANSPORT SERVICES HEADING THAT WAY.
WHAT, ARE YOU JUST GOING TO WALK THERE?!
OH, YOU CAN LEAVE THAT TO ME.

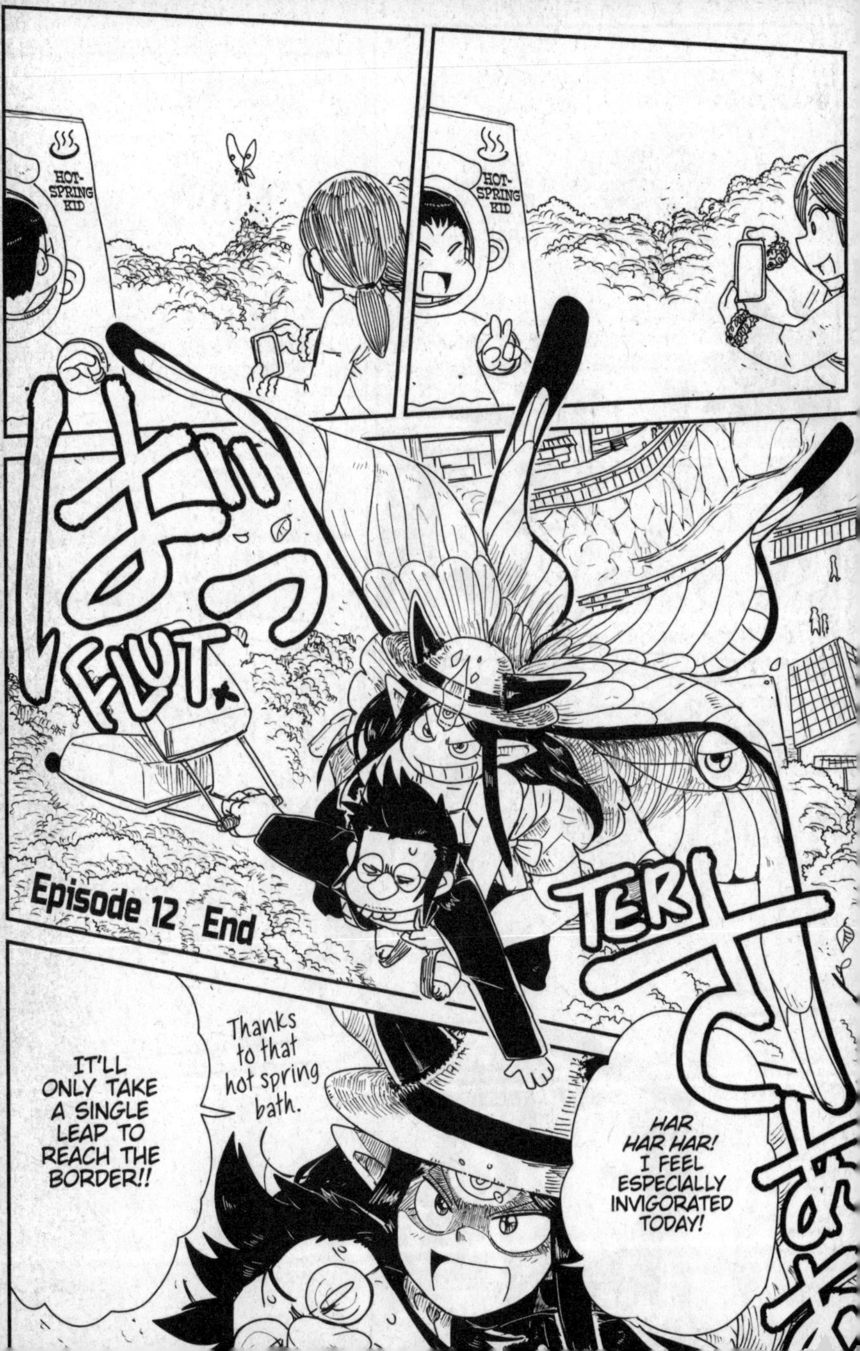
HOT-SPRING KID
HOT-SPRING KID
TERI
ぱっ
FLUT
Episode 12 End
HAR HAR HAR! I FEEL ESPECIALLY INVIGORATED TODAY!
Thanks to that hot spring bath.
IT'LL ONLY TAKE A SINGLE LEAP TO REACH THE BORDER!!

LEVEL 1 DEMON LORD & ONE ROOM HERO

LEVEL 1 DEMON LORD & ONE ROOM HERO

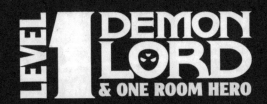

Episode 13: Battle at the Border

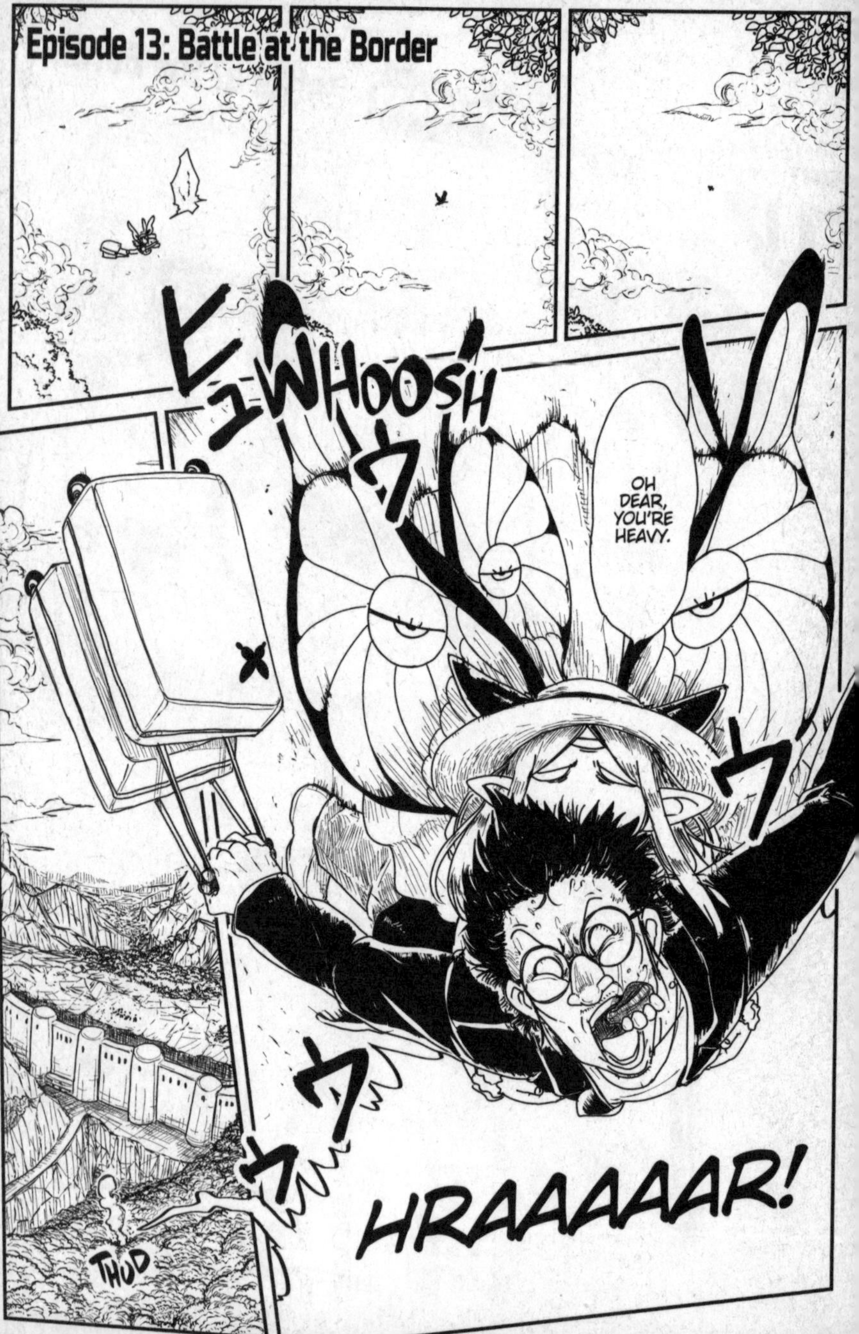
WHOOSH
OH DEAR, YOU'RE HEAVY.
HRAAAAAR!
THUD

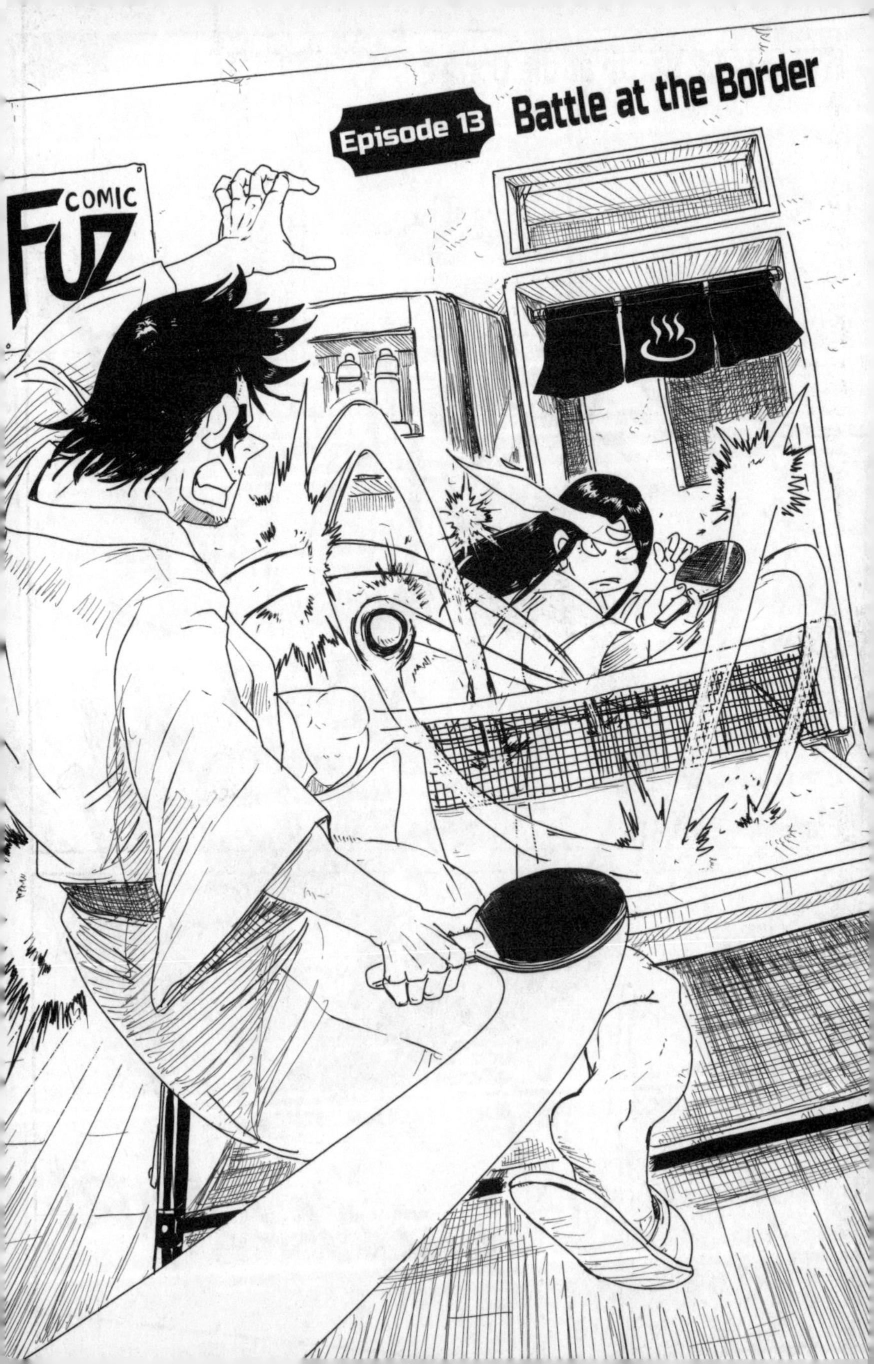
Episode 13
Battle at the Border
COMIC FUZ

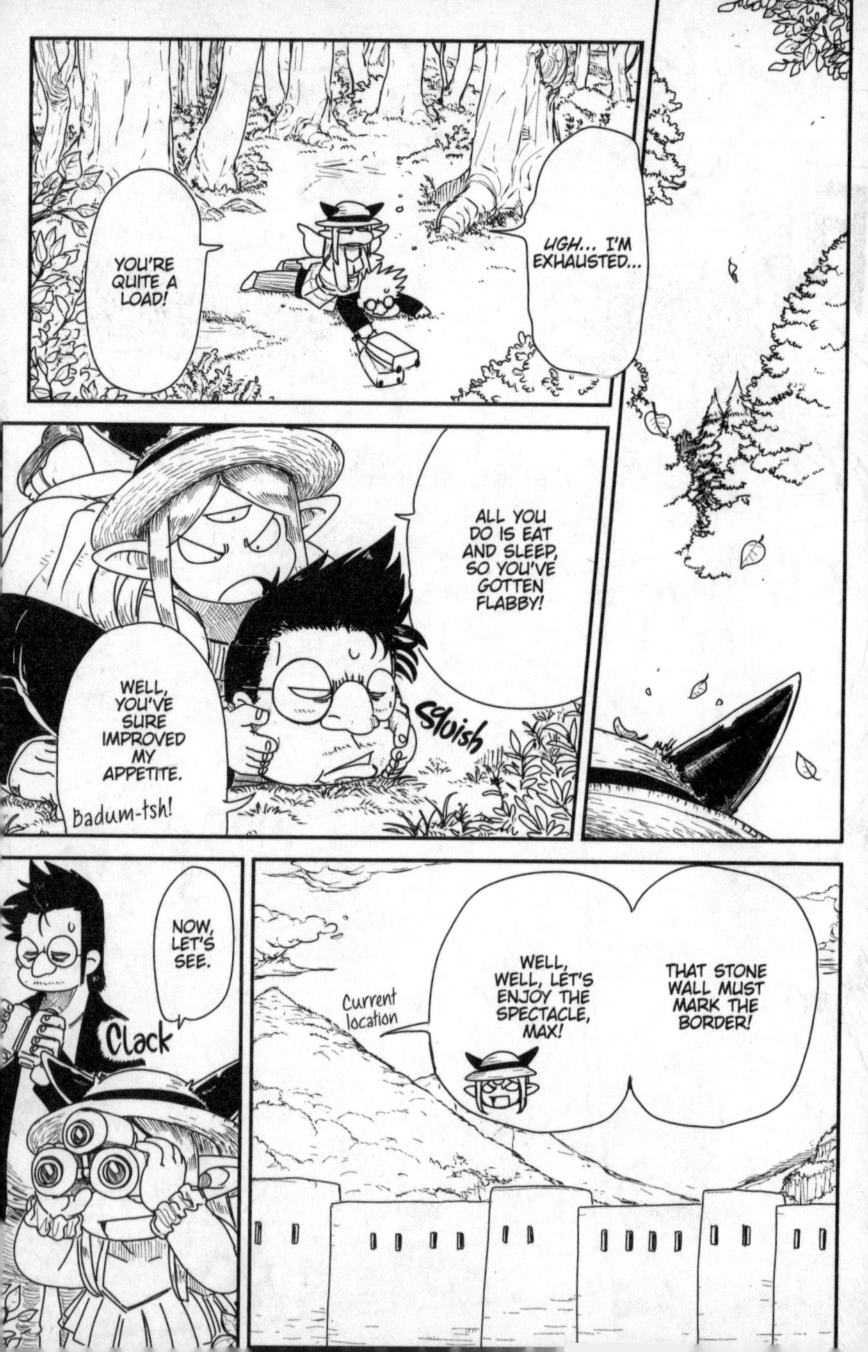
UGH... I'M EXHAUSTED...
YOU'RE QUITE A LOAD!
ALL YOU DO IS EAT AND SLEEP, SO YOU'VE GOTTEN FLABBY!
Squish
WELL, YOU'VE SURE IMPROVED MY APPETITE.
Badum-tsh!
THAT STONE WALL MUST MARK THE BORDER!
WELL, WELL, LET'S ENJOY THE SPECTACLE, MAX!
Current location
NOW, LET'S SEE.
Clack

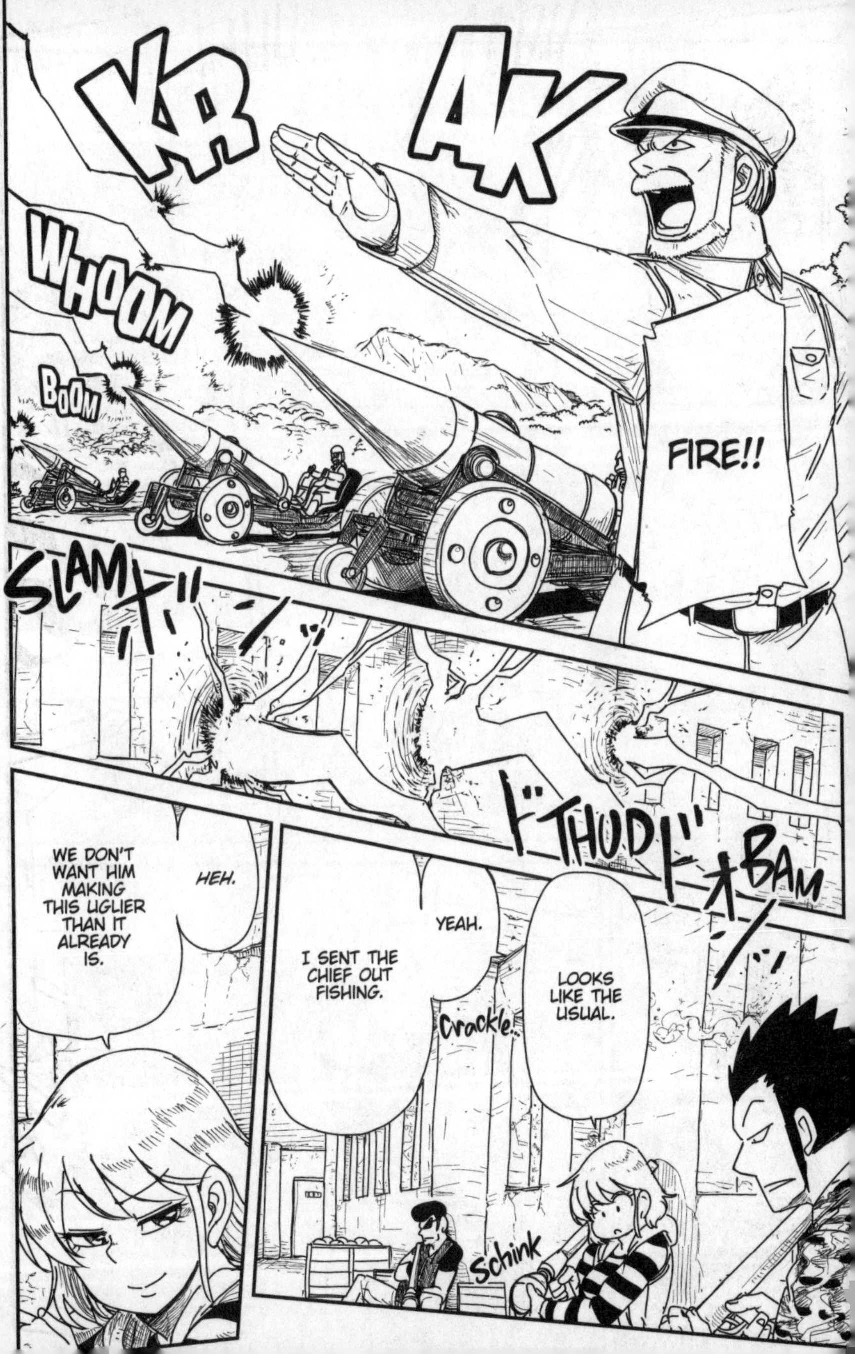
KRAK
FIRE!!
WHOOM
BOOM
SLAM
THUD
BAM
LOOKS LIKE THE USUAL.
YEAH.
I SENT THE CHIEF OUT FISHING.
Crackle...
Schink
HEH.
WE DON'T WANT HIM MAKING THIS UGLIER THAN IT ALREADY IS.

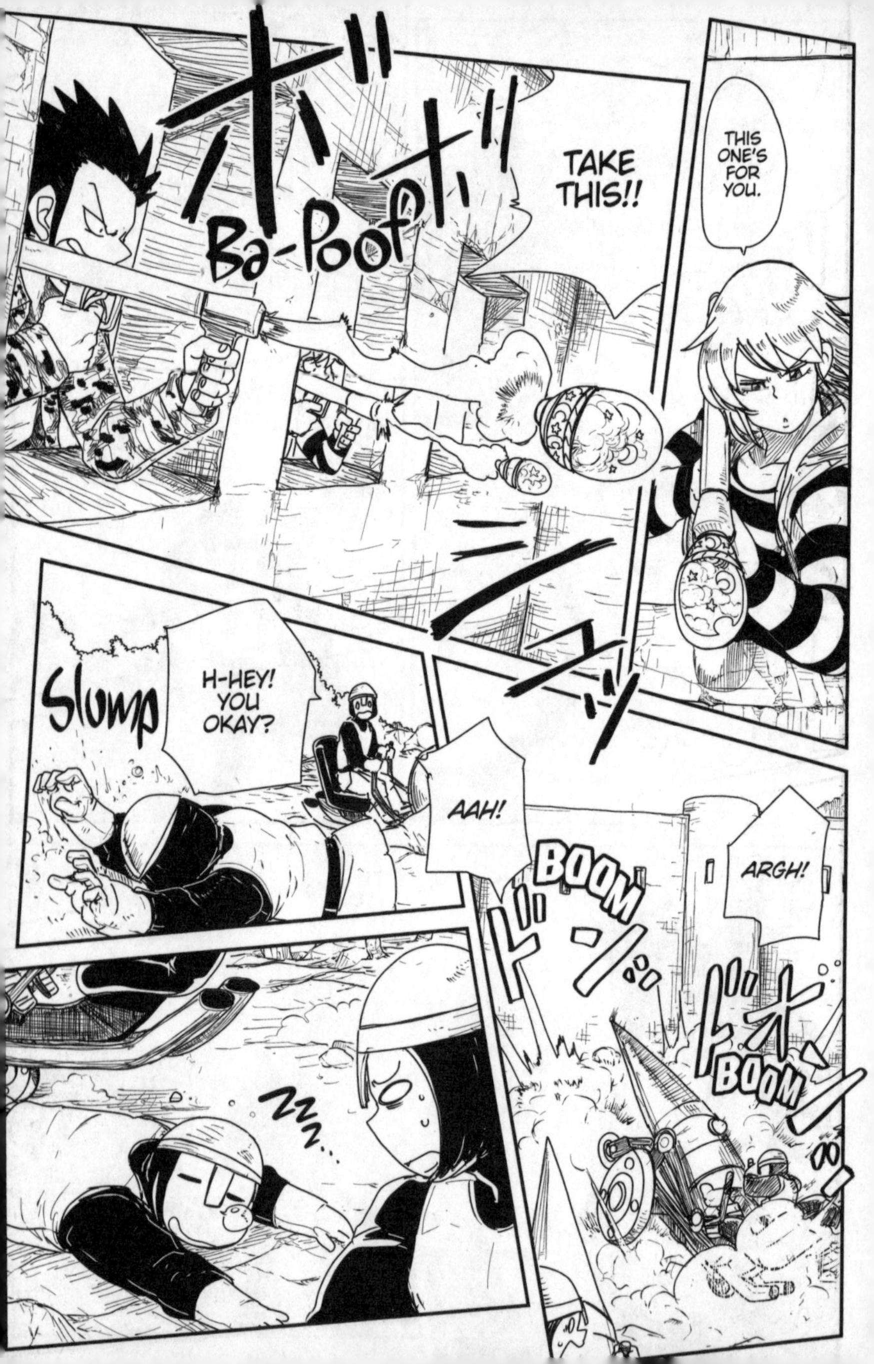
THIS ONE'S FOR YOU.
TAKE THIS!!
Ba-Poof
AAH!
ARGH!
BOOM
BOOM
H-HEY! YOU OKAY?
Slump
ZZZ...

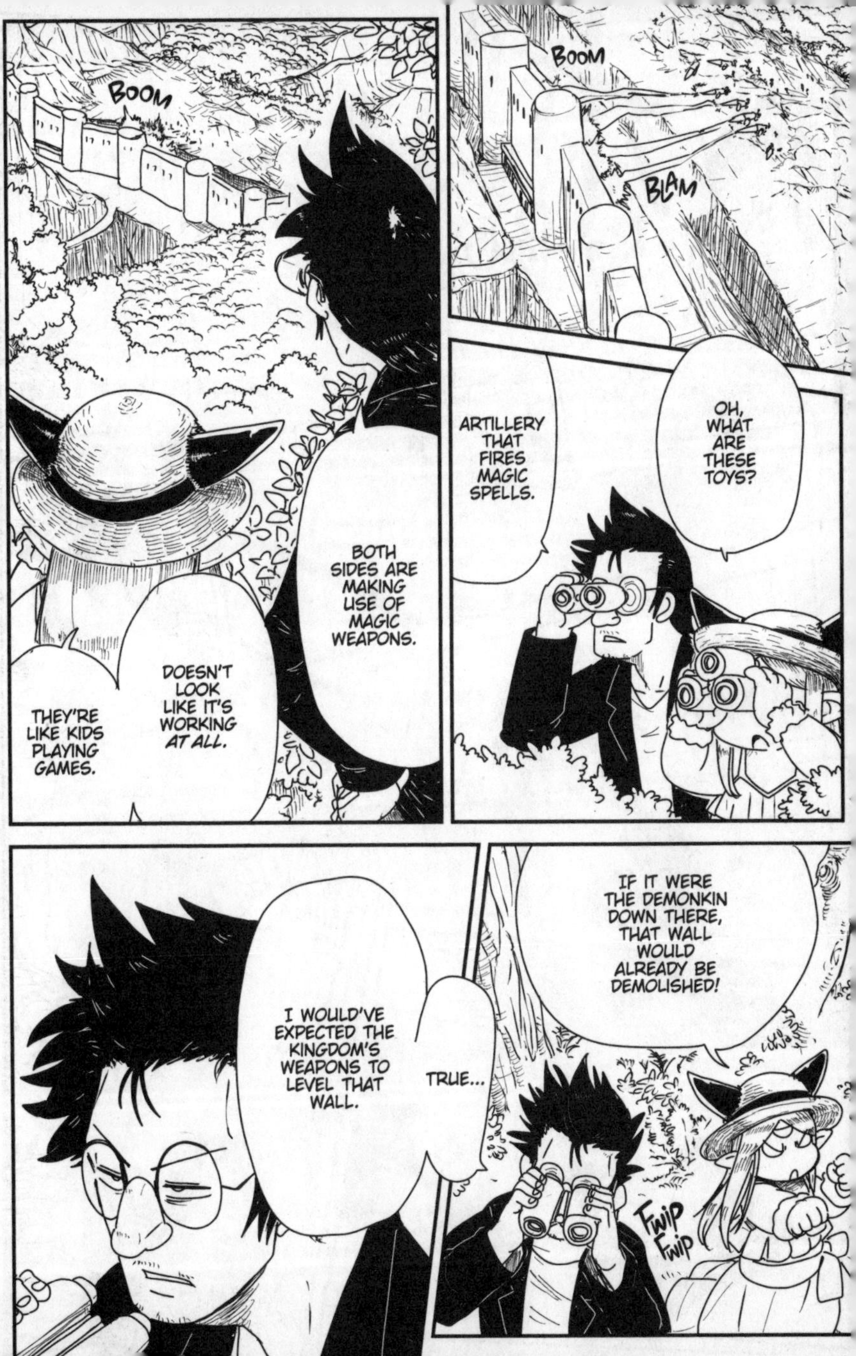
BOOM
BLAM
OH, WHAT ARE THESE TOYS?
ARTILLERY THAT FIRES MAGIC SPELLS.
BOOM
BOTH SIDES ARE MAKING USE OF MAGIC WEAPONS.
DOESN'T LOOK LIKE IT'S WORKING AT ALL.
THEY'RE LIKE KIDS PLAYING GAMES.
IF IT WERE THE DEMONKIN DOWN THERE, THAT WALL WOULD ALREADY BE DEMOLISHED!
FWIP FWIP
TRUE...
I WOULD'VE EXPECTED THE KINGDOM'S WEAPONS TO LEVEL THAT WALL.

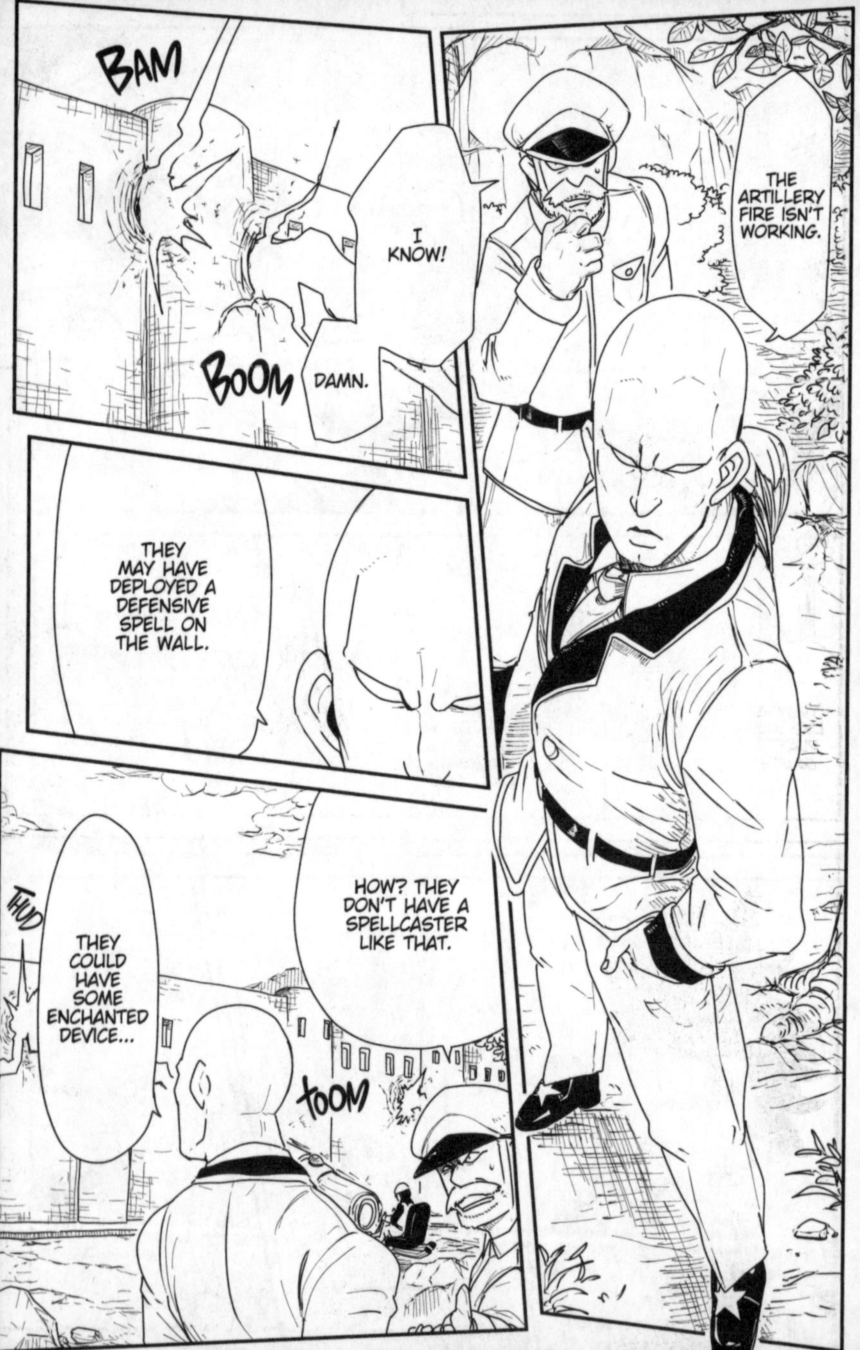
THE ARTILLERY FIRE ISN'T WORKING.
BAM
I KNOW!
DAMN.
BOOM
THEY MAY HAVE DEPLOYED A DEFENSIVE SPELL ON THE WALL.
HOW? THEY DON'T HAVE A SPELLCASTER LIKE THAT.
THEY COULD HAVE SOME ENCHANTED DEVICE...
THUD
TOOM

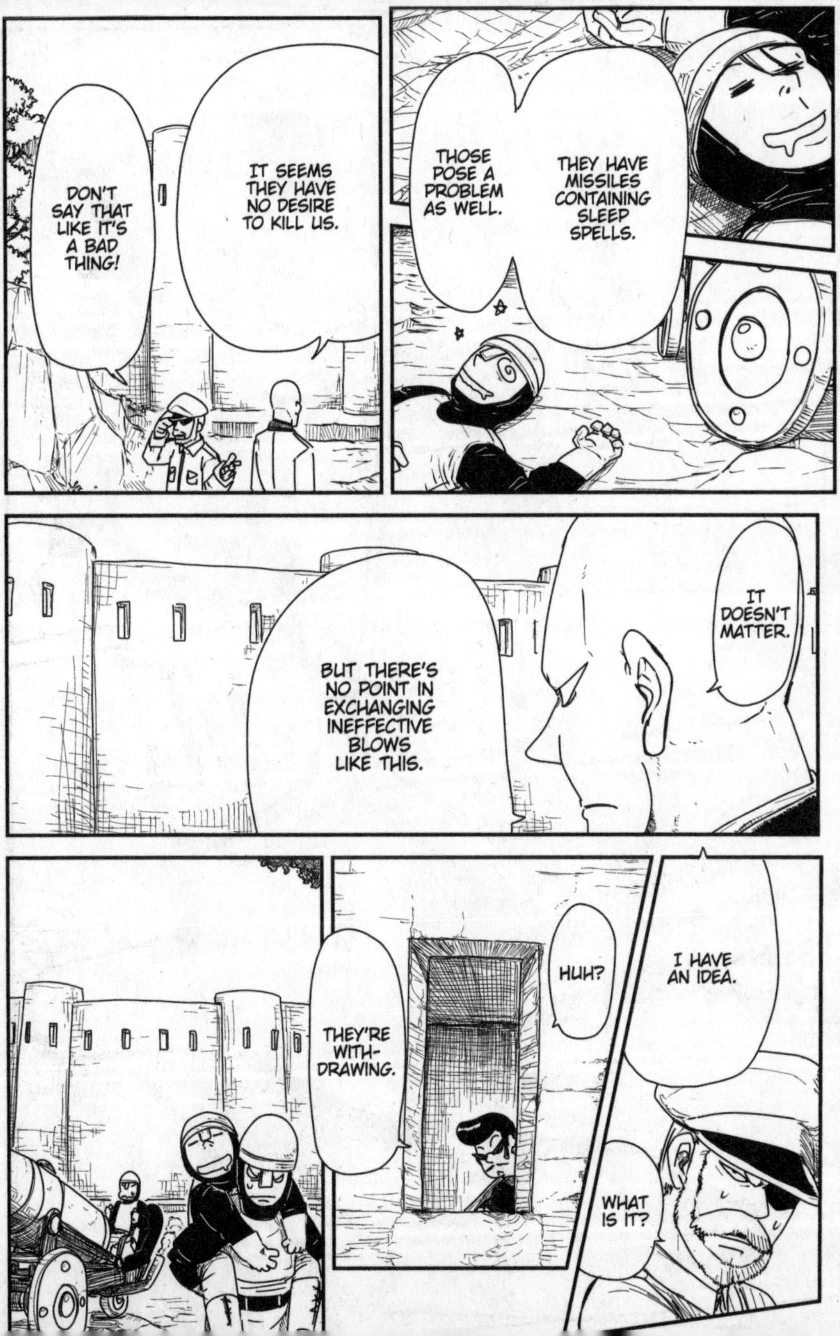
THEY HAVE MISSILES CONTAINING SLEEP SPELLS.
THOSE POSE A PROBLEM AS WELL.
IT SEEMS THEY HAVE NO DESIRE TO KILL US.
DON'T SAY THAT LIKE IT'S A BAD THING!
IT DOESN'T MATTER.
BUT THERE'S NO POINT IN EXCHANGING INEFFECTIVE BLOWS LIKE THIS.
I HAVE AN IDEA.
WHAT IS IT?
HUH?
THEY'RE WITH-DRAWING.

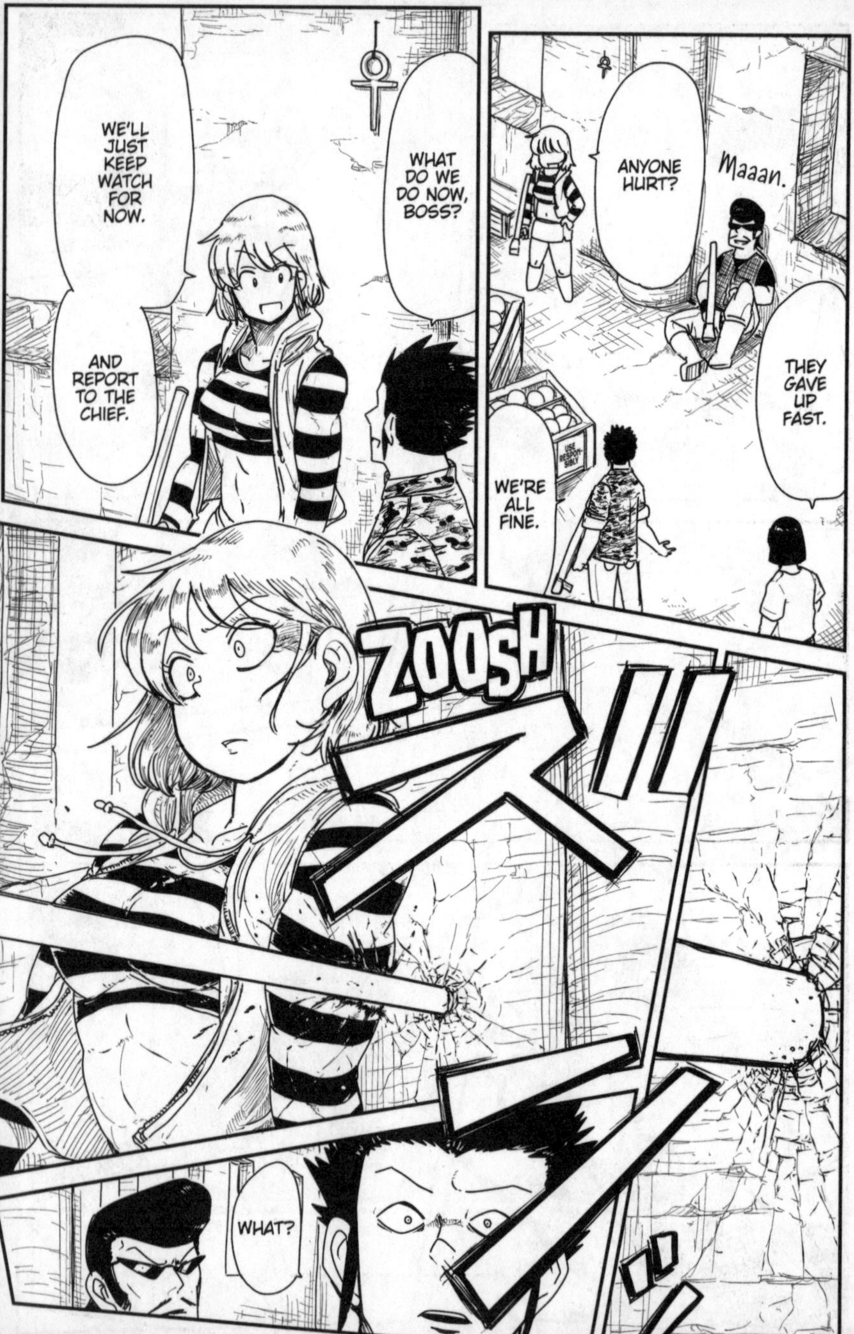
Maaan.
ANYONE HURT?
THEY GAVE UP FAST.
USE RESPON-SIBLY
WE'RE ALL FINE.
WHAT DO WE DO NOW, BOSS?
WE'LL JUST KEEP WATCH FOR NOW.
AND REPORT TO THE CHIEF.
ZOOSH
WHAT?

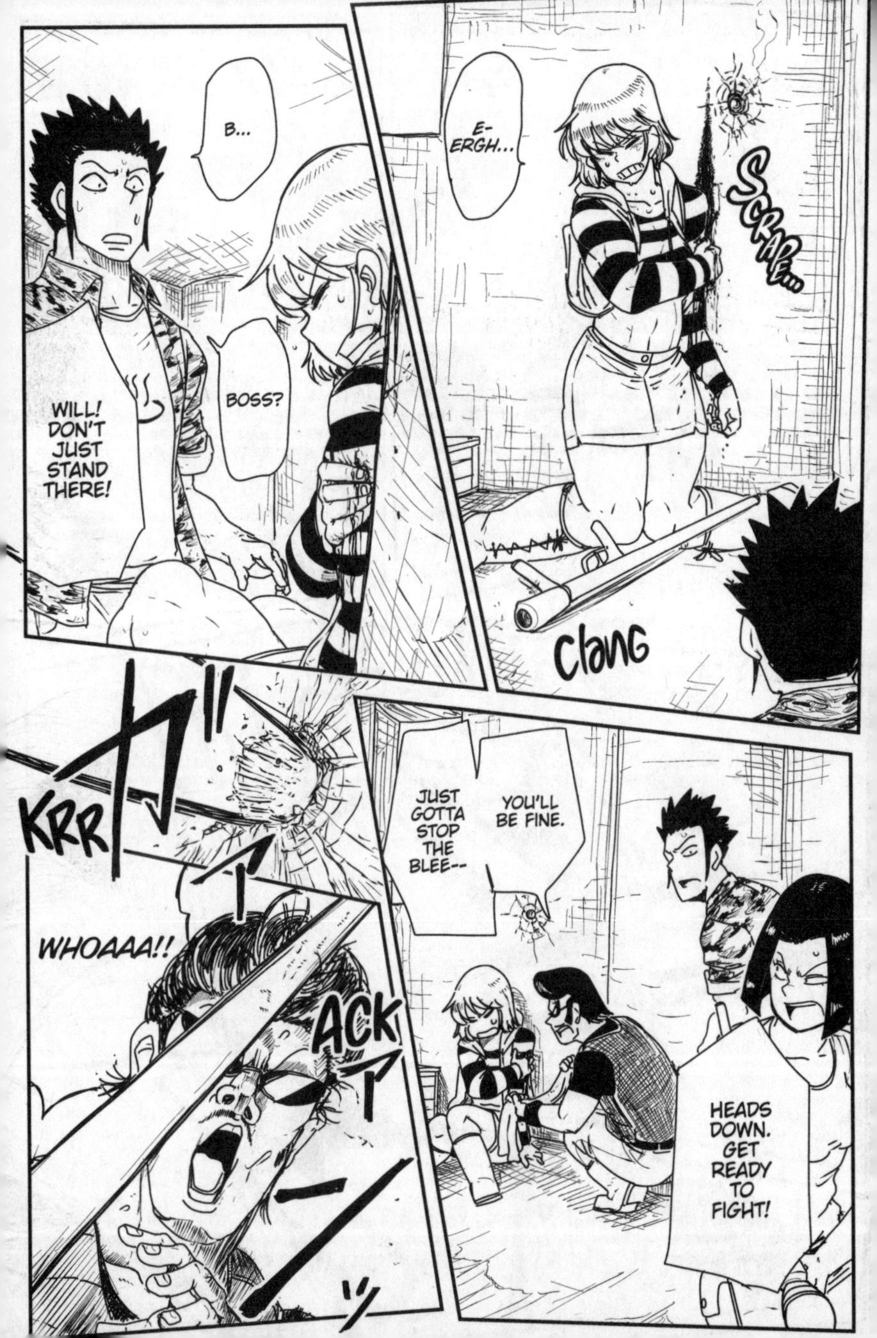
E-
ERGH...
SCRAP...
Clang
B...
BOSS?
WILL! DON'T JUST STAND THERE!
YOU'LL BE FINE.
JUST GOTTA STOP THE BLEE--
HEADS DOWN. GET READY TO FIGHT!
KRR
WHOAAA!!
ACK

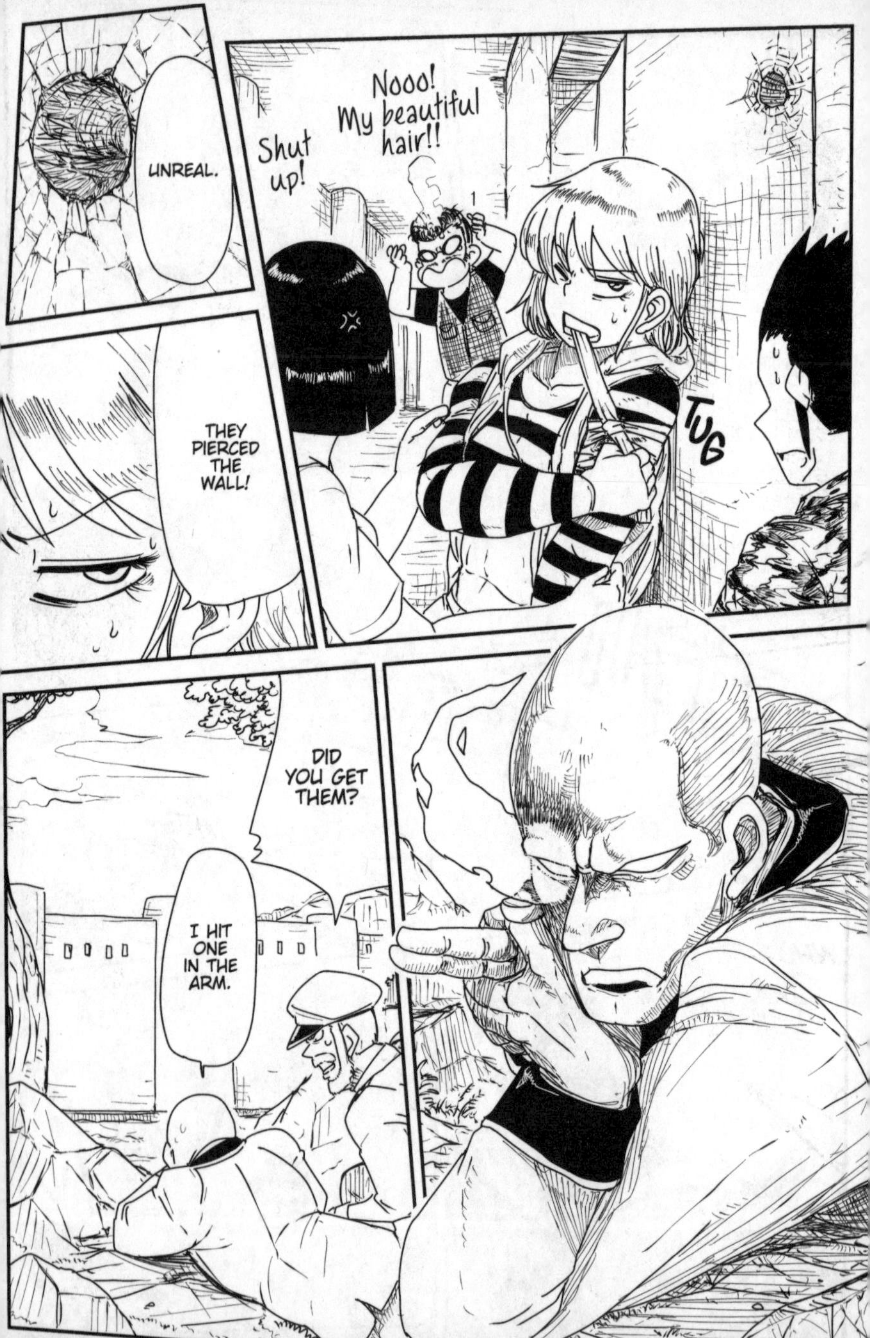
Nooo! My beautiful hair!!
Shut up!
TUG
UNREAL.
THEY PIERCED THE WALL!
DID YOU GET THEM?
I HIT ONE IN THE ARM.

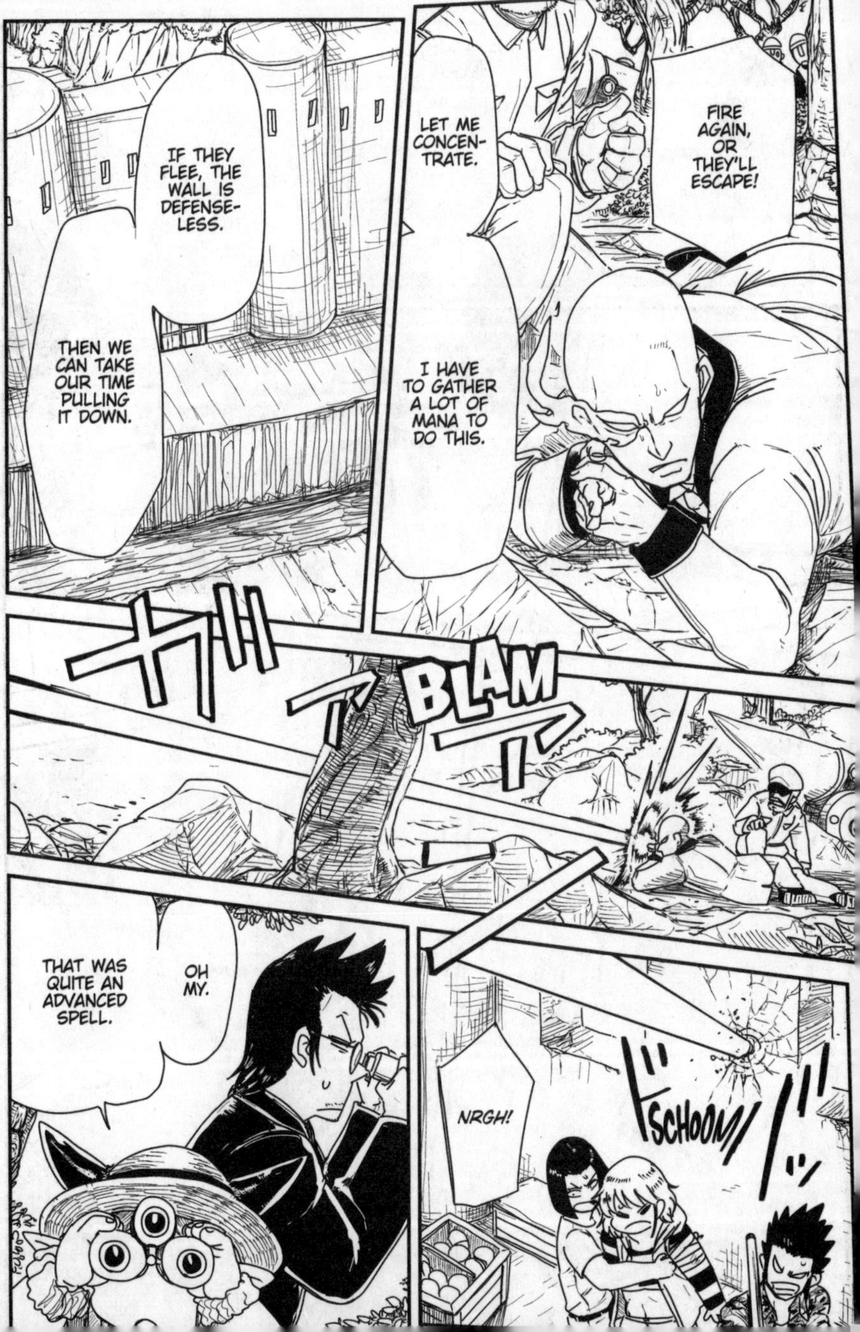
FIRE AGAIN, OR THEY'LL ESCAPE!
LET ME CONCENTRATE.
I HAVE TO GATHER A LOT OF MANA TO DO THIS.
IF THEY FLEE, THE WALL IS DEFENSELESS.
THEN WE CAN TAKE OUR TIME PULLING IT DOWN.
BLAM
NRGH!
SCHOOM
OH MY.
THAT WAS QUITE AN ADVANCED SPELL.

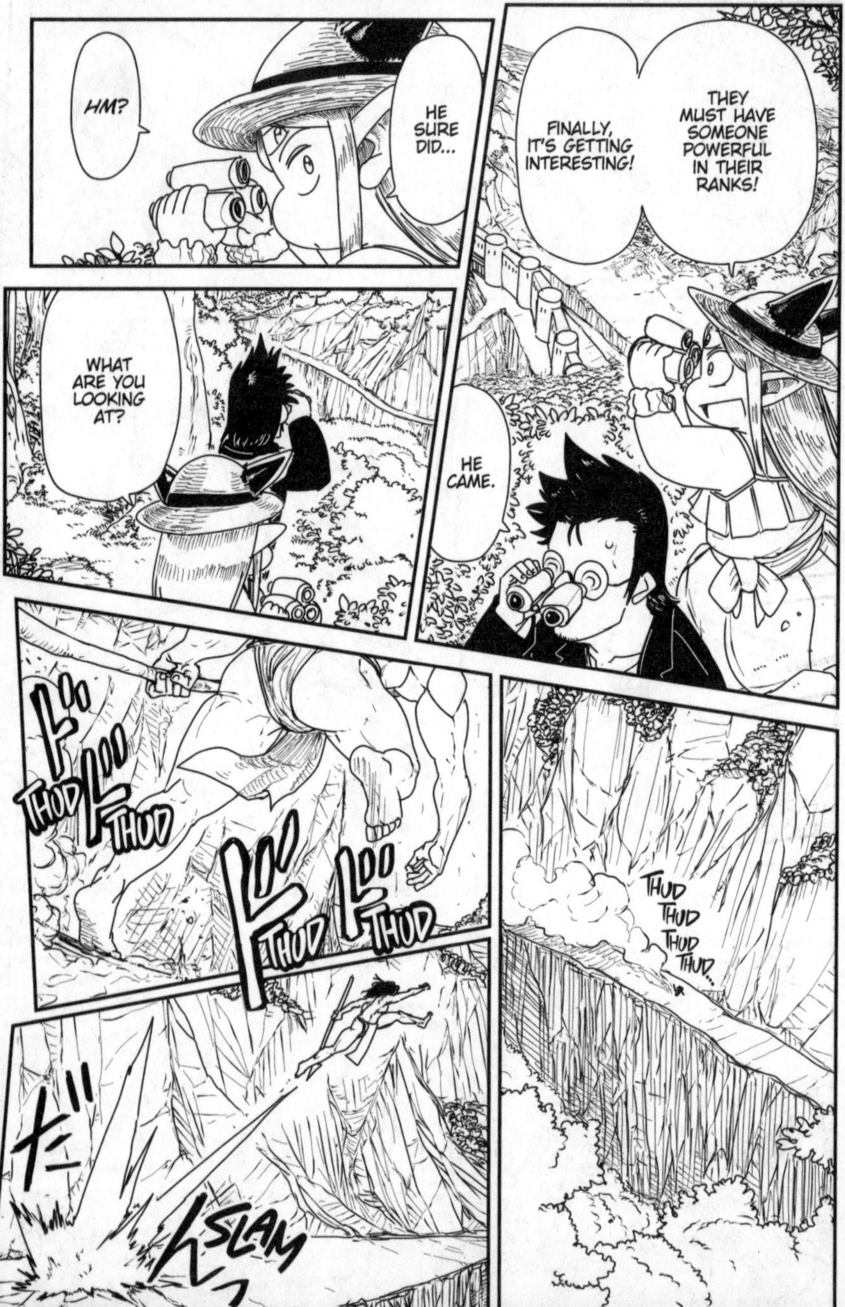

THEY MUST HAVE SOMEONE POWERFUL IN THEIR RANKS!
FINALLY, IT'S GETTING INTERESTING!
HE CAME.
HE SURE DID...
HM?
WHAT ARE YOU LOOKING AT?
THUD THUD THUD THUD...
THUD THUD
THUD THUD
SLAM

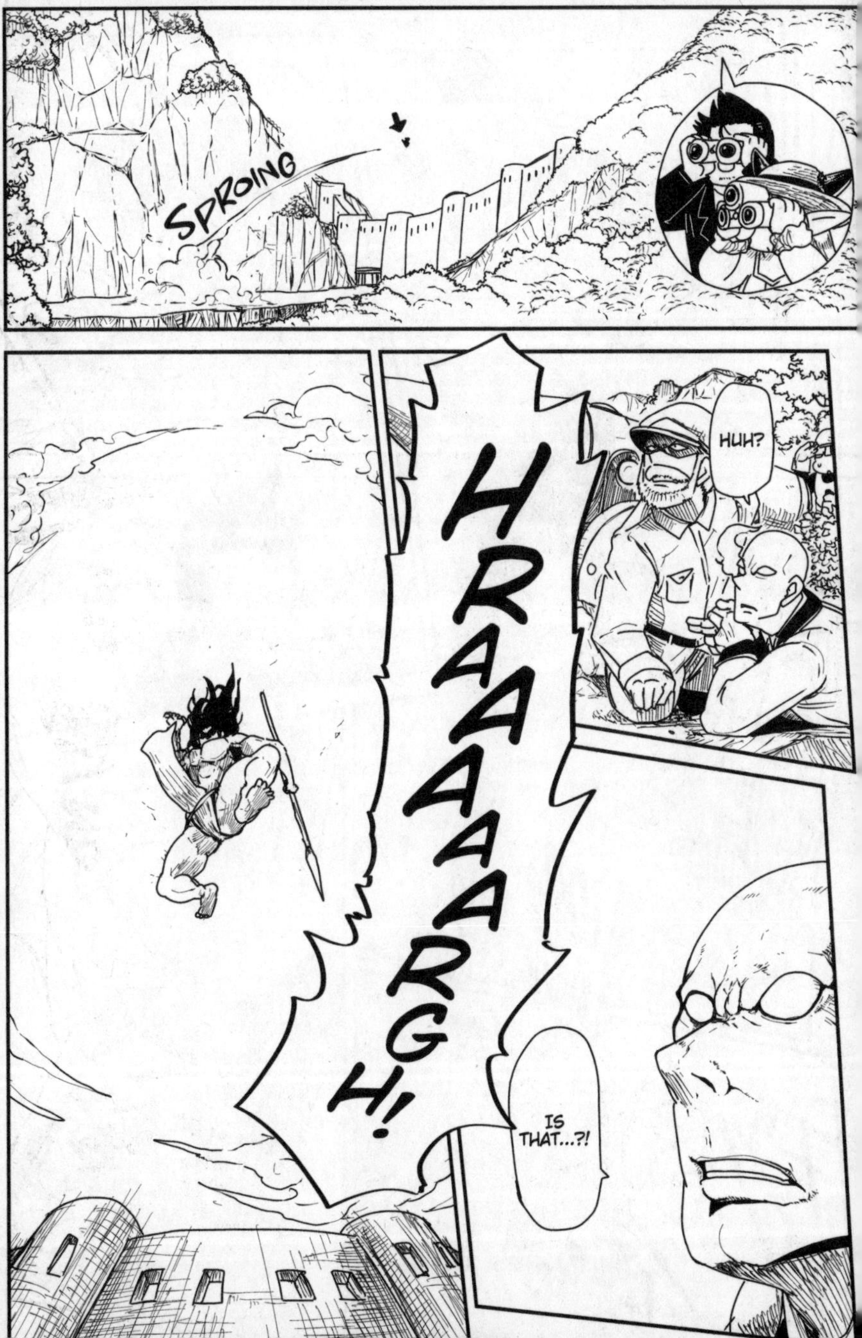
SPROING
HUH?
IS THAT...?!
HRAAAAARGH!

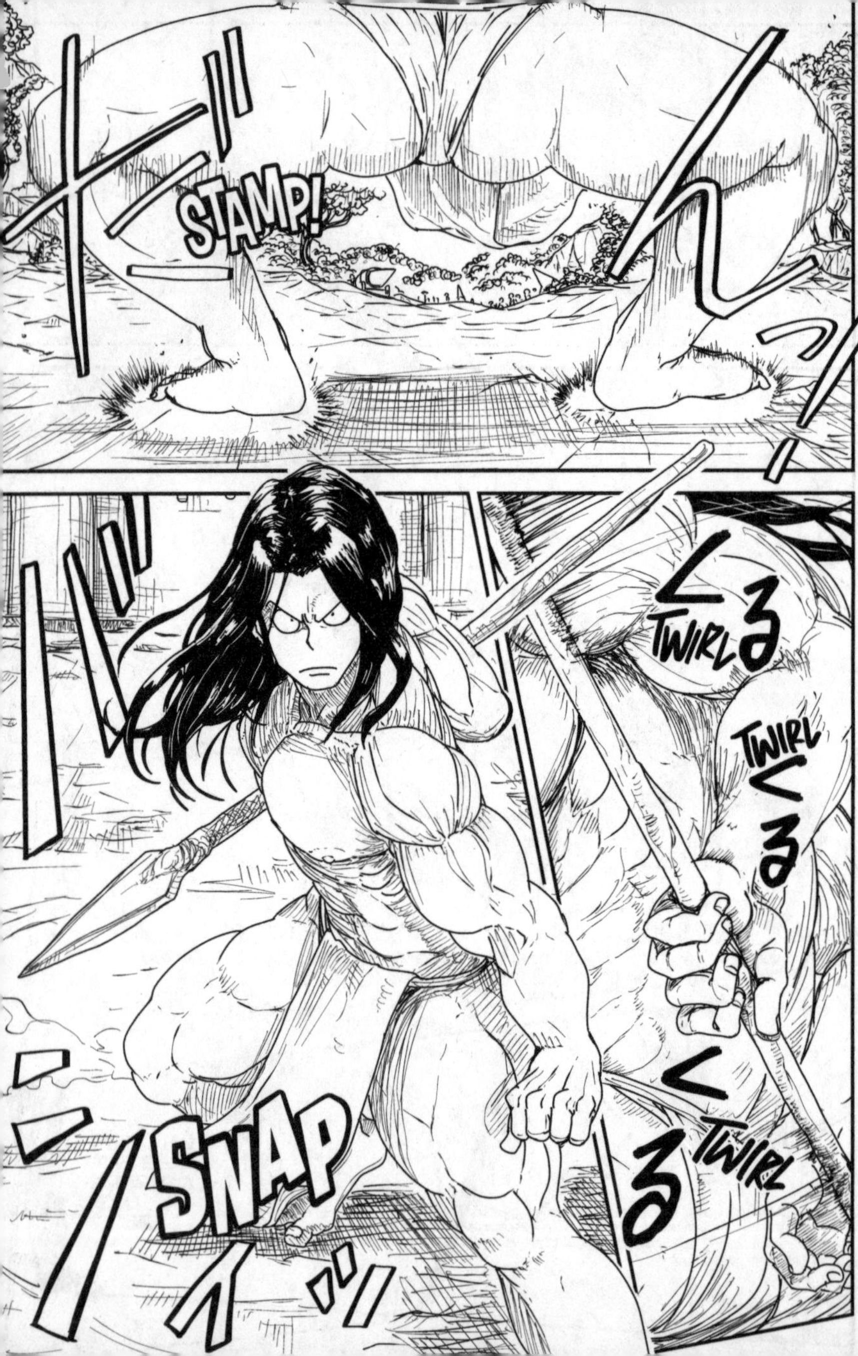
STAMP!
くる TWIRL
TWIRL くる
くる TWIRL
SNAP

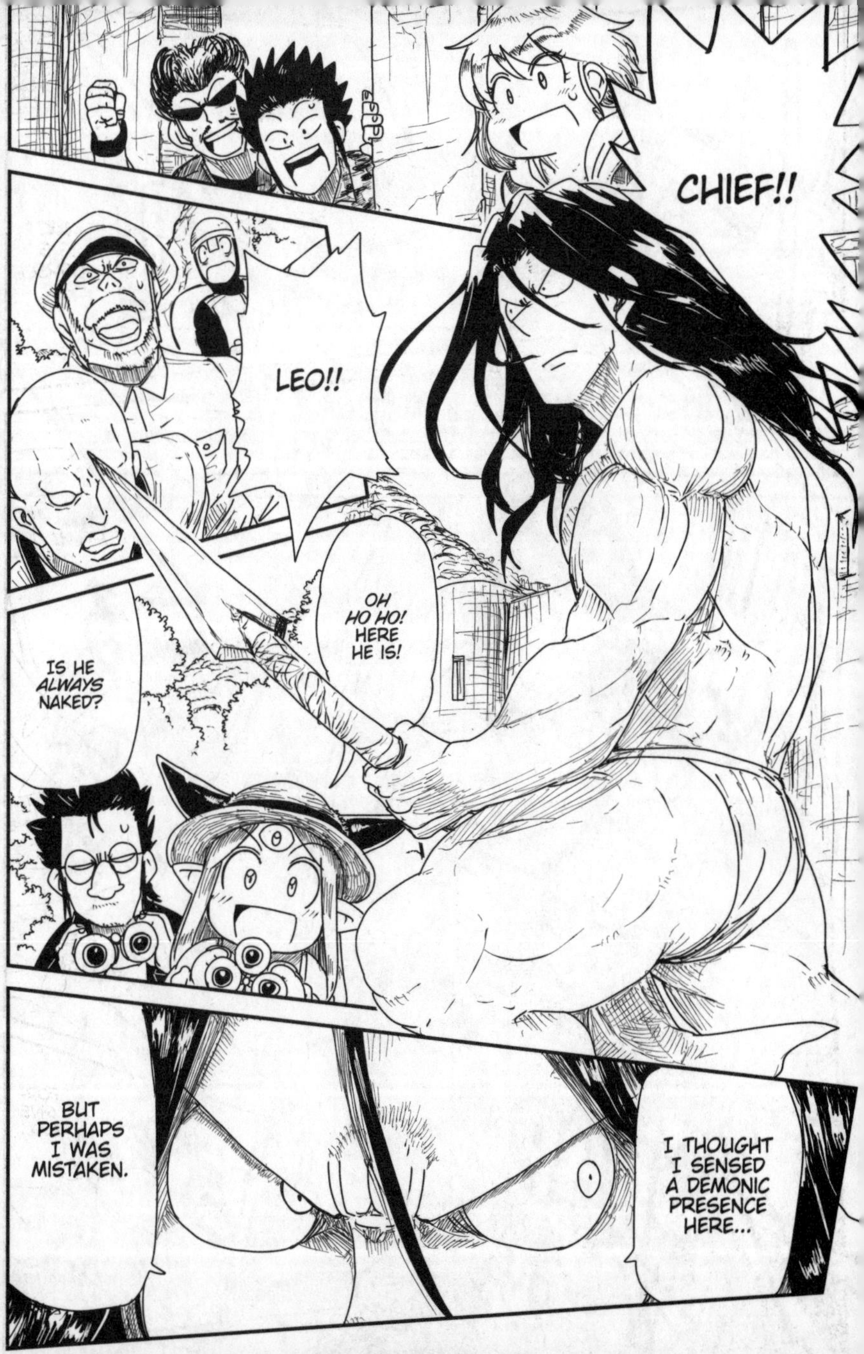
CHIEF!!
LEO!!
OH HO HO! HERE HE IS!
IS HE ALWAYS NAKED?
I THOUGHT I SENSED A DEMONIC PRESENCE HERE...
BUT PERHAPS I WAS MISTAKEN.

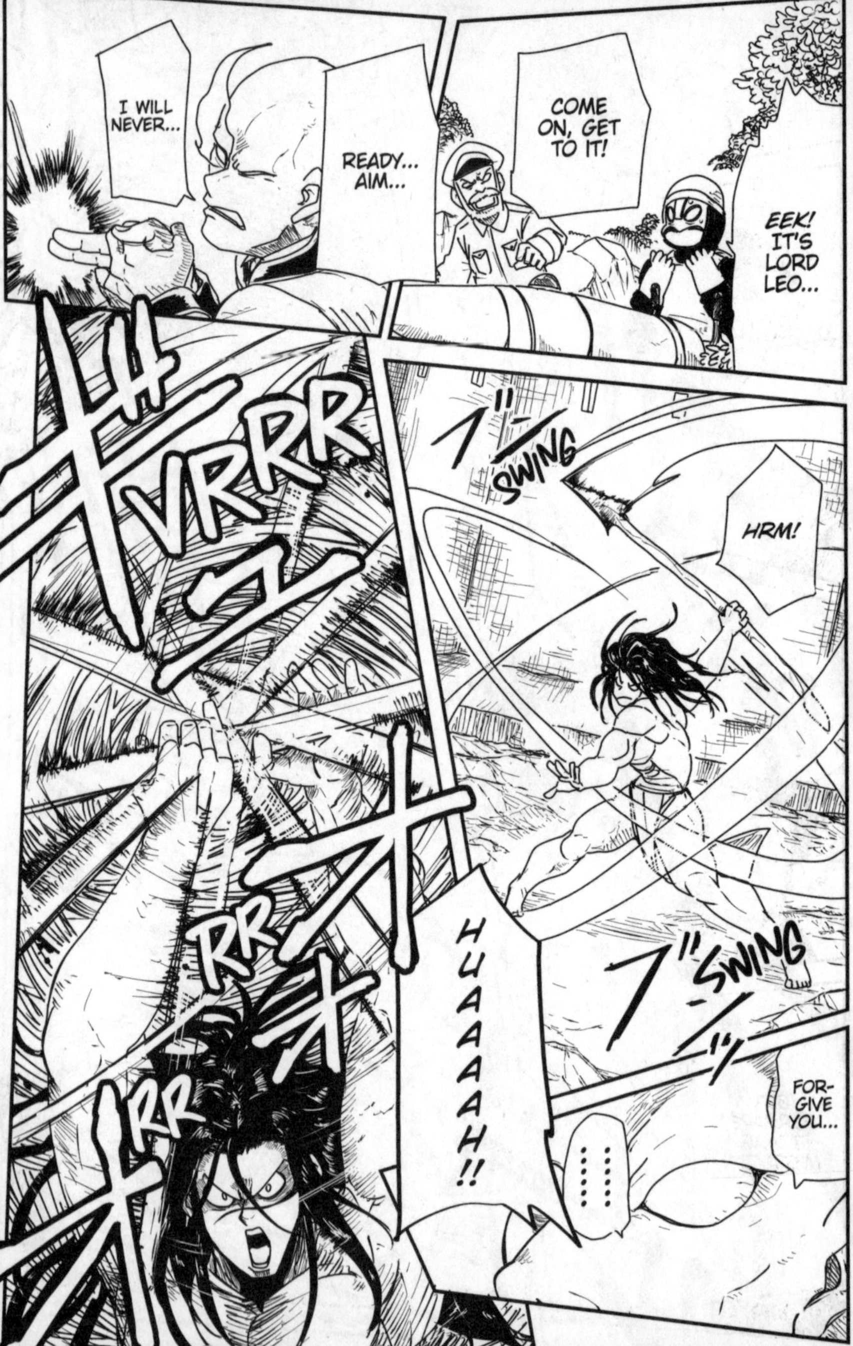
COME ON, GET TO IT!
EEK! IT'S LORD LEO...
READY... AIM...
I WILL NEVER...
SWING
HRM!
SWING
FOR-GIVE YOU...
......
HUAAAAAAH!!
VRRR
RR
RR

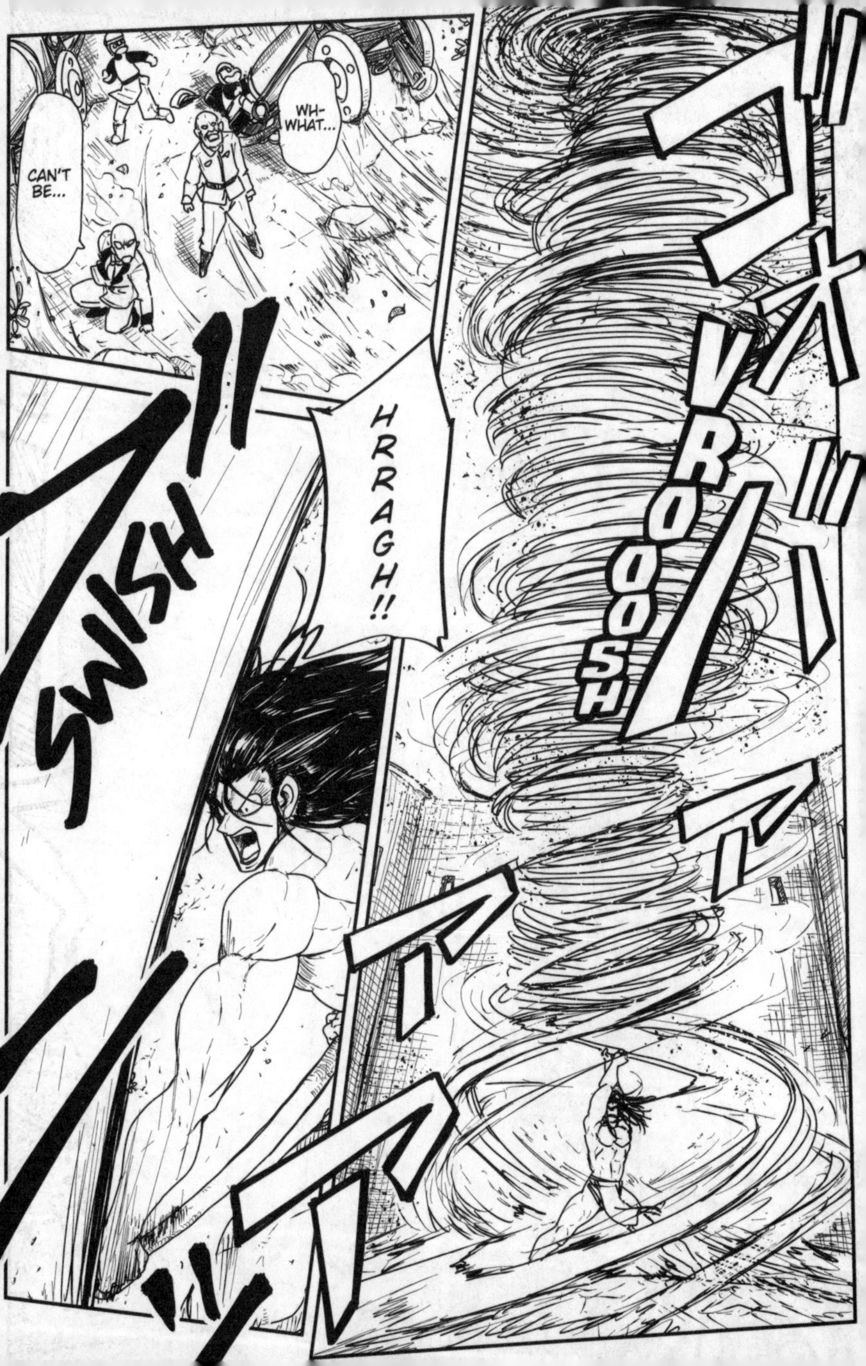
VROOOOSH
WH-WHAT...
CAN'T BE...
HRRAGH!!
SWISH

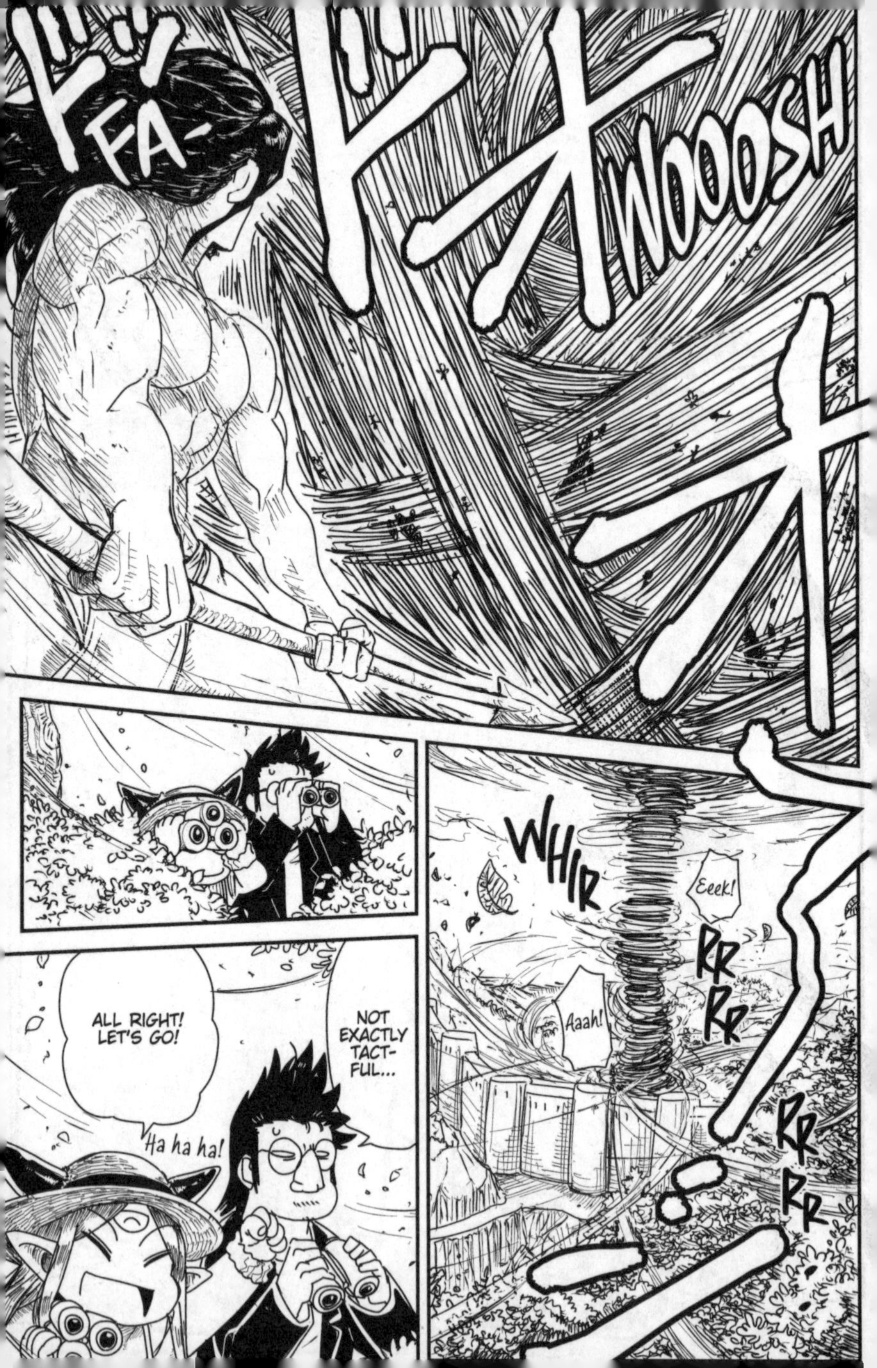

WOOOSH
FA-
WHIR
Eeek!
Aaah!
RR RR
RR RR
NOT EXACTLY TACT-FUL...
ALL RIGHT! LET'S GO!
Ha ha ha!

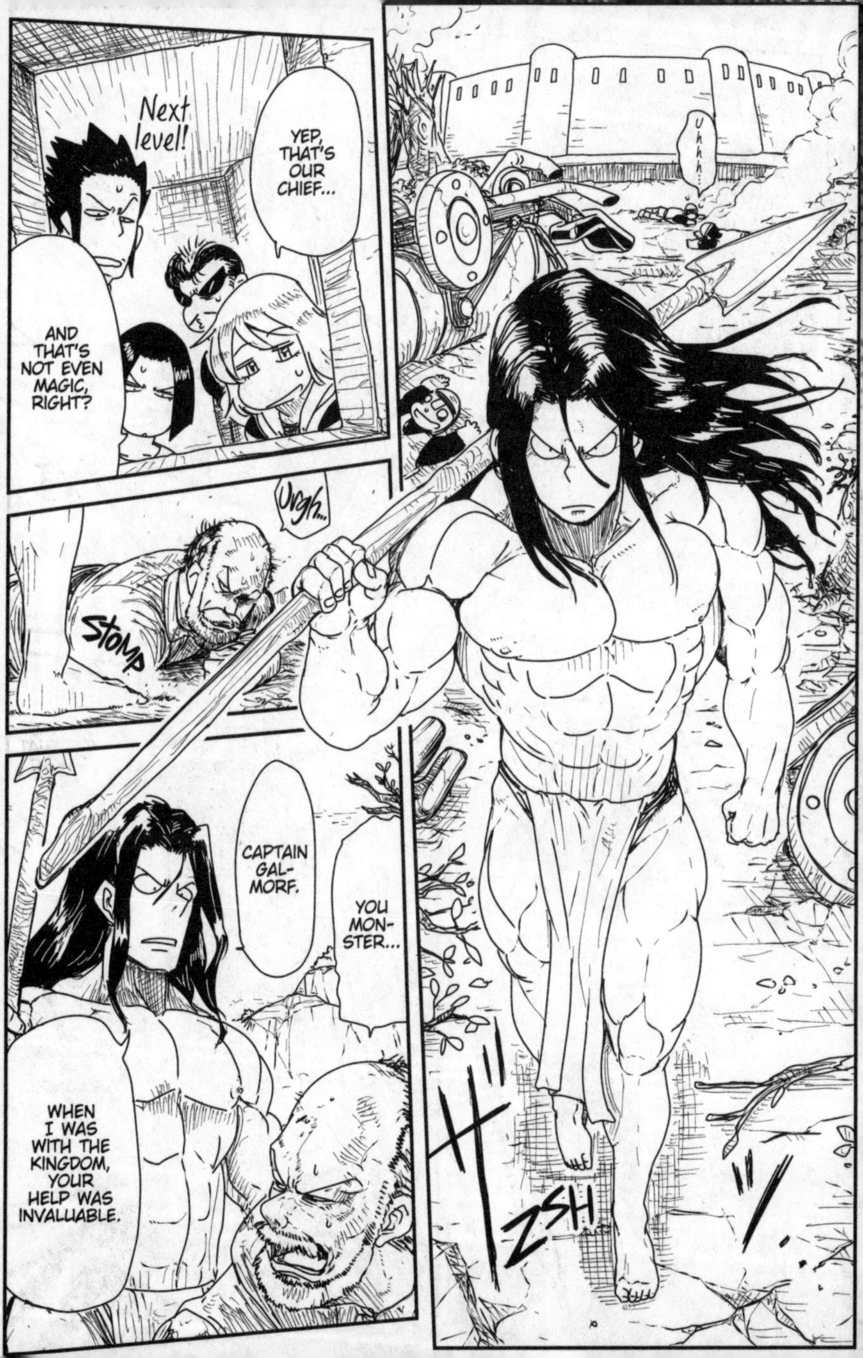
Uhhh...
ZSH
YEP, THAT'S OUR CHIEF...
Next level!
AND THAT'S NOT EVEN MAGIC, RIGHT?
Urgh...
STOMP
CAPTAIN GAL-MORF.
YOU MON-STER...
WHEN I WAS WITH THE KINGDOM, YOUR HELP WAS INVALUABLE.

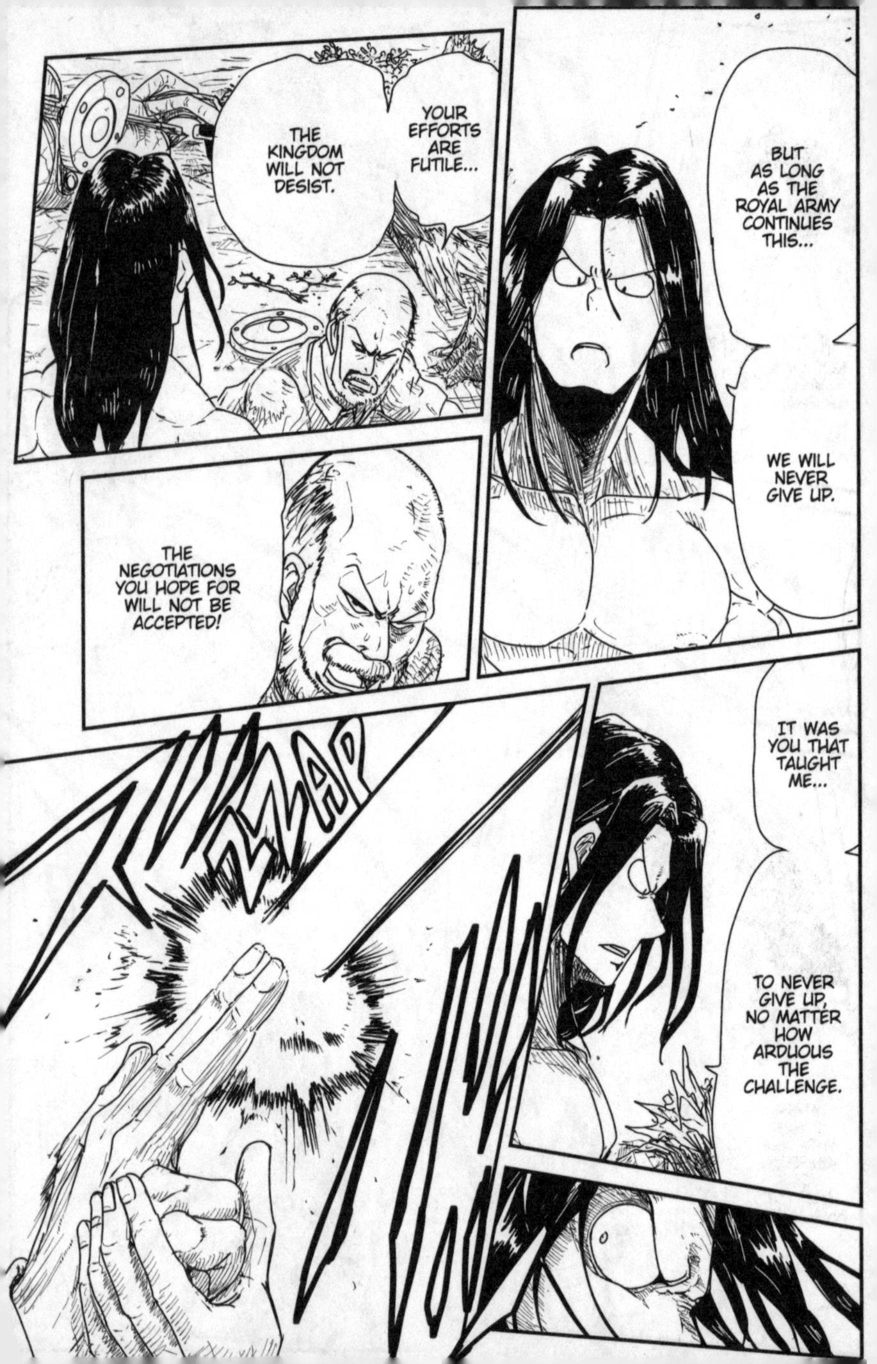
BUT AS LONG AS THE ROYAL ARMY CONTINUES THIS...
WE WILL NEVER GIVE UP.
YOUR EFFORTS ARE FUTILE...
THE KINGDOM WILL NOT DESIST.
THE NEGOTIATIONS YOU HOPE FOR WILL NOT BE ACCEPTED!
IT WAS YOU THAT TAUGHT ME...
TO NEVER GIVE UP, NO MATTER HOW ARDUOUS THE CHALLENGE.
ZAP

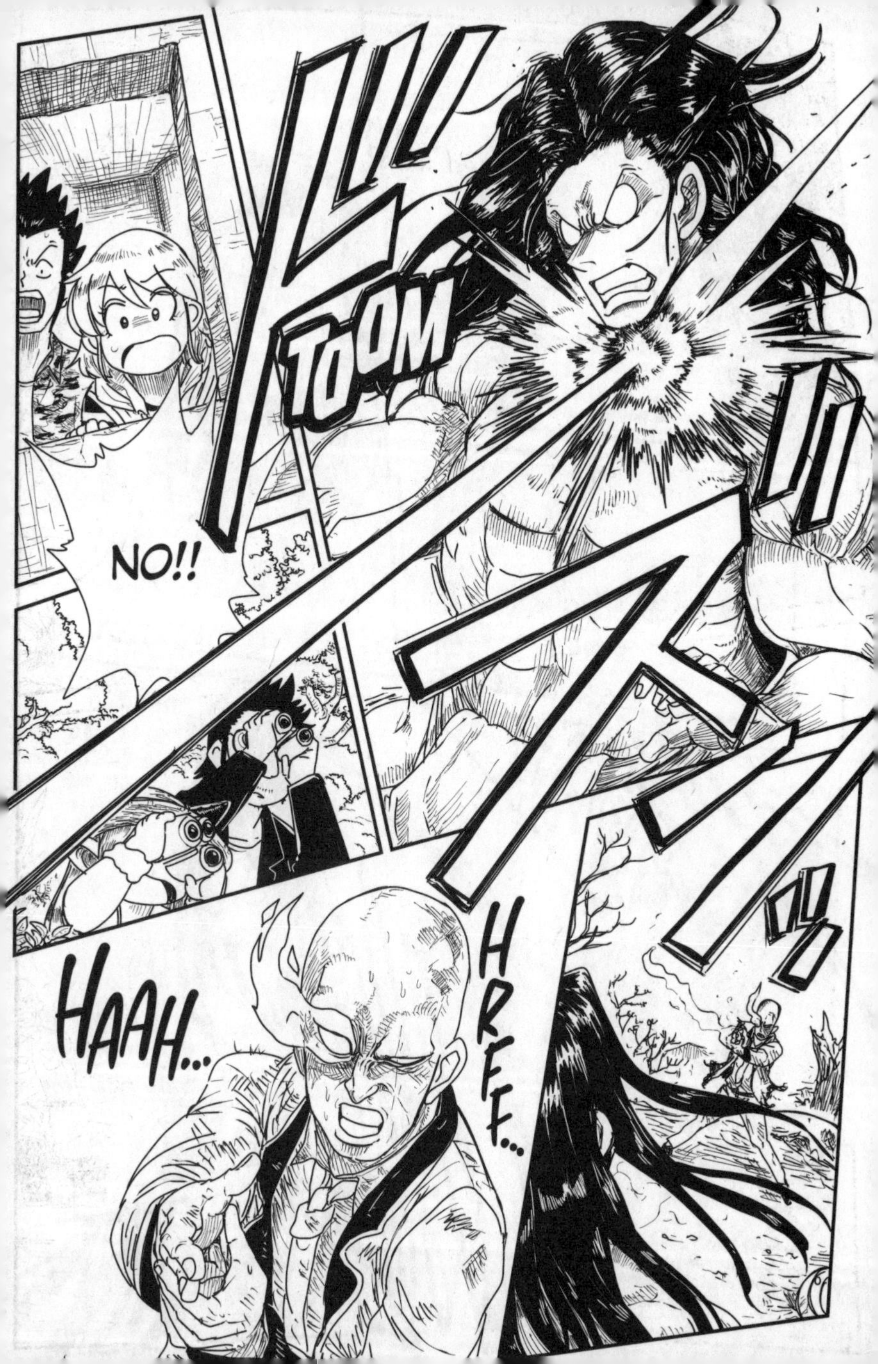
TOOM
NO!!
HRFF...
HAAH...

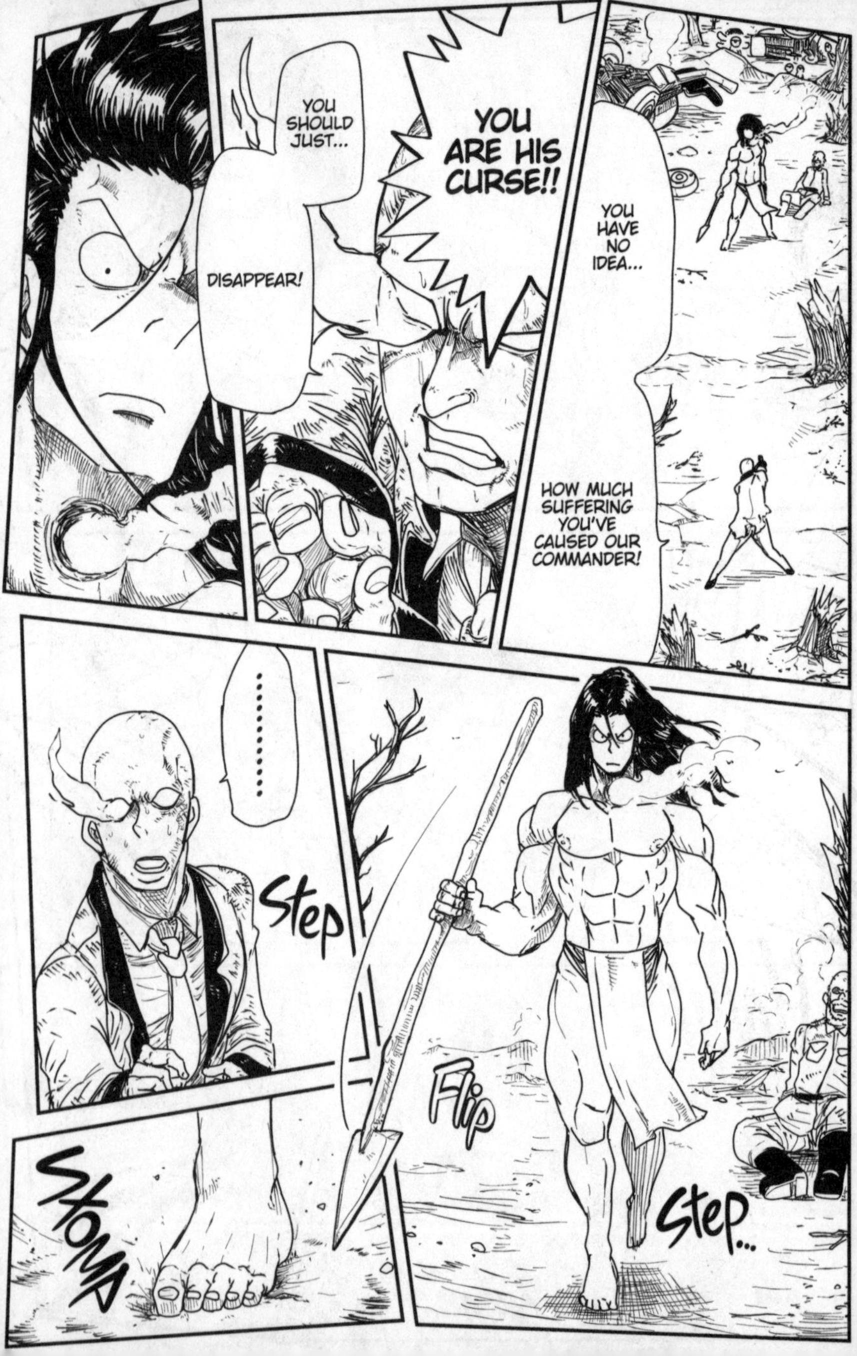
YOU HAVE NO IDEA...
HOW MUCH SUFFERING YOU'VE CAUSED OUR COMMANDER!
YOU ARE HIS CURSE!!
YOU SHOULD JUST...
DISAPPEAR!
Flip
Step...
......
Step
STOMP

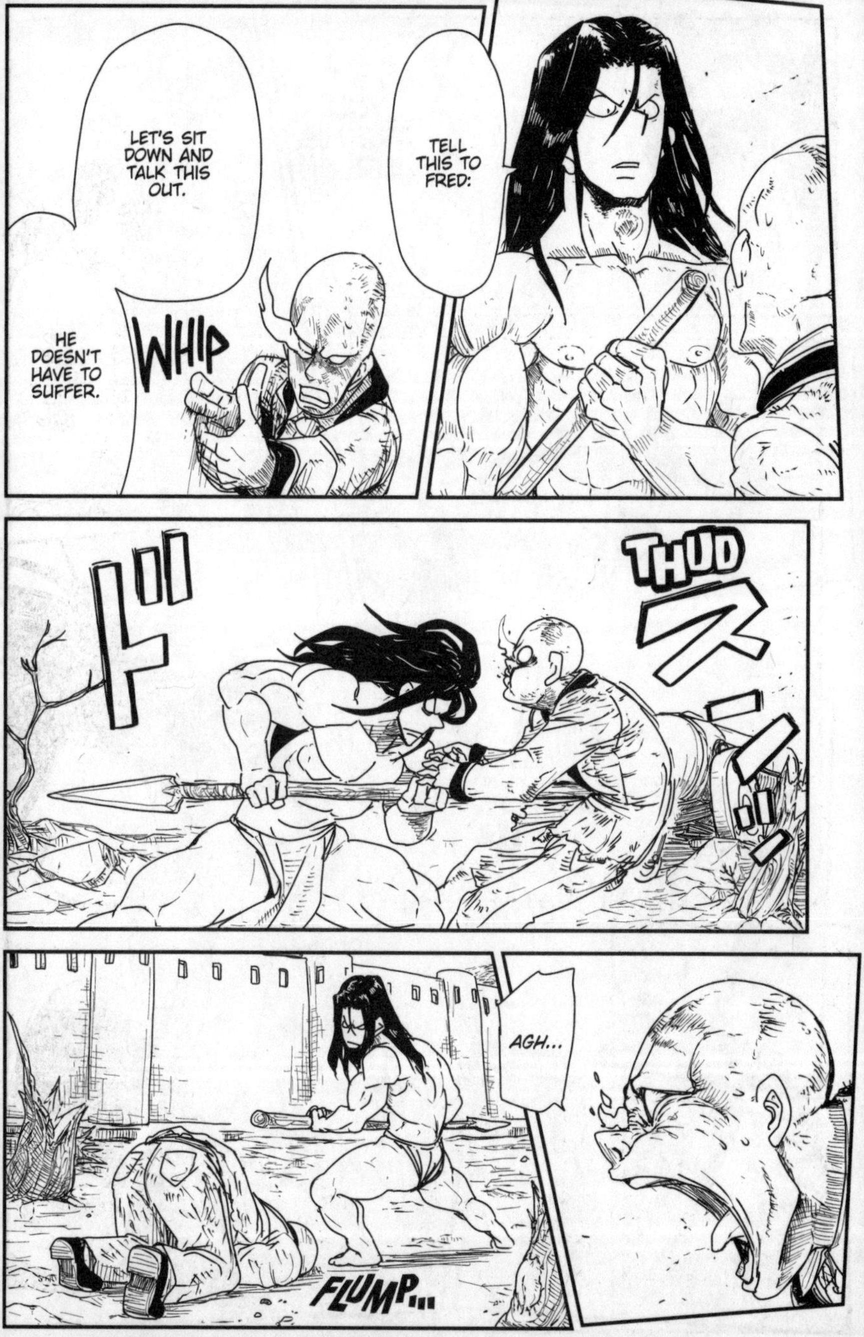
TELL THIS TO FRED:
LET'S SIT DOWN AND TALK THIS OUT.
HE DOESN'T HAVE TO SUFFER.
WHIP
THUD
AGH...
FLUMP...

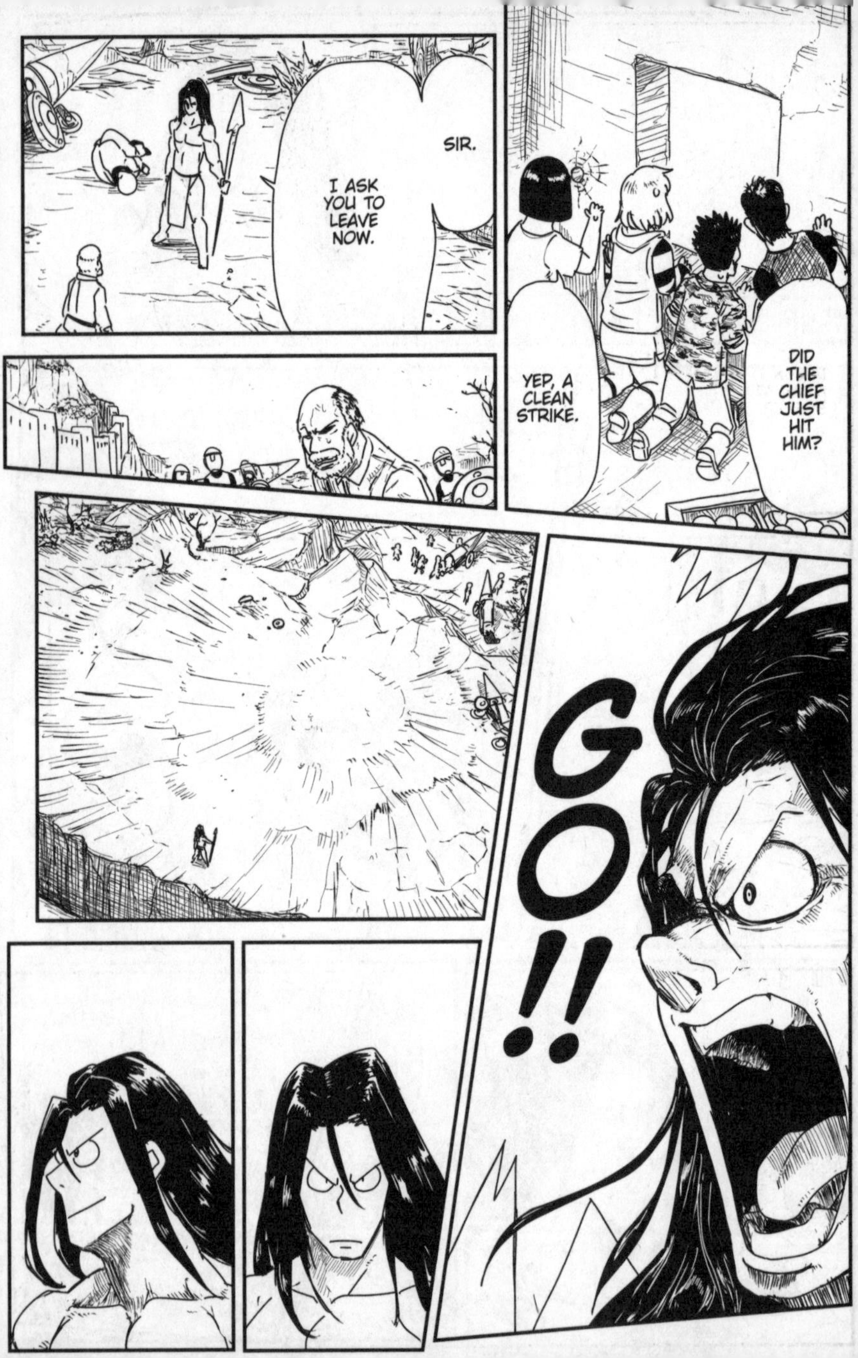
DID THE CHIEF JUST HIT HIM?
YEP, A CLEAN STRIKE.
SIR.
I ASK YOU TO LEAVE NOW.
GO!!

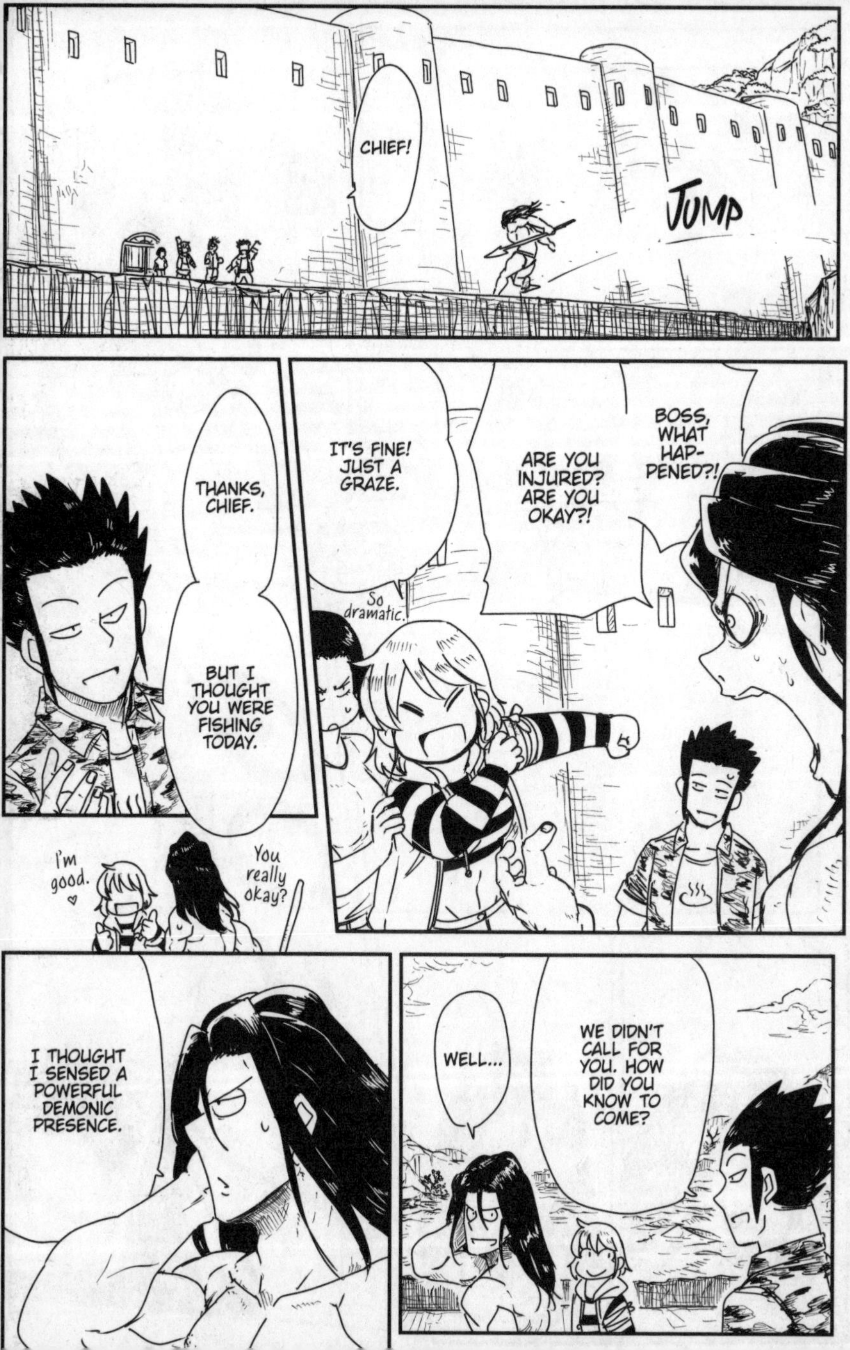
CHIEF!
JUMP
BOSS, WHAT HAP-PENED?!
ARE YOU INJURED? ARE YOU OKAY?!
IT'S FINE! JUST A GRAZE.
So dramatic.
THANKS, CHIEF.
BUT I THOUGHT YOU WERE FISHING TODAY.
You really okay?
I'm good. ♡
WE DIDN'T CALL FOR YOU. HOW DID YOU KNOW TO COME?
WELL...
I THOUGHT I SENSED A POWERFUL DEMONIC PRESENCE.

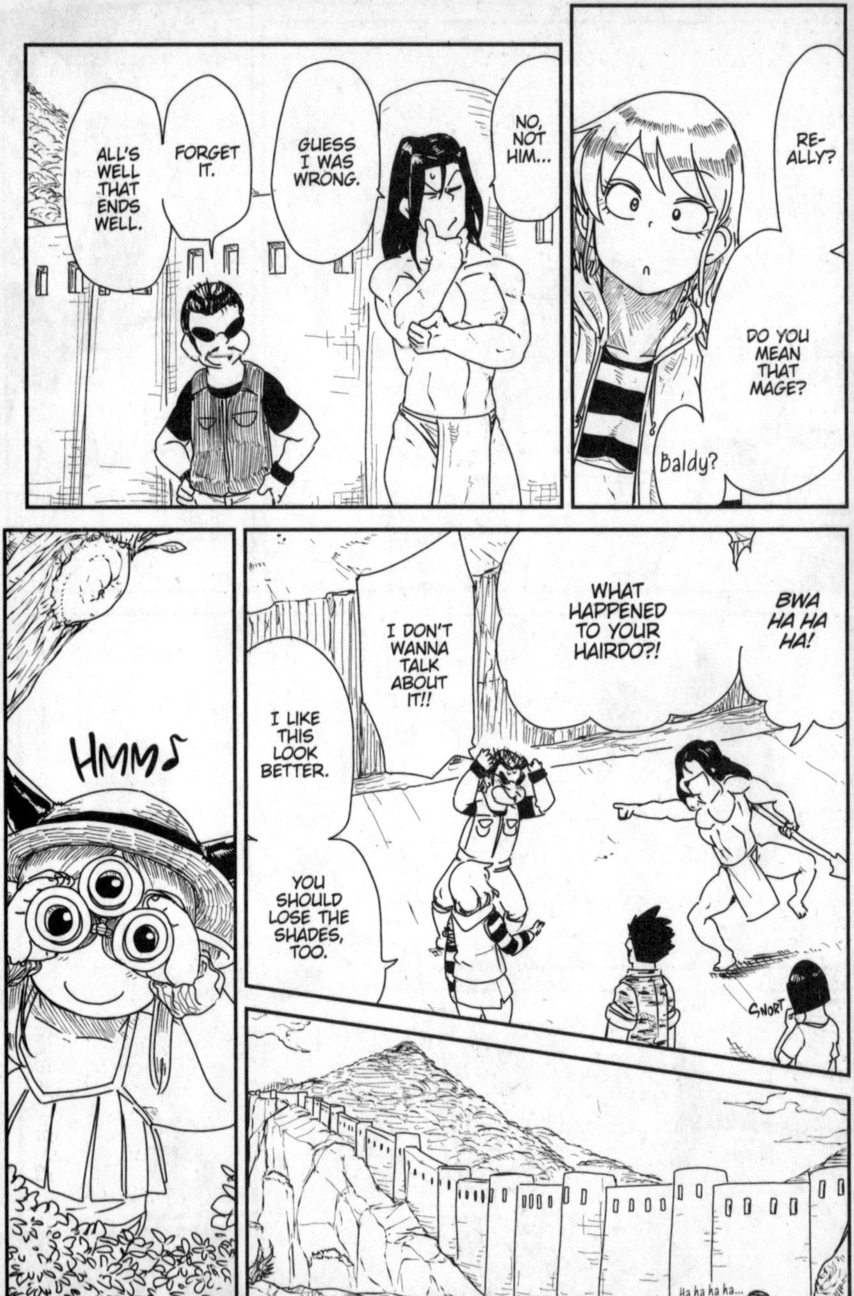
RE-ALLY?
DO YOU MEAN THAT MAGE?
Baldy?
NO, NOT HIM...
GUESS I WAS WRONG.
FORGET IT.
ALL'S WELL THAT ENDS WELL.
BWA HA HA HA!
WHAT HAPPENED TO YOUR HAIRDO?!
I DON'T WANNA TALK ABOUT IT!!
I LIKE THIS LOOK BETTER.
YOU SHOULD LOSE THE SHADES, TOO.
SNORT
Ha ha ha ha...
HMM♪

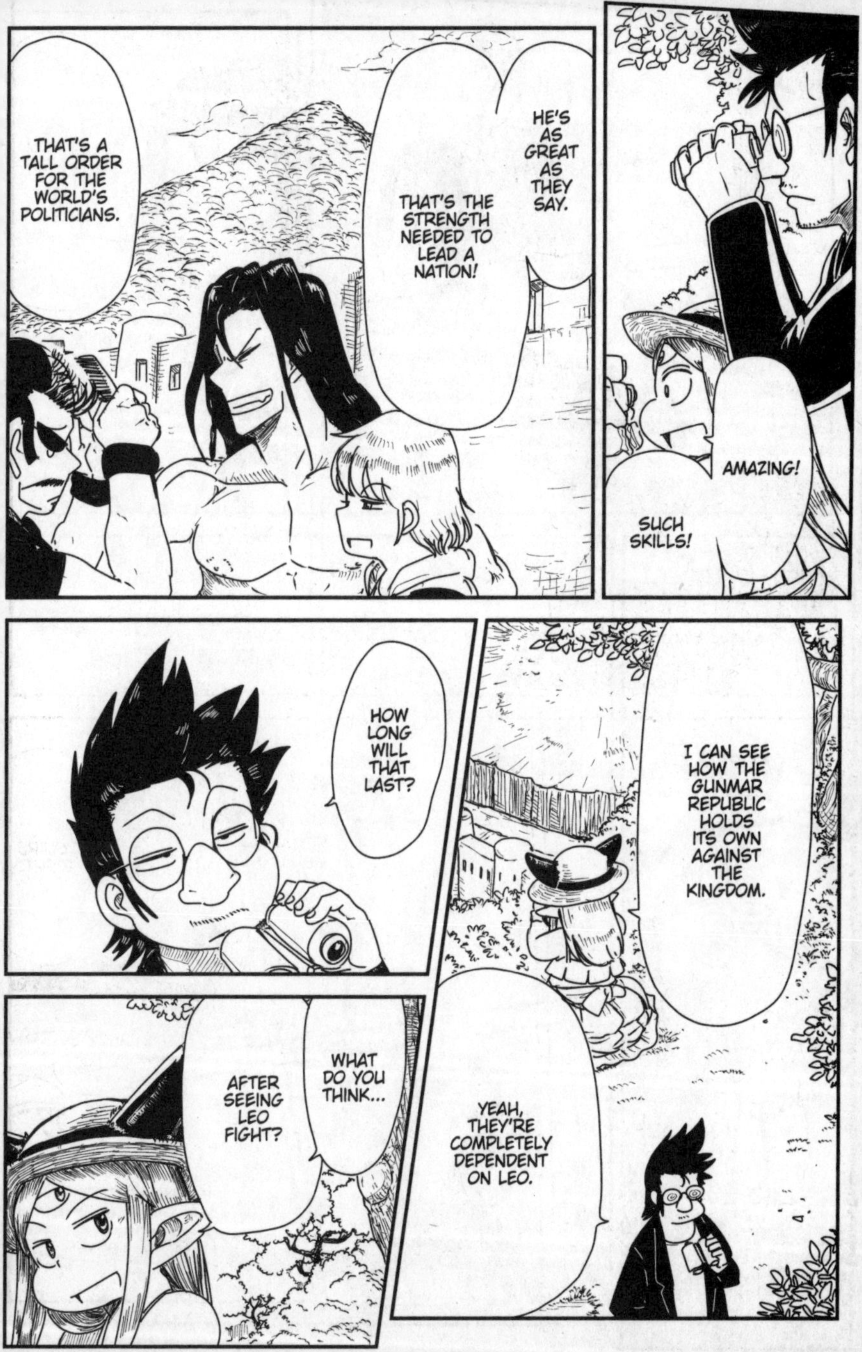
AMAZING!
SUCH SKILLS!
HE'S AS GREAT AS THEY SAY.
THAT'S THE STRENGTH NEEDED TO LEAD A NATION!
THAT'S A TALL ORDER FOR THE WORLD'S POLITICIANS.
I CAN SEE HOW THE GUNMAR REPUBLIC HOLDS ITS OWN AGAINST THE KINGDOM.
YEAH, THEY'RE COMPLETELY DEPENDENT ON LEO.
HOW LONG WILL THAT LAST?
WHAT DO YOU THINK...
AFTER SEEING LEO FIGHT?

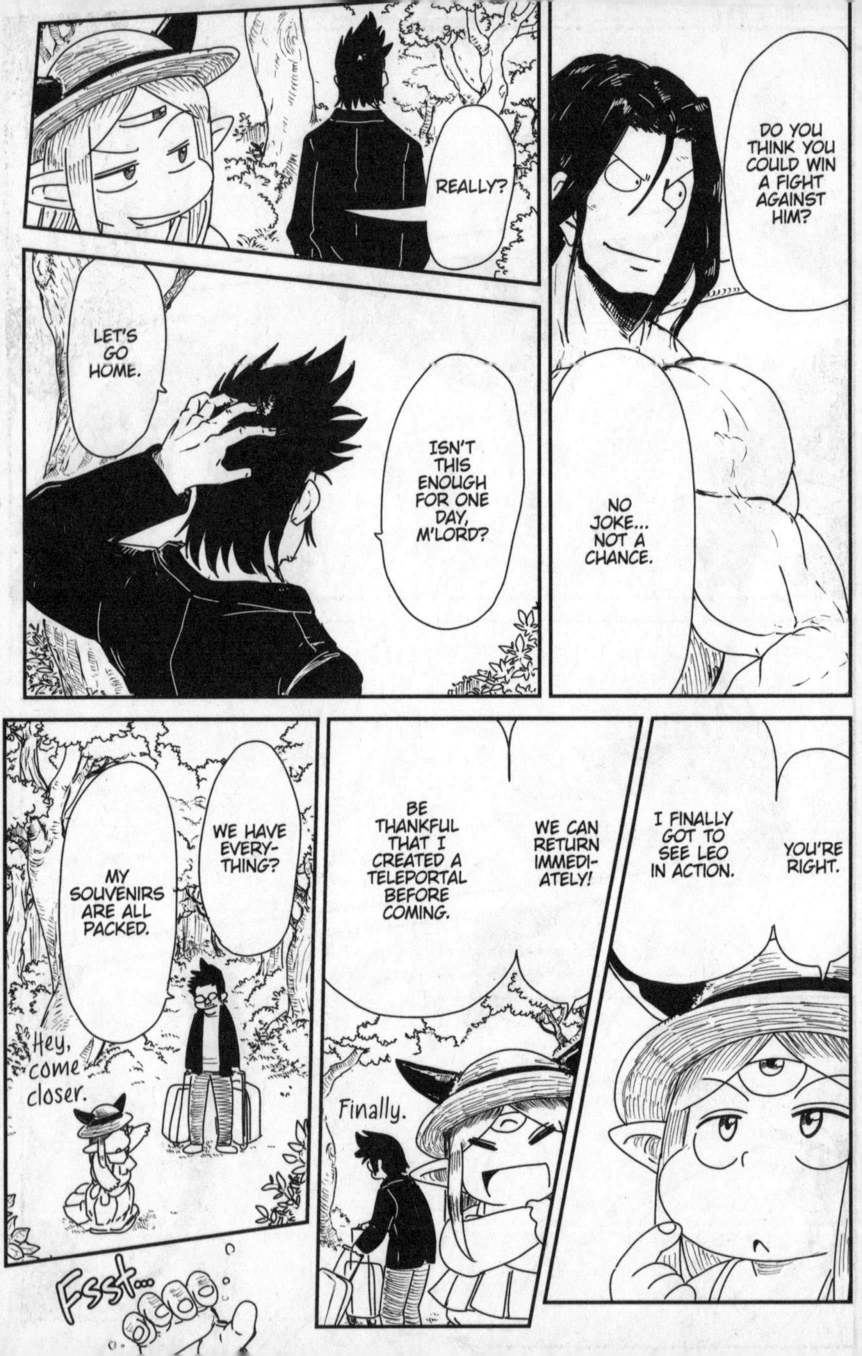
DO YOU THINK YOU COULD WIN A FIGHT AGAINST HIM?
NO JOKE... NOT A CHANCE.
REALLY?
ISN'T THIS ENOUGH FOR ONE DAY, M'LORD?
LET'S GO HOME.
YOU'RE RIGHT.
I FINALLY GOT TO SEE LEO IN ACTION.
WE CAN RETURN IMMEDIATELY!
BE THANKFUL THAT I CREATED A TELEPORTAL BEFORE COMING.
Finally.
WE HAVE EVERYTHING?
MY SOUVENIRS ARE ALL PACKED.
Hey, come closer.
Fsst...

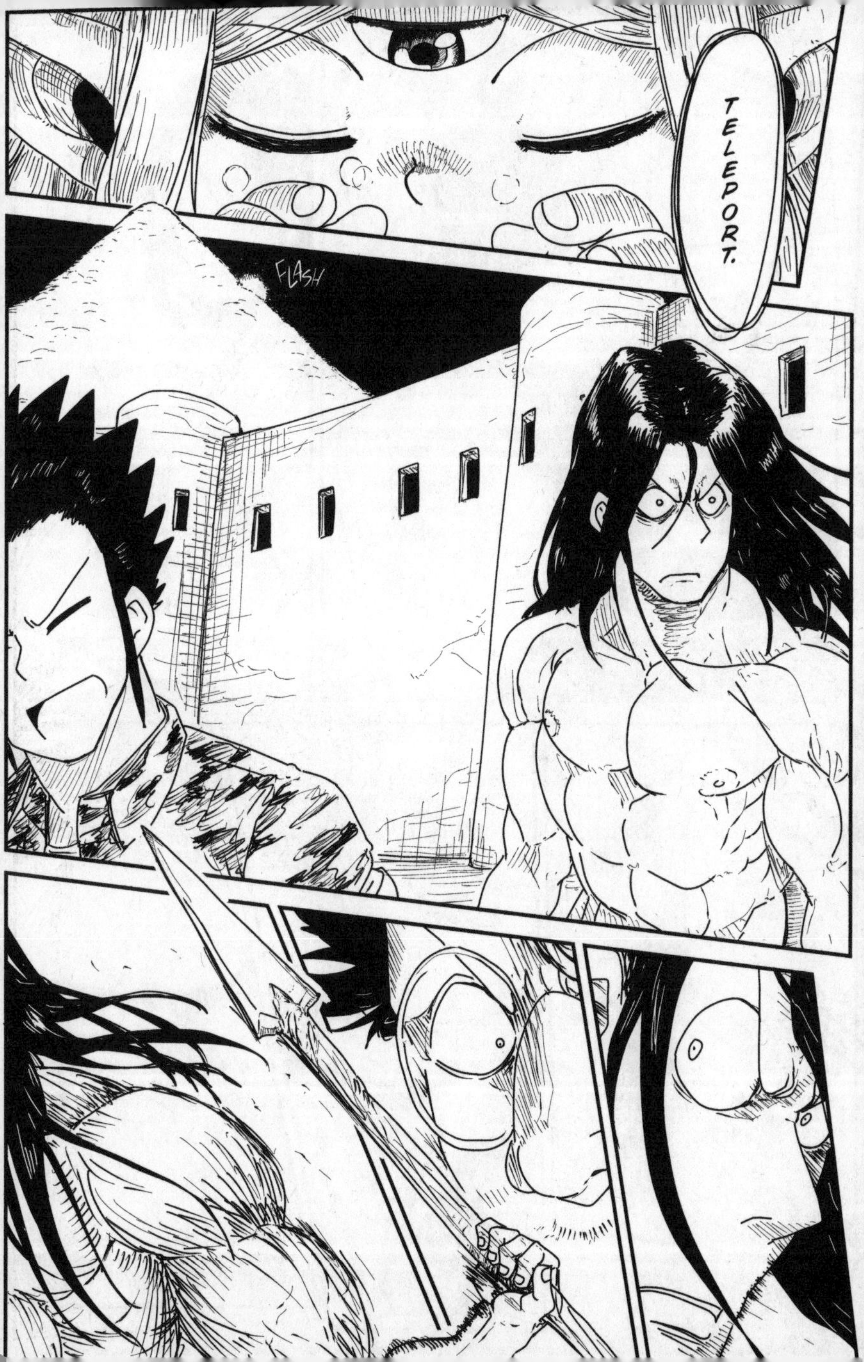
TELEPORT.
FLASH

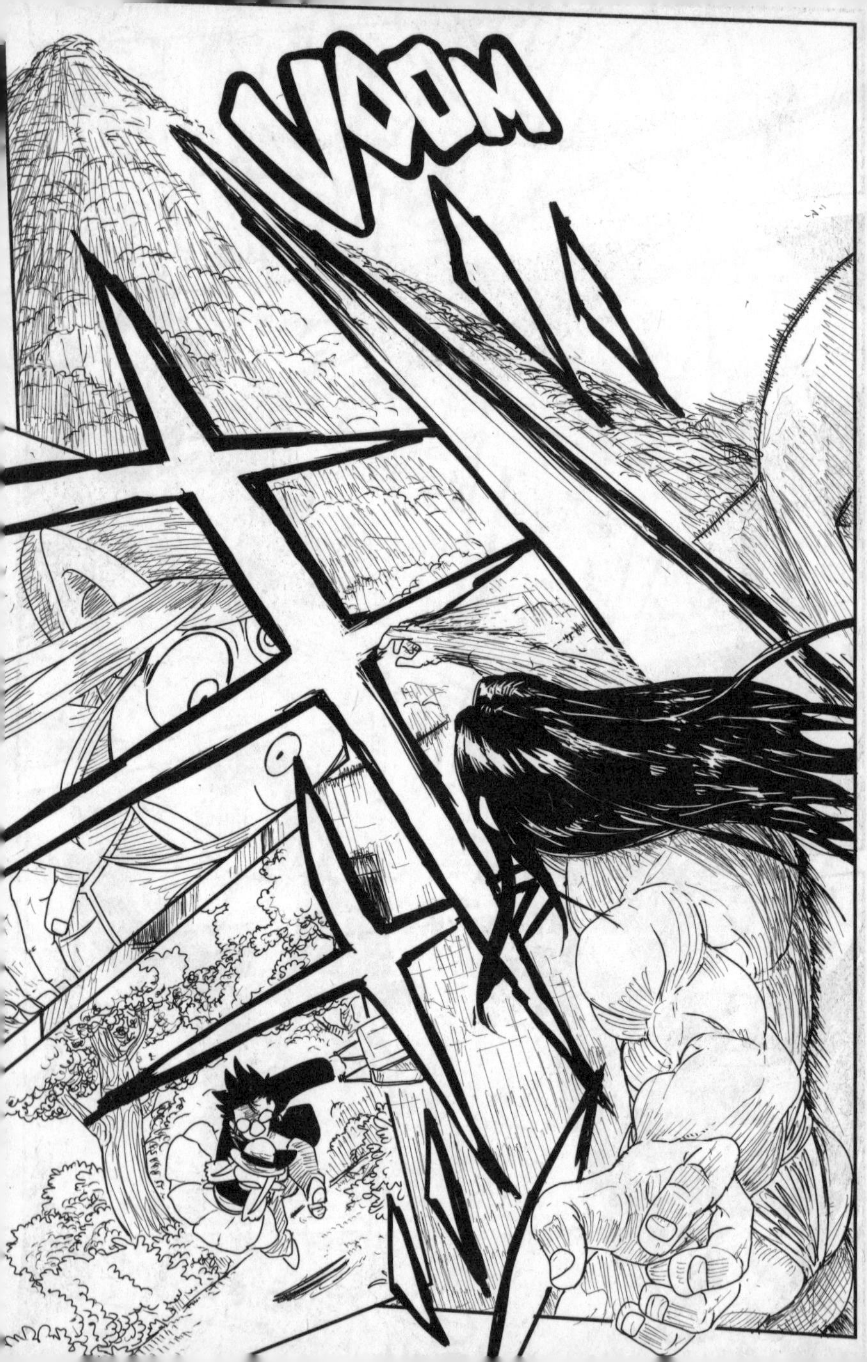
VOOM

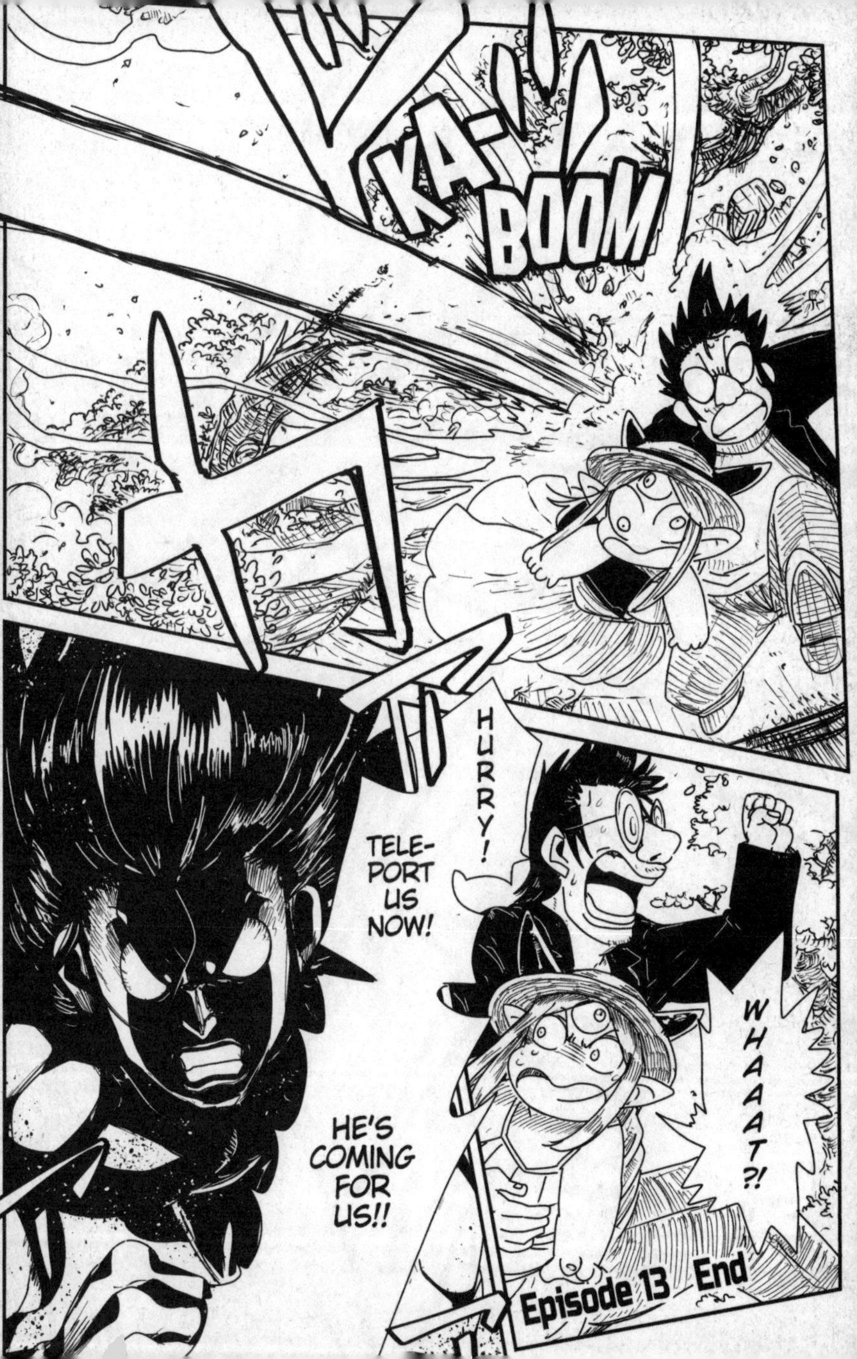
KA-BOOM
HURRY!
TELE-PORT US NOW!
WHAAAT?!
HE'S COMING FOR US!!
Episode 13 End

LEVEL 1 DEMON LORD & ONE ROOM HERO

LEVEL 1 DEMON LORD & ONE ROOM HERO

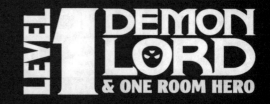

Episode 14: Leo the Warrior

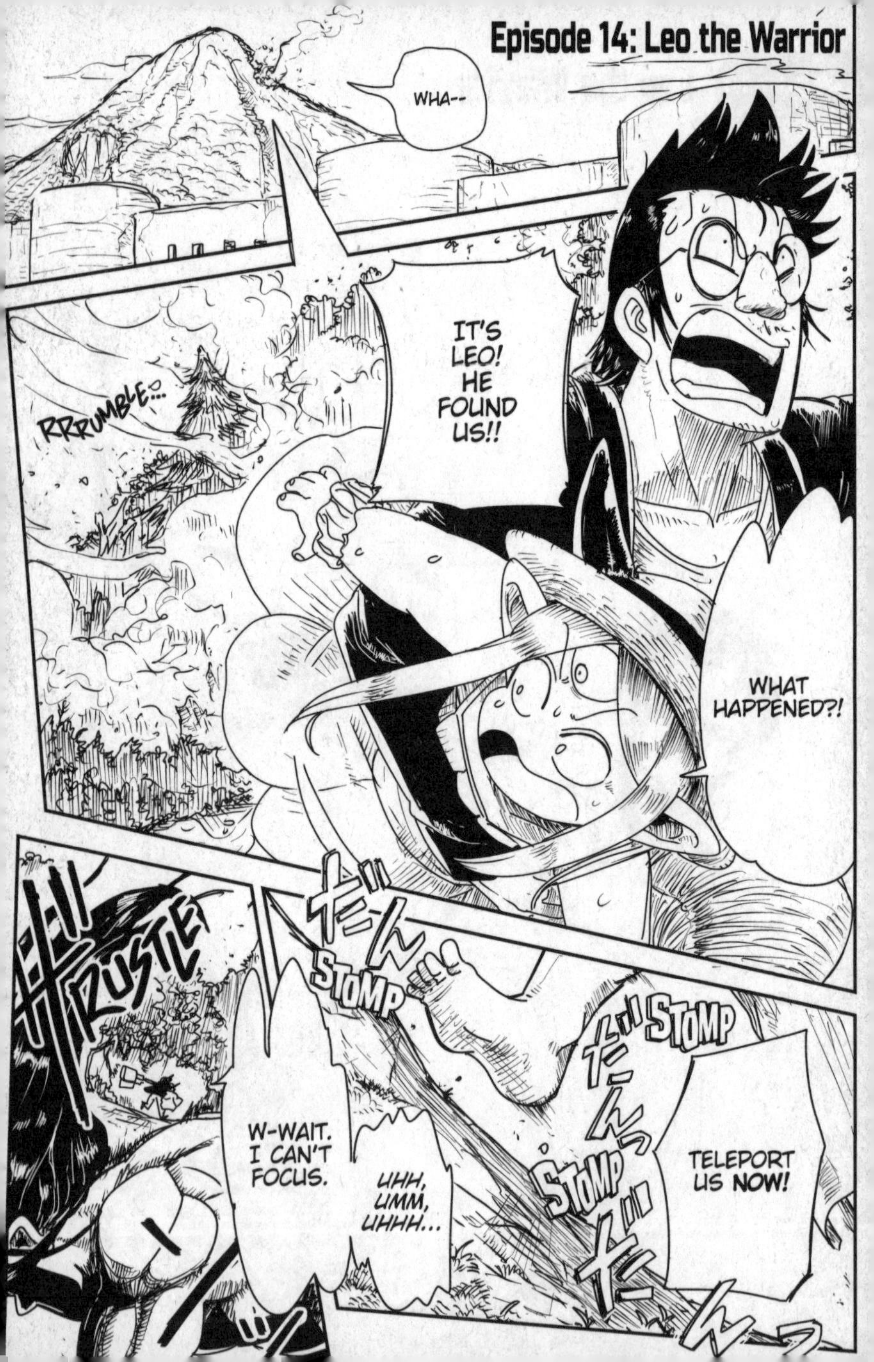
WHA--
WHAT HAPPENED?!
IT'S LEO! HE FOUND US!!
RRRUMBLE...
STOMP
STOMP
TELEPORT US NOW!
UHH, UMM, UHHH...
W-WAIT. I CAN'T FOCUS.
STOMP
RUSTLE

Episode 14 Leo the Warrior

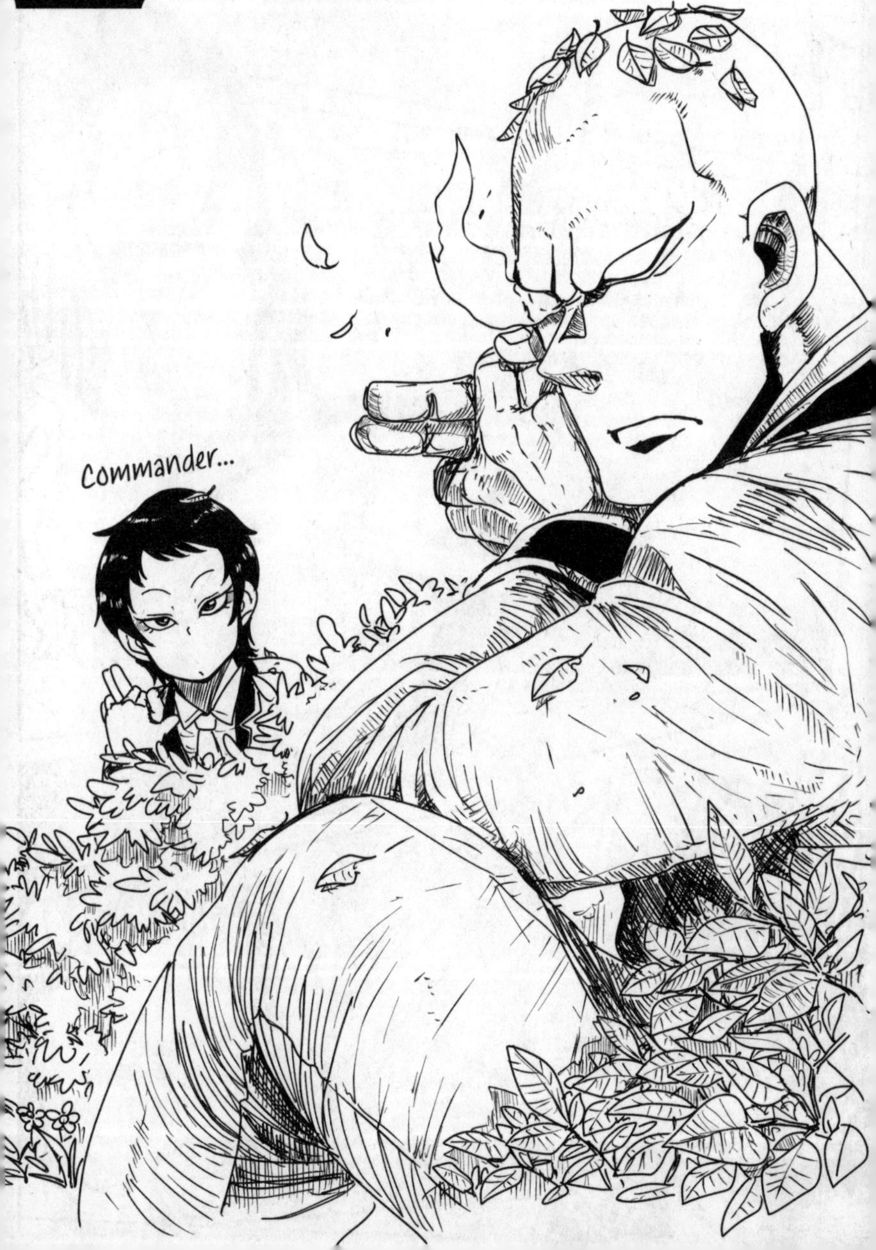
Commander...

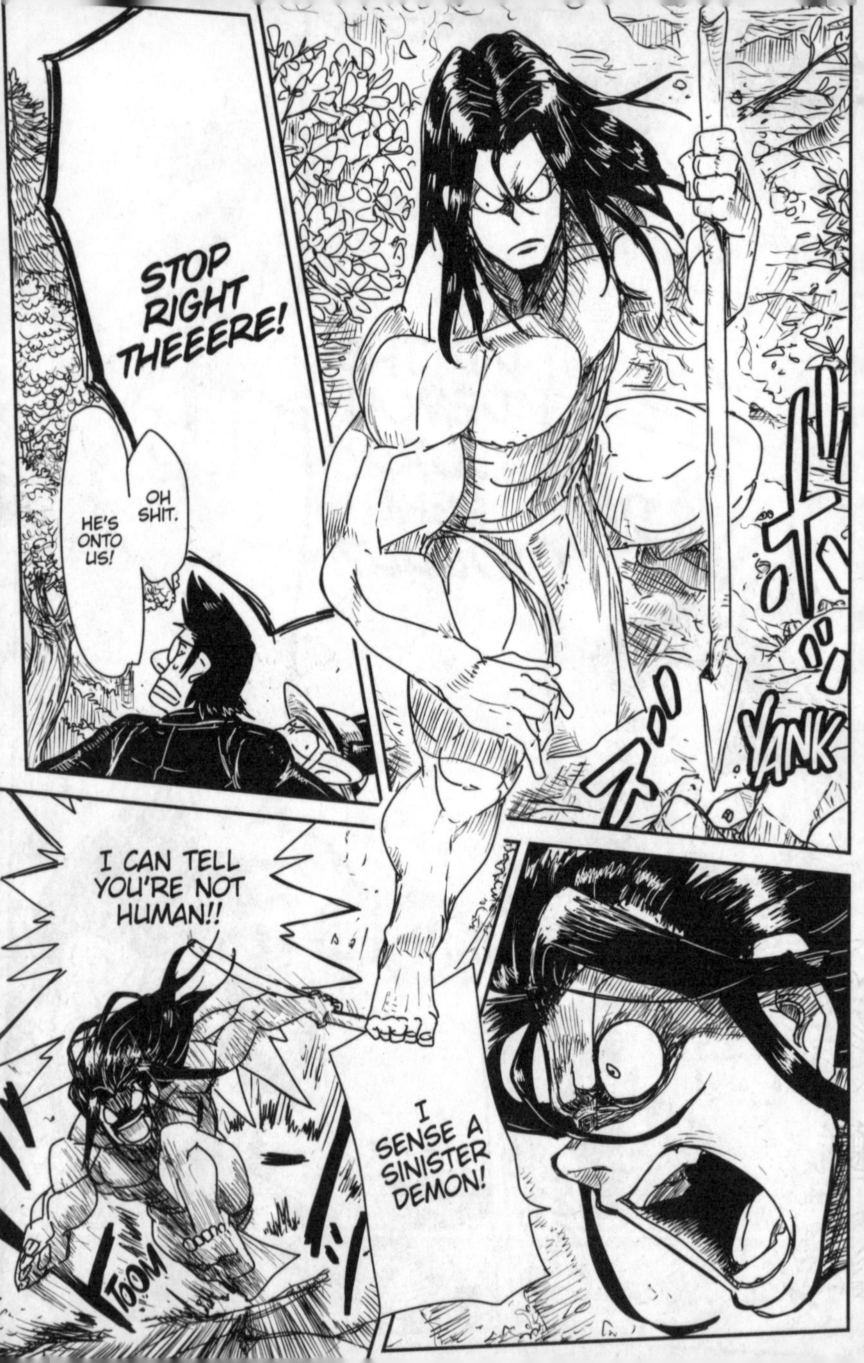
YANK
STOP RIGHT THEEERE!
OH SHIT.
HE'S ONTO US!
I SENSE A SINISTER DEMON!
I CAN TELL YOU'RE NOT HUMAN!!
TOOM

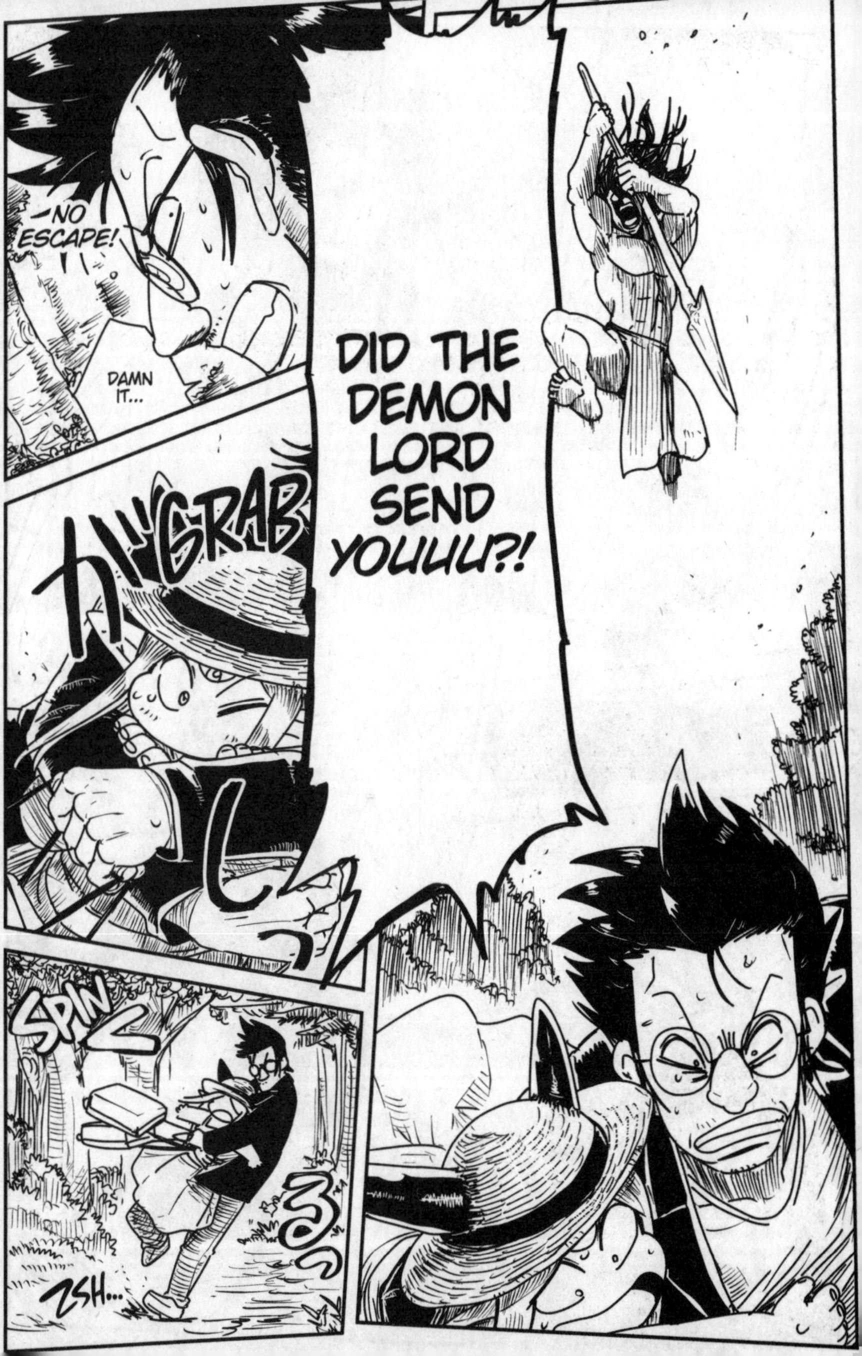
DID THE DEMON LORD SEND YOUUU?!
—NO ESCAPE!
DAMN IT...
GRAB
SPIN
ZSH...

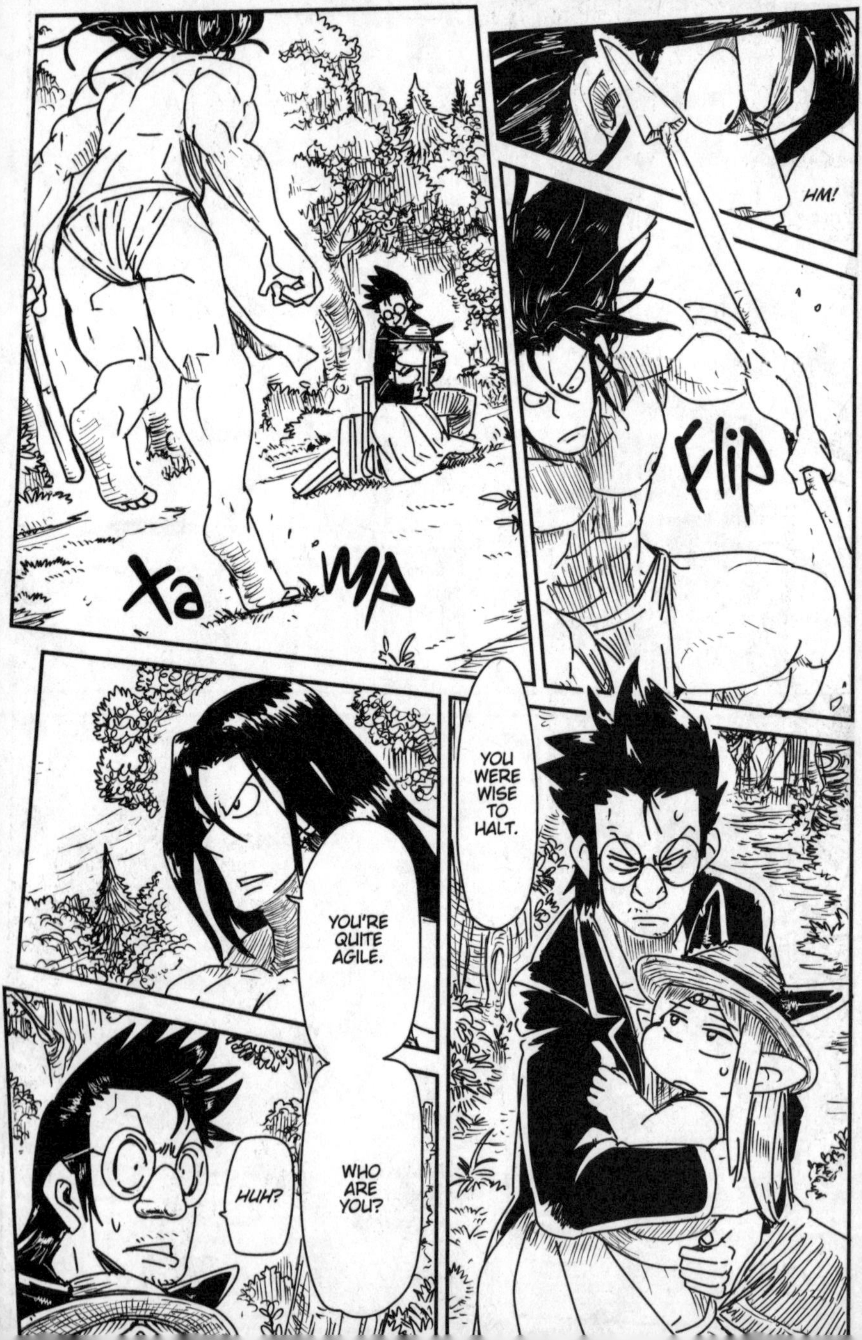
HM!
Flip
ta mp
YOU WERE WISE TO HALT.
YOU'RE QUITE AGILE.
WHO ARE YOU?
HUH?

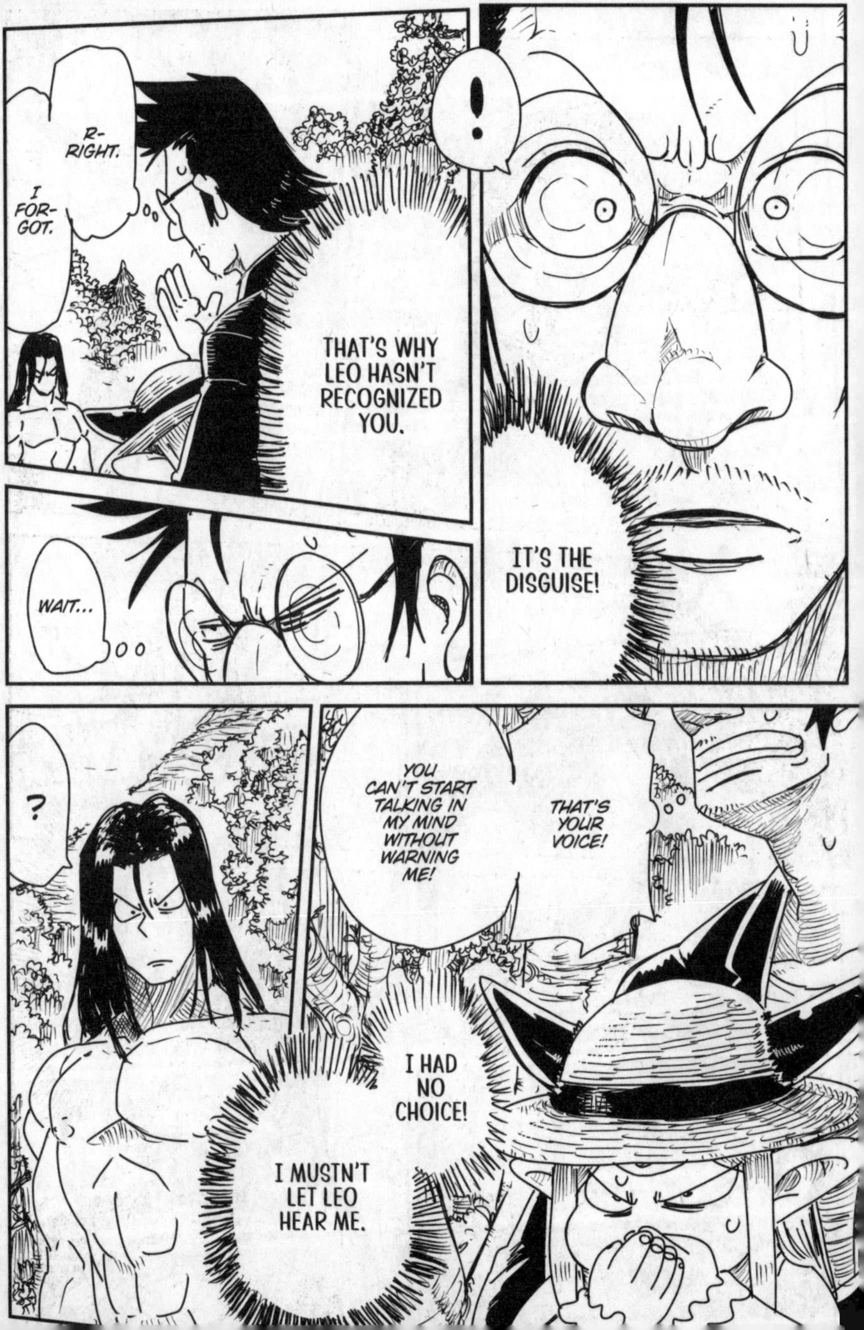
!
IT'S THE DISGUISE!
THAT'S WHY LEO HASN'T RECOGNIZED YOU.
R- RIGHT.
I FORGOT.
WAIT...
THAT'S YOUR VOICE!
YOU CAN'T START TALKING IN MY MIND WITHOUT WARNING ME!
I HAD NO CHOICE!
I MUSTN'T LET LEO HEAR ME.
?

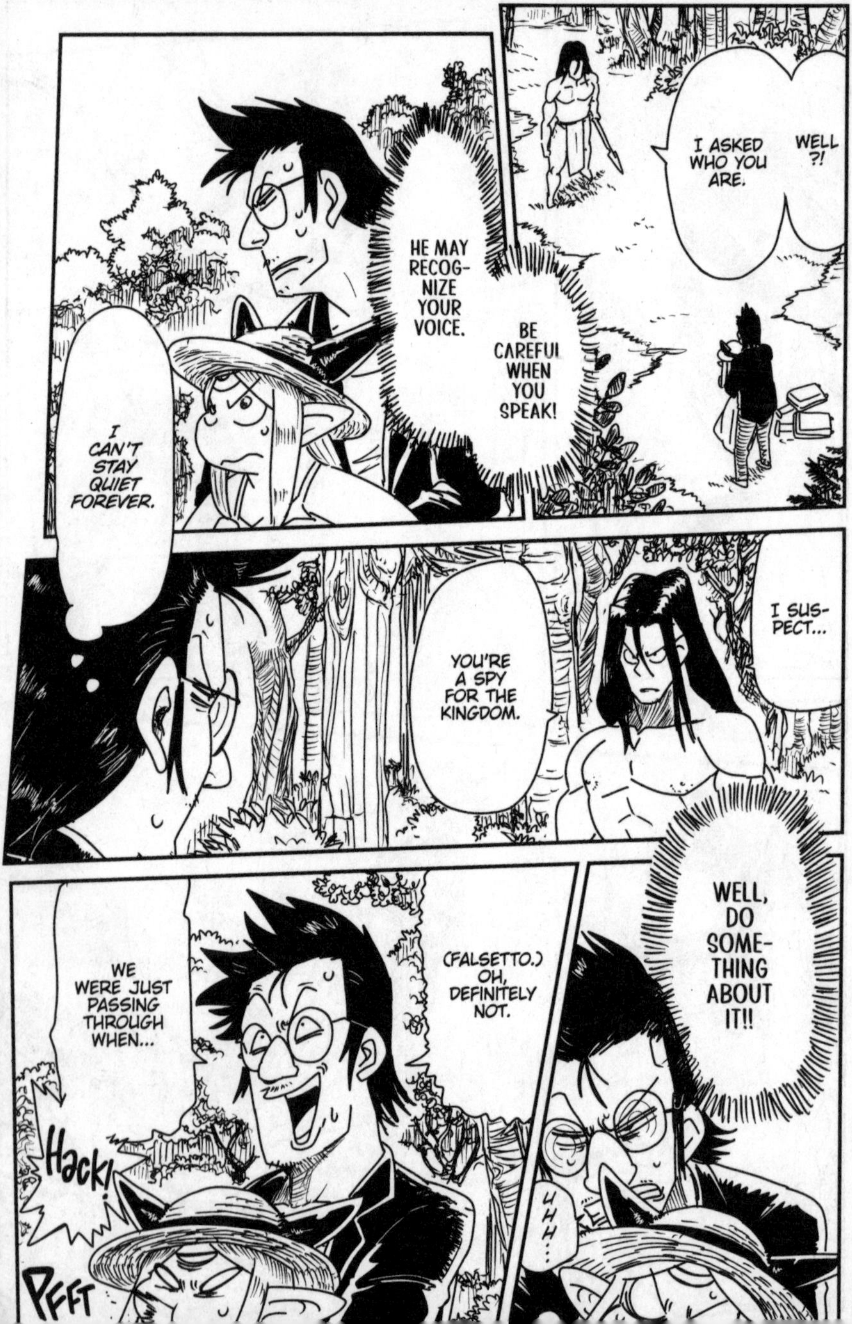
WELL ?!
I ASKED WHO YOU ARE.
BE CAREFUL WHEN YOU SPEAK!
HE MAY RECOGNIZE YOUR VOICE.
I CAN'T STAY QUIET FOREVER.
I SUSPECT...
YOU'RE A SPY FOR THE KINGDOM.
WELL, DO SOMETHING ABOUT IT!!
UHH...
(FALSETTO.) OH, DEFINITELY NOT.
WE WERE JUST PASSING THROUGH WHEN...
Hack!
PFFT

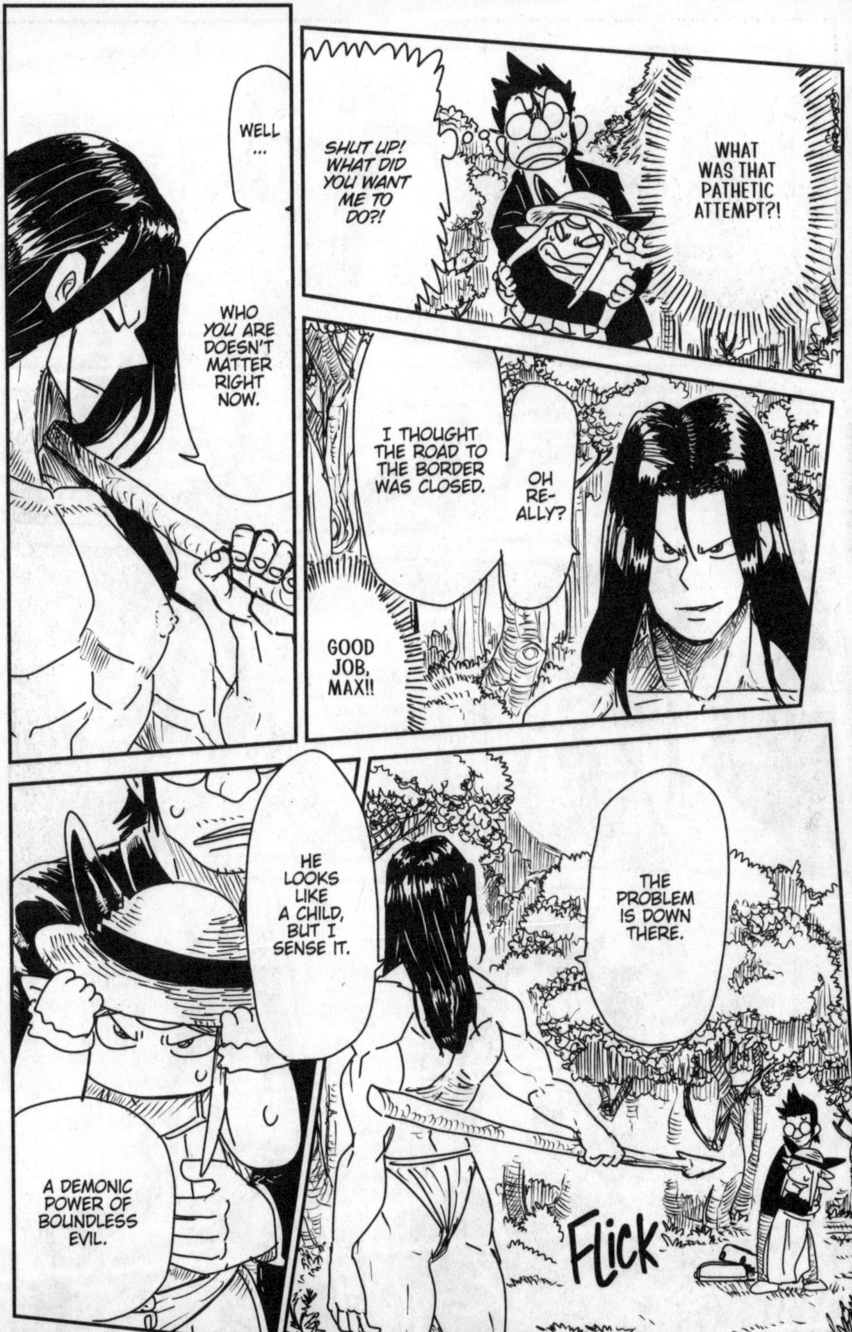
WHAT WAS THAT PATHETIC ATTEMPT?!
SHUT UP! WHAT DID YOU WANT ME TO DO?!
OH RE-ALLY?
I THOUGHT THE ROAD TO THE BORDER WAS CLOSED.
GOOD JOB, MAX!!
WELL ...
WHO YOU ARE DOESN'T MATTER RIGHT NOW.
THE PROBLEM IS DOWN THERE.
HE LOOKS LIKE A CHILD, BUT I SENSE IT.
FLICK
A DEMONIC POWER OF BOUNDLESS EVIL.

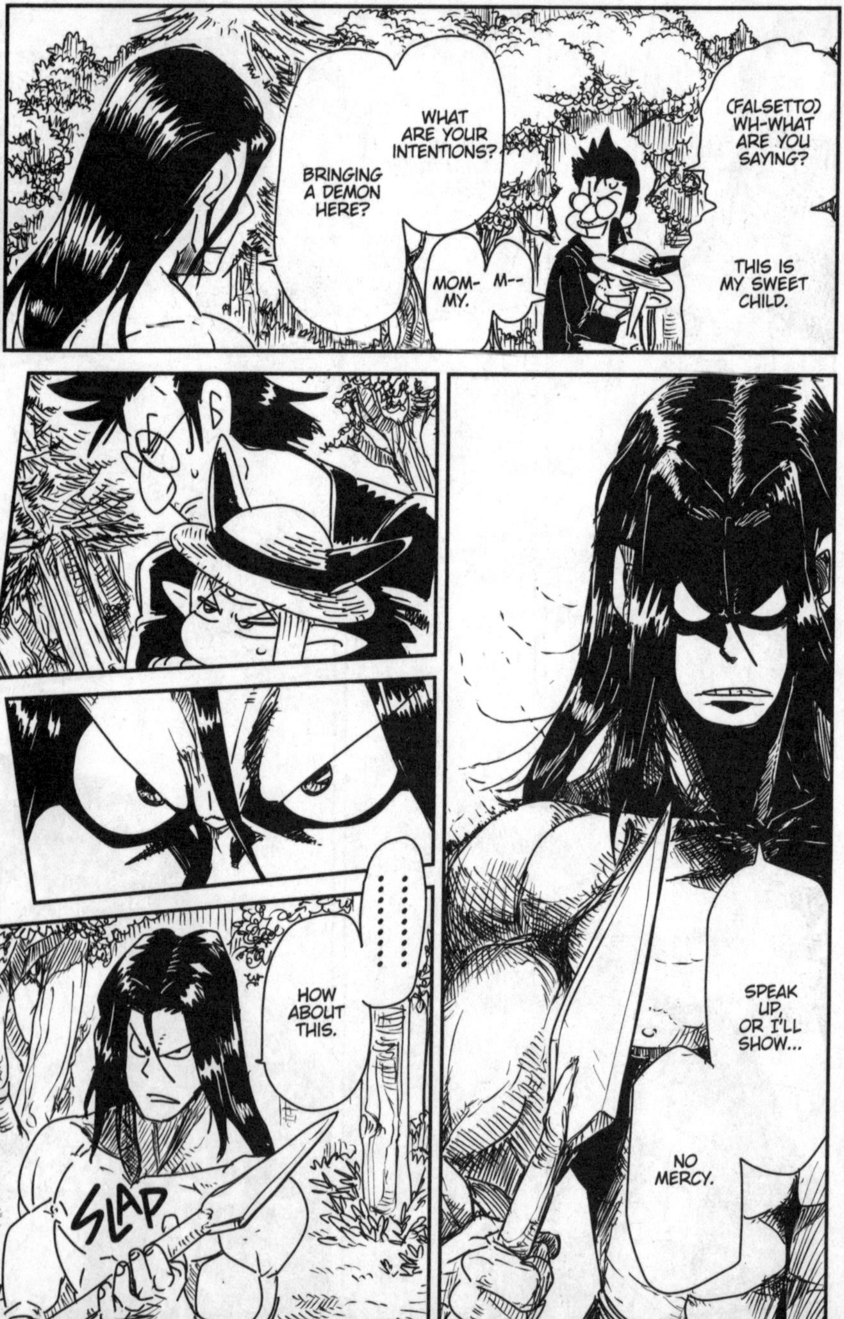
(FALSETTO) WH-WHAT ARE YOU SAYING?
THIS IS MY SWEET CHILD.
M--
MOM-MY.
WHAT ARE YOUR INTENTIONS?
BRINGING A DEMON HERE?
SPEAK UP, OR I'LL SHOW...
NO MERCY.
......
HOW ABOUT THIS.
SLAP

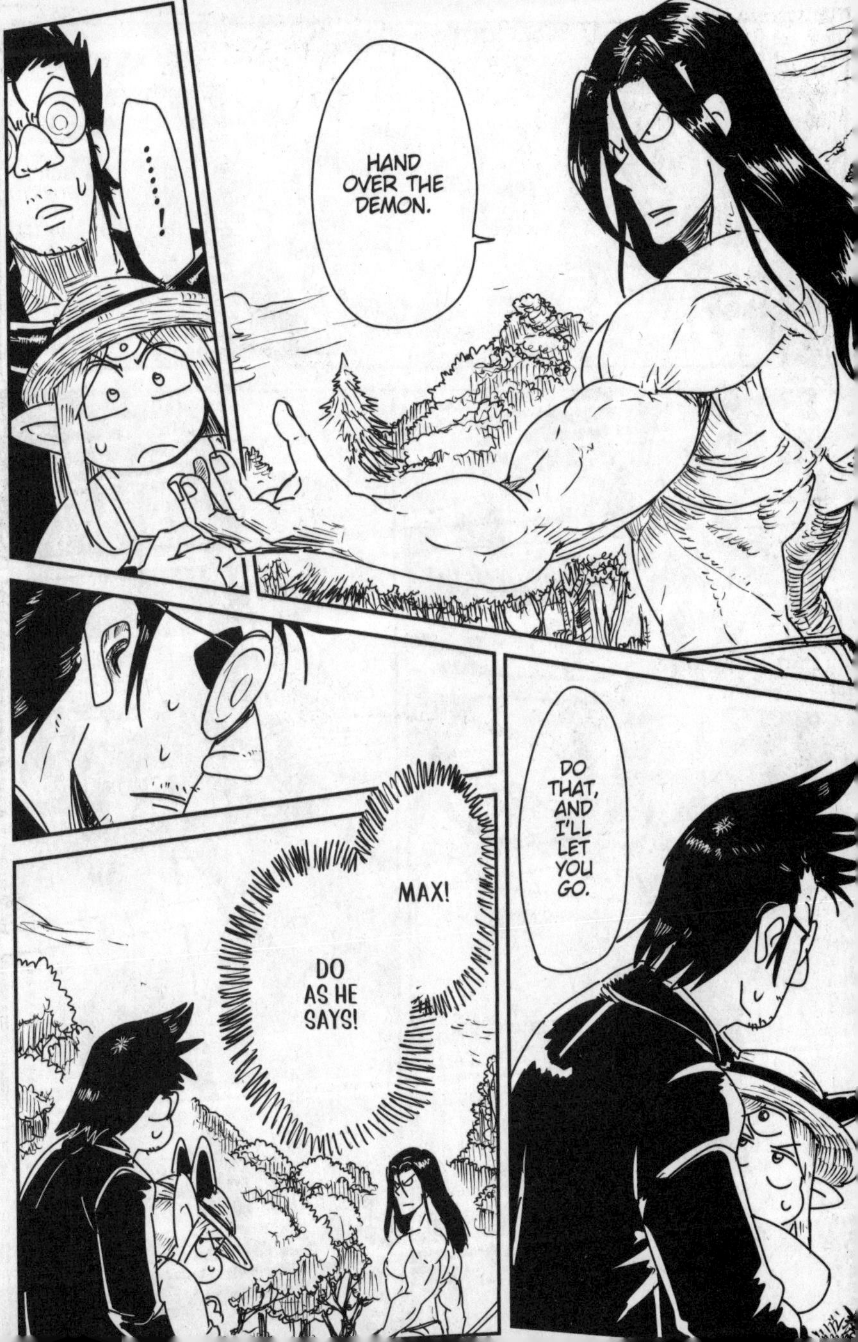
HAND OVER THE DEMON.
......!
DO THAT, AND I'LL LET YOU GO.
MAX!
DO AS HE SAYS!

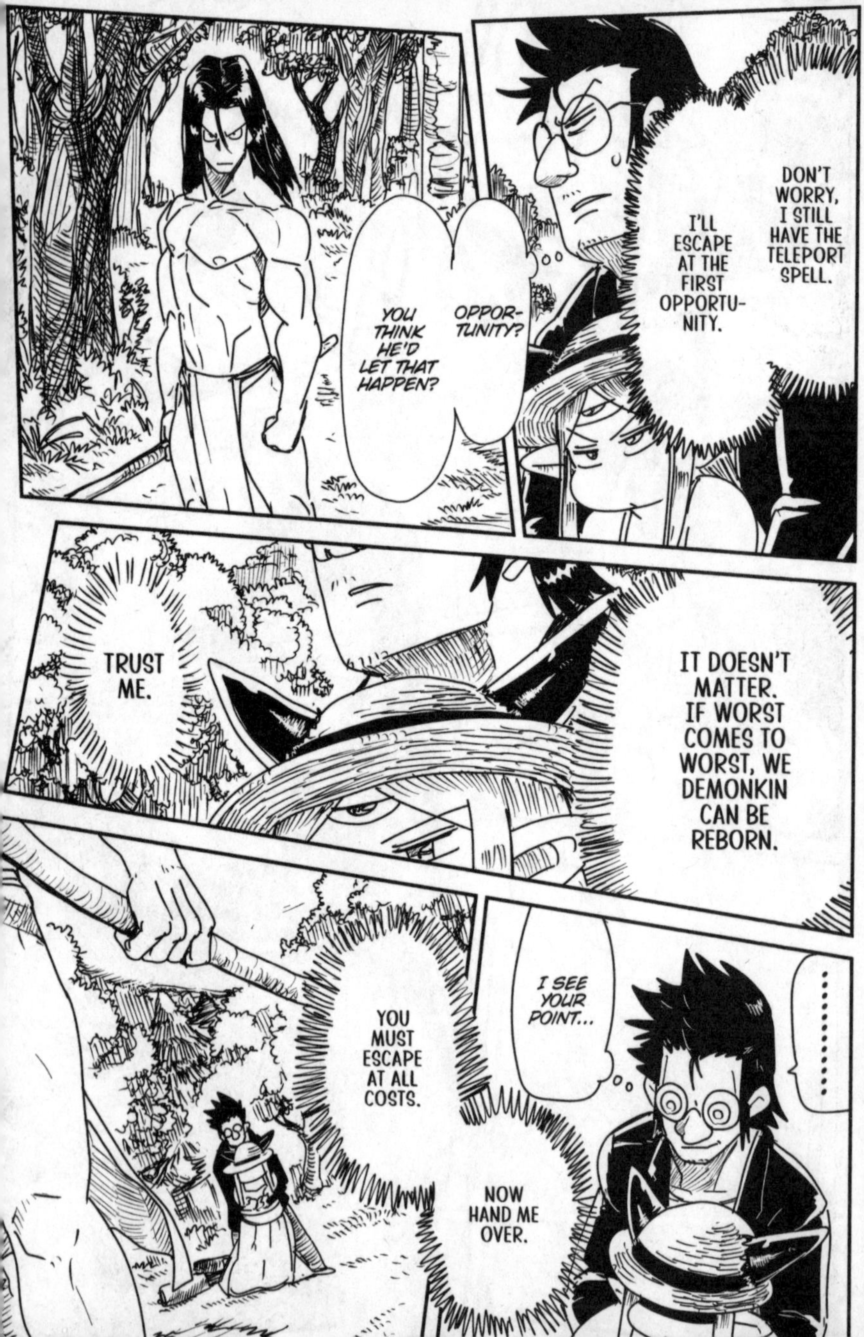

DON'T WORRY, I STILL HAVE THE TELEPORT SPELL.
I'LL ESCAPE AT THE FIRST OPPORTUNITY.
OPPORTUNITY?
YOU THINK HE'D LET THAT HAPPEN?
IT DOESN'T MATTER. IF WORST COMES TO WORST, WE DEMONKIN CAN BE REBORN.
TRUST ME.
......
I SEE YOUR POINT...
YOU MUST ESCAPE AT ALL COSTS.
NOW HAND ME OVER.

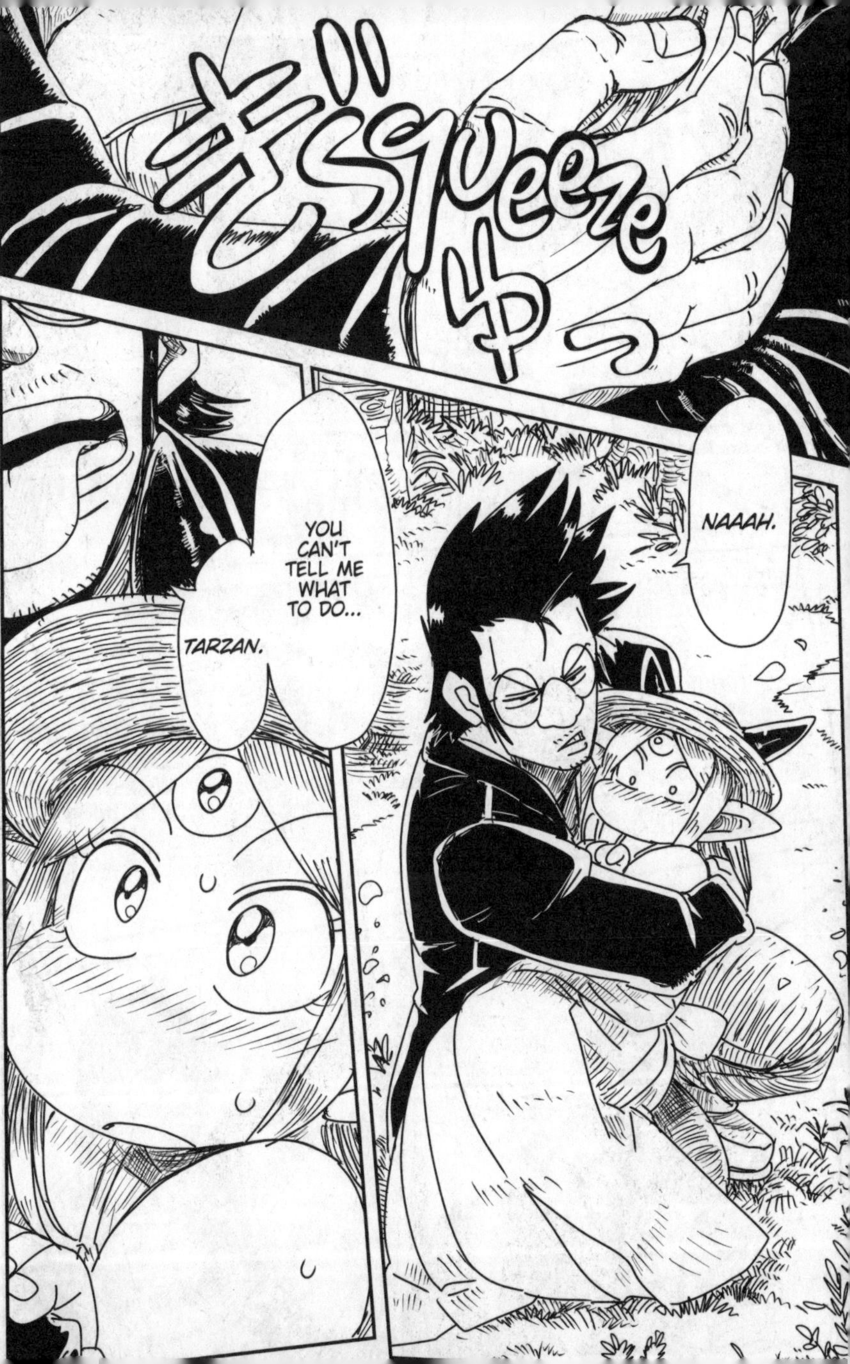
ぎゅっ
Squeeze
NAAAH.
YOU CAN'T TELL ME WHAT TO DO...
TARZAN.

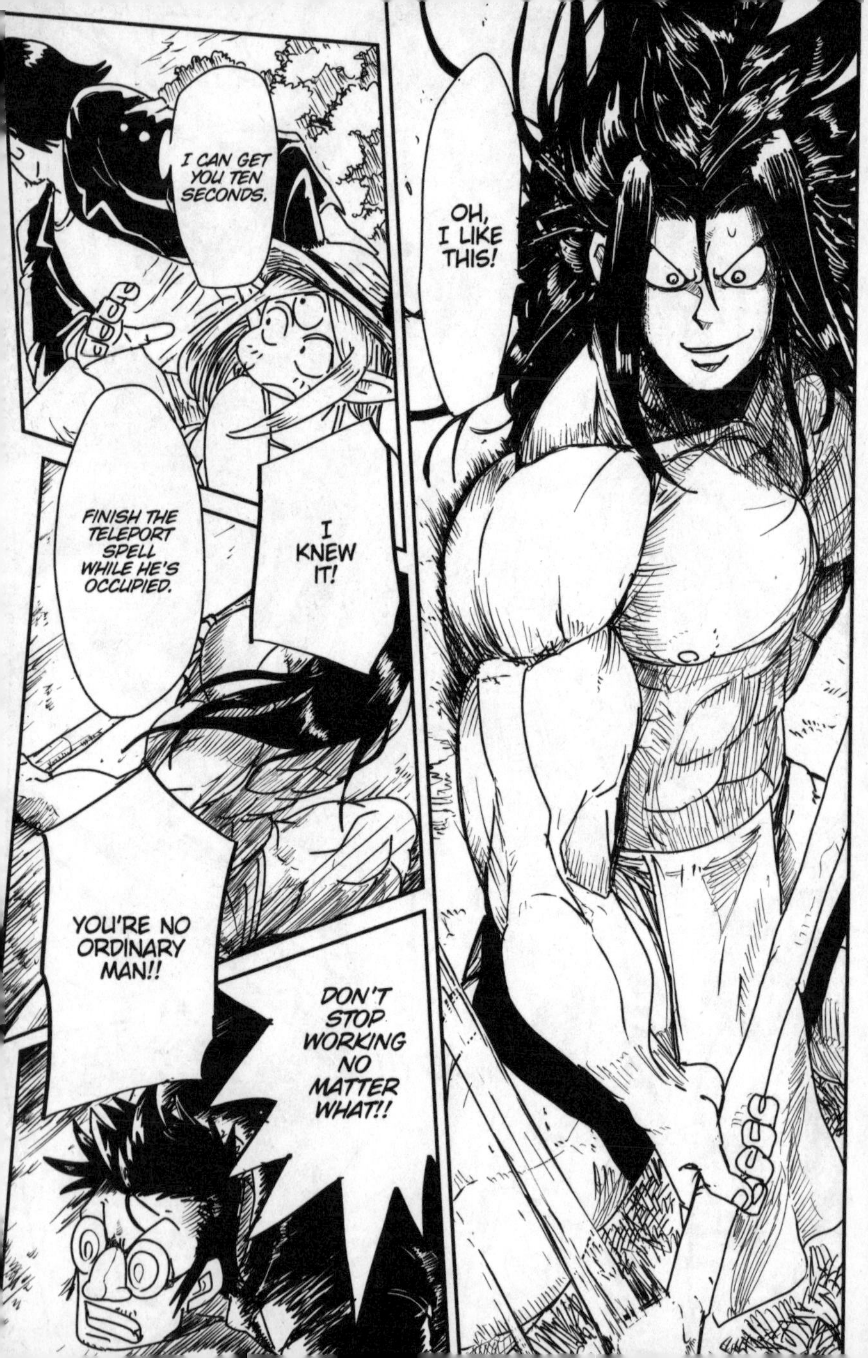
OH, I LIKE THIS!
I CAN GET YOU TEN SECONDS.
I KNEW IT!
FINISH THE TELEPORT SPELL WHILE HE'S OCCUPIED.
YOU'RE NO ORDINARY MAN!!
DON'T STOP WORKING NO MATTER WHAT!!

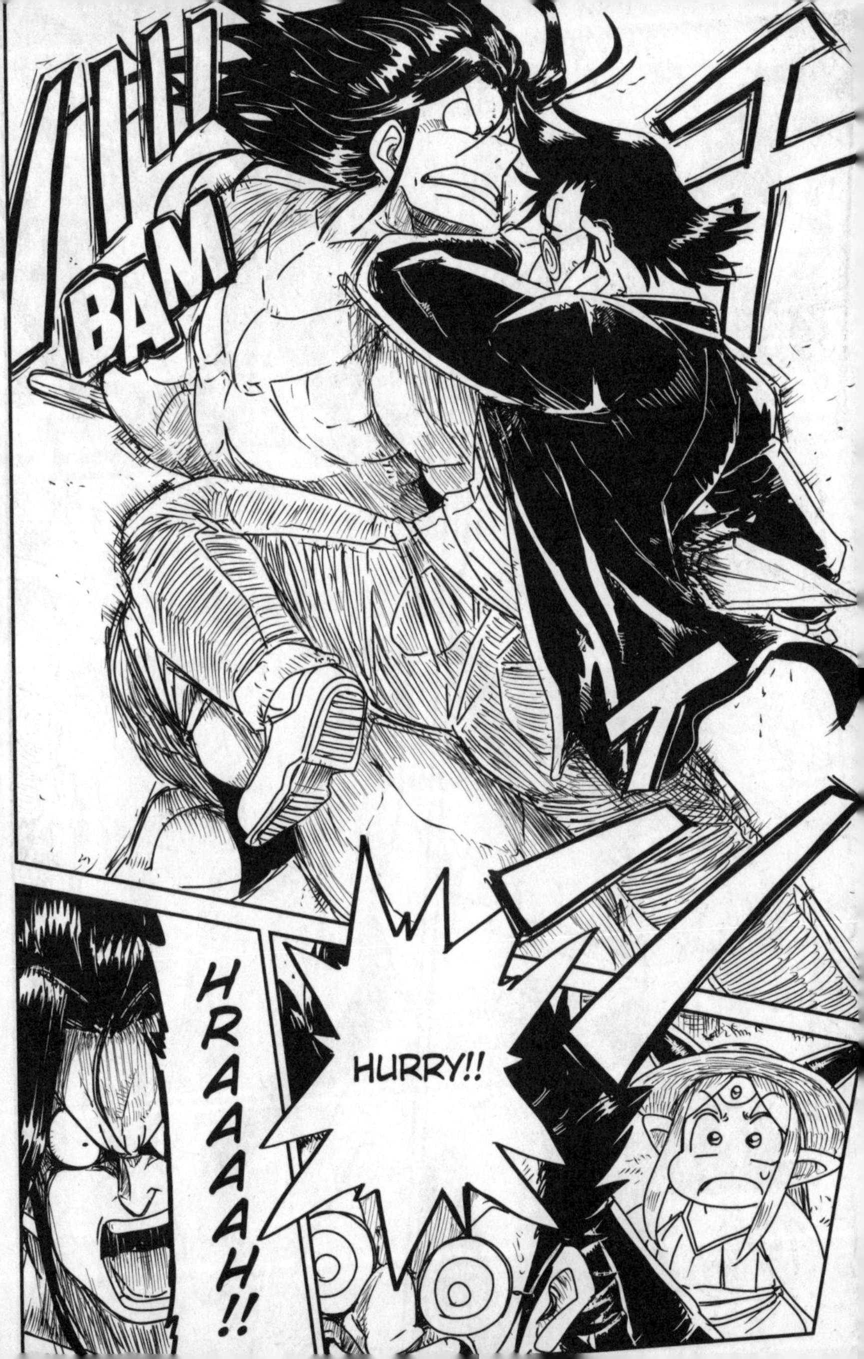
BAM
HURRY!!
HRAAAAH!!

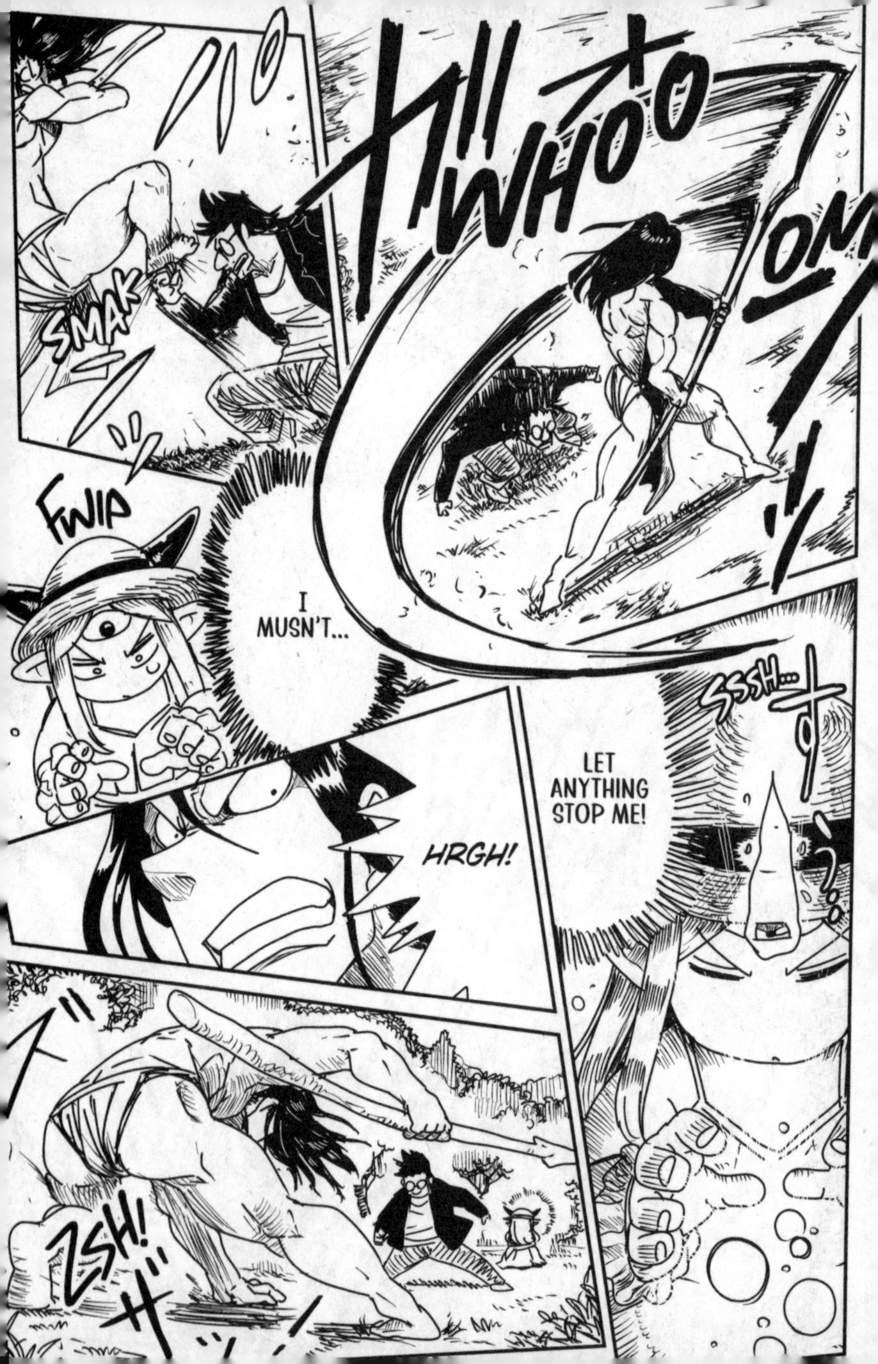
WHOOOOM
SMAK
FWIP
I MUSN'T...
SSSH...
LET ANYTHING STOP ME!
HRGH!
ZSH!

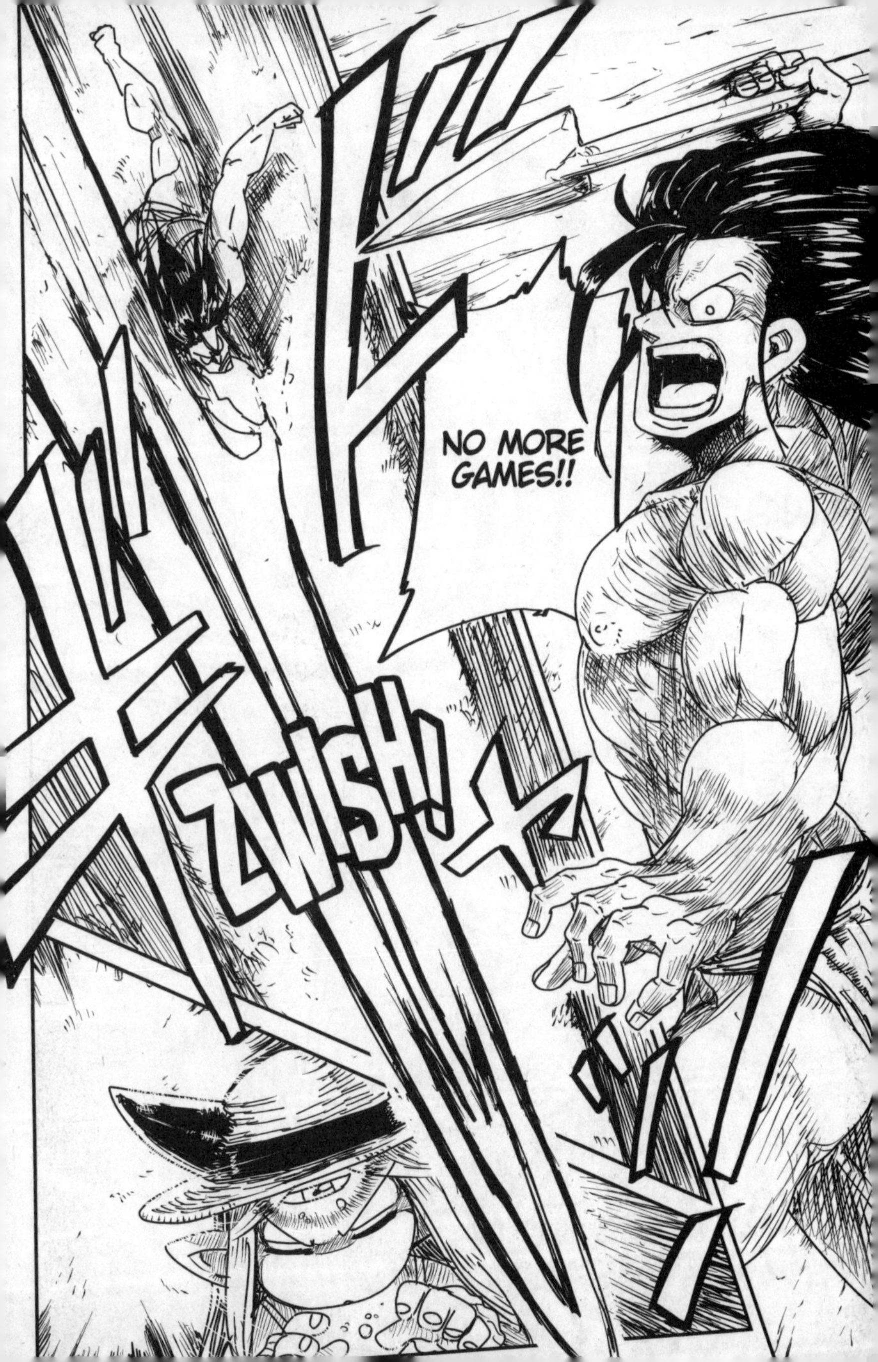
NO MORE GAMES!!
ZWISH!!

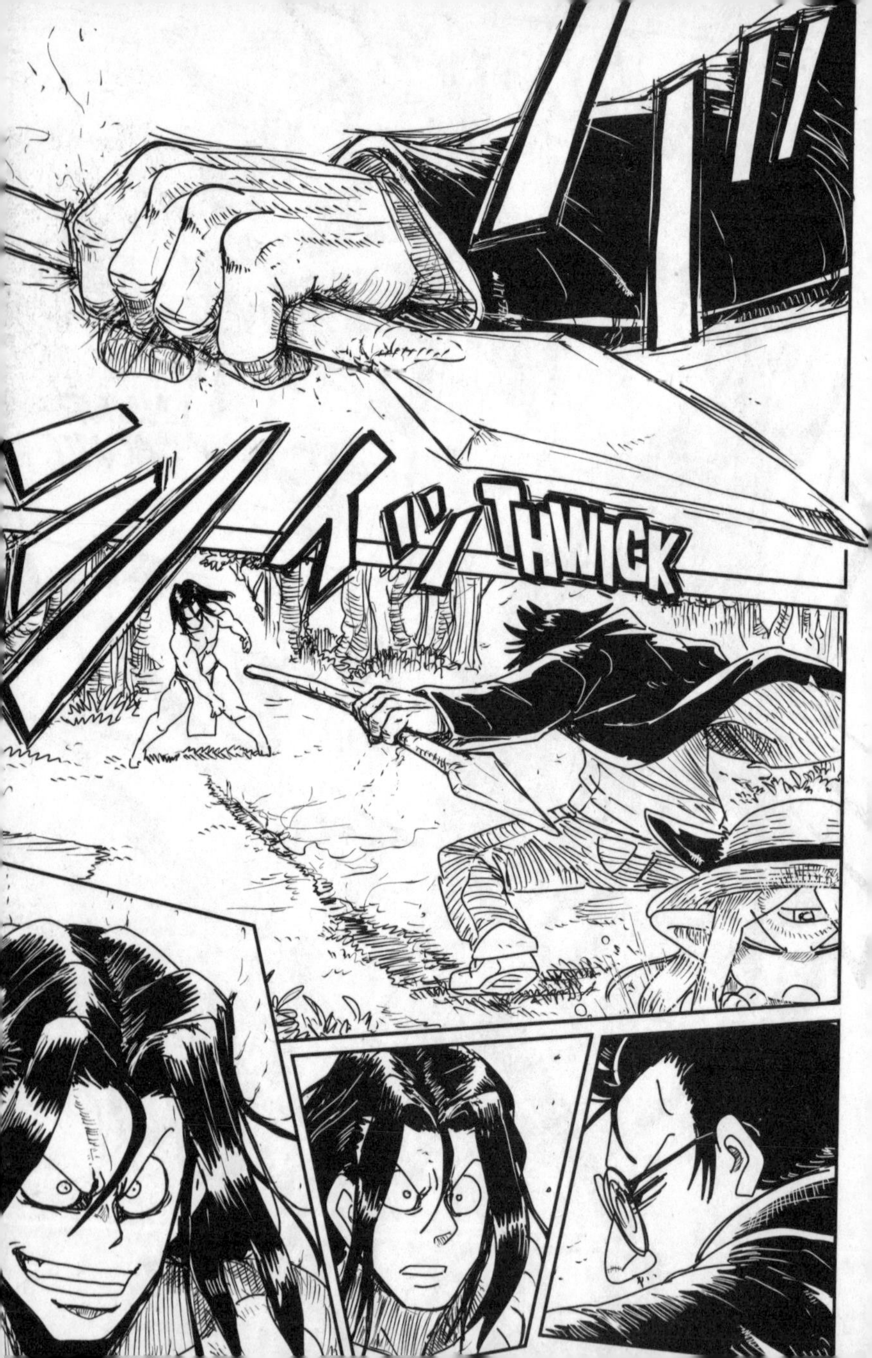
THWICK

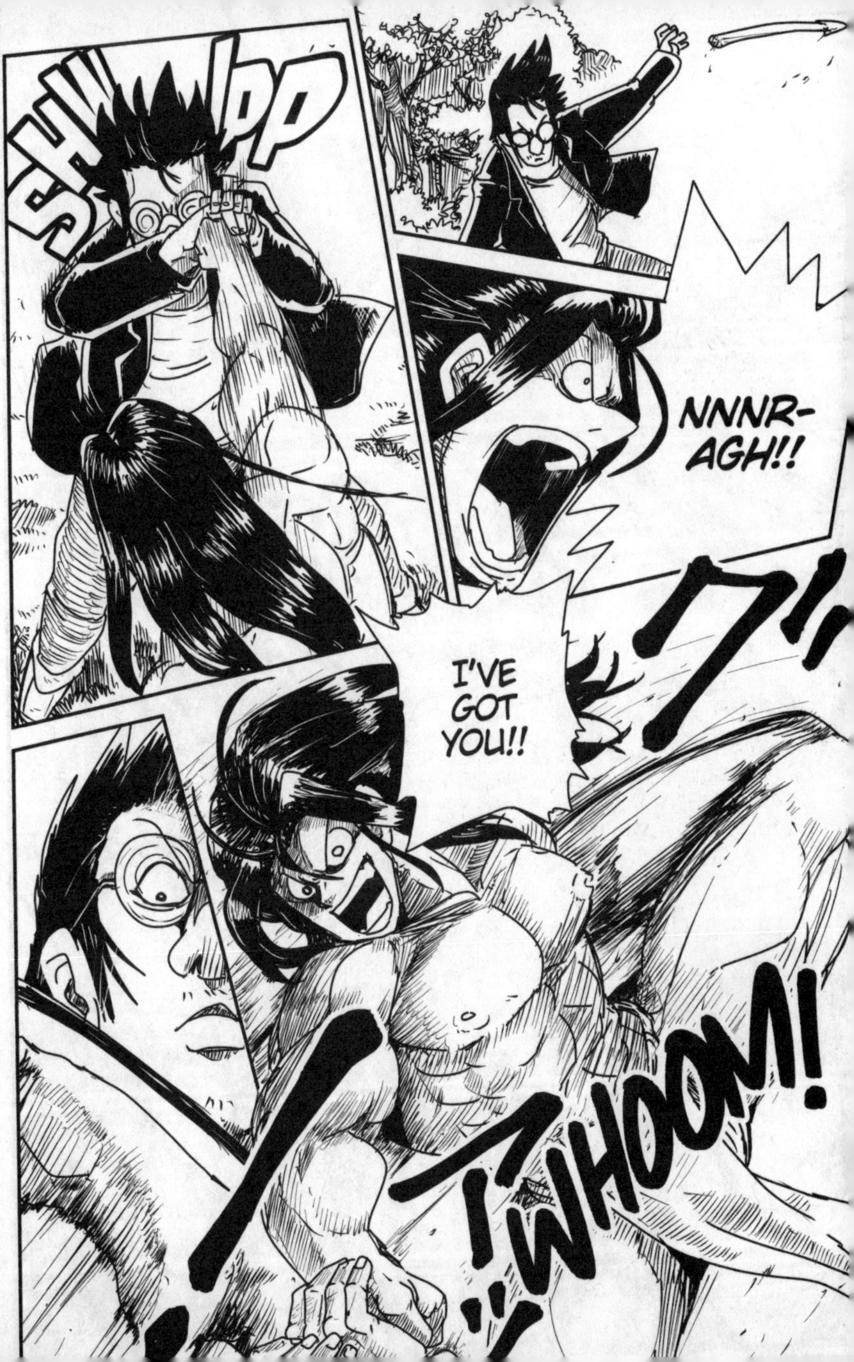
NNNR-
AGH!!
I'VE
GOT
YOU!!
WHOOM!!

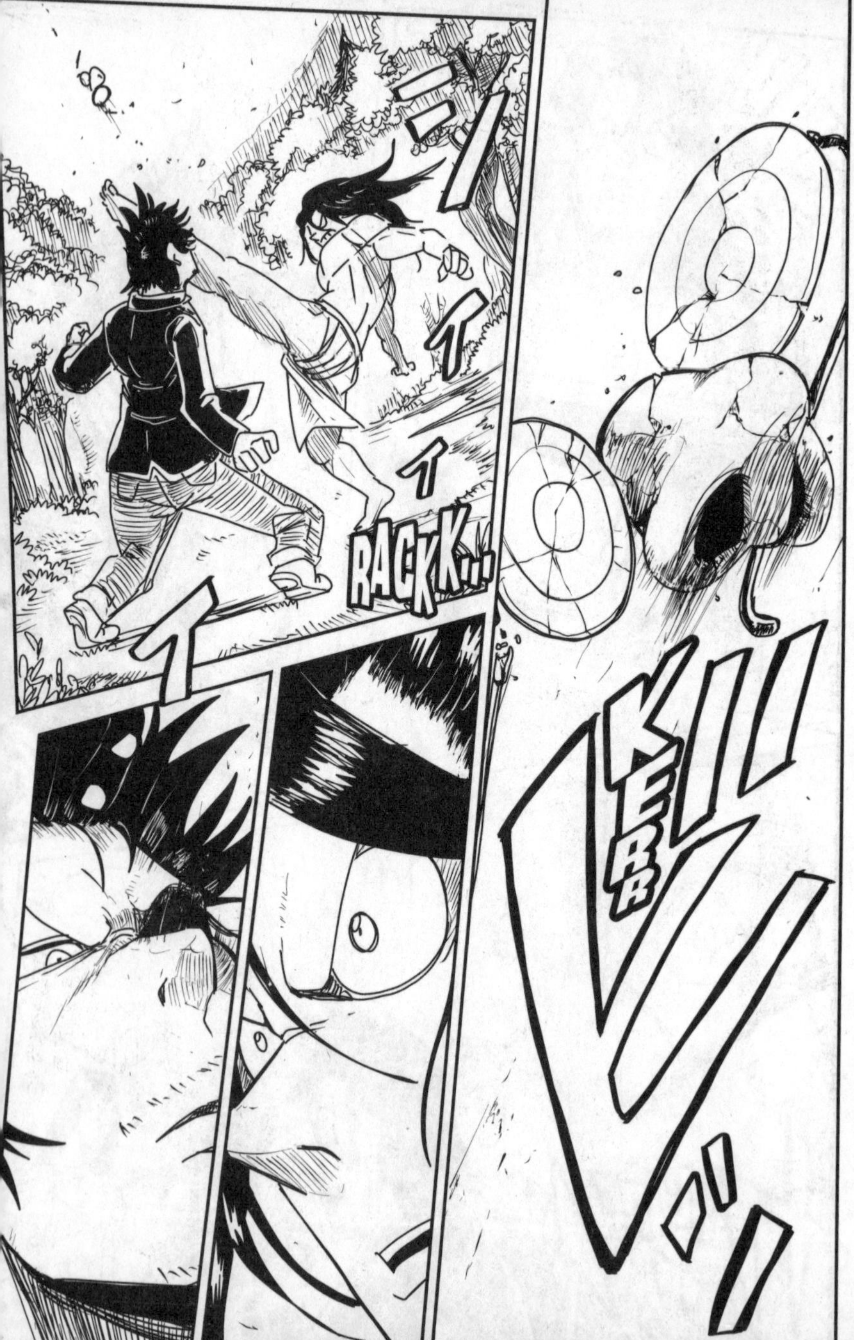
KERR
RACKK...

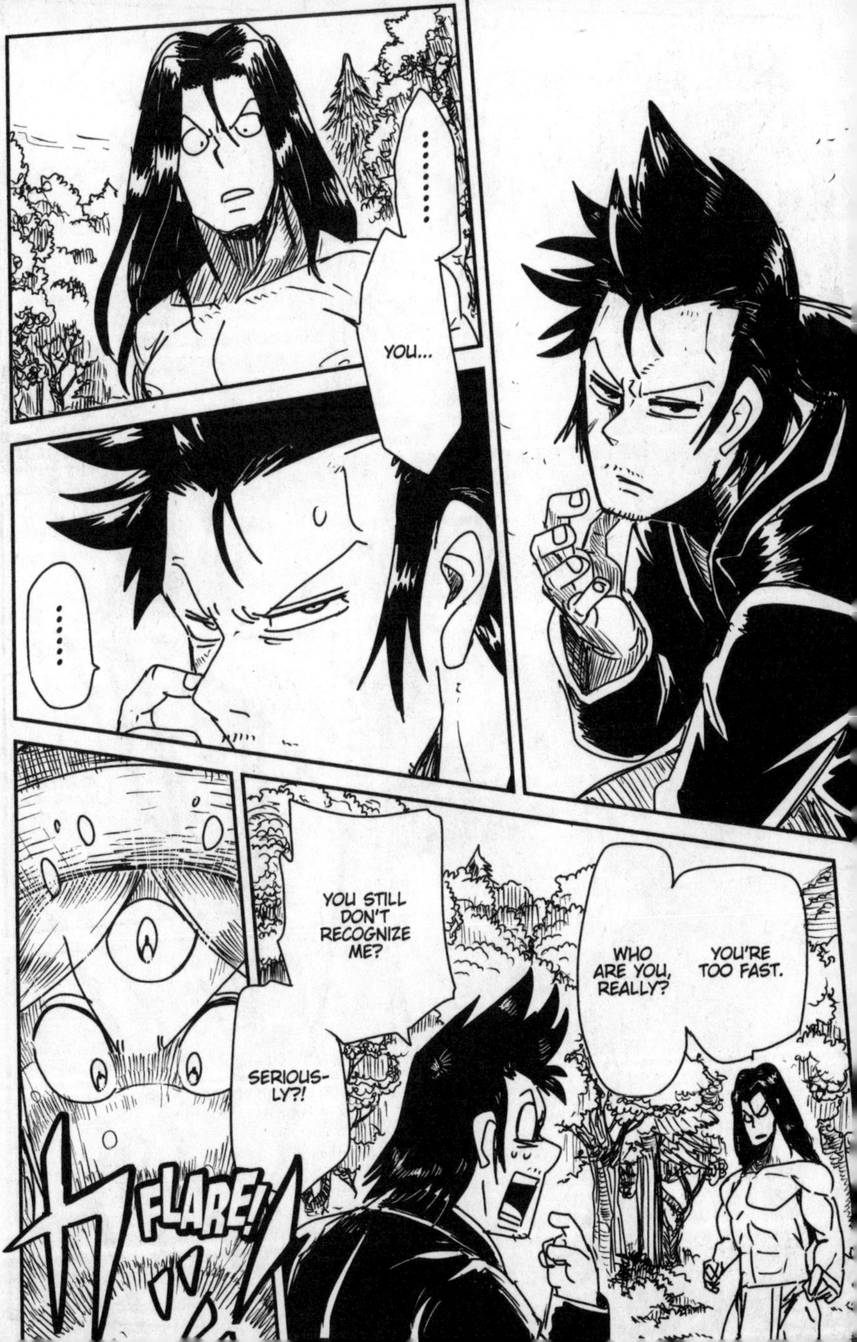
......
YOU...
......
YOU'RE TOO FAST.
WHO ARE YOU, REALLY?
YOU STILL DON'T RECOGNIZE ME?
SERIOUS-LY?!
FLARE!!

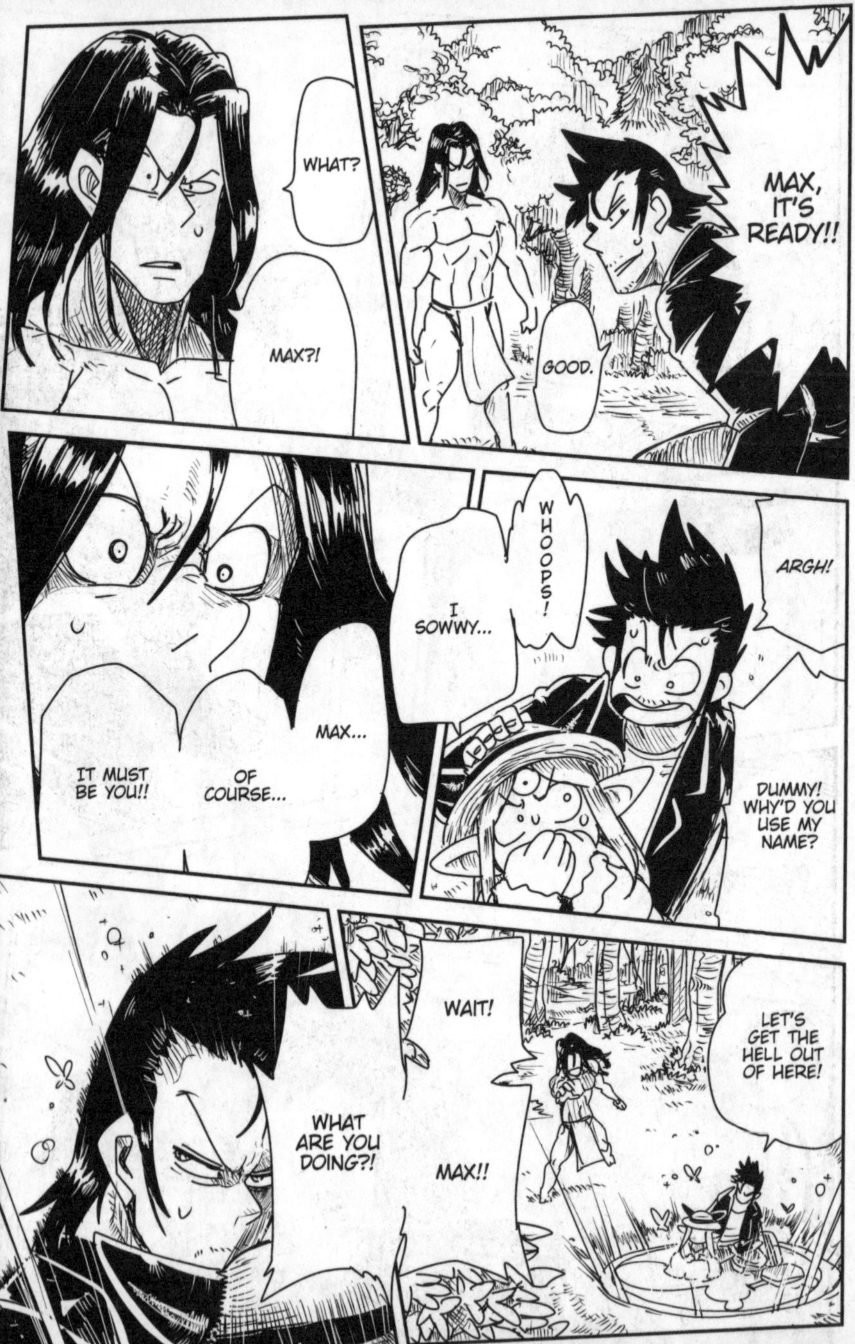
MAX, IT'S READY!!
GOOD.
WHAT?
MAX?!
ARGH!
DUMMY! WHY'D YOU USE MY NAME?
WHOOPS!
I SOWWY...
MAX...
OF COURSE...
IT MUST BE YOU!!
LET'S GET THE HELL OUT OF HERE!
WAIT!
MAX!!
WHAT ARE YOU DOING?!

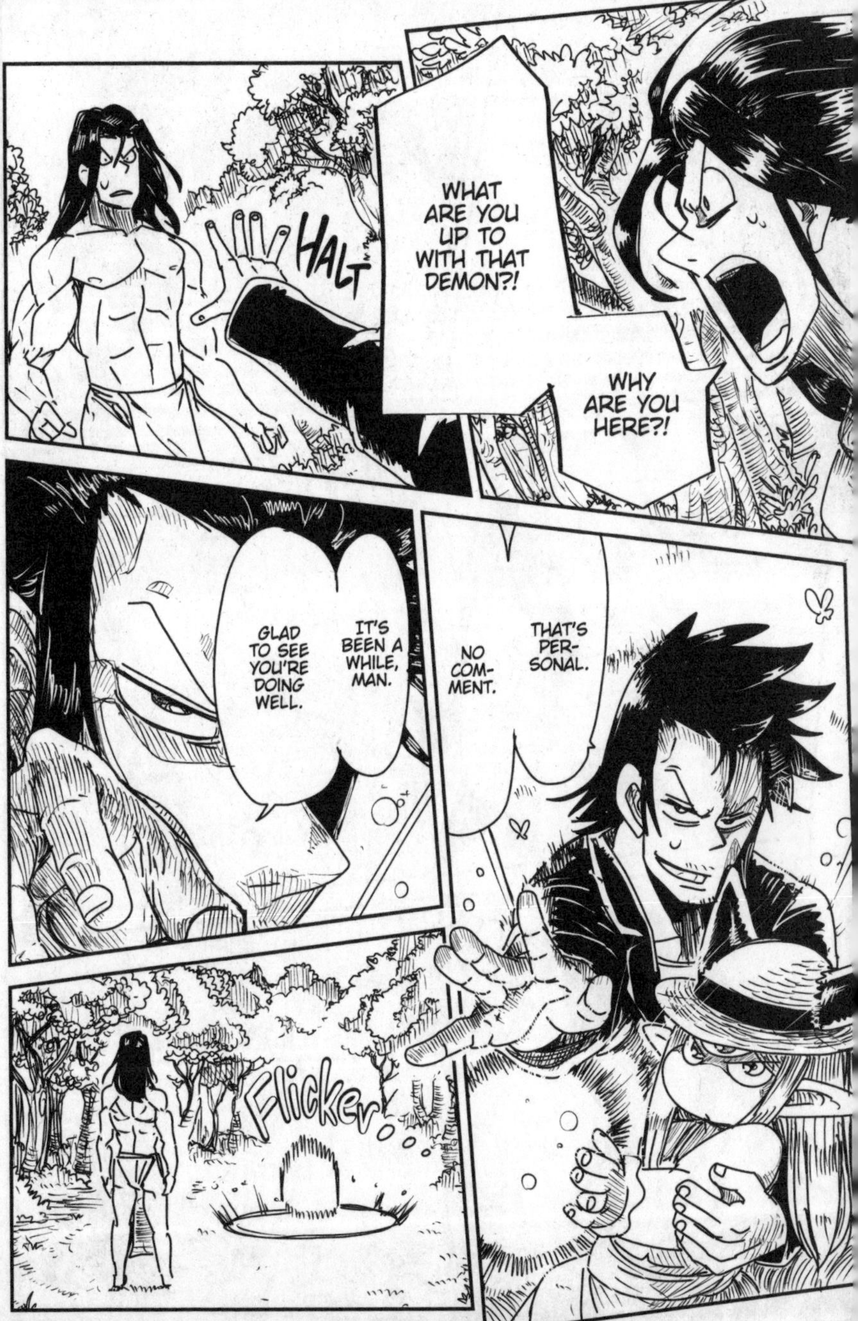
WHAT ARE YOU UP TO WITH THAT DEMON?!
WHY ARE YOU HERE?!
HALT
THAT'S PER-SONAL.
NO COM-MENT.
IT'S BEEN A WHILE, MAN.
GLAD TO SEE YOU'RE DOING WELL.
Flicker

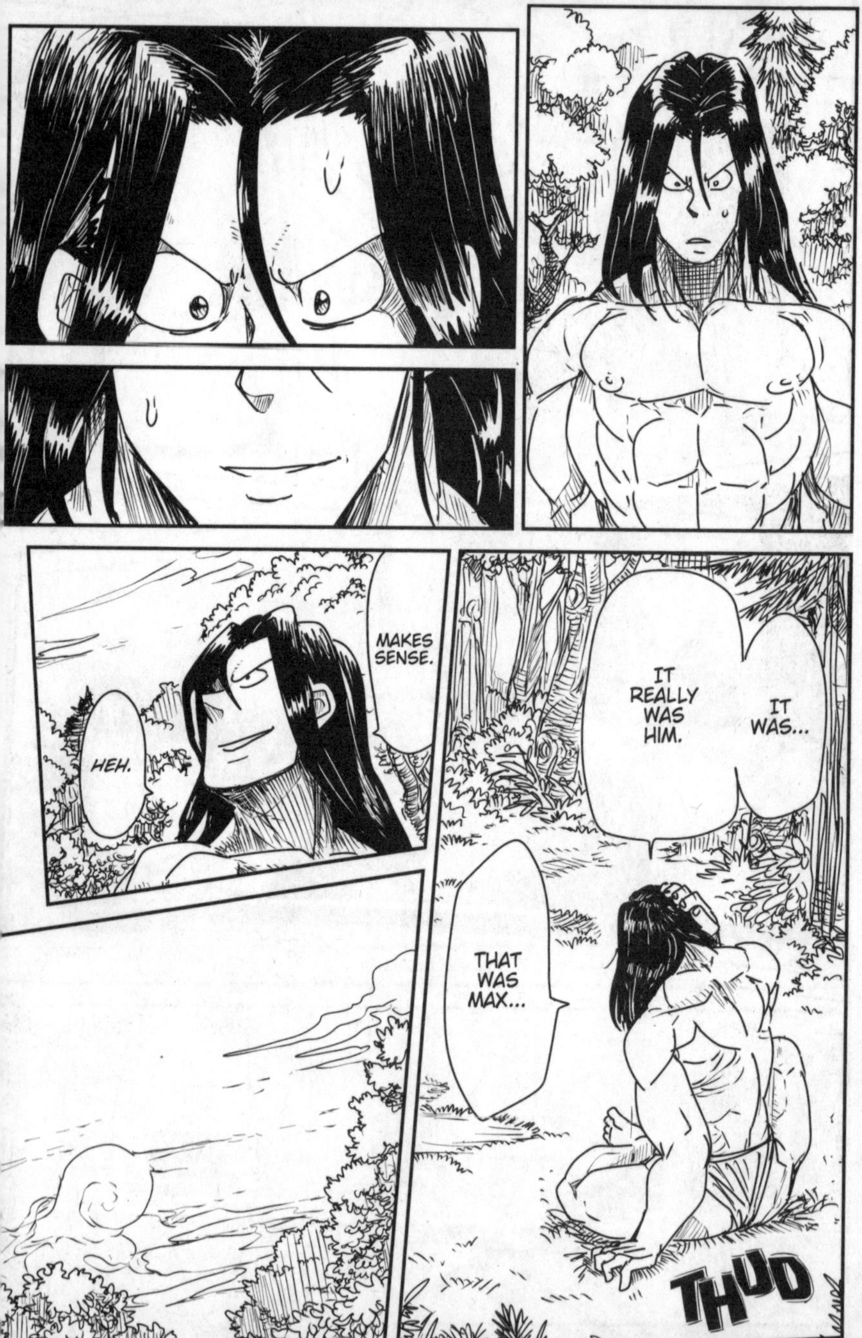
IT WAS...
IT REALLY WAS HIM.
THAT WAS MAX...
THUD
MAKES SENSE.
HEH.

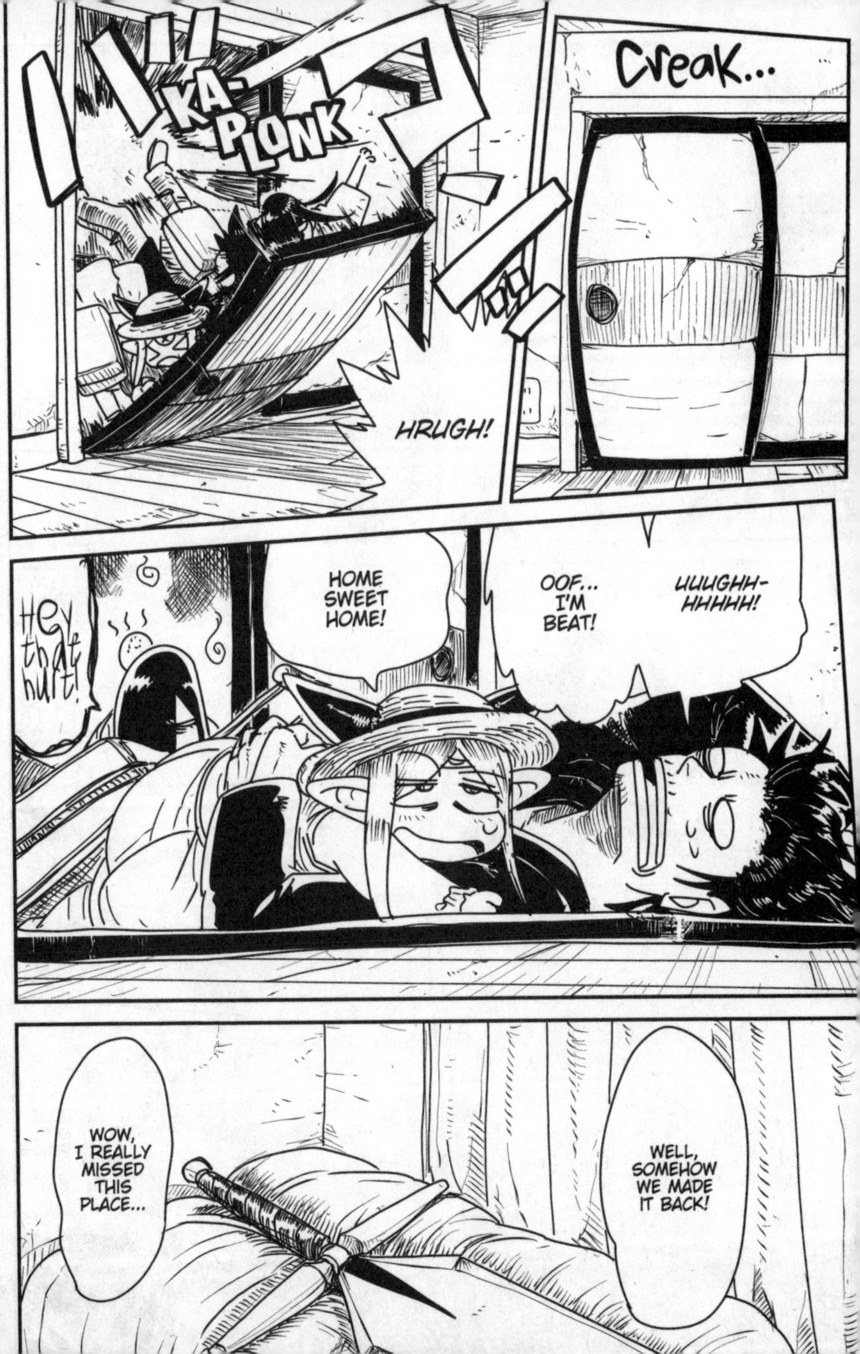
Creak...
KA-PLONK
HRUGH!
UUUGHH-HHHHH!
OOF... I'M BEAT!
HOME SWEET HOME!
Hey that hurt!
WELL, SOMEHOW WE MADE IT BACK!
WOW, I REALLY MISSED THIS PLACE...

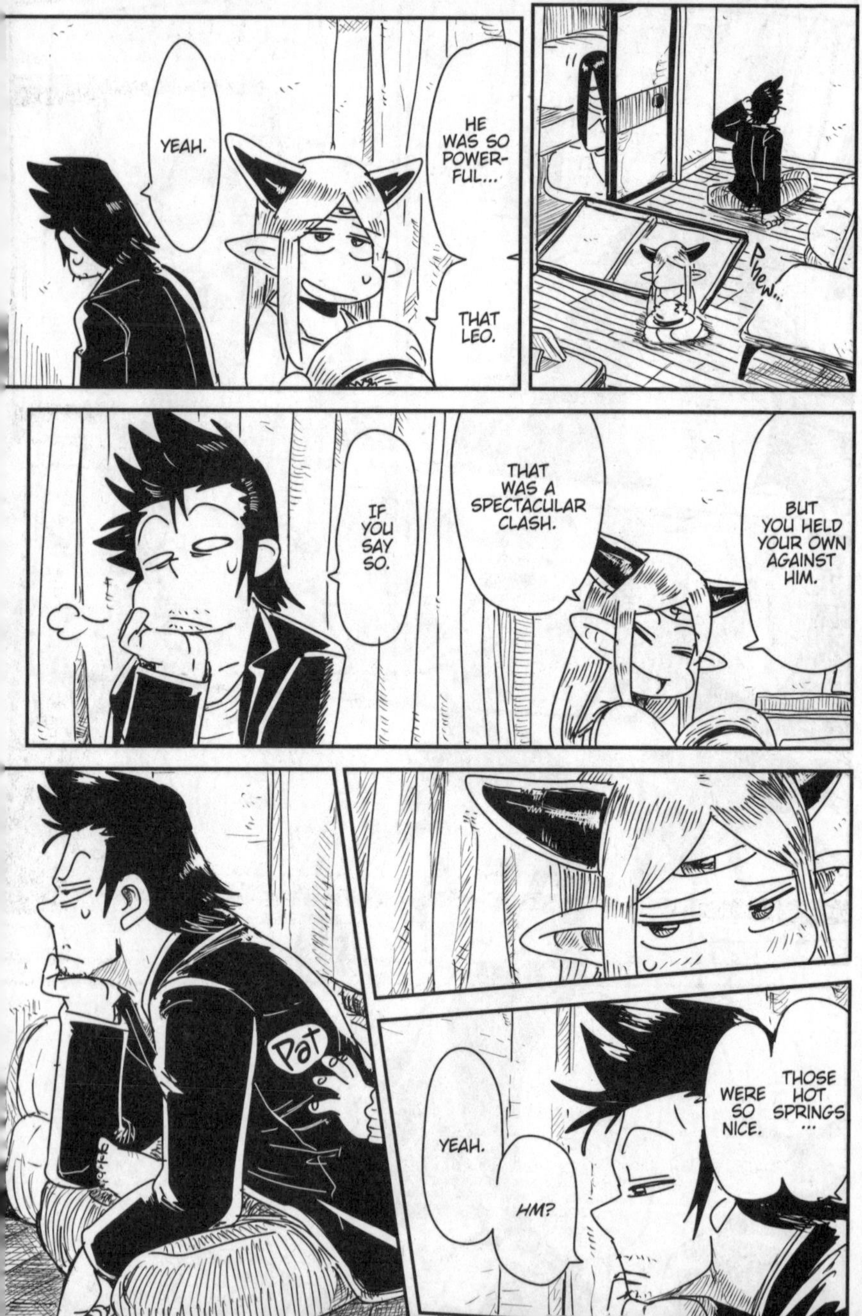
Phew...
HE WAS SO POWERFUL...
THAT LEO.
YEAH.
BUT YOU HELD YOUR OWN AGAINST HIM.
THAT WAS A SPECTACULAR CLASH.
IF YOU SAY SO.
THOSE HOT SPRINGS...
WERE SO NICE.
YEAH.
HM?
Pat

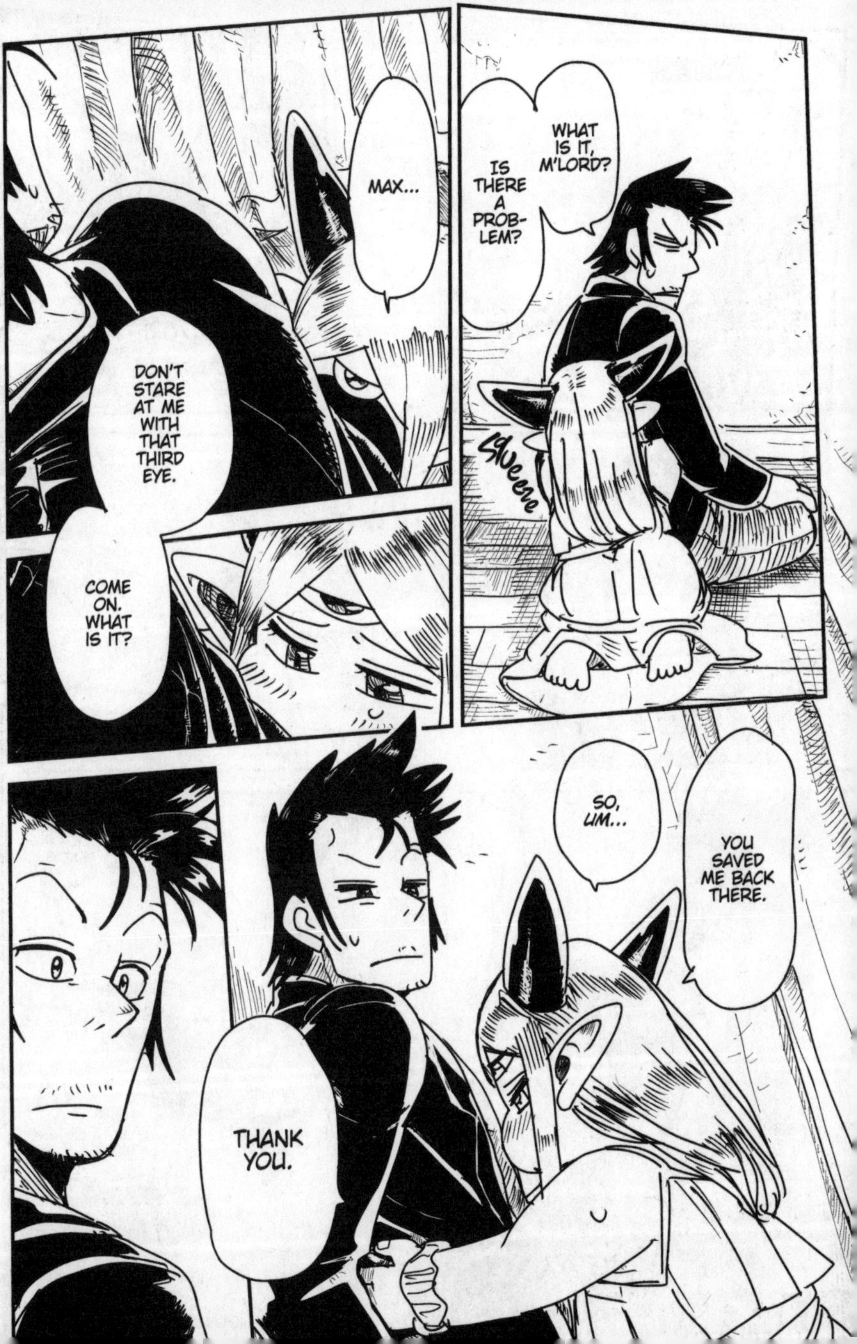
WHAT IS IT, M'LORD?
IS THERE A PROBLEM?
Squeeze
MAX...
DON'T STARE AT ME WITH THAT THIRD EYE.
COME ON. WHAT IS IT?
SO, UM...
YOU SAVED ME BACK THERE.
THANK YOU.

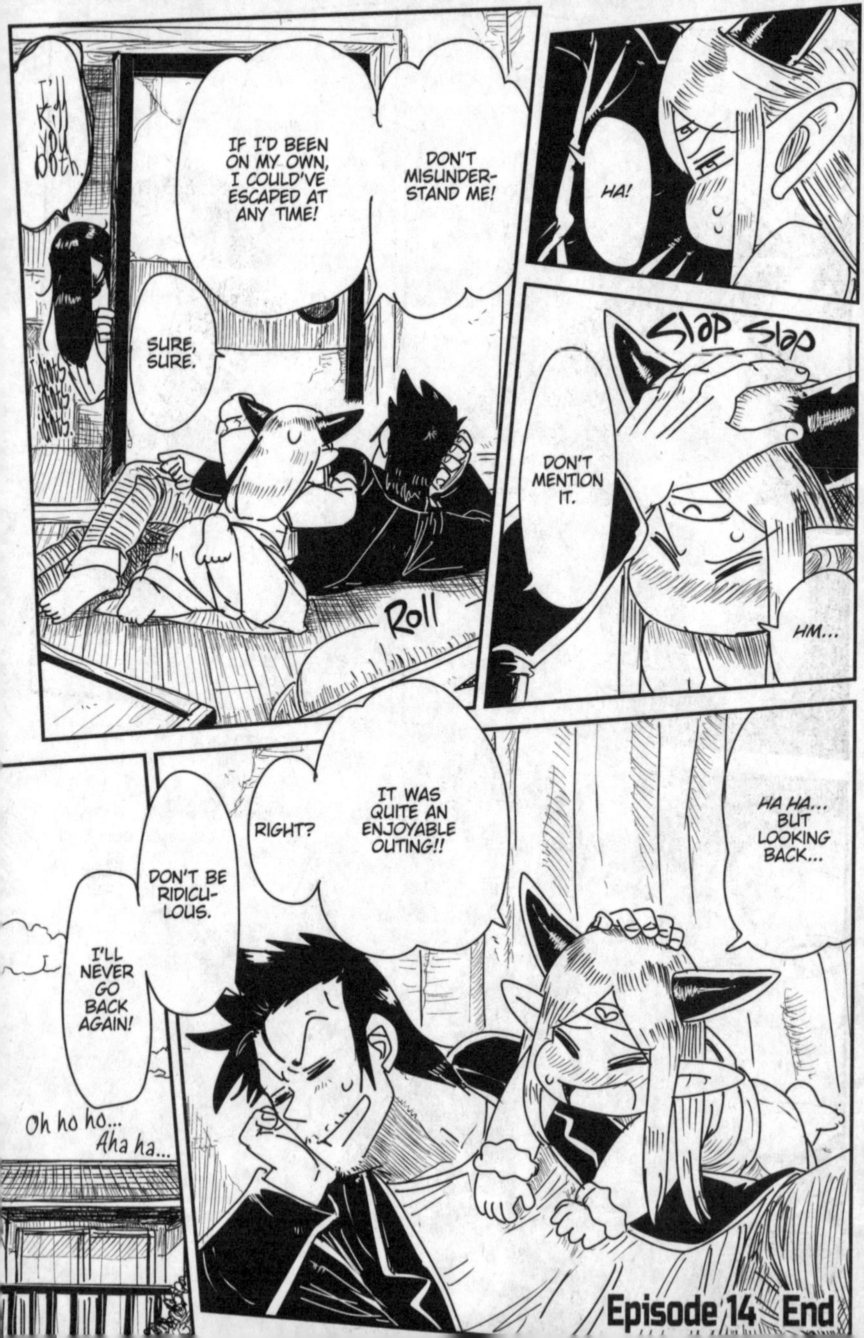
HA!
Slap Slap
DON'T MENTION IT.
HM...
DON'T MISUNDERSTAND ME!
IF I'D BEEN ON MY OWN, I COULD'VE ESCAPED AT ANY TIME!
I'll kill you both.
SURE, SURE.
Idiots idiots idiots.
Roll
HA HA... BUT LOOKING BACK...
IT WAS QUITE AN ENJOYABLE OUTING!!
RIGHT?
DON'T BE RIDICULOUS.
I'LL NEVER GO BACK AGAIN!
Oh ho ho... Aha ha...
Episode 14 End

LEVEL 1 DEMON LORD & ONE ROOM HERO

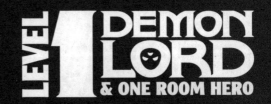

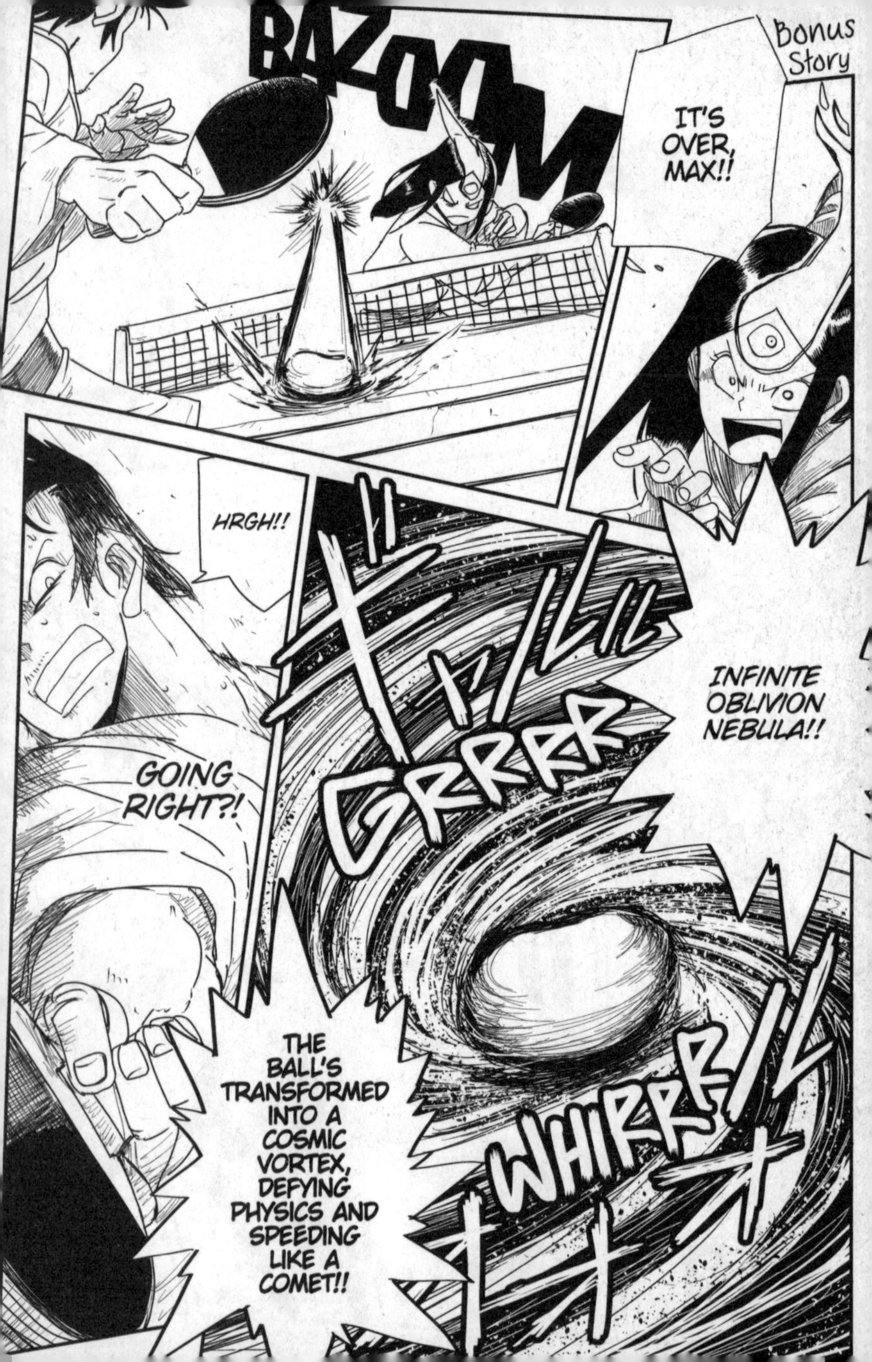
Bonus Story
IT'S OVER, MAX!!
BAZOOM
INFINITE OBLIVION NEBULA!!
GRRRR
HRGH!!
GOING RIGHT?!
THE BALL'S TRANSFORMED INTO A COSMIC VORTEX, DEFYING PHYSICS AND SPEEDING LIKE A COMET!!
WHIRRR

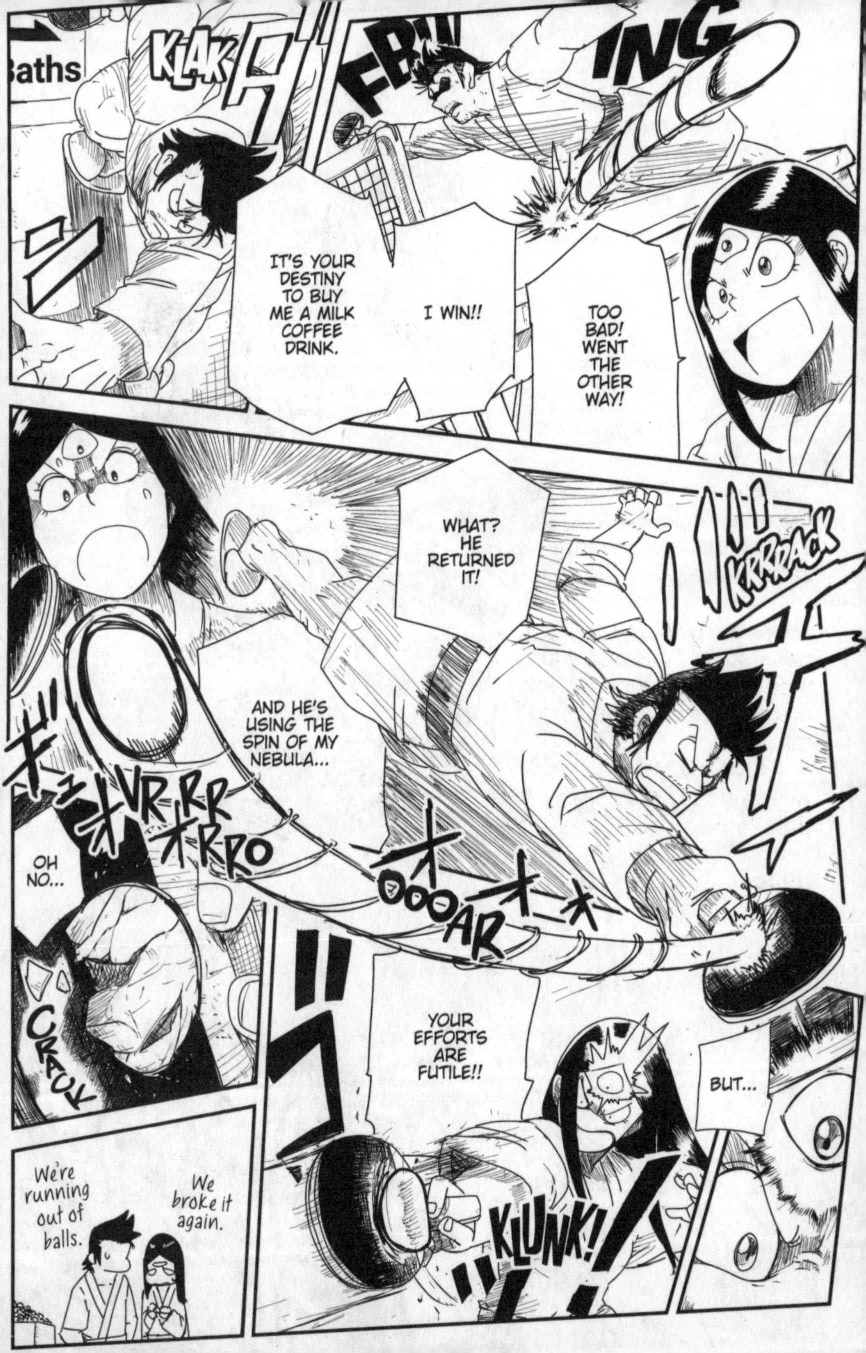
F-B ING
Baths
KLAK
TOO BAD! WENT THE OTHER WAY!
I WIN!!
IT'S YOUR DESTINY TO BUY ME A MILK COFFEE DRINK.
KRRRACK
WHAT? HE RETURNED IT!
AND HE'S USING THE SPIN OF MY NEBULA...
VRRRR
RRO
OOOAR
OH NO...
CRACK
BUT...
YOUR EFFORTS ARE FUTILE!!
KLUNK!
We broke it again.
We're running out of balls.

The Gunmar Republic in the story is based on a town in the Gunma prefecture, called Kusatsu.

There are no scary gangs in Kusatsu, but you might just meet a woman aggressively distributing sweet buns and tea...

Anyway, the hot springs there are very nice.

toufu

LEVEL 1 DEMON LORD & ONE ROOM HERO

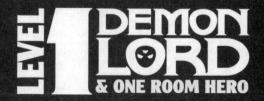

LEVEL 1 DEMON LORD & ONE ROOM HERO

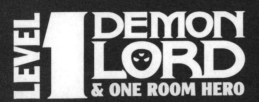

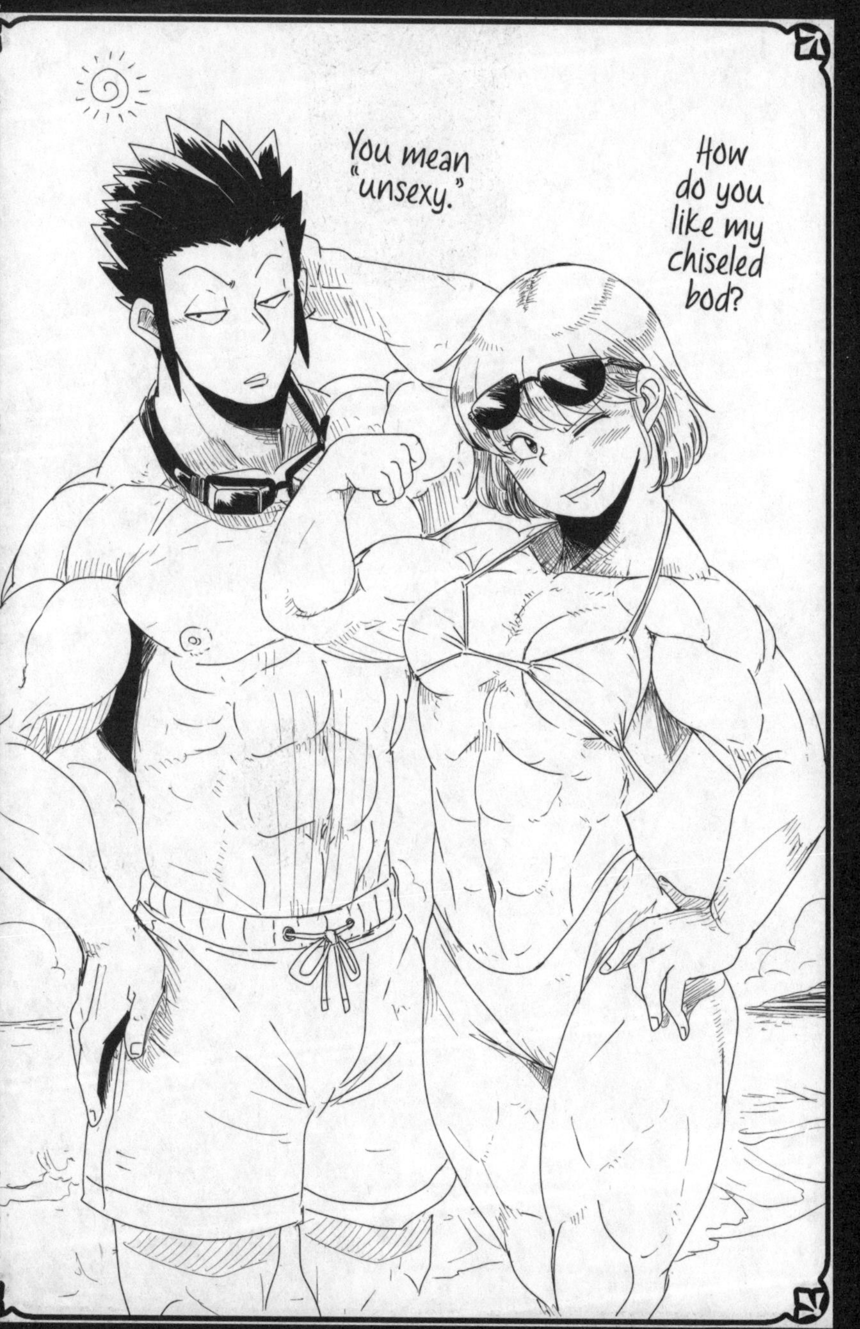
How do you like my chiseled bod?
You mean "unsexy."

& ONE ROOM HERO
LEVEL ONE DEMON LORD

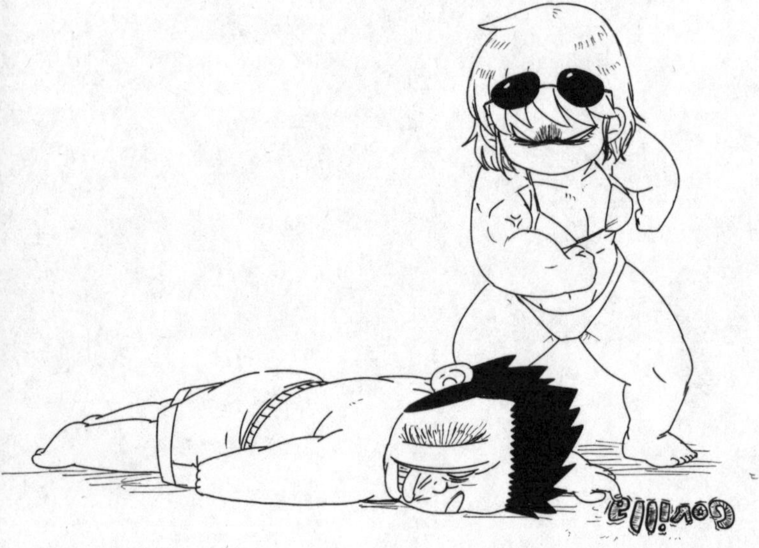
Gorilla

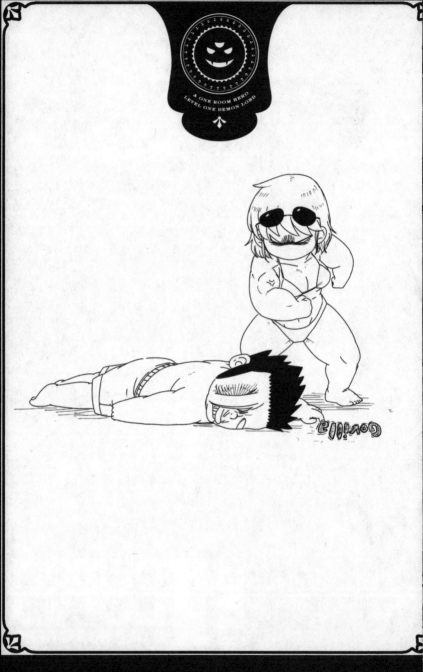

LEVEL 1 DEMON LORD & ONE ROOM HERO